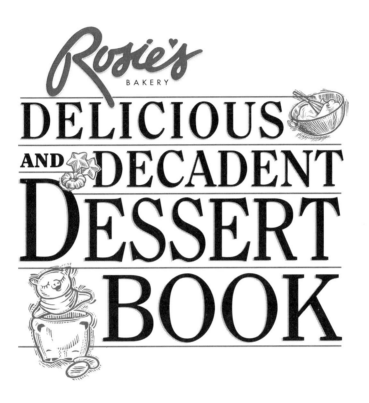

Rosie's BAKERY
DELICIOUS
AND DECADENT
DESSERT
BOOK

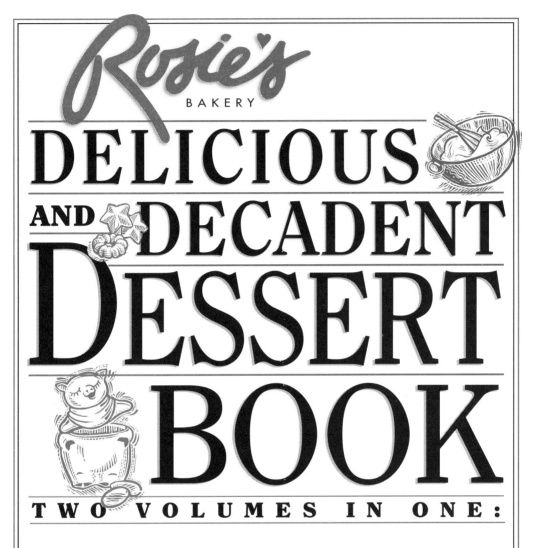

Rosie's BAKERY
DELICIOUS
AND DECADENT
DESSERT
BOOK

TWO VOLUMES IN ONE:

ROSIE'S BAKERY BAKING BOOK AND
ROSIE'S BAKERY COOKIE BOOK

BY JUDY ROSENBERG

Written with Nan Levinson
Illustrations by Barbara Maslen and Sara Love

WORKMAN PUBLISHING • NEW YORK

Dedication

♥

To my mother, and to my father
who is now
loving me from above

Rosie's Bakery Delicious and Decadent Dessert Book
Copyright © 2002 by Judy Rosenberg

Rosie's Bakery All-Butter, Fresh Cream, Sugar-Packed No-Holds-Barred
Baking Book
Copyright © 1991 by Judy Rosenberg
Illustrations © 1991 by Barbara Maslen

Rosie's Bakery Chocolate-Packed, Jam-Filled, Butter-Rich No-Holds-Barred
Cookie Book
Copyright © 1996 by Judy Rosenberg
Illustrations © 1996 by Sara Love

Library of Congress Cataloging-in-Publication Data
Rosenberg, Judy.
Rosie's Bakery delicious and decadent dessert book / by Judy Rosenberg;
written with Nan Levinson; illustrated by Barbara Maslen (baking book)
and Sara Love (cookie book).
p. cm.
Includes index.
Contents: Rosie's Bakery baking book—Rosie's Bakery cookie book.
ISBN 0-7611-2810-7 (alk. paper)
1. Desserts. 2. Rosie's Bakery. I. Levinson, Nan S. II. Title.

TX772 .R653 2002
641.8'6—dc21   2002016790
                                                          CIP

Workman books are available at special discounts when purchased in bulk for premi-
ums and sales promotions as well as for fund-raising or educational use. Special edi-
tions or book excerpts can be created to specification. For details, contact the Special
Sales Director at the address below.

Workman Publishing Company, Inc.
708 Broadway
New York, NY 10003-9555
www.workman.com

First printing April 2002
10 9 8 7 6 5 4 3 2 1

Contents

♥ ♥ ♥ ♥ ♥ ♥ ♥ ♥ ♥ ♥ ♥ ♥ ♥ ♥ ♥ ♥ ♥

Contents

Rosie's BAKERY

ALL-BUTTER
FRESH CREAM
SUGAR-PACKED
No-Holds-Barred
BAKING BOOK

INTRODUCTION

Meet
Rosie

I can't say for sure that I came out of the womb on a diet, but it certainly wasn't long afterward that I was put on one. As far back as I can remember, it was a family ritual to climb on the scale each morning: first my father, blessed with a metabolism that burned up everything he ate; then my mother, with the will power to stay thin; and finally, me, their chubby child. No one would have guessed then that I'd end up a baker, least of all me.

We lived in a huge apartment in the middle of Manhattan. My mother was a theatrical agent, and my father quit teaching English to join her in the business. Our apartment was often full of people, all talking, making music, and eating. I heard the score for "A Funny Thing Happened on the Way to the Forum" way before anyone else. I remember Julie Andrews, Jean Stapleton, and Imogene Coca coming over for auditions. Rob Reiner was at my third birthday party, and, best of all, Marilyn Monroe lived in an apartment upstairs. It seemed ordinary to me.

It also seemed perfectly ordinary that my mother worked. I think of her as forever talking on the phone, making arrangements or organizing some event, so with all that, she didn't have a lot of time to spend in the kitchen. But that was never a problem. A master orchestrator, she'd go through cookbooks to pick out recipes for our housekeeper to make, and her instincts were unerring. Although my mother was anything but domestic, she knew exactly where to shop to get the best meats, the best fish . . . and the best desserts.

Sometimes, as a special treat for me, my mother baked brownies. It was the only thing she did bake, but her grandmother was reputed to have been a master baker in Czechoslovakia, so it may have been an inherited talent. In any event, those wonderful brownies were the stuff of my dreams from early childhood on. I still get a heightened physical reaction, a buzz, when I bite into a spectacular dessert, and lust is probably the only word that accurately describes my relationship to chocolate. So when people ask me how I came up with the name "Chocolate Orgasms" for Rosie's brownies, I don't know how to answer because it seemed the most obvious name in the world to me.

In the 1950s there weren't cookie shops or gourmet ice cream outlets on every corner, even in New York City, where you can get nearly anything you can imagine if you're willing to pay for it. But if you were as serious in your quest for the ideal dessert as I invariably was, you could be well rewarded. There were William Greenberg, Jr.'s, brownies made of that dense, not-too-sweet chocolate that I think of as pure American. There was Reuben's cheesecake, heavy enough to choke on if you didn't drink milk with it, and Serendipity's Frozen Hot Chocolate, which was so cold it gave me a headache, but so good I didn't care. Eclair made a chocolate cake with sour cherries, Ebinger's had rugalah, Bonte's madeleines would have inspired Proust to write another seven books, and even Schrafft's brownies were great in those days. On the home front, there were Hershey's Golden Almond Bars, which my mother hid in her stocking drawer for fear my father and I would consume them in a frenzy. A good number of my childhood memories, it seems, were chocolate-coated.

Majoring in Dessert

*7*hings didn't change much as I grew older. When I went away to college at the University of California at Berkeley in the late sixties, I continued my research into the ultimate dessert and added Crucheon's Fudge Pie, King Pin donuts, and See's candy to my pantheon. Officially I was studying French, but it was the era of the Free Speech movement, communes, and organic food, so I learned a lot of other things on the side. After graduation I moved to Cambridge, Massachusetts, and looked for work. To no one's surprise, I gravitated toward food.

For a while, I waitressed in a coffeehouse in Harvard Square (which I loved and my parents hated), then I went back to school for another degree (which I hated and my parents loved), all of which qualified me to waitress at a classier restaurant and spend a year and a half at the Boston Museum of Fine Arts School (which, at last, pleased both my parents and me).

It was in those days that I developed my philosophy of food, an answer to every glutton's dream, because I figured out how to have my cake and eat it too. It all had to do with balance, a kind of Yin and Yang of calorie consciousness. I lived on a strict diet of brown bread, cheese, fruit, nuts, and vegetables — sensible, healthy, balanced eating. Then I'd polish the meal off with a fat slab of cheesecake from Jack and Marion's, a now-departed Brookline delicatessen. After all, guilty pleasures are still pleasures.

The Awakening

Then on Valentine's Day 1974, all those years of appetite and abstinence were vindicated. I was wondering about life after art school when it popped into my mind to create edible valentines. Until then I had done only the most basic baking: brownies and birthday cakes when the occasion demanded, not much more. Yet once I started, I found that this was how I loved spending the day: creating pastries that would delight the eyes as well as the belly.

I baked heart-shaped sugar cookies, glazed them in lavender and pink, and decorated them with velvet flowers, miniature angels, silver sugar pearls, and colored crystals. They were elaborately campy concoctions that could have been eaten, I suppose, although I thought of them more as romantic gifts to be saved and savored. I arranged them on trays lined with purple satin, and trotted off to present my wares to four Cambridge art galleries and one food shop called Baby Watson Cheesecake.

The cookies were a hit, and Baby Watson called me early the next morning. "What else can you bake?" they demanded. I was on my way. There was the chocolate layer cake I made for birthdays, a carrot cake whose recipe had come from a friend's mother in California, and my own brownies, which I had perfected when I realized that I didn't want to go through life without a really good brownie recipe. Beyond that, I was starting from scratch. I began to investigate recipes, but I was seldom satisfied—too sweet, not chocolaty enough, too many additions. So I experimented and learned. I created Boom Booms, Harvard Squares, Chocolate Orgasms, Queen Raspberries . . . the names entered the Cambridge lexicon. I called them all my BabyCakes and went into the baking business.

I lugged hundred-pound bags of flour up to my second-floor apartment, where every doorknob was coated with chocolate. I learned to sleep with sugar in my bed and ignore that my floor crunched as I walked on it. I invested in a twenty-quart professional mixer and thirty-gallon trash cans to hold the sugar and flour. I woke at five in the morning and baked, took a quick run while the pastries cooled, then delivered them to Harvard Square, where customers were lined up in anticipation. I must have

been quite a sight, almost an emblem of the era, in my hot pants and platform shoes with a hairdo that stuck out about a foot from my head. I was having the time of my life.

Everything moved so quickly in the beginning that within six months I had outgrown the kitchen in my apartment. I built a new kitchen adjacent to Baby Watson, right in the heart of Harvard Square, and enclosed it in glass so that customers buying my goods could see the baking process. It was like a movie set, complete with custom-built cherry cabinets with cut-crystal knobs, an Art Deco lantern with satin shades, Edwardian botanical prints on the walls, and the insistent pulse of Toots and the Maytals in the background.

Hello Rosie's

*A*fter almost three years of working there and selling through Baby Watson, the next obvious step was to market my pastries myself; so I opened my own store in Inman Square in Cambridge and named it Rosie's as a declaration of independence. This new place was a full-range bakery where you could pick up a muffin and coffee on your way to work, a pie to take home for dinner, or a custom-made cake decorated for a special celebration. If you had the time, there were tables where you could indulge in a brownie and cup of tea while you discussed the soaps, a proposal for work, or the meaning of life. Over time Rosie's became the incongruous but appealing combination of a friend's kitchen, a neighborhood bar, and a thriving bakery.

In those first days, though, going from Harvard Square to Inman Square was a shock. The two neighborhoods are less than a mile apart, but when Rosie's arrived, Inman could be most charitably described as "funky." Since restaurants and jazz clubs were opening there, we did a lot of business late at night when people came from all over the city. During the day we were a neighborhood attraction and had our regulars. There was the professor who came in every morning to read his newspaper over coffee and a lemon poppy-seed muffin, and a guy writing his magnum opus—about what I never found out—in daily sessions at one of our tables. We had little kids counting out pennies to buy a treat, mothers with baby carriages converging every afternoon at about three o'clock, doctors and nurses from Cambridge City Hospital who never ordered less than twenty items for take-out, and the firemen of Cambridge Local 30 who gave us a plaque in appreciation of our hospitality and pastries after a particularly bad fire nearby.

Graduate students who had once gotten stoned to the strains of the Velvet Underground stood shoulder-to-shoulder with businessmen who had never heard of the rock group but hungered just as avidly for our dark chocolate cake of the same name. Genteel women ordered Chocolate Orgasms in elegant but unflinching tones, while our nonchocolate products developed equally loyal followings since rugalah, butter cookies, and shortbread seemed appropriate tributes to everyone's grandmother, no matter what her heritage.

In a neighborhood then short on decoration, our pink neon sign in the window drew people, and, once inside, they stayed, mostly for the goodies but also for the homey atmosphere. I had determined from the first that Rosie's would be a treat not just for the taste buds but for all the senses, so I painted and decorated, lugged in overstuffed furniture, and made sure we had fresh flowers every week.

Since those early years, Rosie's has grown larger and more established. What began as a whim in Harvard Square now occupies an entire building in Inman Square, a second store in suburban Chestnut Hill, and a new store in Boston's South Station. In the intervening years, my first customers have cut their hair, put on suits, acquired kids, mortgages, and life insurance, and ventured beyond the rarified atmosphere of "the Square." But they haven't changed their desire for a little something from Rosie's, and they still indulge it, even if that now means having to go out of their way.

So it's sometimes tempting to view Rosie's as an inevitability—you know, the hand of fate gently nudging me in that direction from birth, all that lust and denial as a rite of passage. Or maybe it was bred in the bone, this taking my chocolate very seriously and insisting on the best. Not that it matters, really. When you're having so much fun, it seems greedy to question fate.

CHAPTER ONE

Common Sense Baking

We all have certain conversations that get repeated so often we could conduct them in our sleep. Mine begins, "No kidding! You own Rosie's? Where did you study baking?" When I answer that I didn't but learned on my own, the response is often amazement. But what's amazing to me is that so many people don't believe it's possible. It makes me wonder who has been perpetuating this myth that baking involves a delicate chemical reaction that only the chosen few can control. And, more to the point, it makes me ask where all the hocus-pocus has gotten us. I mean, how many oh-so-stylish Baba au Hazelnut Tortes do we have to try before we admit that both Aunt Esther and our college roommate's mother could whip up better at a moment's notice?

I don't mean to denigrate expertise, but all this training business should be put in perspective. Baking does involve chemical reactions, but so does taking an aspirin. While you may not reach baker's heaven on your first try, if good food is important to you, if you like desserts, and if you can count, none of the recipes in this book is beyond you. It's as simple as that. Baking can also be fun; there are even those among us who find it more therapeutic than a hot bath or a session on the couch, and that's not even considering its more tangible rewards.

Now, about achieving those tangible rewards. Let's start with one basic rule I learned from my years on the baking front: Don't let yourself be intimidated. That may sound simple, but bear in mind that these are the words of a woman who used to panic whenever a recipe called for beaten egg whites. I was sure I had a genetic inability to tell if they were stiff or soft enough, and even if by some miracle I made it past that hurdle, who knew how gently I should be folding the stiff-soft whites into the batter? I had myself convinced that if I beat the egg whites one second too long, the entire enterprise would be a flop. And you know what? It often was, fear of failure being one of those things that fulfills itself with depressing regularity.

Only slightly daunted though, I remembered that old chestnut about learning from my mistakes, and I now stand before you a reformed egg beater. The moral of this story (and the trick with more than just egg whites) is to

Baking Temperatures and Times

— ❖ —

I can't emphasize enough how important it is to remember that oven temperatures vary greatly from oven to oven and sometimes even from week to week in the same oven. Consequently baking times will vary too. Don't take the times suggested in the book too literally; rely on the visual descriptions of the various stages and finished product, as well as the techniques suggested to test for doneness.

develop a feel for what you're doing and the confidence to make adjustments. That's where real creativity comes from, because when you're in control, you feel freer to experiment.

There's something to be said for serendipity, too. I've put too little flour in a cake only to find that it came out lighter, and the time I forgot to add the eggs to pumpkin bread, I ended up liking the texture better without them. Archimedes, on discovering the principle of displacement of water, was said to have run naked through the streets shouting, "Eureka! I have found it!" I merely file my discoveries in the back of my mind to use for future creations.

In addition to goofs, there are lots of factors that affect how a recipe comes out, and you can't be aware of all of them before you start. Your oven may bake differently from mine, your apples may be less juicy, or your eggs larger. That's where adaptability and experience come in.

First you learn that time-honored baking ritual in which you take something out of the oven, hit yourself on the forehead, and say, "Darn, I should have thought of that!" Next you figure out how to adjust your oven temperature so that your cake layers don't have a crust or how much juice to add to keep your apple pies from drying out. One of the joys of baking is that problems have solutions, and they're often a matter of common sense.

Aside from the power of positive thinking and the incantation I chant over each batch of brownies that I'm not at liberty to disclose, I have a few suggestions that should help you avoid basic problems in baking and keep your frustration level within reason.

Method to the Madness

*S*oul and panache go a long way to making a good baker, but it helps to be organized and systematic, too, and I don't make that suggestion lightly. When I left home and my mother's compulsion for tidiness, I realized that by nature I'm a slob. So it wasn't until years later that I also realized my mother was on to something. Chaos makes baking twice as hard. I don't always practice what I preach, but nonetheless I'd like to pass on to you Rosie's Five Steps to Carefree Baking, Longer Life, and Gaining Permission to Use Your Mother's Kitchen.

1. First, read the entire recipe so that there are no surprises. It's a pain to discover halfway through that you're out of an essential ingredient and can't finish baking without a trip to the store.

2. Line up, pour, measure, and count out all your ingredients in advance, replacing boxes and containers as you go along to avoid confusion (as in: Uh oh, is that white mound in the batter baking soda or baking powder?).

3. Avoid distractions: chatty phone calls, drop-in visits, disgruntled children pulling at your apron strings, the soaps, or Oprah Winfrey. You may think you're concentrating, but sooner or later you will be rummaging through the garbage counting egg shells to figure out how many you've cracked.

4. Bake when you're not tense or in a hurry. Otherwise baking becomes a chore, not a pleasure, and you're more likely to make mistakes.

5. Make sure you understand basic baking techniques and try to become comfortable with the procedures explained in the recipes you use so that you can deepen your confidence and expand your creativity.

The Right Stuff

*W*hen you're stocking up on ingredients, keep in mind that it's hard to improve on nature when it comes to food, so you're on firm ground if you rely on fresh, pure items as much as possible. That doesn't mean that you have to buy the most expensive ingredients or that all things imported are heaven-blessed, despite what many gourmet shops would have us believe. But baking with second-rate ingredients is like playing a sonata on a kazoo; it's not the real thing and it's not as good.

Check the pantry box on the facing page for a list of all-important baking ingredients.

Rosie's Pantry

— ❖ —

Most of my recipes call for ingredients that your supermarket stocks regularly, but if you want to be able to bake from this cookbook with a degree of spontaneity ("I think I'll whip up a little chocolate mousse cake tonight in case this blizzard lasts another week"), here are the ingredients you should keep in good supply in your pantry.

— ❖ —

Unbleached all-purpose flour	Honey	Pure vanilla extract
Cake flour (not self-rising)	Corn syrup (light and dark)	Almond extract
Baking soda	Unsalted butter	Salt
Baking powder	Unflavored gelatin	Spices: ground ginger, cinnamon, nutmeg, mace, allspice, cloves
Cornstarch	Fruit preserves	
Granulated sugar	Raisins	Sweetened shredded coconut
Brown sugar (light and dark)	Peanut butter (salted or unsalted)	Semisweet chocolate chips
Confectioner's sugar	Instant espresso or other good-quality coffee powder	Unsweetened chocolate
Molasses		

Equipment

*A*s with ingredients, having the equipment you need on hand will make baking convenient and more spontaneous. It's easy to go overboard on kitchenware, though, what with those seductive displays at kitchen shops and all the fads. Remember fondue pots and yogurt makers, those necessities of the seventies? And before you make major purchases, I suggest you shop around, because prices can vary widely. You might start at a commercial kitchen supply store that usually offers a large selection, sturdy quality, and reasonable prices.

To make the recipes in this book easily and successfully wherever you acquire your tools, I recommend that, as much as possible, you equip your kitchen with the following items:

❖ *Electric mixer* with *paddle and whisk attachments* and *two mixing bowls.* If your budget allows, invest in a mixer mounted on a base, as opposed to a hand-

Some Notes on Ingredients

— ❖ —

BUTTER: Keep in mind as you follow these recipes that melted butter is not equal to solid butter in terms of measurement. For example, 6 tablespoons of melted butter equals approximately 5½ tablespoons of solid butter. Always remeasure the butter once it's melted to make sure you are using the correct amount.

CAKE FLOUR (not self-rising): This flour is lighter than all-purpose flour because it contains less gluten. Although the standard wisdom says that 1 cup of all-purpose flour equals 1 cup plus 2 tablespoons of cake flour, I find that when I substitute all-purpose flour, I often have to adjust other ingredients to avoid getting a powdery texture. So to make life simple, I recommend using cake flour when it's called for. Convenience stores and smaller markets don't usually stock it, but you'll find it at large supermarkets.

SUGAR: Granulated and light and dark brown sugar differ in moisture and mass, though they are the same in weight. This means that the drier granulated sugar tends to produce crunchier cookies and slightly drier cakes when it is substituted for equal amounts of brown sugar. Also, dark brown sugar has a higher molasses content than light brown sugar, so the equivalent cup measure weighs more. When you substitute dark for light, you need smaller amounts. You can make accurate substitutions if you have an ounce scale. In other words, 6 ounces of granulated sugar equals 6 ounces of light of light brown sugar equals 6 ounces of dark brown sugar.

CHOCOLATE: I've spent my lifetime thinking and dreaming about chocolate, and I still swear by Baker's when it comes to baking chocolate. I find the taste to be real, unadulterated, and exactly what I think chocolate should be. You'll find a lot of cookbooks and chefs who recommend imported chocolate, but I haven't found any that's better than our homegrown variety for baking.

That said, I make two exceptions to the rule. For chocolate chips, I like Nestlé's. Whatever brand you buy, make sure that they're real chocolate, not "chocolate flavored." And for making glazes, I've found that the more expensive chocolates do have a smoother texture, so I use Lindt bittersweet chocolate.

EGGS: Recently uncooked eggs have been the source of salmonella, a serious infection. If you are unsure of the quality of the eggs you buy, avoid recipes that use them raw.

held one, for the simple reason that it leaves your hands free. The extra bowl is essential for cakes that require beaten egg whites. The KitchenAid mixer is the absolute best.

❖ *Food processor.* Great for preparing pie crusts, chopping nuts and chocolate, making fillings for tarts or Bavarians, and on and on. I don't know what I did without one.

❖ *Two 8-inch layer cake pans* (2 inches deep) of heavy metal.

❖ *Two 9-inch layer cake pans* (2 inches deep) of heavy metal.

❖ *One 9-inch and one 10-inch springform pan,* although you can usually get away with only the smaller one.

❖ *Standard jelly-roll pan,* $15 \times 10\frac{1}{4}$ inches.

❖ *Four square or rectangular pans:* 11×7 inches, 8×8 inches, 9×9 inches, and 13×9 inches.

❖ *Bundt or tube pan,* 10-inch diameter with a removable bottom.

❖ *Two loaf pans:* $8\frac{1}{2} \times 4\frac{1}{2} \times 2\frac{1}{2}$ inches and $9\frac{1}{2} \times 5\frac{1}{4} \times 3$ inches.

❖ *Two standard pie plates,* $9 \times 1\frac{1}{2}$ inches.

❖ *Deep-dish pie plate,* 9×2 inches, usually made of Pyrex.

❖ *Two cookie sheets,* 15×12 inches, standard, heavy weight. I don't care for the new air-cushion cookie sheets — they tend to take the crunch out and leave the cookies soggy. I'd use them only for baking cake-like cookies.

❖ *Two cooling racks.*

❖ *Two baking dishes* for puddings and custards, preferably ceramic, $1\frac{1}{2}$ quart and $2\frac{1}{2}$ to 3 quart.

❖ *Double boiler,* 3-quart, heavy weight.

❖ *Saucepan,* 3-quart, heavy weight.

❖ *Three or four small bowls,* 2 cup and 4 cup, for cracking eggs, sifting dry ingredients, and measuring nuts. *One large bowl,* 12 to 14 cup, for sifting flour or folding ingredients together.

❖ *Two attractive bowls* for mousses, Bavarians, and puddings, 5 cup and 2 quart.

❖ *Two sets of graduated measuring cups,* $\frac{1}{8}$ cup, $\frac{1}{4}$ cup, $\frac{1}{3}$ cup, $\frac{1}{2}$ cup, and 1 cup for dry ingredients. Metal ones with handles last longest.

❖ *Pyrex measuring cup,* 2-cup measure, for liquids.

❖ *Two sets of metal measuring spoons.*

Some Notes on Equipment

— ❖ —

ELECTRIC MIXERS: The recipes in this book were tested with a KitchenAid mixer, which is more powerful than a standard hand mixer, so your mixing times may vary from the ones noted. When you're mixing batters, use the paddle attachment, if you have one. Save the whisk for whipping cream and egg whites and yolks.

MICROWAVE OVENS: I'm crossing my fingers we won't discover someday that microwaves turn teeth green or make our great-grandchildren grow horns, because I use mine constantly in baking. It's wonderful for melting butter and chocolate; bringing eggs, cold butter, liquids, sour cream, or cream cheese to room temperature; and softening hard brown sugar. Test your microwave to find the best temperatures and times for the results you're looking for, since the ovens vary. But, for the most part, avoid all high temperatures.

❖ *Two sturdy, standard-size rubber spatulas,* 9½ inches long (even better, make your second one commercial-quality, 13½ inches long—available at a kitchen supply store). *One very small rubber spatula,* 2 × 17 inch.

❖ *Standard metal frosting spatula* 10 inches long and 1½ inches wide for leveling off dry ingredients in the measuring cups and for icing cakes.

❖ *Small hand whisk,* 8 inches long, and a standard *domestic-size whisk,* 12 inches long, for beating by hand.

❖ *Standard-size or larger rolling pin.*

❖ *Pie weights.*

❖ *Large wooden spoon* for mixing puddings and custards.

❖ *Timer* and a *clock or watch with a second hand.*

❖ *Pancake spatula* to remove cookies from cookie sheets.

❖ *Two strainers,* about 3 and 5 inches in diameter.

❖ *Two sharp cutting knives;* one thin, one sturdy.

❖ *10- or 12-inch pastry bag* with *writing tips* for decorating cakes.

❖ *Baking parchment* for lining

cookie sheets and cake pans (also consider parchment cake pan liners).

❖ *Plastic wrap* or *waxed paper* for rolling dough.

Bare Essentials

—❖—

Having listed what may appear to be enough equipment to outfit Buckingham Palace, let me say that I know many bakers who wouldn't be able to fit into their kitchen if they followed my suggestions to the letter. Never fear, there's no question that you can bake successfully without purchasing a whole battery of equipment.

Of course, with less equipment, you will have to make some common-sense recipe adjustments. For example, if a recipe calls for baking brownies in an 11 × 7-inch pan and you only have an 8-inch square pan, your brownies will be thicker and therefore should bake more slowly and at a temperature 25°F lower than the one called for. If you bake a recipe calling for 8-inch layers in a 9-inch layer pan, they will require a shorter baking time because the batter level will be lower. Use your judgment; if the results are less than

perfect, you'll know to make further adjustments next time.

If you want to start off easy, here are the important items to have on hand:

1 electric mixer, stationary or hand-held

2 round layer cake pans, 8 or 9 inches

1 springform pan, 9 or 10 inches

2 cookie sheets

1 standard pie plate, 9 × 1½ inches

1 set graduated measuring cups for dry ingredients

1 measuring cup (2 cup size) for liquid ingredients

1 set measuring spoons

1 set small, medium, and large mixing bowls

1 rubber spatula

1 hand-held whisk

1 wooden spoon

1 rolling pin

A Final Word

I confess that I began this book with grand ambitions. It was to be a cookbook that grew dog-eared and smudged with fingerprints from generations of use while the recipes wormed their way into family lore and got trotted out along with the old photos. You know: "I've still never run across anyone who can make brownies as scrumptious as my father's," or "Every time I visited my grandmother, she used to make this really incredible chocolate cake with raspberries."

I still hope for something like that. But, as I mentioned earlier, my more immediate goal is to demystify baking through common sense, because I'm convinced that that is the key to successful and happy baking. In an odd way I was lucky in my baking career. Lacking formal training, I learned what I know through passion, instinct, and trial and error, and these still seem to me to be the best teachers anyone — novice or pro — can find.

So my final advice is to trust my recipes but trust yourself as well. After all, the worst that can happen is that you make a mistake — and one of the joys of baking is that the majority of our mistakes are edible.

CHAPTER TWO

Piece of Cake

In my teenage years, while my friends spent their Saturdays shopping for Villager outfits and Pappagallo loafers, I hung out in Doubleday's, poring over cookbooks with color photos of cakes. Who needed forbidden passages from *Peyton Place* when I could salivate over luscious pictures of double chocolate cakes?

I like to think I learned of the consolations of art early on, but even for those whose pleasures take a different form, cakes are an integral part of the way we celebrate. From birthday cakes adorned with plastic ballerinas or cowboys and Indians, to wedding cakes worthy of Claes Oldenburg, it's hard to imagine a proper anniversary or holiday as a cakeless event. So, early on, Rosie's started developing an array of cakes for every occasion.

I began with a little something chocolate, of course: Rosie's Famous Chocolate Sour-Cream Layer Cake which, when topped with ice cream, was cause for celebration in its own right. That was followed by the Snow Queen, inspired by the yellow cakes with white frosting and raspberry jam that are the perennial mark of an authentic birthday party among the under-ten crinoline set. Next came the Velvet Underground (as decadent as the group it was named after), the Mocha Cake, Queen Raspberry, Cold Fudge Sundae, and Texas Ruby Red, which have become the mainstays of Rosie's menu.

Theme and Variations

I learned quickly an old baker's strategy of taking a basic recipe and adding one or two things to make it into a whole new cake. For instance, once you've perfected a simple chocolate cake, you can layer it with fudge, preserves, whipped cream, mousse, fresh or frozen fruit, bananas and cream, or liqueur, and, *voilà!* have seven additional cakes in your repertoire. Then we have the humble pound cake which, like one of those make-overs in a fashion magazine, can appear plain at morning coffee, dressed tastefully with fruit for afternoon tea, or transformed into a rich layer cake for a ritzy dinner party. And you get to call the cake something different in each of its incarnations — naming is half the fun.

Since getting a cake just right can take some doing, you need something that comes easily at the beginning. Cake batters can be finicky, and a slight variation, such as the sequence in which ingredients are added, mixing technique, or baking time and temperature, can affect the outcome greatly.

Telling someone how to bake a cake gets complicated because nearly every rule has an exception. To try to simplify things in the following sections, I've identified basic rules. So unless you're fond of reading cookbooks cover to cover, I suggest that you glance through each section to find the category that applies to the cake you're making.

Preparing the Pan and the Batter

Layer Cakes

Do yourself a favor and line your baking pans with inserts made of baking parchment, which are larger versions of muffin papers and are usually available at kitchen stores. This way, you won't have to grease or flour your pans, and because the batter doesn't touch the sides of the pan, your cake edges come out moist and spongy. If you don't have ready-made liners, I recommend using parchment rather than waxed paper, which smokes as it heats.

To cut parchment circles from a larger roll, place the baking pan right side up on the paper and trace around the base of the pan with a pen or pencil. Cut out the shape with scissors just inside the outline and place the paper cutout in the bottom of the pan.

Regardless of whether you grease the pan or use parchment, it's best to cool all your cakes on a cooling rack and to leave the layer in the pan until you're ready to frost the cake. If you leave it for any length of time, cover it with plastic wrap after it has cooled.

When you use a pan insert, after the layer has baked and cooled, pick it up by the edge of the insert and lift it out of the pan onto a plate. When you've used circles cut out of parchment, after the cake has baked and cooled, run a frosting spatula around the edge to loosen it. Then turn the pan upside down at a 45° angle and allow the layer to drop onto your hand. Peel the parchment off with your other hand and flip the layer onto a plate.

If you have neither paper inserts nor baking parchment, use a small piece of paper towel or waxed paper to grease the pan lightly and thoroughly with butter or vegetable oil. Then, when the layer has cooled but is still slightly warm, run the spatula along the edge to loosen it, turn the pan over, and, holding the layer in place with your hand, tap the pan lightly on the counter as you rotate it. When the layer has loosened, let it fall onto your palm, then flip it over onto a plate.

Tube and Bundt Pans

Parchment doesn't work here, so grease these pans lightly with butter or oil, paying special attention to where the center tube meets the bottom of the pan because cakes tend to stick there. Pans without removable bottoms require particularly thorough greasing.

When the cake has cooled in the pan, run a flat frosting spatula around its sides. If the bottom is removable, lift it out, then run the spatula between the cake and the bottom of the pan and leave it under one side of the cake. Place a second spatula or a knife under the opposite side of the cake and use both to lift the cake off the pan bottom. (I sometimes press my chin against the top of the tube to help release the tube from the cake too.) Put the cake on a plate and cover it with plastic wrap until you're ready to frost or serve it.

For chiffon and angel food cakes, use a tube pan with a re-movable bottom and don't grease it because grease keeps them from rising. When cooling the cake, rest it upside down on the counter to prevent it from dropping back into the pan. If the tube pan isn't high enough to keep the top of the cake from touching the counter, stick a funnel or bottle into the hole of the pan, then turn it upside down and balance it on the funnel. Either way, after the cake cools for about 1½ hours, run a spatula around the sides and bottom and   remove it the same as you would above.

Springform Pans

This is an either/or situation vis-à-vis inserts or greasing. If you've greased the pan, when the cake has cooled, run a spatula around its edge, release the pan's lock, and remove the side of the pan. Then run a spatula between the cake and the bottom of the pan and use the spatula and your hand or two spatulas to lift the cake onto a plate.

If you have time to chill the cake for a minimum of 6 hours after baking, it will be sturdy enough to turn upside down, so use a parchment cutout. Chill the cake in the pan, then run a spatula around its edge and release the sides. Turn the cake upside down onto a plate or counter, peel off the paper, then flip the cake right side up, if necessary (depending on the type of cake, the bottom can be more attractive than the top and easier to frost).

Square and Rectangular Pans

If you plan to frost your cake in the pan and cut it into squares to serve, then it's best to grease the bottom and sides of the pan with butter or oil. If, however, you want to take the cake out of the pan in one piece and serve it on a plate, I'd go with a parchment liner. Let the cake cool, run a spatula around the edges, turn the pan over onto a plate, drop the cake out, and then remove the parchment. When you don't have parchment but want to remove the cake, grease the pan and remove the cake from the pan while it is still slightly warm with the assistance of your trusty spatula.

Batters with the Right Texture

*S*o much depends on texture that, to me, it contributes as much to a cake's character as does its flavor. Not to panic though; a cake's texture depends largely on the way you mix the batter, and there are basic rules for mixing that will stand you in good stead.

I've found it useful to divide mixing techniques into six categories, and once again, I suggest you find the one that applies to the recipe you're making. This system is imperfect, however (too much order makes me nervous), and a few recipes in this chapter blithely defy all my categories. Where there are exceptions to the rules, I've noted in the recipe how to deal with them.

Before you begin to follow any of these methods, it's very important that all of your ingredients be at room temperature, unless the recipe specifies otherwise. This makes it easier to mix everything together thoroughly.

Creaming Method

This is a standard method for mixing cakes, such as Poppy-Seed Pound Cake and Breakfast Coffeecake, that have a high fat content (for example, eggs, butter, and margarine). You alternate adding liquid and dry ingredients so that the flour helps the butter absorb the liquid. These cakes have a sturdy texture, but vary in lightness and density.

1. Sift all the dry ingredients except for the sugar together into a small bowl.

2. Blend the butter and sugar with the paddle attachment of an electric mixer set on medium or medium-high speed until light and fluffy.

3. Add the eggs one at a time to the butter mixture (unless the recipe says otherwise) and beat at medium-low to medium speed until each one is distributed evenly. Scrape the bottom and side of the bowl with a rubber spatula once during the mixing. The mixture will not be smooth at this time.

4. Add the dry ingredients to the butter, sugar, and egg mixture, alternating with the liquid. To do this, set the mixer on low speed, add one-third of the dry ingredients, and mix just until they are blended. Scrape the bowl with a rubber spatula now and each time new ingredients are blended in. Next add half the liquid; blend and scrape. Follow this with another third of the dry ingredients; blend and scrape. Add the remaining liquid; blend and scrape. Then add the remaining dry ingredients and — do I sound

like a caller at a square dance? — blend just until everything is incorporated and scrape again. If the recipe doesn't call for liquid, add the dry ingredients in two parts, mixing just until blended.

5. Use your rubber spatula to complete the blending by hand.

6. Pour the batter into the prepared pan and bake the cake immediately.

Creaming with Separated Eggs Method

This method is good for recipes such as Sour Cherry Fudge Cake and Pineapple Upside-Down Cake. Because the whites are beaten to a froth before being added to the batter, this method produces a lighter cake.

1. Follow the Creaming Method, but separate the egg yolks from the whites and set the whites apart in a grease-free bowl.

2. Add the yolks to the butter and sugar mixture and beat until incorporated, using the paddle attachment of an electric mixer set on medium-low speed.

3. Add the dry ingredients and liquid alternately as in the standard Creaming Method.

4. Whip the egg whites with the whisk attachment on medium speed until they are frothy.

Gradually add the sugar reserved for the whites over a span of about 20 seconds. Increase the speed to high and beat until they form firm but not dry peaks. Fold them into the batter gently with a rubber spatula.

5. Pour the batter into a prepared pan and bake the cake immediately.

Standard Sponge Method

These cakes, such as the Lemon-Strawberry Sponge Roll and Chocolate-Custard Sponge Roll, usually contain little or no butter or oil and get their sponginess from the air in the eggs. The mixing process begins by foaming the eggs, that is, beating air into them with a whisk or paddle. Sometimes the whole egg is foamed, other times the yolks are foamed separately from the whites, or just the whites are foamed.

1. Sift the dry ingredients together into a small bowl.

2. Separate the egg yolks from the egg whites, and set the whites aside in a grease-free mix-

ing bowl. Put the yolks in a separate medium-size mixing bowl and, with the whisk attachment of an electric mixer, beat them with the sugar at high speed until they are thick and pale.

3. Sift the dry ingredients over the egg yolk mixture, then fold it in with a rubber spatula.

4. Whip the egg whites with the whisk attachment on medium-low speed until they are frothy. Increase the speed to medium and gradually add the sugar reserved for the whites. Beat until they form firm but not dry peaks. Fold the egg whites into the batter gently by hand right away.

5. Pour the batter into the prepared pan and bake immediately.

Butter Sponge Method

These cakes are similar to the ones above but include melted butter, producing a cake that is somewhat denser and richer. Desert Island Butter Cake, for example, uses this method.

1. Sift all the dry ingredients except for the sugar into a small bowl.

2. In a separate medium-size bowl, beat the eggs and sugar with the whisk attachment of an electric mixer at high speed until the mixture is thick and pale, 4 to 5 minutes.

3. While the eggs and sugar are beating, melt the butter.

4. Sift the dry ingredients a second time over the egg and butter mixture and fold them in carefully with a rubber spatula.

5. Fold the melted butter in with a rubber spatula.

6. Pour the batter into the prepared pan and bake immediately.

Two-Bowl Method

Batters containing a lot of sugar and more liquid (for example, eggs, milk, or juice) than usual use this method. The batter is usually runny before baking, and the texture of these cakes can vary considerably. Rosie's Famous Chocolate Sour-Cream Cake Layers and Lemon-Glazed Orange Chiffon Cake both use this method.

Some Notes on Procedures

❖

TO SEPARATE AN EGG: Hold a raw egg over a bowl and crack its shell open around the middle with a knife. Gently separate the two halves of the shell, keeping the yolk in one half while letting the white run through your fingers into the bowl. Take care not to allow any of the yolk to get into the white, then slide the yolk into a separate bowl.

TO DIVIDE A YOLK IN TWO (when you want to halve a recipe): Follow the procedure for separating an egg, but rather than sliding the yolk into a bowl at the end, slide it into the palm of your hand. With a sharp knife — careful, now — slice through the yolk's center and push half off your hand into the cake batter. Save the other half to scramble into your kid's eggs.

TO MELT CHOCOLATE IN A DOUBLE BOILER: Place the chocolate in the top of a double boiler; the water in the bottom shouldn't touch the top pan. Cover the top pot and allow the water to simmer until the chocolate is about two-thirds melted — the shape will still be discernible but the chocolate will be soft. Turn the heat off and let the chocolate continue to melt completely.

TO MEASURE DRY INGREDIENTS: This includes flour, sugar, cocoa, confectioner's sugar and others. Use individual measuring cups (1 cup, ½ cup, ⅓ cup, ¼ cup, ⅛ cup) and spoons (1 tablespoon, 1 teaspoon, etc.) Scoop the ingredients into the cup or spoon, then level the top by scraping off the excess with a frosting spatula.

TO LINE A LOAF PAN: Cut a piece of waxed paper or parchment big enough to overhang the sides and ends by a couple of inches when it is molded into the pan.

1. Sift the dry ingredients together into a medium-size mixing bowl, add the butter or oil, and mix on low speed, using the paddle attachment of an electric mixer.

2. If the recipe calls for melted chocolate, mix it in now.

3. Stir the eggs together with the liquid ingredients in a separate bowl and add the liquid in a stream to the dry ingredients, while mixing at low speed. Mix just until the batter is blended.

4. The batter will be thin, but pour it into the prepared pan and bake immediately.

On the Way to the Oven

*F*ew recipes I've come across pay attention to the steps between mixing the batter and getting it into the oven. Yet how the batter sits in the pan is crucial to the baking process. Pour loose (thin) batters directly into a prepared pan by tipping the mixing bowl at a sharp angle and using your trusty rubber spatula to direct the flow and to scrape the bowl clean. The batter needs to be distributed evenly in the pan to bake well, so rock the pan gently from side to side to

achieve this. For a thicker batter, use a rubber spatula to scoop it from the bowl and to spread it evenly in the pan.

The tricky question though, and one my mother never really answered, is, when is enough enough? Layer, springform, and sheet cake pans should be between one-half and two-thirds full. Bundt and tube pans should be two-thirds full. This is important because too much batter in the pan can overflow, and, even if it doesn't, the edges of the cake will overcook before the center is done. With too little batter, however, the cake won't rise or brown properly. So if you don't have a large enough pan, put the right amount of batter in the one you have and make cupcakes from what's left over. If you don't have a small enough pan, borrow one from your neighbor.

Into the Oven

*S*o now you've got the properly mixed batter properly poured into the proper size pan, and all that's left is to get the cake into the oven — properly. But oven temperature and the position of your oven racks are crucial to attaining the proper taste and texture.

No matter what kind of cake you're baking, you want to place it in the center of a rack that is positioned in the center of your oven, where the heat is most even. When baking layer cakes, make sure that your pans are at least 1 to 1½ inches apart and arrange them on a slight diagonal so that they can both take advantage of this sweet spot in your oven.

The majority of cakes bake at 350°F, but several kinds require a slightly different temperature. When an oven is too hot, a cake rises too quickly, often forming an underdone mound at the center and a dark crust at the edges. When an oven is too cool, a cake, unlike the sun, never rises.

Sponge Rolls

I bake these cakes, Chocolate-Custard Sponge Roll and Lemon-Strawberry Sponge for example, at 400°F. Because there's usually less than an inch of batter in the pan, the cake can bake quickly and evenly without burning or drying out, even at this high temperature.

Flourless and Chiffon Cakes

These cakes, such as Chocolate Truffle Soufflé Cake and Lemon-Glazed Orange Chiffon Cake, contain a number of beaten egg whites and often call for an oven set between 300° and 325°F so that they will bake evenly and rise gently.

Cheesecakes

Because cheesecake batter is heavy and doesn't rise much anyway, I use a lower temperature, usually 300°F. In this cooler oven, cheesecake bakes slowly and evenly and its surface is less likely to crack. Try putting a shallow pan of hot water on the oven rack below; its steam will keep the cake moist. You can turn the oven off when the cake is done and leave it inside to set for 1 hour. By avoiding a quick change in temperature, you can often keep your cake from dropping or cracking. Or you can cool it on a wire rack. I've had success both ways.

And Out of the Oven

*O*vens vary; that's one of those truisms like fish swim and birds fly, only with fewer exceptions. It's for that reason that

I suggest you first look at your cake about ten minutes before the end of the baking time suggested in the recipe. To tell if it's done then, consider three indicators in the following order:

1. How the cake looks.

2. What the cake feels like when you touch it lightly.

3. If a tester inserted into the center comes out dry.

The cake's appearance and feel will vary, depending on your oven: layers will spring back to the touch; cheesecakes will feel firm; bundt cakes will have a rounded crisp top, and cakes baked in jelly-roll pans will be spongy in texture and almost level. Every recipe in this book describes what the finished cake should look like, but the most dependable test is to insert a cake tester or a long skewer in the center of the cake when you think it's done. (I don't use the time-honored toothpick because it's seldom long enough to get to the bottom of the cake.) If the tester comes out dry or with a few crumbs on it, the cake is done. If it comes out at all wet, the cake isn't done and needs to be baked a little longer, after which you should test it again. Don't remove the cake from the oven when performing this test, just slide the cake forward on the rack or gently slide out the rack.

The Eyes Have It

On more than one occasion I have argued for an anatomical connection between the eyes and the appetite, but even if there isn't one, there is surely a sensual relationship. So how your cake looks can add to its appeal. I'm partial to decoration that enhances the taste and appearance of the cake without overwhelming the cake itself. I find desserts that proclaim "Look at me!" are about as appealing as people who do, and it's been my experience that gobs of over-the-top sugar frosting lose their allure shortly after one's tenth birthday.

The simplest decoration for a cake is frosting, although getting the frosting on evenly and neatly takes several steps. Before beginning make sure your cake has cooled to room temperature.

Frosting a Two-Layer Cake

1. To keep the plate clean, cut 4 strips of baking parchment or waxed paper, each 3 inches wide and 2 inches longer than the diameter of your cake. Arrange the strips around the edge of your cake plate to form a square with the ends of the strips overlapping. Put the plate on a turntable or lazy Susan, if you have one.

2. Place one layer right side up on the plate so that the strips of paper are under the outer edge of the cake with their ends sticking out.

3. Using a frosting spatula, spread frosting ¼ inch thick over the top of this layer and then stack the second layer on top.

5. Spread another layer of frosting, no more than a ¼ inch thick, over the sides of the cake and smooth it out with the long, thin edge of the spatula.

4. Apply a thin layer of frosting to the top and sides of the cake to form a base coat which seals the cake, contains the crumbs, and makes it easier to frost.

6. Spread the remaining frosting over the top of the cake, smooth it out, then glide the rounded tip of a frosting spatula across the top of the cake on a diagonal to form parallel ridges. Trim off excess frosting by passing the long edge of the spatula around the circumference of the cake's top.

If you have a cake wheel, you can add a swirl by centering the cake on the wheel and spinning the wheel slowly while holding the top of the spatula at a 45° angle to the cake and gliding it toward the center of the cake in a continuous stroke.

7. Pull the paper strips out carefully. If there are any frosting or finger smudges on the plate, wipe them off with a damp paper towel.

If you were working on a cake wheel, ease your spatula under-

neath the cake and gently lift it. Use both your free hand and the spatula to support the cake as you move it to a serving platter.

Frosting a Four-Layer Cake

Follow the steps above, but in step 2, carefully slice each layer through its middle (see the box below on splitting layers). In step 3, spread frosting between each of these new layers, then continue on to the next step.

Writing on a Cake

Use a number 14 or 15 star tip and a 10- or 12-inch pastry bag. All of the items needed for writing are available at a cake decorating store. Before beginning, write your

Splitting Layers

— ❖ —

To split each layer in two, put the full layers on a piece of waxed paper on a flat surface, such as a counter or table. Place the blade of a long, thin knife at the midpoint of the first layer. With your free hand resting lightly on the top of the layer, slice through the layer evenly, keeping the knife parallel to the flat surface. Repeat with the second full layer.

If you have a cake wheel, follow these instructions, but turn the wheel carefully for a full revolution as you cut through the middle of the layer.

message down on a piece of paper. Check the spelling of all words, especially names.

1. If the pastry bag is new, clip just enough of the tip off so that the plastic cone fits securely, and insert the cone. Put the metal writing tip over the end of the cone and secure it by screwing the ring in place.

2. Fold the top of the bag down once over your left hand and hold it there. With a rubber spatula, fill the bag one-third full with butter cream frosting, then pull the collar back into place.

3. Gather the top of the bag together with your right thumb and forefinger and squeeze out any air bubbles with your palm.

4. Use your left thumb and forefinger to support and guide the bag as you write. If you're left-handed, reverse these directions.

5. Again, practice writing on a piece of baking parchment or waxed paper before you tackle your cake; it's not erasable.

Making a Chain of Rosettes

Fit a 10- or 12-inch pastry bag with a large star tip. All the items needed to make rosettes are available at a cake decorating store.

1. Remove all parchment strips from under the cake.

2. Follow steps 2 and 3 for writing on cakes but fill the bag half full of frosting.

3. Hold the bag as you would for writing, but keep it at a 45° angle with the tip touching the outer edge of the top of the cake. Squeeze the bag enough for a single rosette, then slowly pull the bag away while releasing the pressure. Continue this rocking motion until you have a chain of rosettes around the edge of the entire cake.

4. Repeat this process around the base of the cake, pointing the tip at the edge where the cake meets the plate.

Fresh Flowers

Not all decorations have to be edible. When I first started adorning my cakes, I had no idea how to make those pink, sugary roses bakeries use, and I waited for someone to discover my secret and say, "And you call yourself a baker!" So in self-defense, I found the one lavender plastic orchid in a five-and-ten that didn't look tacky and stuck it on top of a chocolate sour-cream layer cake whose rich brown frosting showed it off to distinction.

Then it dawned on me that there is an alternative to plastic, and I began to decorate cakes with real flowers. I've learned how to make the bakery buds since then, but why bother when a bouquet of fresh flowers is so much prettier?

I generally opt for elegant flowers such as roses, orchids, tiger lillies, dendrobium orchids, freesia, and snapdragons. Delphiniums and sweet peas are lovely as well although they do not last more than a couple of hours. Statice, baby's breath, and any frilly or lacy flower and the like can cover stems and create texture between flowers and greens such as various ferns, fica leaves, palm spears, and ivy. The greens provide accent and structure to the bouquet. Look for variety in color, texture and shape when you're choosing your flowers and avoid lillies of the valley and the berries on holly leaves because of their toxicity.

It is essential when decorating with fresh flowers and leaves that they look fresh and crisp; slightly browned or wilted petals must be removed, frosting smudges or crumbs must be cleaned off, and placement should be such that these beauties of nature rise above the surface of the cake if only by a fraction of an inch.

Flowers stay fresh for a surprisingly long time on a cake, but still add them as close to serving time as possible.

The Center Bouquet: This bouquet should give the feeling that it is growing right out of the cake's center, bursting forth with freshness. The bouquet is most dramatic when a few primary flowers such as roses, tiger lilies or tulips are placed at slightly varying heights to form the center of the bouquet. To insert the flowers, make a fresh cut across the stems leaving 1½ to 3 inches to insert in the cake depending on placement and the desired height of each flower. After the primary flowers have been placed, secondary flowers such as Peruvian lilies and freesia

can be used to surround the primary flowers, once again imbedded at slightly different heights to make the bouquet more interesting. Next use statice or baby's breath to fill in some of the spaces between and around the base of the bouquet, and to add a more impressionistic texture that softens the bouquet.

Positioning the leaves is the next step; these darker accents can shoot out from the base of the bouquet as if to be almost supporting it and they can be placed inside the bouquet to contribute to the texture and color.

The Arched Bouquet: This bouquet is particularly nice for cakes that are going to have an inscription. The arch can span anywhere from one-quarter to halfway around the outer edge of the top of the cake on the right hand side (just inside the frosting rosettes if the cake has them). For this bouquet you generally need more flowers than for the center bouquet. Use primary flowers in the middle of the arch and smaller flowers tapering out to the ends or make the arch using only smaller delicate flowers and filler and dainty leaf accents.

Dotting with Statice: On frosted cakes that have been piped with rosettes and are going to be inscribed, I like to pinch off little pieces of statice and place them in between every 3 to 4 rosettes. Then I choose an inscription color that complements the statice.

Log Cakes, Bundt Cakes, and Loaf Cakes: These cakes can be decorated as well. On log cakes, such as Tom's Birthday Roll or the Lemon-Strawberry Roll, flowers can be placed in little whipped cream rosettes accented by leaves as well as at the base of the cake. Bundt and loaf cakes look lovely on paper lace doilies, surrounded at the base with greens and an occasional flower.

Fresh Fruit

Fruits in season (and, for some varieties, out of season) add decoration, taste, and extra freshness to your baking. Try strawberries or raspberries arranged around the top of a frosted cake (I'm partial to berries with chocolate), or intersperse flowers with fruit. For a special touch, you can dip the strawberry peaks in melted bittersweet chocolate, allow the chocolate to harden, and then arrange the strawberries point side up on top of the cake.

You can slice citrus fruits thin and press them along the sides of a frosted cake or at the base of a bundt cake. Or you can slit the slices up the center, twist them and place them on top of the cake to give it height. Put the fruit on the cake just before serving so it won't dry out.

Chocolate Shavings

Chocolate shavings are a perfect final touch for any cake with chocolate in it. Use an ounce of Baker's unsweetened chocolate or any other dark chocolate. Using the fine side of a standard kitchen grater, first dust the top of the cake with shavings, then accent it with coarser gratings. For a dramatic effect, shave larger flakes onto the cake from an ounce or bar of chocolate. Use a sharp thin knife and allow the flakes to fall randomly over the top or around the outer edge of the cake.

Salvaging

*E*ven the best of cooks goof on occasion; layers can come out overcooked and cakes sometimes crumble as you transfer them to a plate. That's when you revert to a salvage operation. You can slice a layer through the middle so that you have two layers half as thick, and then smother each half with frozen berries in juice and whipped cream. If that won't work, cut the layers into chunks, toss them with wet fruit—raspberries, strawberries, ripe peach cubes— maybe mix in some vanilla pudding or custard, and put the whole thing in custard cups, crowning it with a piece of fruit and a dollop of whipped cream. Because you need the liquid to moisten the cake, pour the fruit's juice over the chunks as early before serving as possible.

Serving

*P*resentation doesn't stop with what's *on* the cake but includes what the cake is *presented* on as well. I swear by decorative plates which I pick up everywhere from china shops to garage sales. I'm lavish with lacy paper doilies, but cutting a frosted cake on a paper doily can be a messy business, so I avoid it by putting the doily under the plate instead. Make sure that your doilies are crisp and clean, your flowers, berries, and nuts are fresh, and all your toppings are perched lightly *on* the cake, not imbedded in the frosting and looking like ships foundering at sea.

If it's theatricality you want, present your cake on a pedestal cake server and maybe add the circular straw or cloth placemat or a crocheted doily underneath. When you're serving several cakes at once, create tiers by putting one or two on a pedestal and others on flat plates or baskets turned upside down.

Consider serving a bundt cake or a loaf cake in slices, or with half of it whole and the other half in overlapping slices like felled dominoes. If you're serving part of a bundt or tube cake, cut thin slices and arrange them in concentric circles on a round plate. Then dress them up by sprinkling confectioner's sugar over the top and strewing strawberries or flowers over all.

Cut frosted cakes with a sharp long, thin knife. To make each slice come out neatly, dip the knife in hot water and wipe it dry

Baking Cupcakes

❖

You don't have to be a kid to love cupcakes, They're portion controlled, transportable, festive, and best of all, fun to eat.

You can make cupcakes from almost any cake recipe. If you're a cupcake fan, keep a couple of muffin tins and a package of muffin cup liners on hand. I find that the paper liners keep the outside of the cupcake moist and make life very easy when it comes to removing the cupcakes from the tin. I also love peeling the paper away as I eat the cupcake. If you don't have liners, just be sure that each muffin cup is well greased with vegetable oil before pouring in the batter.

I fill each muffin cup to the top of the paper liner or three-quarters of the way up if I have no papers. This will produce a nice full cupcake. Bake them at the temperature called for in the cake recipe (usually 350°F) until the top is firm and a tester inserted in the center comes out dry, 30 to 35 minutes.

Cool the cupcakes in the pan. If you've used paper liners, the cupcakes should lift right out. If you've greased the pan, run a thin knife or spatula around the cupcakes and gently pick them up by their tops. Sometimes it's necessary to place the pan on an angle and tap it lightly on the counter to release the unpapered cupcakes.

Once cooled, frost the cupcakes, if desired, with a spatula.

before you make each cut. But if this means bringing a bowl of water to the table, just wipe the knife well after each cut.

Pound cakes, chiffon cakes, sponge cakes, and unfrosted bundt cakes, which are somewhat fragile, are best cut with a serrated knife, which puts less pressure on them. I find cake servers — slightly wedged-shaped spatulas — useful, especially for removing the first slice or when I'm serving frosted rectangular or square cakes from the pan.

Storing

To keep a frosted cake that has been sliced, pat plastic wrap against the cut surfaces. The wrap will stick to the frosting and help keep the cake moist. If you plan to finish the cake in a day or two, keep it at room temperature, preferably under a cake dome. Longer than that, a cake needs to be refrigerated, but bring it to room temperature before you serve it again. (Cold cakes usually taste dry and bland.)

Unfrosted cakes don't have a built-in sealer, so they should be kept under a cake dome or covered completely with plastic wrap. Most unfrosted cakes will stay moist for two or three days if they're well covered.

You can freeze any cake (although a cake that's been frozen won't taste as fresh or flavorful), but you have to seal it from the air. Tupperware dome containers work best placed over cakes wrapped in plastic. But if your generation missed out on Tupperware parties, you can wrap your cake in a layer of plastic wrap, followed by a layer of aluminum foil. Finally, put it in a heavy plastic bag and use one of those twisty things to close it up tight.

Relaxing

All these directions and admonitions — do this, don't do that — may leave you reeling and wondering why anyone in his or her right mind would bother. Bring on the Hostess Twinkies, you say, but the truth is that much of baking becomes second nature quickly.

Perhaps that's why, more than any other class of desserts, cakes seem to bear the individual stamps of their creators. Each has its own style and each has a mystique which I'd be the last to try to analyze. Instead I recommend that you follow these recipes with care, unleash your imagination when the cake comes out of the oven, and then flash a Mona Lisa smile as everyone asks you how you did it.

Rosie's Famous Chocolate Sour-Cream Cake Layers

I've read that chocolate contains a chemical similar to the one our bodies produce when we fall in love. This doesn't surprise me because I've never had any doubt that chocolate has transcendent powers. I wish my readers all the love they need, but in a pinch I offer this recipe. Baking the layers a bit below 350°F keeps them moist. In my well-considered opinion, these are the perfect chocolate layers: dark and not too sweet compared to other chocolate cakes, quintessentially American. The variations that follow match them up with rich fillings and frostings for unbeatable delicious layer cakes.

4 ounces unsweetened chocolate
2 cups sugar
1½ cups sifted all-purpose flour
¾ teaspoon baking soda
½ teaspoon salt
1 cup hot strong brewed coffee or 5 teaspoons instant coffee powder dissolved in 1 cup hot water
½ cup sour cream, at room temperature
½ cup vegetable oil
2 large eggs, lightly beaten with a fork, at room temperature

1. Preheat the oven to 345°F. Lightly grease two 8-inch layer cake pans with vegetable oil or butter, or line them with parchment circles or inserts.

2. Melt the chocolate in the top of a double boiler placed over simmering water, then turn off the heat.

3. Sift the sugar, flour, baking soda, and salt together into a large mixing bowl.

4. In a separate bowl, blend the hot coffee, sour cream, and vegetable oil with a whisk.

5. With the mixer on low speed, add the coffee mixture in a stream to the dry ingredients and mix until blended, about 35 seconds. Stop the mixer to scrape the bowl several times with a rubber spatula.

6. Add the eggs one at a time and mix on medium-low speed after each addition until smooth, about 15 seconds. Scrape the bowl each time. Add the chocolate and mix until the batter is uniform in color, about 10 seconds more.

7. Divide the batter evenly between the prepared pans and place them on the center rack of the oven.

8. Bake until the cake springs back to the touch and a tester inserted in the center comes out dry (do not wait for a crust to form), 35 to 38 minutes.

9. Cool the layers in the pans on a rack before frosting.

Makes 12 to 16 servings when frosted

Fudge Cake

*T*wo layers and one terrific frosting stack up to the simplest and dreamiest of the chocolate cakes. It's the ultimate at birthday time — copacetic with ice cream — need I say more?

I N G R E D I E N T S

*1 recipe Rosie's Famous Chocolate
    Sour-Cream Cake Layers (recipe
    precedes)*
1 recipe Fudge Frosting (page 83)

Follow the procedure for frosting a two-layer cake on page 27.

Makes 12 to 16 servings

Velvet Underground Cake

A deep dark inside of layers of chocolate cake and hot fudge concealed by a velvety buttercream.

I N G R E D I E N T S

*1 recipe Rosie's Famous Chocolate
    Sour-Cream Cake Layers (facing
    page), split into 4 layers (page
    29)*
1 recipe Hot Fudge Filling (page 87)
*About 1½ cups Rosie's or Mocha
    Buttercream (page 85 or 86)*
1 ounce dark chocolate for shaving

1. Following the procedure for frosting a four-layer cake (page 29), spread all interior layers with fudge filling, and the outside of the cake with the buttercream.

2. Shave the dark chocolate over the surface of the cake with a fine grater, then use the knife method of shaving (page 33) to make darker accents on the top of the cake.

*Makes
12 to 16 servings*

Queen Raspberry Cake

*A*n elegant cake which combines chocolate and raspberries with mocha or vanilla buttercream. I decorate it very simply: a dab of raspberry preserves on the center of the top and chocolate shavings around the top edge.

INGREDIENTS

1 recipe Rosie's Famous Chocolate Sour-Cream Cake Layers (page 36), split into 4 layers (page 29)

⅔ cup raspberry preserves, plus 1 teaspoon for garnish

⅓ recipe (¼ cup) Hot Fudge Filling (page 87)

About 1½ cups Rosie's or Mocha Buttercream (page 85 or 86)

1 ounce dark chocolate for shaving

1. Following the procedure for frosting a four-layer cake, spread the preserves, fudge filling, and buttercream as follows: cake layer, ⅓ cup preserves, layer, fudge filling, layer, ⅓ cup preserves, layer, buttercream on the top and sides.

2. Using the knife method for shaving chocolate (page 33), shave a wreath of dark chocolate around the top edge of the cake and place the remaining 1 teaspoon preserves in the center before serving.

Makes 12 to 16 servings

Cold Fudge Sundae Cake

I like to serve this cake—a new twist on the classic soda fountain treat—for celebrations, New Year's Eve for instance, accompanied by Champagne. It's particularly festive looking because the sides are not frosted and the whipped cream ruffles out like crinolines between the dark chocolate layers.

INGREDIENTS

1 recipe Rosie's Famous Chocolate Sour-Cream Cake Layers (page 36), split into 4 layers (page 29)

1 recipe Hot Fudge Filling (page 87)

1 double recipe Whipped Cream (page 86)

1½ cups frozen raspberries, thawed

1 ounce dark chocolate for shaving

12 fresh raspberries

1. Following the procedure for frosting a four-layer cake (page 29), spread the fudge filling, whipped cream, and raspberries as follows: cake layer, ¼ cup fudge filling, ½ cup frozen raspberries (leave a ½-inch border of plain fudge to prevent raspberry juice from dripping down the sides of the cake), ½ cup whipped cream (it should extend just beyond the edge of the cake), layer, ¼ cup fudge filling, ½ cup frozen raspberries, ½ cup whipped cream, layer, remaining ¼ cup fudge filling, remaining frozen raspberries, ½ cup whipped cream, layer, and the remaining whipped cream on top. As you stack each layer, press down lightly with your hand so that the whipped cream is squeezed out from between the layers a little.

2. Shave the dark chocolate over the top of the cake and crown it with the fresh raspberries.

Makes 12 to 16 servings

Texas Ruby Red Cake

*L*ayers of chocolate cake, raspberry preserves, and fudge frosting make this a very rich choice.

I N G R E D I E N T S

---

1 recipe Rosie's Famous Chocolate Sour-Cream Cake Layers (page 36), split into 4 layers (page 29)
⅔ cup raspberry preserves
1 recipe Fudge Frosting (page 83)
½ pint fresh raspberries (optional)
1 recipe Whipped Cream (page 86)

1. Following the procedure for frosting a four-layer cake (page 29), spread the preserves and frosting as follows:

cake layer, ⅓ cup preserves, layer, ½ cup fudge, layer, remaining ⅓ cup preserves, layer, remaining fudge on top and sides.

2. Crown the cake with fresh raspberries and serve each slice with a dollop of whipped cream.

Makes 12 to 16 servings

Snowball Cake

*R*emember those soft fluffy pink and white mounds covered with coconut? Well, this is a more sophisticated version, but we only make it in white!

I N G R E D I E N T S

---

1 recipe Rosie's Famous Chocolate Sour-Cream Cake Layers (page 36)
1 recipe Rosie's Buttercream (page 85)
2 cups shredded coconut

1. Following the procedure for frosting a two-layer cake (page 27), frost the chocolate layers with buttercream.

2. Pat the coconut gently around the sides of the cake and sprinkle it generously over the top.

Makes 12 to 16 servings

Mocha Cake

*T*he wonderful combination of chocolate cake, fudge filling, and mocha buttercream produces one of our all-time favorite cakes at Rosie's.

INGREDIENTS

1 recipe Rosie's Famous Chocolate Sour-Cream Cake Layers (page 36), split into 4 layers (page 29)
1 recipe Hot Fudge Filling (page 87)
1 recipe Mocha Buttercream (page 86)

1. Following the procedure for frosting a four-layer cake (page 29), spread the fudge filling and buttercream as follows: cake layer, ¼ cup fudge filling, layer, ½ cup plus 2 tablespoons buttercream, layer, ¼ cup fudge filling, layer, remaining buttercream on top and sides.

2. Heat the remaining ¼ cup fudge filling until it's syrupy but not hot and drizzle it over the cake with a spoon or a pastry bag fitted with a fine tip.

Makes 12 to 16 servings

Chocolate Buttermilk Cake

A light chocolate cake that I like to frost with Marshmallow Frosting.

INGREDIENTS

4 ounces unsweetened chocolate
¾ cup plus 2 tablespoons cake flour
¼ cup all-purpose flour
¾ teaspoon baking soda
12 tablespoons (1½ sticks) unsalted butter, at room temperature
1¼ cups sugar
1 teaspoon vanilla extract
2 large eggs, at room temperature
¾ cup buttermilk, at room temperature
1 recipe Marshmallow Frosting or German Chocolate Topping (page 83 or 84)

1. Melt the chocolate in the top of a double boiler placed over simmering water, then set aside.

2. Preheat the oven to 350°F. Grease an 11 × 7-inch baking pan lightly with vegetable oil or butter.

3. Sift both flours and the baking soda together into a small bowl.

4. Cream the butter, sugar, and vanilla in a medium-size mixing bowl with an electric mixer on medium-high speed until light and fluffy, about 2 minutes. Stop the mixer once or twice to scrape the bowl with a rubber spatula.

5. Add the eggs one at a time and mix on medium speed after each addition, about 10 seconds. Scrape the bowl each time.

6. Add the chocolate on medium-low speed and mix until blended, about 8 seconds. Scrape the bowl.

7. With the mixer on low speed, add the dry ingredients in three additions alternating with the buttermilk in two additions, starting and ending with the dry ingredients. Beat for 2 or 3 seconds after each addition except the last and scrape the bowl. After the last addition, beat the batter till everything is well blended, about 5 seconds.

8. Spoon the batter into the prepared pan and spread it evenly. Bake the cake on the center oven rack until the top is firm and a tester inserted in the center comes out dry, 30 to 35 minutes. Allow the cake to cool completely before frosting.

Makes 12 servings

Sour Cherry Fudge Cake

*A*n odd combination of tastes, you say? Not once you try it. The tartness of the cherries contrasts wonderfully with the sweetness of the chocolate, and all together it makes a dense substantial cake. You can make it for Passover by substituting matzoh cake flour for the all-purpose flour in the recipe.

I N G R E D I E N T S

8 ounces semisweet chocolate chips
4 ounces unsweetened chocolate
¼ cup water
1 cup (2 sticks) unsalted butter, at room temperature
2 cups sugar
2 teaspoons vanilla extract
6 large eggs, separated, at room temperature
1 cup all-purpose flour, sifted
2 cups canned or frozen sour red cherries, drained well and patted dry with a paper towel

1. Preheat the oven to 300°F. Lightly grease the bottom of a 9-inch springform pan with butter or vegetable oil.

2. Melt both chocolates with the water in the top of a double boiler placed over simmering water. Set aside to cool to room temperature.

3. Cream the butter, 1½ cups of the sugar, and the vanilla in a medium-size bowl with an electric mixer on medium speed until light and fluffy, about 2 minutes. Stop to scrape the bowl several times with a rubber spatula.

4. Using a whisk, stir the egg yolks into the chocolate and add this mixture to the butter mixture. Beat on medium speed until smooth, about 2 minutes, stopping to scrape the bowl once or twice.

5. With the mixer on low speed add the flour and mix until incorporated, about 20 seconds.

6. Beat the egg whites in another mixing bowl until frothy, about 30 seconds. Gradually add the remaining ½ cup sugar and continue beating until the whites form soft peaks, about 45 seconds more.

7. Whisk one-third of the whites into the chocolate mixture to loosen it, then fold the remaining egg whites into the batter with a rubber spatula. Place the cherries evenly over the surface of the batter and fold them in very gently with several slow strokes of the spatula.

8. Pour the batter into the prepared pan. Bake the cake on the center oven rack until it has risen and set and a tester inserted in the center comes out with a moist crumb, about 2 hours 10 minutes. Cool in the pan.

Makes 12 to 16 servings

Note: The cake will form a crust on top while baking; when the cake cools it will drop and the crust will crack. If you are bothered by its appearance, spread a layer of whipped cream on top and sprinkle chocolate shavings over the whipped cream or just sprinkle confectioner's sugar over the cake and eat it plain.

Chocolate Mousse Cake

*A*fter indulging in my first piece of chocolate mousse cake on a visit to New York several years ago, I decided that Rosie's could go no longer without our own version. By definition, the cake is rich and a little piece goes a long way, so I aimed to balance its richness with a deep semisweet chocolate flavor. A thin base of flourless cake supports a thick layer of mousse, which I accent with rum (though brandy or framboise will work too), then it's topped off with a veneer of whipped cream. The result looks very fancy, making this a perfect dessert for a dinner party or any celebration. Because this cake is made with uncooked eggs, be sure to prepare the mousse quickly and to refrigerate it while the base is baking.

INGREDIENTS

8 ounces semisweet chocolate
3 ounces unsweetened chocolate
1 cup (2 sticks) unsalted butter
5 large eggs, separated
¼ cup rum
1 teaspoon vanilla extract
⅓ cup plus 1 teaspoon sugar
1¾ cups heavy (whipping) cream, chilled
1 ounce dark chocolate for shaving

1. Preheat the oven to 350°F. Line the bottom of a 9-inch springform pan with a parchment or waxed paper circle.

2. Melt both chocolates and the butter in the top of a double boiler placed over simmering water.

3. Transfer the chocolate mixture to a large mixing bowl and allow it to cool to room temperature.

4. Add the egg yolks, rum, and vanilla to the chocolate mixture and whisk briskly until blended, 5 seconds.

5. Beat the egg whites in a medium-size mixing bowl with an electric mixer on medium-high speed until frothy, about 30 seconds. Gradually add ⅓ cup sugar and continue beating just until the peaks are stiff but not dry, about 1 minute more.

6. Add one-third of the egg whites to the chocolate mixture and whisk

gently to lighten this batter. Add the rest of the egg whites and whisk until blended.

7. To form the cake base, spread one-third of the chocolate mixture evenly in the prepared pan with a rubber spatula. Refrigerate the rest immediately.

8. Bake the base until it rises and then drops, 18 to 20 minutes. Cool it in the pan in the refrigerator, 15 minutes.

9. Meanwhile whip 1 cup of the cream until stiff in a medium-size mixing bowl with an electric mixer on medium-high speed. Fold the cream into the remaining chocolate mixture using a rubber spatula.

10. Scoop the chocolate mixture onto the cooled base and smooth the surface with a spatula. Stretch a piece of plastic wrap over the top of the pan and place the cake in the freezer overnight.

11. The next morning run a frosting spatula around the sides of the springform pan and remove the side.

12. Place a large plate upside down on the top of the cake and flip the cake onto the plate. Remove the bottom of the pan and the paper. Then flip the cake right side up onto a second large plate.

13. Beat the remaining ¾ cup of cream with 1 teaspoon sugar in a mixing bowl with an electric mixer on medium-high speed until stiff peaks are formed.

14. Spread half the whipped cream gently over the top of the mousse cake.

15. Place the remaining whipped cream in a pastry bag fitted with a decorative tip. Pipe rosettes of whipped cream around the top edge of the cake.

16. Shave the dark chocolate over the top of the cake and refrigerate it for 8 hours.

17. Remove the cake from the refrigerator 1 hour before serving.

Makes 16 servings

Chocolate Nut Torte

*T*his is a luxuriously rich cake which I often garnish with whipped cream, although, on its own, it is dark and moist and glazed with bittersweet chocolate. You can substitute matzoh cake flour for the all-purpose flour in the recipe and have an elegant Passover cake. Have all the ingredients prepared before starting because the chocolate starts to harden immediately when added to the egg yolks.

INGREDIENTS

CAKE
8 ounces semisweet chocolate
4 ounces unsweetened chocolate
1½ cups (3 sticks) unsalted butter
1 cup ground almonds (about 1⅓ cups slivered almonds ground in a food processor)
¼ cup slivered almonds for the top
9 large eggs, separated, at room temperature
1½ cups sugar
½ cup sifted all-purpose flour

GLAZE
6 ounces semisweet chocolate
3 ounces unsweetened chocolate
4 tablespoons (½ stick) unsalted butter
1½ tablespoons light corn syrup
3 teaspoons boiling water

1. Preheat the oven to 300°F. Lightly grease a 10-inch springform pan with butter or vegetable oil.

2. For the cake, melt both chocolates and the butter in the top of a double boiler placed over simmering water. Let cool slightly.

3. Place the ground almonds on half of a cookie sheet and place the slivered almonds on the other half. Toast them in the oven until they are golden, about 10 minutes. Leave the oven on.

4. Beat the egg yolks and 1 cup of the sugar with an electric mixer on medium-high speed until they are thick and lemon colored, 4 minutes.

5. Beat the egg whites in another mixing bowl on medium-high speed until frothy, 45 seconds to 1 minute. Gradually add the remaining ½ cup sugar and continue beating until the whites have soft peaks, about 45 seconds more. Set them aside.

6. Add the chocolate mixture to the egg yolks and mix on low speed until blended, 5 to 8 seconds. Scrape the bowl with a rubber spatula and mix on low speed again until blended, about 5 seconds more. Transfer the mixture to a large bowl.

7. Combine the ground almonds and the flour and sprinkle them on top of the chocolate mixture.

8. Place the beaten whites on top of the nuts and flour and with gentle strokes of a rubber spatula, fold everything together.

9. Pour the batter into the prepared pan. Bake the cake on the center oven rack until a tester inserted in the center comes out with very moist crumbs, 1¼ hours. Allow the cake to cool in the pan.

10. When the cake has cooled, prepare the glaze. Melt both chocolates and the butter in the top of a double boiler placed over simmering water.

11. Dissolve the corn syrup in the boiling water and stir this into the chocolate mixture.

12. Turn the cake upside down on a cutting board or plate and pour the glaze over the cake. Use a frosting spatula to spread the glaze to the edge of the top so it can drip down the sides of the cake.

13. Crush the toasted slivered almonds in your hand or chop them and sprinkle them around the top edge of the cake. Allow the glaze to set before slicing the cake.

Makes 12 to 16 servings

Chocolate Fruitcake

*S*ince chocolate is a hallmark of Rosie's, I decided to take the traditional fruitcake recipe and gussy it up a little. Like its forebears, this is a dense cake aged in liquor, but the chocolate and unsweetened dried fruits (not those cloying candied ones) make it stand out even in the special category of fruitcakes.

INGREDIENTS

*2 cups chopped mixed dried fruits,
such as apricots, dates, prunes,
pears, and raisins (½-inch pieces)*

*6 tablespoons Grand Marnier or other
orange liqueur*

2 tablespoons Cognac

3 ounces unsweetened chocolate

*½ cup plus 1 tablespoon all-purpose
flour*

½ teaspoon baking powder

*8 tablespoons (1 stick) unsalted butter,
at room temperature*

1 cup sugar

3 large eggs, at room temperature

*½ cup chopped walnuts, almonds, or
pecans*

¼ cup Cognac for brushing the cake

1. Combine the dried fruits, Grand Marnier, and Cognac in a small bowl or container and allow it to sit covered for 24 hours. Toss the fruit occasionally to ensure that it is completely saturated.

2. The next day melt the chocolate in the top of a double boiler placed over simmering water. Let it cool.

3. Preheat the oven to 325°F. Line a 9½ × 5½ × 2-inch baking pan with a piece of greased waxed paper that overhangs both long sides of the pan by 2 inches.

4. Sift the flour and baking powder together into a small bowl and set aside.

5. Beat the butter and sugar in a medium-size mixing bowl with an electric mixer on medium speed until light and fluffy, about 2 minutes.

6. Add the chocolate to the butter mixture and beat on medium speed until completely blended, about 10 seconds. Scrape the bowl with a rubber spatula.

7. Add the eggs one at a time and mix on low speed after each addition for 10 seconds. Scrape the bowl each time. Increase the speed to medium and mix 15 seconds more.

8. Add the flour mixture and mix on low speed just until blended, about 8 seconds. Scrape the bowl.

9. Stir the fruit (and any remaining liquid) and the nuts in by hand with a wooden spoon.

10. Spoon the batter into the prepared pan. Bake on the center oven rack until a tester inserted in the center comes out with a moist crumb, 1 to 1¼ hours.

11. Allow the cake to cool in the pan, then remove it from the pan. Remove the paper.

12. Using a pastry brush, brush some of the Cognac over all surfaces of the cake. Wrap the cake in cheesecloth or a light cotton cloth and brush the cloth with the liqueur.

13. Place the cake in a container or Ziploc bag and refrigerate it. If you plan to keep it for several weeks or months, brush it with more Cognac when the cloth is dry. The cake gets better and better as it ages.

Makes 12 to 14 servings

Golden Cake Layers

*R*emember the beautiful slice of cake on the box of Betty Crocker cake mix? I used to look at it and think that I could never make anything quite so perfect, but this cake not only looks good, it tastes a whole lot better. Although all-purpose flour can, in most cases, be substituted for cake flour (1 cup all-purpose equals 1 cup plus 2 tablespoons cake), I highly recommend using cake flour in this recipe — it greatly contributes to the delicacy of texture.

INGREDIENTS

2¼ cups plus 3 tablespoons sifted cake flour (measure after sifting)
¾ teaspoon baking soda
¾ teaspoon baking powder
½ teaspoon salt
1 cup plus 2 tablespoons (2 sticks plus 2 tablespoons) unsalted butter, at room temperature
1¼ cups plus 1 tablespoon sugar
2 teaspoons vanilla extract
4 large yolks, at room temperature
1 large whole egg, at room temperature
¾ cup sour cream, at room temperature

1. Preheat the oven to 350°F. Lightly grease two 8-inch round layer pans with vegetable oil or butter, or line them with parchment circles or inserts.

2. Resift the flour with the baking soda, baking powder, and salt into a small bowl.

3. Cream the butter, sugar, and vanilla in a medium-size mixing bowl with an electric mixer on medium-high speed until light and fluffy, about 2 minutes. Stop the mixer twice to scrape the bowl with a rubber spatula.

4. Add the yolks one at a time, blending for 5 seconds on medium-low speed after each addition. Scrape the bowl each time. Then add the whole egg and mix until blended, 10 seconds.

5. Add one-third of the dry ingredients to the butter mixture by stirring them in lightly with the rubber spatula so that the liquid is absorbed. Then turn the mixer on low to blend partially, about 5 seconds. Scrape the bowl.

6. Add half of the sour cream and blend in with several broad strokes of the spatula. Then fold in one-third more dry ingredients by hand, followed by the remaining sour cream, then the rest of the dry ingredients. Turn the mixer to low and blend until the batter is velvety in texture, 10 seconds.

7. Divide the batter evenly between the prepared pans and place them on the center rack of the oven.

8. Bake until the layers are golden in color and spring back to the touch, and a tester inserted in the center comes out dry, 35 minutes.

9. Cool the layers in the pans on a rack before frosting.

Makes 12 to 16 servings when frosted

Summertime Cake

*T*his delicately light cake is one of my favorites. It combines the tartness of lemon filling with the sweetness of buttercream icing.

INGREDIENTS

1 recipe Golden Cake Layers (page 47), split into 4 layers (page 29)
1 recipe Lemon Custard Filling (page 88)
About 1½ cups Rosie's Buttercream (page 85)
1 lemon for garnish

1. Following the procedure for frosting a four-layer cake (page 29), spread the lemon custard over all interior layers.

Frost the outside of the cake with the buttercream. The custard may cause the layers to slip from side to side, so I suggest placing one hand on the top of the cake while you frost the sides using the base coating method on page 28.

2. Refrigerate the cake after the base coat and allow the custard to set for an hour before completing the frosting.

3. Cut thin slices of lemon and place them on top of the frosted cake as suggested on page 32.

Makes 12 to 16 servings

Snow Queen Cake

*T*his is a golden butter cake layered with raspberry preserves. Probably because I'm getting sentimental in my old age, it tickles me to see that it's the dream cake of both the 10-year-old birthday girl and the bride planning her wedding feast. There will be those with quite different ideas of how to celebrate momentous occasions, I know, but keep in mind that this is the cake those fat little birds were busy festooning in Disney's *Sleeping Beauty*. And who am I to argue with Walt Disney?

**1 recipe Golden Cake Layers
(page 47), split into 4 layers
(page 29)**
⅔ cup raspberry preserves
**1 recipe Rosie's Buttercream
(page 85)**

Following the procedure for frosting a four-layer cake (page 29), spread preserves and buttercream as follows: cake layer, ⅓ cup preserves, layer, buttercream, layer, remaining preserves, layer, and the remaining buttercream on the top and sides.

Makes 12 to 16 servings

Harvard Mocha Cake

*P*eople who like their chocolate in moderation love this cake, which gives them four layers of golden cake layered with mocha buttercream and frosted all over with fudge. I'm not sure why I named it after Harvard.

**1 recipe Golden Cake Layers
(page 47), split into 4 layers
(page 29)**
2 cups Mocha Buttercream (page 86)
1 recipe Fudge Frosting (page 83)

Following the procedure for frosting a four-layer cake (page 29), spread ½ cup buttercream over each interior layer. Frost the top and sides of the cake with fudge frosting and crown the cake with mocha buttercream rosettes (page 30).

Makes 12 to 16 servings

Boston Cream Pie Cake

*M*ore Boston than baked beans (which seem to exist mostly in cans around here), this cake creates the taste of Boston cream pie with layers of golden cake iced with a rich vanilla custard. It's frosted with a dark fudge, and, since Boston is the home of America's first chocolate factory, you can't get more authentic than that.

**1 recipe Golden Cake Layers
(page 47), split into 4 layers
(page 29)**
1 recipe Fudge Frosting (page 83)
**1 recipe Vanilla Custard Filling
(page 87)**

1. Following the procedure for frosting a four-layer cake (page 29), spread the frosting and custard as follows:

cake layer, half the custard, layer, ½ cup fudge, layer, remaining custard, layer, remaining fudge on top and sides. The custard may cause the layers to slip from side to side, so I suggest placing one hand on the top of the cake while you frost the sides using the base coating method on page 28.

2. Refrigerate the cake after the base coat and allow the custard to set for an hour before completing the frosting.

Makes 12 to 16 servings

Pineapple Upside-Down Cake

I wonder about the mind that first conceived of an upside-down cake, although something is right side up about it, since I've yet to meet an American who hasn't tasted a pineapple upside-down cake. It was a staple of dorm food during my college years, but I don't hold that against it. This version is a light yellow cake topped with pineapple chunks that have caramelized in brown sugar and butter.

INGREDIENTS

TOPPING
¾ cup (lightly packed) light brown sugar
½ teaspoon salt
3 tablespoons unsalted butter, melted
1½ cans (20 ounces each) pineapple chunks, drained, patted dry with paper towels, then wrapped in more paper towels, and set in a bowl for several hours

CAKE
1 cup all-purpose flour
½ teaspoon baking soda
½ teaspoon baking powder
¼ teaspoon salt
6 tablespoons (¾ stick) unsalted butter, at room temperature
1 cup granulated sugar
1½ teaspoons vanilla extract
2 large eggs, separated, at room temperature
½ cup buttermilk, at room temperature

1. Preheat the oven to 350°F.

2. For the topping, mix the brown sugar, salt, and butter in a medium-size bowl with a spoon. Add the pineapple and toss the chunks in the mixture.

3. Spread the topping evenly in an 8-inch square pan and set aside.

4. For the cake, sift the flour, baking soda, baking powder, and salt together into a small bowl.

5. Cream the butter, ¾ cup of the granulated sugar, and the vanilla in a medium-size mixing bowl with an electric mixer on medium speed until light and fluffy, about 2 minutes. Stop the mixer once or twice to scrape the bowl with a rubber spatula.

6. Add the egg yolks and beat the mixture on low speed until they are incorporated, about 30 seconds. Scrape the bowl.

7. With the mixer on low speed, add half the dry ingredients to the butter mixture and blend just until incorporated, about 10 seconds. Scrape the bowl. Add the buttermilk and mix on low speed for about 8 seconds. Scrape the bowl. Fold in the rest of the dry ingredients by hand, then turn the mixer to low for several spins. Scrape the bowl.

8. In another medium-size mixing bowl, whisk the egg whites on medium-high speed until frothy, about 15 seconds. Gradually add the remaining ¼ cup sugar and continue beating the whites to soft peaks, about 15 seconds more.

9. Stir one-third of the whites into the batter with a wooden spoon, to loosen the mixture. Fold in the remaining whites with a rubber spatula.

10. Spread the batter evenly over the pineapple and place the pan on a rack in the oven just below the center. The higher heat allows the topping to caramelize better. Bake the cake until the top is golden and springs back to the touch, and a tester inserted in the center comes out dry, about 50 minutes.

11. Remove the cake from the oven and allow it to cool for about 2 hours. Run a frosting spatula around the sides and turn the pan upside down onto a plate.

Makes 9 to 12 servings

Carrot-Pineapple Layer Cake

*7*his is a wonderfully moist, fruity cake, delicious plain or frosted with a Cream Cheese Frosting.

INGREDIENTS

2 cups all-purpose flour
2 teaspoons baking powder
1½ teaspoons baking soda
1 teaspoon salt
2 teaspoons ground cinnamon
½ teaspoon ground cloves
½ teaspoon ground allspice
½ teaspoon ground mace
1 cup drained crushed pineapple
2 cups grated carrots (about 4 carrots)
½ cup chopped walnuts
1¾ cups sugar
1½ cups vegetable oil
1 teaspoon vanilla extract
4 large eggs, at room temperature
1 recipe Cream Cheese Frosting (optional; page 85)

1. Preheat the oven to 350°F. Lightly grease two 9-inch layer cake pans with butter or vegetable oil or line them with parchment inserts.

2. Sift the flour, baking powder, baking soda, salt, and spices together into a small bowl and set aside.

3. Pat the pineapple dry and place it in a medium-size bowl. Add the grated carrots and the nuts to the pineapple and mix them together.

4. Mix the sugar, oil and vanilla together in a medium-size mixing bowl using an electric mixer on medium speed until completely blended, 20 seconds. Stop the mixer to scrape the bowl twice with a rubber spatula.

5. Add the eggs one at a time and mix on medium speed after each addition until blended, 10 seconds. Scrape the bowl each time.

6. Add the dry ingredients and beat on low speed for 5 seconds. Scrape the bowl, then mix the batter by hand until the dry ingredients are incorporated.

7. Blend in the pineapple mixture with several turns of the mixer at low speed.

8. Pour the batter into the prepared pans and bake on the center rack until the top is golden and springs back to the touch, and a tester inserted in the center comes out dry, about 45 minutes. Place the cake on a rack to cool completely.

9. Eat as is or frost with Cream Cheese Frosting.

Makes 8 to 12 servings

Bittersweet Orange Cake with a Lemon Glaze

*I*f a cake can contradict itself, this one does: It combines the bite of the citrus fruits with the sweetness of the raisins, the crunch of the nuts with a moist texture. To me, though, that's what makes this cake special.

INGREDIENTS

CAKE

3 cups all-purpose flour
1½ teaspoons baking soda
1½ teaspoons baking powder
¾ teaspoon salt
1½ oranges with rind, cut into
    chunks and seeds removed
1½ cups raisins
¾ cup walnut pieces
12 tablespoons (1½ sticks) unsalted
    butter, at room temperature
1½ cups sugar
1 tablespoon grated lemon zest
3 large eggs, at room temperature
1½ cups buttermilk, at room temperature

GLAZE

½ cup fresh lemon juice
¼ cup fresh orange juice
5 tablespoons sugar

1. Preheat the oven to 350°F. Generously grease a 10-inch bundt pan with vegetable oil or butter.

2. Sift the flour, baking soda, baking powder, and salt together into a small bowl and set aside.

3. Put the oranges and raisins in a food processor and process with short pulses until the ingredients are chopped but not puréed, about 30 pulses. Add the nuts and pulse 6 more times.

4. Cream the butter, sugar, and lemon zest together in a medium-size mixing bowl with an electric mixer on medium speed until light and fluffy, about 1½ minutes. Stop the mixer once or twice to scrape the bowl with a rubber spatula.

5. Add the eggs one at a time and mix on medium speed after each addition until blended, 8 seconds. Scrape the bowl each time.

6. Fold the orange mixture in by hand. The batter will appear curdled.

7. Fold in the dry ingredients by hand alternating with the buttermilk as follows (to prevent overmixing, do not completely blend each addition): one-third of the dry ingredients, half the buttermilk, another third of the dry ingredients, the remaining buttermilk, and then the rest of the dry ingredients. Mix on low speed just until blended, several seconds.

8. Pour the batter into the prepared pan. Bake the cake on the center oven rack until the top is a deep golden color and a tester inserted in the center comes out dry, about 1¼ hours. Allow the cake to cool completely in the pan on a wire rack.

9. Meanwhile prepare the glaze: Whisk both juices and the sugar together in a small bowl until blended.

10. When the cake has cooled, remove it from the pan, put it on a plate, and poke holes over the entire surface with a fork. Then use a pastry brush to baste the glaze repeatedly over the surface of the cake until all the glaze has been absorbed. (You can also pour the glaze over the entire cake, reusing the excess that has dripped onto the plate to pour onto the cake again.)

Makes 12 to 16 servings

Apple Cake

Since apples taste best in fall or winter, this cake is a seasonal treat and one that can be stored nearly forever — if it makes it as far as the fridge.

INGREDIENTS

3 cups all-purpose flour
2 teaspoons ground cinnamon
1 teaspoon baking soda
1 teaspoon salt
1 cup (2 sticks) unsalted butter,
    at room temperature
¼ cup vegetable oil
2 cups sugar
2 teaspoons vanilla extract
3 large eggs, at room temperature
4 cups apples (3 to 4 large apples),
    peeled, cored, and cut into
    ½-inch cubes
1 teaspoon cinnamon mixed with
    1 tablespoon sugar for topping

1. Preheat the oven to 350°F. Lightly grease a 10-inch tube pan with a removable bottom with butter or vegetable oil.

2. Sift the flour, cinnamon, baking soda, and salt into a small bowl.

3. Cream the butter, oil, sugar, and vanilla in a medium-size mixing bowl with an electric mixer on medium speed until the ingredients are blended, about 2 minutes. Stop to scrape the bowl twice with a rubber spatula.

4. Add the eggs one at a time, and mix on medium-low speed after each addition until blended, 10 seconds. Scrape the bowl each time. Once the eggs are added, mix again for 10 seconds.

5. Add half the dry ingredients and blend on low speed for 15 seconds. Scrape the bowl, add the rest of the dry ingredients, and mix on low speed until blended, about 5 seconds more.

6. Add the apples with a few turns of the mixer or by folding them in by hand with a wooden spoon.

7. Spoon the batter into the pan and sprinkle the cinnamon-sugar over the top. Bake the cake on the center oven rack until the top is firm and golden and a tester inserted at the cake's highest point comes out dry, about 1 hour 5 minutes.

Makes 12 to 16 servings

Applesauce-Raisin Cake

Dark and hearty, this cake is a great fall and winter treat. I like to use unsweetened applesauce because the cake doesn't need the extra sweetness.

I N G R E D I E N T S

CAKE
2 cups all-purpose flour
1½ teaspoons baking soda
½ teaspoon salt
8 tablespoons (1 stick) unsalted butter,
*   at room temperature*
1 cup granulated sugar
½ cup (lightly packed) light brown
*   sugar*
1½ teaspoons ground cinnamon
1½ teaspoons ground nutmeg
1 teaspoon ground cloves
½ teaspoon ground ginger
½ teaspoon ground allspice
3 tablespoons unsweetened cocoa
*   powder*
2 large eggs, at room temperature
1½ cups applesauce, at room
*   temperature*
¾ cup raisins
¾ cup chopped walnuts or pecans

GLAZE
1½ cups sifted confectioner's sugar
1 tablespoon ground allspice
2 teaspoons ground ginger
1 teaspoon ground cinnamon
6 tablespoons (¾ stick) unsalted
*   butter*
3 tablespoons heavy (whipping)
*   cream*

1. Preheat the oven to 350°F. Generously grease a 10-inch bundt pan with vegetable oil or butter.

2. For the cake, sift the flour, baking soda, and salt together into a small bowl.

3. Cream the butter, both sugars, the spices, and cocoa together in a medium-size mixing bowl with an electric mixer on medium-high speed

until light and fluffy, about 2 minutes. Stop the mixer once or twice to scrape the bowl with a rubber spatula.

4. Add the eggs one at a time and mix on medium-low speed after each addition until blended, 8 to 10 seconds. Scrape the bowl each time. After the final scraping mix again on medium speed, about 10 seconds.

5. Add the applesauce and blend it in with a rubber spatula. Turn the mixer to medium for 2 complete spins.

6. Fold in the dry ingredients by hand with the spatula until they are almost incorporated. Then turn the mixer to medium speed and blend the ingredients until the batter is well mixed, about 8 seconds.

7. Fold in the raisins and nuts by hand with the rubber spatula.

8. Pour the batter into the prepared pan. Bake the cake on the center oven rack until the top is firm to the touch and a tester inserted in the center comes out dry, about 1 hour 10 minutes.

9. Allow the cake to cool completely in the pan.

10. To make the glaze, sift the confectioner's sugar and spices together into a small bowl.

11. Melt the butter in a small saucepan over low heat, add the cream when the butter has melted, and cook just until the cream is hot.

12. Stir the butter mixture vigorously into the dry ingredients with a whisk until they are absorbed. There will be lumps.

13. Pour the glaze into an electric blender and blend on medium speed until smooth, about 20 seconds.

14. Remove the cake from the pan and place it on a cake plate. Pour the glaze over the top of the cake, allowing it to run down the outer sides and down the center hole. Allow the glaze to set for an hour before cutting the cake.

Makes 12 to 16 servings

Banana Cake

*B*anana cake par excellence: a sheet cake that's perfect in flavor, delicate and moist in texture, and delicious plain or with Cream Cheese Frosting.

I N G R E D I E N T S

2¼ cups sifted cake flour
5 tablespoons all-purpose flour
1½ teaspoons baking soda
½ teaspoon salt
1 cup plus 2 tablespoons buttermilk,
    at room temperature
¾ cup mashed banana
    (about 2 very ripe bananas,
    skin should be brown)
10 tablespoons (1¼ sticks) unsalted
    butter, at room temperature
6 tablespoons vegetable oil
¾ cup (lightly packed) light brown sugar
¾ cup granulated sugar
1 teaspoon vanilla extract
3 large eggs, at room temperature
1 recipe Cream Cheese Frosting
    (optional; page 85)

1. Preheat the oven to 350°F. Grease a 13 × 9-inch baking pan lightly with butter or vegetable oil.

2. Sift both flours, the baking soda, and salt together into a small bowl and set aside.

3. In a second small bowl, stir the buttermilk into the mashed banana and set aside.

4. Cream the butter, oil, both sugars, and vanilla in a medium-size mixing bowl with an electric mixer on medium speed until light and fluffy, about 2 minutes. Scrape the bowl with a rubber spatula.

5. Add the eggs one at a time to the butter mixture and mix on medium speed after each addition until blended, about 10 seconds. Scrape the bowl each time.

6. Add one-third of the dry ingredients with the mixer on low speed, and mix for 8 seconds. Scrape the bowl. Add half the banana mixture, mix 10 seconds, and scrape the bowl. Add the rest of the dry ingredients and the rest of the banana mixture and mix for 10 seconds. Scrape the bowl and stir the batter several times by hand to mix thoroughly.

7. Pour the batter into the prepared pan. Bake on the center oven rack until the top is golden, springs back to the touch, and a tester inserted in the center comes out dry, 30 to 35 minutes. Place the cake on a rack to cool completely.

8. Eat as is or frost with Cream Cheese Frosting.

Makes 12 to 18 servings

Mustard Gingerbread

*I*n my opinion this is the classic American gingerbread: dark, moist, sharp in flavor, and not gummy the way some gingerbreads are. Serve it hot with whipped cream or vanilla ice cream.

INGREDIENTS

2½ cups sifted cake flour
1¼ teaspoons baking soda
½ teaspoon salt
¾ teaspoon mustard powder
2 tablespoons plus 2 teaspoons ground ginger
2 teaspoons ground cinnamon
¼ teaspoon ground allspice
10 tablespoons (1¼ sticks) unsalted butter, at room temperature
⅓ cup (lightly packed) light brown sugar
2 large eggs, at room temperature
¾ cup unsulphured molasses, at room temperature
1 cup strong brewed coffee

1. Preheat the oven to 350°F and lightly grease a 10-inch springform pan with butter or vegetable oil.

2. Sift the flour, baking soda, salt, mustard powder, and spices together into a medium-size bowl.

3. Cream the butter and sugar together in a medium-size mixing bowl with an electric mixer on medium speed until light and fluffy, about 2 minutes. Stop the mixer twice to scrape the bowl with a rubber spatula.

4. Add the eggs one at a time to the butter mixture and mix on medium speed after each addition until the eggs are blended but not smooth, 8 to 10 seconds. Scrape the bowl each time.

5. Add the molasses with the mixer on medium-low speed and mix for 5 seconds. The batter will look very separated.

6. Add half the dry ingredients to the batter with the mixer on low speed and mix just until they have absorbed the liquid but are not thoroughly blended, about 10 seconds. Add half the coffee and fold it into the mixture with a rubber spatula.

7. Add the remaining dry ingredients on medium-low speed and blend until they are almost incorporated, 10 seconds. Pour in the remaining coffee, then fold it in by hand with a rubber spatula. Turn the mixer to low and blend until the batter is smooth, 5 seconds.

8. Pour the batter into the prepared pan. Bake the cake on the center oven rack until the top springs back to the touch and a tester inserted in the center comes out dry, about 45 minutes. Cool slightly in the pan before serving.

Makes 12 to 16 servings

Coconut-Pecan Oatmeal Cake

7his is a hearty cake, almost more of a fall or winter snack than a dessert. Be careful not to let the oatmeal stand or it will coagulate. Serve this cake soon after it has baked—it's great warm.

INGREDIENTS

CAKE
1⅓ cups all-purpose flour
1 teaspoon baking soda
½ teaspoon baking powder
1 teaspoon salt
½ teaspoon ground cinnamon
1 cup quick-cooking oats
8 tablespoons (1 stick) unsalted butter, at room temperature
1 cup plus 3 tablespoons sugar
2 teaspoons vanilla extract
2 large eggs, at room temperature
1⅓ cups boiling water

TOPPING
6 tablespoons (¾ stick) unsalted butter, at room temperature
1 cup (lightly packed) light brown sugar
¼ cup light cream, half and half, or milk
1 teaspoon vanilla extract
½ cup chopped pecans
½ cup shredded coconut

1. Preheat the oven to 350°F. Lightly grease an 11×7-inch broiler-proof baking pan with butter or vegetable oil.

2. For the cake, sift the flour, baking soda, baking powder, salt, and cinnamon together into a small bowl. Place the oats in a medium-size bowl.

3. Cream the butter, sugar, and vanilla together in a second medium-size mixing bowl with an electric mixer on medium speed until light and fluffy, about 2 minutes. Stop the mixer twice to scrape the bowl with a rubber spatula.

4. Add the eggs one at a time to the

butter mixture and mix on medium speed after each addition until blended, 10 seconds. Scrape the bowl each time.

5. Pour the boiling water over the oatmeal and stir several times with a wooden spoon. Add the oatmeal to the egg mixture and mix on medium speed until blended, about 6 to 7 seconds.

6. Partially fold in the dry ingredients by hand with the spatula, using several broad strokes. Then mix on medium speed until all the ingredients are blended, about 10 seconds. Scrape the bowl.

7. Pour the batter into the prepared pan. Bake the cake on the center oven rack until the top is golden and springs back to the touch, 25 to 30 minutes. Remove the cake from the oven and allow it to cool for 15 minutes.

8. Meanwhile prepare the topping. Put all the ingredients in a medium-size mixing bowl and stir vigorously with a whisk until they are blended.

9. Preheat the broiler.

10. Spread the topping over the cake with a spatula, then place the cake on a cookie sheet (to catch any drips). If your broiler is part of your oven, place the cake on the center rack of the oven. If you have a separate broiler unit, place the cake as far as possible from it. With the oven or broiler door open, broil, rotating the pan several times, until the topping bubbles to a deep golden color, 5 to 6 minutes. Watch it carefully.

Makes 12 servings

Breakfast Coffeecake

A classic sour-cream coffeecake layered and topped with a sweet, crunchy pecan mixture.

INGREDIENTS

TOPPING
1 1/3 cups (lightly packed) light brown sugar
1 tablespoon ground cinnamon
1 1/2 cups chopped pecans
8 tablespoons (1 stick) unsalted butter, cool but not cold

CAKE
2 2/3 cups all-purpose flour
1 1/4 teaspoons baking powder
1 teaspoon baking soda
1/2 teaspoon salt
12 tablespoons (1 1/2 sticks) unsalted butter, at room temperature
1 cup plus 2 tablespoons granulated sugar
2 teaspoons vanilla extract
4 large eggs, at room temperature
1 1/3 cups sour cream, at room temperature

1. Preheat the oven to 350°F. Grease a 9-inch springform pan lightly with butter or vegetable oil.

2. For the topping, combine the brown sugar, cinnamon, and pecans in a medium-size bowl and rub the butter into this mixture with your fingertips until it is incorporated. Set aside.

3. For the cake, sift the flour, baking

powder, baking soda, and salt into a small bowl.

4. Cream the butter, sugar, and vanilla in a medium-size mixing bowl with an electric mixer on medium speed until light and fluffy, about 2 minutes. Stop the mixer twice to scrape the bowl with a rubber spatula.

5. Add the eggs one at a time to the butter mixture and mix on medium-low speed after each addition until blended, 5 seconds. Scrape the bowl each time.

6. By hand add the dry ingredients in 4 additions alternately with the sour cream in 3 additions, beginning and ending with the dry ingredients. Do not blend each addition in fully before adding the next. When everything has been added, turn the mixer on low and blend until smooth, 5 seconds.

7. Spread half of the batter in the prepared pan and distribute half the topping over it. Spoon the remaining batter on top, smooth it out evenly, and distribute the remaining topping over the top.

8. Place a piece of foil or a cookie sheet on the bottom oven rack, then place the cake on the center rack. Bake the cake until the top turns golden, about 40 minutes. Gently place a piece of aluminum foil over the top of the cake (do not mold it) and continue to bake the cake until a tester inserted in the center comes out dry, about 40 minutes more. Serve warm or at room temperature.

Makes 12 to 16 servings

Fresh Blueberry-Muffin Breakfast Cake

*7*his is really a blueberry muffin masquerading as a cake, which makes it perfect for brunch or snacking—anytime you want something to accompany a cup of tea or coffee or a glass of milk. The cake should be served quite warm, soon after it comes out of the oven, and I especially like my piece with a thin veneer of sweet butter. Cranberries can be substituted for blueberries when they are in season.

INGREDIENTS

CAKE
2 cups all-purpose flour
2 teaspoons baking powder
¾ teaspoon salt
10 tablespoons (1¼ sticks) unsalted butter, at room temperature
1½ cups granulated sugar
1½ teaspoons vanilla extract
2 large eggs, at room temperature
¾ cup milk, at room temperature
1¾ cups fresh blueberries

TOPPING

8 tablespoons (1 stick) unsalted
    butter, cut into 8 pieces,
    at room temperature
¼ cup all-purpose flour
½ cup granulated sugar
½ cup (lightly packed) light brown
    sugar
¼ teaspoon ground cinnamon
Pinch of salt

1. Preheat the oven to 350°F. Grease a 9-inch square baking pan lightly with butter or vegetable oil.

2. For the cake, sift the flour, baking powder, and salt together into a small bowl.

3. Cream the butter, sugar, and vanilla in a medium-size mixing bowl with an electric mixer on medium speed until the mixture is light and fluffy, about 2 minutes. Stop the mixer once or twice to scrape the bowl with a rubber spatula.

4. Add the eggs one at a time to the butter mixture and mix on medium speed after each addition until blended, 8 to 10 seconds. Scrape the bowl each time.

5. Fold one-third of the dry ingredients in by hand just until they have absorbed the liquid but are not thoroughly blended. Fold in half the milk by hand with several strokes, then the rest of the dry ingredients, folding just until they are absorbed. Add the rest of the milk and fold it in just until the batter is smooth.

6. Fold the blueberries in gently.

7. Pour the batter into the prepared pan. Bake the cake on the center oven rack until the top is just set but not golden, 25 to 30 minutes.

8. Meanwhile prepare the topping: Place all the ingredients in a food processor and pulse until blended, about 10 pulses. Or mix all the dry ingredients in a small bowl and rub the butter into the mixture with your fingers.

9. When the top of the cake is set, cover the surface with spoonfuls of topping and return the cake to the oven until the topping spreads and begins to get crunchy, 15 to 20 minutes.

10. Remove the cake from the oven and serve it hot. It is good eaten plain or buttered like a muffin.

Makes 9 to 12 servings

Cream Cheese Pound Cake

I dedicate this dessert to my sister-in-law Laura, who is such a fan that when she first tasted it, she devoured nearly the entire cake. The cream cheese combines with the other ingredients to make it velvety and moist, but it doesn't overpower the flavor of the butter.

INGREDIENTS

3 cups cake flour
1½ cups (3 sticks) unsalted butter, at room temperature
1 package (8 ounces) cream cheese, at room temperature or warmed lightly in a microwave
3 cups sugar
1 tablespoon vanilla extract
6 large eggs, at room temperature

1. Preheat the oven to 325°F. Lightly grease a 10-inch tube pan with butter or vegetable oil.

2. Sift the cake flour into a small bowl and set aside.

3. Cream the butter, cream cheese, sugar, and vanilla in a medium-size mixing bowl with the mixer on medium-high speed until light and fluffy, about 2 minutes. Stop the mixer once or twice to scrape the bowl with a rubber spatula.

4. Add the eggs one at a time to the butter mixture and mix on medium speed after each addition until blended, about 10 seconds. Scrape the bowl each time. When all the eggs are added, mix 30 seconds more.

5. Stir the flour gently into the batter with a rubber spatula. Then mix on low speed 5 seconds, scrape the bowl, and blend until the batter is smooth and even, 5 to 10 seconds.

6. Pour the batter into the prepared pan. Bake the cake on the center oven rack until golden and firm to the touch, and a tester inserted in the center comes out dry, about 1 hour 35 minutes.

7. Allow the cake to cool completely in the pan before unmolding and serving.

Makes 12 to 16 servings

Almond Pound Cake

H ere is a simple butter pound cake with a distinctive almond taste. I top it with an almond glaze and crushed almonds.

I N G R E D I E N T S

CAKE

1½ cups plus 3 tablespoons cake flour
¾ teaspoon baking powder
½ teaspoon baking soda
¼ teaspoon salt
10 tablespoons (1¼ sticks) unsalted
    butter, at room temperature
¾ cup granulated sugar
2 teaspoons almond extract
1 teaspoon vanilla extract
3 large eggs, at room temperature
½ cup plus 1 tablespoon sour cream

GLAZE

1 cup confectioner's sugar, sifted
2¼ teaspoons almond extract
2 tablespoons hot water
¼ cup chopped slivered almonds

1. Preheat the oven to 350°F. Grease an 8½ × 4½ × 2½-inch loaf pan lightly with butter or oil.

2. For the cake, sift the cake flour, baking powder, baking soda, and salt together into a small bowl.

3. Cream the butter, sugar, and both extracts in a medium-size mixing bowl with an electric mixer on medium speed until light and fluffy, about 2 minutes. Stop the mixer once or twice to scrape the bowl with a rubber spatula.

4. Add the eggs one at a time to the butter mixture and mix on medium speed after each addition until blended, 10 seconds. Scrape the bowl each time. The eggs will not be fully mixed into the batter at this point.

5. Add half the dry ingredients and mix on low speed for 10 seconds. Add half the sour cream and mix for 5 seconds. Add the remaining dry ingredients and mix 5 seconds, then add the remaining sour cream and mix another 5 seconds. The batter should be velvety.

6. Pour the batter into the prepared pan. Bake on the center oven rack until the top is firm and golden, and a tester inserted in the center comes out dry, about 50 minutes. The top will crack slightly. Let the cake cool completely.

7. Prepare the glaze: Stir the confectioner's sugar, almond extract, and water together in a small bowl with a small whisk until the sugar is completely dissolved.

8. Remove the cake from the pan and place it on a cookie sheet. Pour the glaze over the cake slowly so that it covers the top and drips down the sides. Sprinkle the almonds over the top immediately. When the glaze hardens, transfer the cake to a pretty serving plate.

Makes 8 to 12 servings

Poppy-Seed Pound Cake

*P*ound cakes got their name because originally they were made with a pound of each ingredient. For this recipe, I kept the name but changed the weight to come up with a remarkably versatile cake. It's ideal sliced thin as a tea cake, as a chunk cut for an after-school snack, served with fresh fruit as dessert, or dunked into coffee in place of a breakfast doughnut. That probably accounts for its popularity, although the crunchiness of the whole poppy seeds also has something to do with it. You can also substitute 1¼ cups blueberries, cranberries, chocolate chips, or nuts for the poppy seeds, and have an equally scrumptious cake.

INGREDIENTS

4 cups all-purpose flour
2 teaspoons baking soda
1 tablespoon baking powder
½ teaspoon salt
1 cup (2 sticks) unsalted butter, at room temperature
2 cups sugar
1 tablespoon vanilla extract
4 large eggs, at room temperature
2 cups sour cream, at room temperature
½ cup plus 1½ tablespoons poppy seeds

1. Preheat the oven to 350°F. Lightly grease a 10-inch tube pan with vegetable oil or butter.

2. Sift the flour, baking soda, baking powder, and salt together into a medium-size bowl.

3. Cream the butter, sugar, and vanilla in a large mixing bowl with an electric mixer on medium speed until light and fluffy, about 2 minutes. Stop the mixer once or twice to scrape the bowl with a rubber spatula.

4. Add the eggs one at a time to the butter mixture and mix on medium-low speed after each addition until blended, 5 seconds. Scrape the bowl each time. When all the eggs are added, beat the mixture for 10 seconds. It will not appear smooth at this point.

5. Add one-third of the dry ingredients to the egg mixture and fold them in lightly with a rubber spatula so that the liquid is absorbed. Mix on low speed 5 seconds until partially blended. Scrape the bowl.

6. Add half the sour cream, and mix on low speed for 5 seconds until partially blended. Mix the batter with several broad strokes of the spatula and scrape the bowl. Add another third of the dry ingredients, the remaining sour cream, and then the remaining dry ingredients with this same procedure. Mix the batter on low speed until it is velvety, about 15 seconds.

7. Add ½ cup of the poppy seeds on low speed and mix just until blended.

8. Pour the batter into the prepared pan and sprinkle the remaining poppy seeds over the top.

9. Bake the cake on the center oven rack until it is high and golden, about 1 hour 10 minutes. A cake tester inserted at the highest point should come out clean.

10. Remove the cake from the oven and allow it to cool in the pan on a rack for several hours before unmolding and serving.

Makes 12 to 16 servings

Poppy-Seed Chocolate-Chip Cake

*7*he name is complicated, but the cake is a straightforward butter cake embroidered with chocolate and poppy seeds, a surprisingly complementary combination.

INGREDIENTS

2¹/₂ cups all-purpose flour
2 teaspoons baking powder
1 teaspoon baking soda
¹/₄ teaspoon salt
*1 cup (2 sticks) unsalted butter,
    at room temperature*
1 cup plus 4 tablespoons sugar
2 teaspoons vanilla extract
1 teaspoon ground cinnamon
*4 large eggs, separated,
    at room temperature*
*1 cup buttermilk, at room
    temperature*
*1 cup semisweet chocolate chips,
    coarsely chopped by hand*
*1¹/₂ ounces unsweetened chocolate,
    grated*
¹/₄ cup poppy seeds
Confectioner's sugar for garnish

1. Preheat the oven to 350°F. Grease a 10-inch bundt pan with butter or vegetable oil.

2. Sift the flour, baking powder, baking soda, and salt together into a small bowl.

3. Beat the butter, 1 cup plus 1 tablespoon of the sugar, the vanilla, and cinnamon in a medium-size mixing bowl with an electric mixer on medium speed until blended, about 2 minutes. Stop the mixer once or twice to scrape the bowl with a rubber spatula.

4. Add the egg yolks to the butter mixture and beat on medium speed until blended, about 10 seconds. Scrape the bowl once during the mixing and again at the end. The batter will not be smooth at this point.

5. Fold in one-third of the dry ingredients with a rubber spatula. Then fold in half the buttermilk, another third of the dry ingredients, the remaining buttermilk, and the remaining dry ingredients. Do not fully blend in the ingredients after each addition until the end.

6. Beat the egg whites in another medium-size mixing bowl with an electric mixer on medium-high speed until frothy, about 30 seconds. Gradually add the remaining 3 tablespoons sugar and continue beating until the whites form soft peaks, about 30 seconds more. Stir one-third of the whites into the batter to loosen it, then fold in the rest of the whites with a rubber spatula. Fold in the chocolate chips, grated chocolate, and poppy seeds.

7. Scoop the batter into the pan and distribute it evenly. Bake the cake on the center oven rack until it is golden and a tester inserted in the center comes out dry, about 1 hour.

8. Let the cake cool completely in the pan. Sift confectioner's sugar over the top before serving.

Makes 12 to 16 servings

Desert Island Butter Cake

*T*his cake got its name because it would be my choice if I were stranded on a desert island and could have only one sweet. (How come no one ever gets stranded on a desert island?) This cake is unbelievably easy and quick to make with a flavor and texture halfway between a sponge and a pound cake. You can gussy it up with strawberries or cut off a chunk to eat plain with an occasional dunk in your coffee.

INGREDIENTS

1 cup (2 sticks) unsalted butter
3 large eggs, at room temperature
1 cup sugar
1 cup sifted all-purpose flour
Frozen strawberries, thawed, or fresh
*   strawberries, hulled and lightly*
*   sugared to make a juice,*
*   for serving (optional)*

1. Preheat the oven to 350°F. Lightly grease an 8-inch springform pan with butter or vegetable oil.

2. Melt the butter in a saucepan over low heat.

3. Beat the eggs and sugar in a medium-size mixing bowl with an electric mixer on high speed until the mixture is thick and pale, about 4 minutes.

4. Resift the flour over the egg mixture and fold it in gently with a rubber spatula.

5. When the flour is almost but not completely incorporated, slowly fold in the melted butter with gentle strokes.

6. Pour the batter into the prepared pan. Bake the cake on the center oven rack until the center of the top puffs up and then falls level with the outer edges, 35 to 40 minutes. The center will drop slightly as the cake cools to room temperature.

7. For the best flavor, serve the cake the next day with the strawberries, if desired.

Makes 12 to 15 servings

Fresh Berry Sponge Cake

*W*henever I make this dessert for Passover, people are always surprised that a cake made with matzoh flour could taste so wonderful. The lemony sponge cake makes a lovely change from the usual berry shortcake.

6 tablespoons potato starch
10 tablespoons matzoh cake flour
½ teaspoon salt
6 large eggs, separated,
    at room temperature
2 tablespoons water
1¼ cups plus 1 tablespoon sugar
2 tablespoons fresh lemon juice
1 tablespoon grated lemon zest
2 teaspoons vanilla extract
1½ cups hulled, sliced fresh or
    frozen strawberries, or raspberries, thawed if frozen
1 double recipe Whipped Cream
    (page 86)
12 fresh whole strawberries or
    24 fresh whole raspberries
    for garnish

1. Preheat the oven to 350°F. Line two 8-inch layer pans with waxed paper or parchment circles or inserts.

2. Sift the potato starch, matzoh flour, and salt together into a small bowl.

3. Beat the egg yolks, water, 1 cup plus 1 tablespoon sugar, the lemon juice and zest, and vanilla in a medium-size mixing bowl with an electric mixer on medium speed until blended, about 10 seconds. Scrape the bowl with a rubber spatula.

4. Blend the dry ingredients into the egg yolk mixture on low speed until incorporated, about 10 seconds. Scrape the bowl.

5. Beat the egg whites in another mixing bowl on medium-high speed until frothy, about 30 seconds. Gradually add the remaining ¼ cup sugar and continue beating the whites to firm peaks, about 90 seconds more.

6. Stir one-third of the egg whites into the batter to loosen it, then gently fold the remaining egg whites into the batter. Divide the batter evenly between the prepared pans. Shake the pans gently to level off the batter.

7. Bake the layers on the center oven rack until they are a rich golden color, spring back to the touch, and a tester inserted in the center comes out dry, about 25 minutes.

8. Cool the layers completely in the pans on a wire rack.

9. Remove the layers from the pan and remove the paper liners. Place one layer right side up on a cake plate. Slice it horizontally through the middle so that you have 2 layers. Spread ½ cup of the berries over the bottom layer, leaving a ½-inch border at the edge.

10. Put one-third of the whipped cream around this outer edge, like a wreath, and gently spread the cream toward the center of the layer with a frosting spatula. (This keeps the berries and the juice from dripping down the sides of the layer as you spread the cream.) Cut the other cake in half as well. Place 1 layer over the cream and continue layering the cake with the remaining berries and another one-third of the cream.

11. Place the last layer on the cake. Before frosting the top, press down

lightly on the top layer with your hand to make the whipped cream between each layer ooze out a little and form a ruffle. Then frost the top layer with the rest of the whipped cream. Stud the top of the cake decoratively with the 12 fresh strawberries or 24 fresh raspberries.

Makes 12 to 14 servings

Lemon-Glazed Orange Chiffon Cake

*T*his bundt cake is light and spongy with an orange flavor and a refreshing lemon glaze. I like to serve it with fresh or frozen strawberries.

INGREDIENTS

CAKE
2¼ cups cake flour
2 cups granulated sugar
1 tablespoon baking powder
½ teaspoon salt
6 large eggs, separated,
*   at room temperature*
1 tablespoon grated orange zest
¾ cup orange juice
½ cup vegetable oil

GLAZE
9 tablespoons unsalted butter
2¼ cups confectioner's sugar
4½ tablespoons hot water
5½ tablespoons fresh lemon juice
*   (1½ to 2 lemons)*

Frozen strawberries, thawed, or fresh
*   strawberries, hulled and lightly*
*   sugared to make a juice,*
*   for serving (optional)*

1. Preheat the oven to 325°F. Have ready a 10-inch tube pan with a removable bottom. Do not grease it.

2. For the cake, sift the flour, 1½ cups of the sugar, the baking powder, and salt together into a large bowl.

3. In a small bowl, whisk the egg yolks, orange zest and juice, and oil together until blended.

4. Add the egg mixture to the dry ingredients and mix with an electric mixer on low speed until the batter is smooth, 1½ to 2 minutes, stopping the mixer once to scrape the bowl. Do not overmix.

5. Beat the egg whites in a medium-size bowl with an electric mixer on medium-high speed until frothy, about 30 seconds. Gradually add the remaining ½ cup sugar and continue beating until the whites form firm peaks, about 1 minute more. Stir one-third of the egg whites into the batter, then fold in the remaining whites with a rubber spatula.

6. Pour the batter into the tube pan and bake on the center oven rack until the top of the cake is golden and springs back to the touch, 1 hour.

7. Cool the cake upside down on a funnel or bottle (page 20).

8. Meanwhile prepare the glaze: Melt the butter in a small saucepan over low heat and transfer it to a small bowl.

9. Add the confectioner's sugar and water and whisk until blended. Add the lemon juice and whisk again. Pour the mixture through a strainer into a second small bowl.

10. When the cake has completely cooled, remove it from the pan and place it upside down on a cake plate. Pour half the glaze over the top of the cake so that it drips down the outside and down the inside of the hole. Allow this to set 30 minutes.

11. Whisk the remaining glaze in the bowl and pour it over the cake for a second coating. Eat the cake that day accompanied by strawberries, if desired.

Makes 12 to 14 servings

Tom's Birthday Roll

*M*y neighbor Tom can always be counted on to stop by and sample the results of whatever recipe I've been working on, so he's tasted my desserts in every stage from batter and scraps to *pièce de résistance*. I made this cake especially for his birthday, and it seems only appropriate that after all the leftovers he's consumed, he should get something special named for him. Made without flour, this moist chocolate cake is rolled into a log with a coffee whipped cream filling.

INGREDIENTS

CAKE
4 ounces semisweet chocolate
2 ounces unsweetened chocolate
3 tablespoons strong brewed coffee
5 large eggs, separated, at room temperature
½ cup plus 2 tablespoons sugar

FILLING
5 teaspoons instant coffee powder
1 tablespoon water
1 tablespoon sugar
1 cup heavy (whipping) cream, chilled

2 tablespoons unsweetened cocoa powder for sprinkling
Fresh strawberries or raspberries for garnish

1. Preheat the oven to 350°F. Grease a jelly-roll pan (15 × 10 inches) with vegetable oil or butter, line it with waxed paper, and grease the paper.

2. For the cake, melt both chocolates with the coffee in the top of a double boiler placed over simmering water. Cool until tepid.

3. Beat the egg yolks with ½ cup sugar in a medium-size bowl with an electric mixer on medium speed until thick and yellow in color, 3 to 4 minutes. Add the chocolate mixture and blend thoroughly, for about 10 seconds, stopping the mixer to scrape the bowl with a rubber spatula.

4. In a deep mixing bowl beat the egg whites to soft peaks, about 30 seconds. Add the remaining 2 tablespoons sugar, and continue beating until the whites are stiff but not dry, about 30 seconds more. Carefully fold the egg whites into the chocolate mixture with a rubber spatula.

5. Pour the batter into the prepared pan and spread it evenly. Bake the cake on the center oven rack until the surface is spongy and the cake springs back to the touch, about 15 minutes. Remove the pan from the oven and cover it with a damp kitchen towel for 1 hour.

6. Ten minutes before the hour is up, prepare the filling: In a medium-size mixing bowl, dissolve the instant coffee in the water. Add the sugar and cream and beat with an electric mixer on medium speed until firm peaks form.

7. Sprinkle the cocoa over a sheet of waxed paper or a damp kitchen towel (not terrycloth) that is 4 inches longer than the cake.

8. Remove the towel from the cake pan. Run a thin knife around the edge of the cake to loosen it. Flip the pan upside down onto the waxed paper. Carefully peel off the waxed paper lining from the bottom of the cake.

9. Spread the whipped cream filling over the cake, leaving a ½-inch strip uncovered along the length of one long side.

10. Roll up the cake, starting from one long side toward the clean strip, using the waxed paper to help. There will be cracks in the cake, but they give the surface an interesting texture. Twist the ends of the waxed paper like a hard candy wrapper and refrigerate the cake a minimum of 3 hours.

11. When ready to serve, remove the cake from the refrigerator and unwrap it. Trim the edges if they appear irregular or unattractive. Place it on an oval or rectangular platter that has been covered with a white lace doily, and garnish with green leaves at the base and fresh strawberries or raspberries if desired.

Makes 12 to 16 servings

Chocolate Custard Sponge Roll

*7*his is a moist chocolate sponge cake rolled with custard and finished with whipped cream, which you can spread over its surface like icing or serve as a garnish with each slice.

INGREDIENTS

CAKE
3 tablespoons cake flour
2 tablespoons all-purpose flour
¼ cup unsweetened cocoa powder
¾ teaspoon baking soda
¼ teaspoon salt
4 large eggs, separated, at room temperature
½ cup plus 1 tablespoon (9 tablespoons) sugar
1 teaspoon instant espresso powder
1 teaspoon water

FILLING
2 tablespoons cornstarch
1 cup milk
2 ounces unsweetened chocolate, chopped
½ cup sugar
1 large egg yolk

TOPPING
1 recipe Whipped Cream (page 86)
1 ounce unsweetened chocolate for shaving or 12 fresh raspberries for garnish

1. Preheat the oven to 400°F. Line a jelly-roll pan (15 × 10 inches) with waxed paper that has been greased lightly with vegetable oil.

2. For the cake, sift both flours, the cocoa, baking soda, and salt together in a medium-size bowl.

3. Beat the egg yolks with ¼ cup sugar in a medium-size mixing bowl with an electric mixer on medium-high speed until light in color, 3 to 4 minutes.

4. Dissolve the espresso powder in the water and add it to the egg yolk mixture on medium speed. Beat until it is incorporated, 10 seconds.

5. Beat the egg whites in another mixing bowl on medium-high speed until frothy, about 30 seconds. Gradually add 3 tablespoons of the remaining sugar and continue beating to medium-firm peaks, about 1 minute more. Fold the whites gently into the yolks. *Do not overmix!*

6. Sift the dry ingredients (again) over the egg mixture and fold them in gently until the batter is uniform in color.

7. Pour the batter into the prepared pan and tip the pan gently back and forth so that the batter is evenly distributed. Bake the cake on the center oven rack until it springs back to the touch but has not formed a crust, about 12 minutes.

8. Allow the cake to cool for 10 min-utes, then sprinkle the remaining 2 tablespoons of sugar over a sheet of waxed paper or a damp kitchen towel that is 4 inches longer than the cake.

9. Run a thin knife around the edge of the cake to loosen it. Flip the pan upside down onto the waxed paper. Carefully peel off the waxed paper lining from the bottom of the cake.

10. Roll up the cake in the waxed paper, starting from one long side, using the waxed paper to help. The cake should never roll onto itself. Twist the ends of the waxed paper like a hard candy wrapper and refrigerate the cake a minimum of 3 hours.

11. Meanwhile prepare the filling: Dissolve the cornstarch in ¼ cup of the milk and set aside.

12. Heat the remaining milk with the chopped chocolate over medium-low heat in a small saucepan until the chocolate is completely melted, about 5 minutes. Stir the mixture vigorously with a whisk for the last few minutes to ensure that the mixture is uniform in color and all specks of chocolate are gone.

13. Vigorously whisk the sugar and the dissolved cornstarch into the chocolate, then whisk in the egg yolk.

14. Heat, stirring or whisking constantly, over low heat until the mixture begins to boil, 3 to 4 minutes. Remove it from the heat, stir it several times in the pan and pour it into a small bowl. Allow it to sit for 20 minutes, stirring it gently several times to release steam. Then cover the surface directly with plastic wrap and refrigerate until it is cool.

15. When you're ready to fill the cake, remove it from the refrigerator and unroll it on a counter so that it is lying on the waxed paper in which it was rolled.

16. Spread the filling over the cake but leave a ½-inch strip along one side uncovered. Starting from the opposite side, roll up the cake, using the waxed paper to help. The roll should end up resting on its seam.

17. Rewrap the roll in the waxed paper and refrigerate it for several hours.

18. Just before serving, prepare the whipped cream. Unwrap the cake and place it on an oval or rectangular serving platter. Frost the cake with the cream and grate chocolate shavings over the top or use the whipped cream as a side garnish with fresh raspberries.

Makes 16 servings

Lemon- Strawberry Sponge Roll

I don't know any blues singers paying tribute to my sweet lemon jelly roll, but maybe

that's because they haven't tasted this one yet. It's a springy roll, with tart lemon custard and strawberries substituted for the jelly inside. Then it's frosted with whipped cream. Try it in the spring or summer.

INGREDIENTS

CAKE
3 whole large eggs, at room
    temperature
3 large eggs, separated, at room
    temperature
15 tablespoons granulated sugar
2 teaspoons grated lemon zest
1½ teaspoons vanilla extract
2 tablespoons fresh lemon juice
¾ cup plus 3 tablespoons all-purpose
    flour
1 rounded tablespoon sifted confec-
    tioner's sugar for sprinkling

FILLING
4 large egg yolks
⅓ cup plus 1½ tablespoons sugar
¼ teaspoon unflavored gelatin powder
¼ cup plus 3 tablespoons fresh lemon
    juice
4 tablespoons (½ stick) unsalted
    butter, cut into small chunks
8 to 10 fresh strawberries, sliced
    ¼ inch thick

TOPPING
1 recipe Whipped Cream (page 86)
6 whole fresh strawberries

1. Preheat the oven to 350°F. Line a jelly-roll pan (15 × 10 inches) with waxed paper that has been greased lightly with butter or vegetable oil.

2. For the cake, mix the whole eggs and the 3 yolks in a medium-size mixing bowl with an electric mixer on medium-high speed until blended.

3. Add 11 tablespoons sugar and the lemon zest and beat the mixture on high speed until it is pale and thick, about 3½ minutes. (It may be necessary to hold a dish towel around the bowl to contain splatters until the mixture thickens.) Stop the mixer several times to scrape the bowl with a rubber spatula. Beat in the vanilla and the lemon juice.

4. Fold in the flour with a rubber spatula until it is incorporated.

5. Beat the egg whites in another mixing bowl with the mixer on medium-high speed until frothy, about 30 seconds. Gradually add the remaining 4 tablespoons sugar and continue beating just to soft peaks, about 30 seconds more. Fold the whites into the batter.

6. Pour the batter into the prepared pan and tip the pan gently back and forth so that the batter is evenly distributed. Bake the cake on the center oven rack until it is light golden and spongy and springs back to the touch, about 16 minutes.

7. Allow the cake to cool for 10 minutes. Sprinkle the confectioner's sugar over a sheet of waxed paper or a damp kitchen towel (not terrycloth) that is 4 inches longer than the cake.

8. Run a thin knife around the edge of the cake to loosen it. Flip the pan upside down onto the waxed paper.

Carefully peel off the waxed paper lining from the bottom of the cake.

9. Roll up the cake in the waxed paper, starting from one long side, using the waxed paper to help. The cake should never roll onto itself. Twist the ends of the paper like a hard candy wrapper and refrigerate the cake a minimum of 3 hours.

10. Meanwhile prepare the filling: In a small saucepan mix the egg yolks and the sugar with a whisk until they are blended. Warm the lemon juice slightly in another small saucepan. Add the gelatin to the lemon juice and stir to blend.

11. Add the gelatin mixture to the egg yolk mixture and cook over medium heat, stirring constantly with a wooden spoon, until the mixture thickens, about 3 minutes. When you run your finger across the wooden spoon, it should leave a path in the mixture.

12. Remove the lemon curd from the stove and strain into a small bowl. Add the butter, and stir until blended.

13. Allow the lemon curd to cool for 20 minutes, stirring occasionally. Puncture a piece of plastic wrap in several places, and use it to cover the surface of the filling. Allow the filling to set at room temperature until it is of spreading consistency, 30 to 40 minutes.

14. When the filling is set, remove the cake roll from the refrigerator and unroll it.

15. Spread the filling evenly over the cake but leave a 1-inch strip along one long side uncovered. Distribute the sliced strawberries evenly over the filling. Roll the cake toward the clean strip, peeling the waxed paper off as you roll. Put the roll in a fresh piece of waxed paper or plastic wrap and refrigerate it for several hours.

16. Just before serving, transfer the cake to a long serving tray and frost it with the whipped cream. Place the whole strawberries, points up, on top of the log. For a special look, arrange ferns around the base of the log.

Makes 16 servings

Lemon Pudding Cake

A layer of light lemon cake sitting atop a layer of tart lemon pudding, this dessert is wonderful served warm right out of the oven or at room temperature. But it is just as delicious cold on day two when its texture has become like that of a cheesecake.

INGREDIENTS

½ cup plus 4 tablespoons sugar
¼ cup all-purpose flour
⅛ teaspoon salt
3 tablespoons melted unsalted butter
1 tablespoon plus 2 teaspoons grated lemon zest
6 tablespoons fresh lemon juice
3 large eggs, separated, at room temperature
1½ cups heavy (whipping) cream, at room temperature

1. Preheat the oven to 350°F. Have ready an 8-inch square baking pan and a larger baking pan in which the smaller pan fits comfortably.

2. Whisk ½ cup plus 1 tablespoon of the sugar, the flour, and salt together in a medium-size mixing bowl. Add the butter and lemon zest and juice to the flour mixture.

3. In a small bowl, whisk the egg yolks and cream until blended.

4. Add the yolk mixture to the flour mixture and blend with an electric mixer on medium-low speed until the batter is velvety, about 15 seconds. Set aside.

5. Whisk the egg whites at medium-high speed in a medium-size mixing bowl until frothy, about 30 seconds. Gradually add the remaining 3 tablespoons sugar and continue beating the egg whites to firm peaks, 45 seconds more. Gently fold them into the flour mixture.

6. Pour the batter into an 8-inch

square baking pan. Place the pan in the larger baking pan. Pour water into the larger pan to come about halfway up the sides of the smaller pan. Place on a rack in the center of the oven.

7. Bake the cake until the top is golden and springs back to the touch, 35 to 40 minutes. Spoon it immediately onto individual dessert plates or allow to cool to room temperature before serving.

Makes 9 servings

Lemon Icebox Cake with Fresh Strawberries

*Y*ou've invited people over for dinner on what turns out to be the hottest day of the year, and you avoid turning on your oven by barbecuing. Great, now what do you do about dessert?

You make this cake: light from the egg whites and whipped cream, tart from the lemon, and fresh out of the fridge with no baking involved. It's good after a heavy meal on a cooler day, too, when you want a strong flavor but not a lot of heft in your dessert.

INGREDIENTS

CAKE
About 30 (when split) ladyfingers
2 envelopes unflavored gelatin powder
¾ cup plus 5 tablespoons fresh lemon juice (5 to 6 lemons)
¾ cup water
4 large eggs, separated, at room temperature
1 cup sugar
1¼ cups heavy (whipping) cream, chilled

TOPPING
1 quart fresh strawberries, hulled and sliced
¼ to ⅓ cup sugar

1. Line the bottom and sides of a 9-inch springform pan with the ladyfingers.

2. Combine the gelatin and 5 table-spoons lemon juice in a small bowl and let it soften, 1 to 2 minutes.

3. Bring the water to a boil and add it along with the remaining ¾ cup lemon juice to the gelatin mixture.

4. Beat the egg yolks and ¾ cup of the sugar in a medium-size mixing bowl with an electric mixer on medium speed until thick and light, about 3 minutes. Blend the gelatin mixture into the egg mixture on low speed.

5. Place the bowl of gelatin mixture in a larger bowl that is filled one-quarter full with cold water and a couple of ice cubes. Stir the mixture intermittently until it resembles a thick syrup, about 10 minutes. (It is important to keep a close eye on this. If the mixture stays in the ice water too long it will get lumpy.)

6. While the gelatin mixture is thickening, beat the cream in another mixing bowl with an electric mixer on medium speed to soft peaks and set aside (see Note).

7. Beat the whites in another mixing bowl with an electric mixer on medium-high speed until frothy, about 30 seconds. Gradually add the remaining ¼ cup sugar and continue beating the whites to soft peaks, about 30 seconds more.

8. Remove the bowl with the gelatin mixture from the ice water. Fold the cream, then the whites, into the lemon mixture with a rubber spatula.

9. Pour the mixture into the springform pan lined with the ladyfingers. Place the pan in the refrigerator to set overnight.

10. For the topping, toss the strawberries with the sugar several hours before serving the cake and set aside.

11. To remove the cake from the pan, run a frosting spatula between the sides of the pan and the cake, then release the sides.

12. To serve, top each slice with a generous helping of the strawberries.

Makes 12 to 14 servings

Note: This recipe requires several mixing bowls. If you do not have enough, transfer the whipped cream to a small bowl, thoroughly wash and dry the mixing bowl, and use it for the egg whites.

Traditional Cheesecake à la Reuben's

*W*hen I was a kid in New York City, a Sunday treat was lunch at Reuben's: a to-die-for corned beef sandwich topped off with a fat slice of cheesecake. Their cake was so creamy, it stuck to the roof of my mouth until I washed it down with several gulps of milk. Frankly, I think Reuben's broke the mold when they created their cheesecake, but I've tried with this recipe to recreate both the cheesecake and my childhood memory. (You're on your own with the milk.)

INGREDIENTS

CRUST

1¼ *cups vanilla wafer crumbs*
1 *tablespoon sugar*
6 *tablespoons (¾ stick) unsalted*
    butter, melted
½ *cup ground almonds, walnuts, or*
    pecans (optional)

CAKE

3 *pounds cream cheese, at room*
    temperature or warmed slightly in
    the microwave
1½ *cups sugar*
2 *teaspoons vanilla extract*
3 *whole large eggs, at room*
    temperature
2 *large egg yolks, at room temperature*
1 *tablespoons fresh lemon juice*

1. Preheat the oven to 375°F.

2. For the crust, place the cookie crumbs, sugar, melted butter, and nuts, if using, in a small bowl and toss them lightly with a fork until they are well blended.

3. Press this mixture firmly over the bottom of a 10-inch springform pan. Bake it on the bottom oven rack until crisp and golden, about 15 minutes. Remove it from the oven and cool.

4. Reduce the oven heat to 300°F and place a roasting pan or baking dish filled with hot water on the bottom rack of the oven to create moisture.

5. Meanwhile prepare the cake filling: Beat the cream cheese, sugar, and vanilla in a medium-size mixing bowl with an electric mixer on medium speed until light and fluffy, 30 to 60 seconds, depending on the temperature of the cream cheese. Scrape the bowl with a rubber spatula, then beat 45 seconds more.

6. Lightly whisk the whole eggs and egg yolks together and add them to the cream cheese mixture with the lemon juice. Mix on low speed until they are incorporated and the batter is velvety, about 30 seconds. Scrape the bowl with a spatula, then mix at medium-high speed for 10 seconds more.

7. Pour the filling over the crust. Bake the cake on the center oven rack until it appears golden, set, and a tester inserted in the center comes out dry, about 1¼ hours.

8. Cool the cake in the pan on a wire rack. When it is cool, refrigerate it overnight in the pan and serve it the next day.

Makes 12 to 16 servings

Pumpkin Cheesecake

I was weaned on Reuben's cheesecake, and, as a result, I remained an uncompromising purist when it came to variations on the theme. Let them keep their Kahlua, Amaretto, Grand Marnier variations, I scoffed; real cheesecake is dense and creamy and unadulterated. Then in 1985 I tasted Pam Ososky's (a former Rosie's baker) pumpkin cheesecake and relented. I bid farewell to pumpkin pie at Thanksgiving and replaced it with this rich and flavorful concoction, which I top with sour cream and pecans. I serve it on a large round cake plate or platter lined with a white paper lace doily, garnished with bits of holly or evergreen and topped with whole cranberries for a festive holiday look.

I N G R E D I E N T S

CRUST
*2 cups gingersnap crumbs
    (35 Nabisco gingersnaps)
3 tablespoons sugar
6 tablespoons (¾ stick) unsalted
    butter, melted
¼ cup pecans, finely chopped*

CAKE
*1½ cups canned pumpkin purée
1 tablespoon plus 1½ teaspoons
    ground cinnamon
1 tablespoon ground ginger
2½ teaspoons ground cloves
2½ teaspoons ground nutmeg
1 teaspoon ground allspice
2½ pounds cream cheese, at room
    temperature
1⅓ cups sugar
1 teaspoon vanilla extract
5 whole large eggs, at room
    temperature
2 large egg yolks, at room temperature*

TOPPING
*1 cup sour cream, at room temperature
3 tablespoons sugar
¼ cup pecans, finely chopped
14 pecan halves*

1. Preheat the oven to 375°F.

2. For the crust, place the gingersnap crumbs, sugar, butter, and nuts in a small bowl and toss lightly with a fork until well blended.

3. Press this mixture firmly over the bottom of a 10-inch springform pan. Bake it on the bottom oven rack until golden, 5 to 7 minutes. Remove it from the oven and cool.

4. Reduce the oven heat to 300°F and place a roasting pan or baking dish filled with hot water on the bottom rack of the oven to create moisture.

5. For the cake filling, lightly whisk together the pumpkin and spices in a small bowl until blended. Set aside.

6. Beat the cream cheese, sugar, and vanilla in a medium-size mixing bowl with an electric mixer on medium speed until light and fluffy, about 30 seconds. Scrape the bowl with a rubber spatula, then beat 30 seconds more.

7. Add the whole eggs, then the egg yolks, one at a time to the cream cheese on low speed. Blend each egg until incorporated, about 30 seconds. Scrape the bowl after each addition.

8. Add the pumpkin mixture to the

cream cheese batter and blend on medium speed until the mixture is velvety, about 1 minute. Scrape the bowl and beat another minute.

9. Pour the filling over the crust. Bake the cake on the center oven rack until the top is set and a tester inserted in the center comes out dry, about 1 hour 40 minutes. Turn off the oven and leave the cake in the oven for an additional hour. Remove the cake from the oven, place it carefully on a wire rack, and let cool for several hours.

10. While the cheesecake is cooling, prepare the topping: Mix the sour cream and sugar together in a small bowl.

11. Preheat the oven to 350°F.

12. Spread the sour cream mixture evenly over the surface of the cake with a spatula and sprinkle the chopped pecans on top. Evenly space the pecan halves around the top edge of the cake.

13. Bake the cheesecake in the oven for 5 to 7 minutes to set the topping. Remove the cheesecake from the oven and refrigerate before serving.

Makes 14 to 16 servings

Brownie Cheesecake

*I*ntroduced to me by my neighbor Susan, this brownie cheesecake is a direct translation of dark, fudgy brownies into cheesecake—how's that for truth in advertising? I like this cake in a vanilla crust, but it's also good with a chocolate cookie crust or a graham cracker crust.

INGREDIENTS

CRUST
1¼ cups vanilla wafer crumbs (about 30 cookies)
1 tablespoon sugar
6 tablespoons (¾ stick) unsalted butter, melted
½ cup chopped walnuts or pecans

CAKE
12 ounces semisweet chocolate chips
½ cup hot very strong brewed coffee
1 pound cream cheese, at room temperature
1 cup sugar
2 teaspoons vanilla extract
¼ teaspoon salt
4 large eggs, at room temperature

1. Preheat the oven to 350°F.

2. For the crust, place the wafer crumbs, sugar, butter, and nuts in a small bowl and toss them together with a fork. Press this mixture over the bottom of a 9-inch springform pan and bake for 10 minutes. Remove it from the oven and cool.

3. Reduce the oven heat to 300°F and place a roasting pan or baking dish filled with hot water on the bottom rack of the oven to create moisture.

4. For the cake filling, melt the chocolate in the coffee in the top of a double boiler placed over simmering water.

5. Cream the cream cheese, sugar, vanilla, and salt in a medium-size mixing bowl with an electric mixer on medium speed until light and fluffy, about 2 minutes. Stop the mixer once or twice to scrape the bowl with a rubber spatula.

6. Add the eggs and beat the mixture on medium-high speed for 30 seconds. Scrape the bowl and beat on medium speed 30 seconds longer.

7. Add the chocolate mixture to the egg mixture and beat on medium speed for 15 seconds. Scrape the bowl and then mix until the batter is smooth and uniform in color, about 10 more seconds.

8. Pour the filling over the crust. Bake the cake on the center oven rack until it is set and a tester inserted in the center comes out clean, about 1 hour 25 minutes.

9. Allow the cake to cool completely on a wire rack, then refrigerate the cake overnight.

Makes 12 to 16 servings

Caramel-Topped Pecan Cheesecake

*Y*ou might call this the southern cousin of traditional New York cheesecake, its creaminess interrupted by a generous helping of nuts.

INGREDIENTS

CRUST
1¼ cups graham cracker crumbs
6 tablespoons (¾ stick) unsalted
    butter, melted
3 tablespoons granulated sugar

CAKE
1½ pounds cream cheese, at room
    temperature
1¼ cups (lightly packed) light brown
    sugar
3 large eggs, at room temperature
1½ teaspoons vanilla extract
2 tablespoons all-purpose flour
1 cup chopped pecans

TOPPING
½ cup (lightly packed) light brown
    sugar
¼ cup heavy (whipping) cream
¾ teaspoon unsalted butter, melted

1. Preheat the oven to 375°F.

2. For the crust, place the cracker

crumbs, butter, and sugar in a small bowl and toss them together with a fork. Press this mixture over the bottom of a 9-inch springform pan. Bake the crust until it is crisp and golden in color, about 10 minutes. Let cool.

3. Reduce the oven heat to 300°F. Place a roasting pan or baking dish filled with hot water on the bottom rack of the oven to create moisture.

4. For the cake filling, cream the cream cheese in a medium-size mixing bowl with an electric mixer on medium speed for 1 minute. Scrape the bowl with a rubber spatula.

5. Add the brown sugar and beat on medium-high speed until the cream cheese is fluffy, about 1 minute. Scrape the bowl.

6. Add the eggs and the vanilla and beat the mixture on medium-low speed until smooth, about 45 seconds. Scrape the bowl.

7. Add the flour and mix on low speed for 5 seconds. Add the pecans and mix to blend, 15 to 20 seconds.

8. Pour the filling over the crust. Bake the cake on the center oven rack until the top is set and a tester inserted in the center comes out dry, about 1¾ hours.

9. Remove the cake from the oven, allow it to cool on a wire rack for 1½ hours, then refrigerate it overnight.

10. Two hours before serving the cake, prepare the topping: Place the brown sugar, cream, and butter in a small saucepan over medium heat and stir until the sugar is dissolved. Bring the mixture to a boil and continue to boil for 1½ minutes, stirring occasionally. The mixture will look like a thick golden syrup.

11. Remove the pan from the heat and pour the topping into a small bowl to stop the cooking process. When it stops bubbling, pour it over the cheesecake. Tip the springform pan from side to side so that the topping coats the cake evenly. Keep the cake at room temperature until ready to serve.

Makes 12 to 16 servings

Fudge Frosting

*I*f Rosie's house is built on chocolate, this frosting is the foundation—or is it the roof? Whatever the metaphor, it's the perfect frosting: dark and glossy and it looks as good as it tastes on any layer cake or brownie.

INGREDIENTS

6 ounces unsweetened chocolate
1 cup plus 2 tablespoons evaporated milk
1½ cups sugar

1. Melt the chocolate in the top of a double boiler placed over simmering water. Cool slightly.

2. Blend the evaporated milk and sugar in a blender on medium speed for 2 seconds.

3. Add the chocolate to the sugar mixture in the blender and blend on high speed until the frosting is thick and shiny, 1 to 1½ minutes. The mixer's sound will change when the frosting has thickened.

4. Spoon the frosting into a bowl and allow it to set at room temperature for 30 minutes. Then cover the bowl with plastic wrap and allow the frosting to set for 1 hour more before frosting. Do not refrigerate the frosting, even if you don't plan to use it for several days.

Makes 1¾ cups, enough to fill and frost a two-layer cake

Note: This recipe can only be made in a blender.

Marshmallow Frosting

*T*his is a frosting that takes me right back to childhood and that much coveted jar of Marshmallow Fluff! Use the back of a spoon to form little peaks in the frosting once it is on the cake. Note: This recipe can be easily doubled to frost a two-layer cake.

INGREDIENTS

2 large egg whites, at room temperature
¼ cup plus 2 tablespoons sugar
3 tablespoons light corn syrup
½ teaspoon vanilla extract

1. Put the egg whites, sugar, and corn syrup in the top of a double boiler placed over rapidly boiling water and beat with a hand-held mixer (electric or rotary) until soft peaks form, about 4 minutes.

2. Transfer the mixture to a medium-size mixing bowl. Add the vanilla and beat with an electric mixer (whisk attachment, if possible) on medium-high speed until soft peaks form, about 30 seconds. Use immediately.

Makes 1⅔ cups, enough to frost an 11 × 7-inch sheet cake

German Chocolate Topping

My friends Susan and Stanley were visiting from Seattle when I was working on this topping, and they were so enamored of it that they insisted that it accompany every dessert I served them. An extreme reaction, perhaps, but not wholly improbable. This topping is creamy, strong on butterscotch, and full of coconut and pecans. In addition to keeping Susan and Stanley happy, I use it to frost Rosie's Famous Chocolate Sour-Cream Layer Cake and Chocolate Buttermilk Cake (see Index).

INGREDIENTS

1 tablespoon plus 1 teaspoon cornstarch
1 cup evaporated milk
½ cup granulated sugar
½ cup (lightly packed) light brown sugar
6 large egg yolks, at room temperature
4 tablespoons (½ stick) unsalted butter
⅛ teaspoon salt
¾ teaspoon vanilla extract
⅓ cup chopped walnuts
1 cup shredded coconut

1. Dissolve the cornstarch in the milk.

2. Place the cornstarch mixture, both sugars, the egg yolks, butter, and salt in a medium-size saucepan over medium-low heat. Cook, stirring constantly, until the mixture thickens and just starts to bubble, about 7 minutes.

3. Transfer the mixture to a blender and blend on medium-low speed for 7 seconds. Scrape the sides of the blender with a rubber spatula and blend several more seconds.

4. Transfer the mixture to a medium-size bowl and stir in the vanilla. Put a piece of plastic wrap directly over the surface and allow it to cool to room temperature or refrigerate it. When the mixture is cool, stir in the nuts and coconut.

Makes about 2 cups, enough to fill and frost a two-layer cake (not including the sides)

Cream Cheese Frosting

A fluffy white frosting that's sweet yet slightly tart.

INGREDIENTS

10 ounces cream cheese, at room temperature
³/₄ cup confectioner's sugar
2 tablespoons unsalted butter, at room temperature
¹/₄ cup plus 1 tablespoon heavy (whipping) cream, at room temperature

1. Cream the cream cheese, sugar, and butter in a medium-size mixing bowl with an electric mixer on medium speed until light and fluffy, 3 to 4 minutes. Scrape the bottom and side of the bowl with a rubber spatula.

2. With the mixer on low speed, add the cream in a stream and mix until it is incorporated. Scrape the bowl.

3. Increase the speed to medium-high and beat the frosting until it is light and fluffy, 5 to 10 minutes. Stop to scrape the bowl several times with a rubber spatula. Keep the frosting at room temperature until you are ready to frost the cake, a maximum of 1 hour.

Makes 2 cups, enough to fill and frost a two- or four-layer cake

Rosie's Buttercream

A fluffy white frosting not overly sugary, this recipe is one you'll use often. It lasts for several days out of the refrigerator, but will require rewhipping after it sits for a while to restore its fluffy texture.

INGREDIENTS

*8 tablespoons (1 stick) unsalted butter,
  at room temperature*
1¼ cups confectioner's sugar
*¾ cup plus 2 tablespoons heavy
  (whipping) cream, chilled*

1. Place all the ingredients in a food processor and process until light and fluffy, about 5 minutes. Stop the machine several times to scrape down the sides of the bowl with a rubber spatula.

2. Transfer the buttercream to a medium-size mixing bowl and, using the paddle attachment of an electric mixer, continue to beat on medium-high speed, until the buttercream is white and fluffy, 15 to 20 minutes. Stop the mixer to scrape the bowl several times with a rubber spatula. (If you do not have a paddle attachment, you can use the whisk.) Use the buttercream for frosting within an hour or it will need rewhipping.

*Makes 2 to 2¼ cups, enough to fill
and frost a two- or four-layer cake*

Mocha Buttercream

*F*lavored lightly with coffee, this variation on Rosie's Buttercream has a lovely café au lait color.

INGREDIENTS

¼ cup instant coffee powder
4½ teaspoons water
*8 tablespoons (1 stick) unsalted butter,
  at room temperature*
1¼ cups confectioner's sugar
*¾ cup plus 2 tablespoons heavy
  (whipping) cream, chilled*

Dissolve the coffee in the water and place all the ingredients in a food processor. Proceed as directed for Rosie's Buttercream (recipe precedes).

*Makes 2 to 2¼ cups, enough to fill
and frost a two- or four-layer cake.*

Whipped Cream

*W*hipped cream may be rich, but it's not too sweet and is the perfect accent to so many desserts. Be sure not to overwhip the cream, you want it to have a fluffy texture.

INGREDIENTS

*1 cup heavy (or whipping) cream,
  chilled*
*1 to 2 tablespoons granulated
  or confectioner's sugar*

Using the whisk attachment (if possible) of an electric mixer, beat the cream and the sugar on high speed until soft peaks (1 minute) or firm peaks (1 minute 15 seconds) are formed. This will vary depending on the recipe.

Makes just over 2 cups

Hot Fudge Filling

*T*radition has it that the hot fudge sundae was invented in Boston at Bailey's, which puts this recipe in honored company. It's a wonderful bittersweet filling for layer cakes, be they chocolate or golden, and it's great ladled warm over ice cream.

I N G R E D I E N T S

2 ounces unsweetened chocolate
2 tablespoons unsalted butter
5 tablespoons plus 1½ teaspoons sugar
6 tablespoons hot water
½ teaspoon vanilla extract

1. Place all the ingredients except the vanilla in the top of a double boiler placed over simmering water and cook uncovered, stirring occasionally, until the chocolate is melted and the sugar

is dissolved, 30 minutes. The mixture will be smooth and velvety.

2. Pour the fudge into a small bowl, stir in the vanilla, and refrigerate until the mixture is thick and of spreading consistency, 2 hours.

Makes ¾ cup, enough to fill a four-layer cake

Vanilla Custard Filling

A thick, creamy filling for layer cakes and tarts, this is also delicious spooned over a bowl of fresh berries.

I N G R E D I E N T S

10 tablespoons milk
¾ cup heavy (whipping) cream
6 tablespoons sugar
2 tablespoons cornstarch
1 large egg yolk
1 teaspoon vanilla extract

1. Scald 4 tablespoons of the milk, the cream, and the sugar in a medium-size saucepan over medium-low heat.

2. Dissolve the cornstarch in the remaining 6 tablespoons milk.

3. Add the egg yolk to the cornstarch mixture and stir it rapidly with a fork or whisk. Add this mixture to the scalded cream mixture and whisk over medium-low heat constantly until it thickens, 1½ to 2 minutes, and then for 30 seconds more.

4. Remove the custard from the heat, stir in the vanilla, and pour it into a ceramic or plastic bowl. Allow it to cool for 10 minutes, stirring it gently several times.

5. Put a piece of plastic wrap that has been punctured several times directly over the surface of the custard and refrigerate until completely chilled or overnight.

Makes 1¼ cups, enough to fill
a four-layer cake

Lemon Custard Filling

I put this thick custard filling between layers of cakes because I like the way its tartness contrasts with a sweet butter-cream frosting.

INGREDIENTS

3 tablespoons cornstarch
1 cup water
2 large eggs
11 tablespoons sugar
⅛ teaspoon salt
5 tablespoons fresh lemon juice

1. Dissolve the cornstarch in ½ cup of the water in a small bowl. Add the eggs and whisk until blended.

2. Heat the remaining water, the sugar, and the salt in a medium-size saucepan over medium-low heat until the sugar dissolves and the mixture is hot, about 2 minutes.

3. Add the cornstarch mixture to the hot liquid, whisking constantly. Add the lemon juice and continue to cook, whisking constantly, until the mixture thickens, 3 to 4 minutes, and then for 30 seconds longer.

4. Pour the custard into a small bowl. Allow it to cool for 10 minutes, stirring it gently several times.

5. Put a piece of plastic wrap that has been punctured several times directly over the surface of the custard and refrigerate for at least 6 hours.

Makes about 1½ cups, enough to fill
a four-layer cake

CHAPTER THREE

Smart Cookies

Cookies may be a Dutch invention, but to me, they are quintessentially American. Even the word calls up memories of a steamy kitchen on a wet November afternoon with a treat fresh out of the oven and a glass of milk standing by. Never mind if your November afternoons weren't like that. The image is a part of the collective nostalgia, and cookies remain a way of reliving the wonderful innocence of eating till you think you're about to burst.

When I was a kid, cookies mostly came in packages from Keeblers or Nabisco; they were all the same size and shape and, not knowing any better, we took their uniformity for a sign of quality. One of my favorite tricks was to stroll down the aisle of the grocery store looking for open packages of cookies to sample. I was never bold enough to open one myself, but if there were cookies just sitting there waiting to be thrown away, far be it from me to let them go to waste. I told myself it was a way to deepen my expertise.

All these years later, I can still conjure up the taste of the cookies I liked best just by reciting their names: Lorna Doones, Social Teas, Vienna Fingers, Pecan Sandies, and Nutter Butters. But my favorites were Oreos because I could be magnanimous and let someone else have the white icing while I hoarded the chocolate wafers for myself.

Still, the cookies that were worth making a fuss over were those baked fresh, and my fondest cookie memories come from William Greenberg's in New York City where Mr. Greenberg made sure you got a free cookie whenever you bought something at one of his shops. I still remember the thrill of complicity when he leaned over the counter to hand one down to me. Maple cookies rolled in sugar, linzer cookies — two big, spicy cookies sandwiched together with jam and covered with confectioner's sugar — elegantly thin and crisp chocolate cookies. Just thinking about them makes me want to catch the next plane to New York.

Then came the day the cookie world finally caught up with my craving when chains such as David's and Mrs. Fields arrived to usher in our current cookie craze. As with any commodity that's hot, the quality of these designer cookies varies, and some aren't worth crossing the aisle of a shopping mall for. But even the crummy ones haven't stopped

Americans from devouring cookies in overwhelming abundance over the past decade.

It probably has something to do with how portable they are and the pleasure of noshing on the run. Whatever, cookies are our first treats and often our first word, and they remain among the easiest pastries to make so that the desire for a cookie is never too far from the satisfaction.

Cookies in General

*7*he cookie recipes in this book fall into six categories; each type has different characteristics, so each has its own requirements. But cookies are democratic creatures, and on some levels, they're all created equal. Hence, before we specialize, here are a few general principles.

Preparing Cookie Sheets: Baking parchment is a wonderful invention that saves you the time and bother of greasing your cookie sheets. On top of that—or on bottom, to be accurate—lining the sheets with this paper protects the bottoms of the cookies from overcooking. If you don't have parchment, grease your cookie sheets lightly with butter or oil. Very buttery cookies like shortbread are the exception;

their pans don't need any greasing.

When you drop or place your dough on the cookie sheets, rest the sheets on a counter or table, not on a hot stove. If the dough melts before it goes into the oven, it can affect the baking time.

Oven Temperatures: Although the oven temperature varies from cookie to cookie, a few simple measures apply in most cases. First, it's always a good idea to have your oven preheating for at least 15 minutes before you put your cookies in.

Second, if you have any question about your oven's dependability, test its temperature against the one recommended in the recipe by baking a couple of cookies for the time called for before you do the whole batch. If the suggested temperature is off, you can adjust it for the remainder before it's too late.

Third, baking time will vary depending on the size of the cookies, large cookies obviously taking more time than small ones. If you choose to make your cookies a different size from the one suggested in the recipe, remember to adjust the baking time accordingly.

Finally, I never bake more than one cookie sheet at a time because the center rack of the oven is the only place that bakes evenly in a domestic oven. It takes longer, but it's worth it.

Handling the Dough: Generally, cookie doughs are hardier than batters for cakes or pastries, so, in most cases, mixing them requires much less caution. The less moisture a dough has, the longer you can beat it without having to worry about your cookies coming out tough or dry, especially when the recipe doesn't use eggs. Rosie's Butter Cookies and Chocolate-Dipped Pecan Logs, for example, can be beaten for a long time.

Classic cookies like chocolate chip or oatmeal, which contain eggs and a bit more liquid, need more delicate beating. But the cookies that require the greatest caution are cakelike cookies because they use a substantial amount of liquid and come out tough and rubbery, just like cake, if they're beaten too long.

Storing Cookies: All cookies should be stored in airtight containers. If you plan to eat them within two days, you can leave them at room temperature. Otherwise, they should be refrigerated.

To keep chewy cookies moist, I have a great trick. I place the cookies in the container, spreading parchment or waxed paper between the layers. Then I moisten a sponge or crumpled-up paper towel and place it on a piece of plastic wrap in the container with the cookies, but not lying directly on them, and snap on the lid.

When you want to restore the crunch in crisp cookies that have gone soggy, place them in a 275°F oven for 10 to 15 minutes. This works especially well for shortbread cookies.

Freezing works very well with all cookies, but frozen cookies need to be kept at room temperature for several hours before eating to allow their flavor to come out. If you don't have that much time, pop them into a 200°F oven until they're warm or microwave them lightly.

Cookie Types

ß eyond these generalizations, it's every cookie for itself, so I suggest that you find the category that applies to the recipe you're making and read it through before you begin.

Traditional Drop Cookies

Drop cookies form the bedrock of cookiedom: chocolate chip, oatmeal, peanut butter, gingersnaps. You make them by dropping dollops of dough (usually made from the standard butter, sugar, egg, leavening, flour mixture) onto the cookie sheet. They're easy and quick to whip up. Texture can vary from thin and crispy like the Oatmeal Lace Cookies to thick and chewy in the center like the Chocolate Chips.

Oven Temperature: A cookie that's chewy at the center and slightly crunchy around the edges requires an oven temperature of between 350° and 375°F, with the exception of meringues, which bake at a lower heat. I find that in some cases it's best to chill the dough before baking so the cookie flattens out less and stays thick and chewy at its center. Crisp cookies like Oatmeal Lace and Crispy Orange Oatmeal Wafers bake faster with a higher oven temperature of 400°F.

Pan Preparation: Line cookie sheets with baking parchment or grease them lightly with butter or oil.

Shaping: Scoop a heaping tea-spoon or tablespoon or a level ice cream scoop of dough from the bowl. Drop the spoonful of dough onto the cookie sheet, using your index finger or another spoon to loosen it. The cookies should be 1½ to 2 inches apart, depending on the size of the spoonful.

I prefer most drop cookies to be large so they can have that combination of crunchy outside and chewy middle (small cookies bake quicker and more uniform-ly). It also makes it easier to fool yourself into thinking that you're eating less by having only one. But if you prefer these classic cookies to be crisp through and through, flatten the dough with the palm of your hand after you've dropped it onto the cookie sheet. If you do this, remember to space the cookies farther apart on the cookie sheet. Bake the cookies at 350°F until the centers drop and the tops are uniform in color.

Testing for Doneness: The edges of these cookies will be the first to bake and change color, fol-lowed by the center, which will puff up but remain lighter col-ored. If you like a chewy center, remove the cookies from the oven at this point. If the cookies bake longer, their centers will drop in the oven and darken like the edges and the cookie will be crunchy throughout.

Cooling: Cooling these cookies on the sheet contributes to a crisp bottom, but they cool well on a rack too.

Eating: As soon as they're cool enough to put in your mouth, pour yourself a glass of milk and indulge. They're equally good later that day or the next, but are best eaten within two days of baking.

Storing: When they are completely cooled, store these cookies in a plastic container or an airtight plastic bag. You can freeze or refrigerate them but bring them to room temperature again before eating, maybe popping them in the toaster oven or regular oven to give them a just-baked aura. The batter can be stored for 4 to 5 days in the refrigerator or it can be frozen.

Cakelike Drop Cookies

These cookies, such as Lemon Cake Cookies and Butter-Glazed Nutmeg Mounds are appropriately named because they have the airier texture of cakes.

Oven Temperature: The oven is usually set high, around 375° to 400°F, so that the cookie rises. Bake the batter right after mixing so that the cookie achieves the right texture.

Pan Preparation: These cookies bake best on parchment, which protects them just enough from the heat of the pan and keeps them from getting crusty. Air-cushion pans work beautifully too because they never get as hot, so the cookie doesn't develop a crust on the bottom.

Shaping: This thick, wet batter drops easily in generously rounded tablespoons onto a cookie sheet. Leave 2 inches between cookies.

Testing for Doneness: Remove the cookies from the oven when they are firm and spring back to your touch like a cake or when a cake tester inserted in the center comes out dry. Make sure that they don't cook long enough to form a hard crust.

Cooling: If these cookies sit on a hot surface after they're baked, their bottoms will continue cooking, so I remove them from the baking sheet immediately with a pancake spatula and place them on a cooling rack.

Eating and Storing: Cakelike cookies taste delicious the first day but can also be stored in an airtight plastic container overnight. Place a piece of parchment or waxed paper between layers of cookies, and if they are glazed, be sure that the glaze has hardened completely before you stack them. On the second day, the cookies will be more moist and, to my way of thinking, even better. This batter cannot be stored, though, because its leavening will get overactive in the moisture.

Log Cookies

Log cookies, such as Pecan Crunchies and Butterscotch-Cinnamon Icebox Cookies, are made of a stiff dough that is rolled, chilled, sliced, and then baked. They hold their shape well during baking and come out of the oven nice and crunchy.

Oven Temperature: Log cookies usually call for a low temperature (between 275° and 325°F) so the cookies bake evenly and get crisp.

Pan Preparation: Line cookie sheets with baking parchment or grease them lightly with butter or oil.

Shaping: When the dough is mixed, form it into logs about 2 inches in diameter. (You may want to dip your hands in flour before molding so that the dough doesn't stick to them.) Place a log near the edge of a piece of waxed paper that has been cut slightly longer than the log. Roll the log inside the waxed paper and twist the paper ends like a hard candy wrapper.

Chill the log for 2 hours, then while it is still in its waxed paper wrapping, roll it gently back and forth on a counter with the palms and fingers of your hands until it forms a smooth cylinder. Return the log to the fridge for several hours more. Finally, cut the log into slices ¼ to ⅜ inch thick and place them about 1½ inches apart on a cookie sheet.

Testing for Doneness: Log cookies are done when they are lightly golden and crisp to the touch. Because they need to bake throughout, I take one from the oven and break it in two to make sure that it's done. A doughy strip in the cookie's middle means that it needs to bake longer.

Cooling: These cookies can cool on the sheet or a cooling rack since they are sturdy and can be transferred easily.

Eating: Let the cookies cool completely before you eat them or, better yet, wait until the next day. They can taste a little doughy when they're warm, but that disappears soon.

Storing: Log cookies stored in an airtight plastic container remain fresh and can be stacked on each other if they're not frosted or adorned with jam. If they get soggy, simply put them in a preheated 275°F oven for 10 minutes to restore their crispness. These cookies freeze well too but taste best at room temperature. The unbaked logs can be stored for 4 to 5 days in your refrigerator, or they can be frozen for up to several weeks.

Shortbread Cookies

This category includes cookies such as Chocolate-Dipped Pecan Logs, Very Short Shortbread, and Noah Bedoahs. Their doughs contain no liquid, so they can be beaten without worry.

Oven Temperature: I like to bake these cookies at a low temperature (250° to 300°F) for a long time to ensure crunchiness throughout. As a rule of thumb, the bigger the cookie, the lower the oven temperature.

Pan Preparation: Line cookie sheets with parchment or place the batter directly on the cookie sheets. Because of the cookies' high butter content and the absence of liquid, the sheets do not need greasing.

Shaping: These cookies can be molded by hand or dropped from a spoon onto the cookie sheets.

Testing for Doneness: The cookies should be lightly golden and baked throughout, so I test for doneness by cutting one in half to insure that there is no doughy strip.

Cooling and Eating: These cookies taste best when they're well cooled or even the next day when the flavors have settled.

Storing: Stored in an airtight container in or out of the refrigerator, these cookies last for weeks. If they do get soggy, you can crisp them again by warming them in a preheated 275°F oven for 10 minutes.

Rolled Cookies

Rolled cookies, such as Ruby Jems, are made from a stiff dough that has been chilled before it is rolled out and cut. You can mix the dough in a food processor, with an electric mixer, or by hand.

Oven Temperature: This varies between 350° and 400°F depending on the recipe.

Pan Preparation: Line cookie sheets with parchment or grease them lightly with butter or oil. Use an ungreased sheet for cookies that contain a lot of butter.

Shaping: Chill the dough in slabs and then roll it out ⅛ to ¼ inch thick; the thickness will vary with the recipe. Use cookie cutters to make special shapes or the top of a glass dipped in flour for round cookies. I usually don't like to reroll the scraps left when the cookies have been cut out because the dough gets tough with overworking, so I cut the cookies as close together as possible. I use a pancake spatula to lift the cut-out cookies onto the cookie sheets.

Testing for Doneness: Rolled cookies are ready when they have just begun to turn golden around the edges.

Cooling: These cookies cool best directly on the cookie sheet. They're delicate and may break if you try to move them while they're hot.

Eating: Let rolled cookies cool before you eat them to allow the floury taste to settle down.

Storing: Use your trusty airtight plastic container for storing these cookies in the freezer or refrigerator. The dough also stores well for 4 to 5 days in the refrigerator, or it can be frozen.

Filled Pastry Cookies

Pastry cookies, which include such delicacies as Rugalah and Maya's Pocketbooks, are made from a rich dough filled with fruit, jam, nuts, cheese, or whatever and rolled into distinctive shapes.

Oven Temperature: Use a hot oven, 375° to 400°F. The dough must be chilled before baking, then cooked quickly so that the considerable amount of butter doesn't melt out of the dough and these pastries keep their shape.

Pan Preparation: Line cookie sheets with parchment or grease them lightly with butter or oil.

Shaping: This varies depending on the cookie.

Testing for Doneness: The dough should be lightly golden in color.

Cooling: Remove pastries with filling from the cookie sheet immediately; use a pancake spatula to place them on a plate or cooling rack. If they sit on the sheet, their filling may harden and stick to the pan or parchment.

Eating: The texture of some pastry cookies is better on the second day (Rugalah is an example). Crisp pastries, such as Maya's Pocketbooks, taste best the day they're made.

Storing: Store pastry cookies in an airtight plastic container. You can freeze or refrigerate them with no problem. The dough, too, can be stored for 4 to 5 days in the fridge and can be frozen for up to several weeks.

Serving

*W*hatever the taste or shape of cookie, I encourage you to think creatively when it comes to serving them because, contrary to conventional wisdom, cookies can provide an elegant closing to a dinner party as well as a casual snack after school. Even hearty cookies like Soho Globs or Chocolate Chips or Oatmeal Raisin work well as a dessert if you make them small and dainty, and most cookies complement sorbet or ice cream perfectly as a garnish.

In fact, the well-dressed cookie can go anywhere. Cover a platter with a doily and build a cookie mosaic using a variety of sizes, shapes, and colors or go for an Ali Baba's cave effect and pile them high on a plate in an embarrassment of riches.

Or maybe forget about entertaining altogether and whip up a batch of your favorite cookies the next time you crave a little something sweet and need to summon up those days of childhood.

Chocolate Chip Cookies

*T*here is little doubt that the chocolate chip or Toll House cookie is America's favorite; so much so that it may qualify as one of the basic food groups. This adaptation is crisp around the edges and chewy in the middle. To achieve that consistency, it's crucial that you take the cookies out of the oven when the centers are light colored and puffy and the edges are golden. The slightly underdone centers will drop when they cool and become chewy. With these cookies, I always figure on ending up with fewer than the stated recipe yield because everyone who wanders into the kitchen can't seem to resist sticking a fingerful of the dough into their mouths. But then, neither can I.

INGREDIENTS

- *2 cups plus 1 tablespoon all-purpose flour*
- *1 teaspoon baking soda*
- *¾ teaspoon salt*
- *1 cup (2 sticks) unsalted butter at room temperature*
- *1 cup plus 1 tablespoon (lightly packed) light brown sugar*
- *½ cup plus 2 tablespoons granulated sugar*
- *1 teaspoon vanilla extract*
- *2 large eggs, at room temperature*
- *1½ cups semisweet chocolate chips*

1. Preheat the oven to 375°F. Line several cookie sheets with parchment paper or grease them lightly with butter or vegetable oil.

2. Sift the flour, baking soda, and salt together into a small bowl and set aside.

3. Using an electric mixer on medium speed, cream the butter, both sugars, and the vanilla together in a medium-size bowl until light and fluffy, 1½ to 2 minutes. Stop the mixer twice to scrape the bowl with a rubber spatula.

4. Add the eggs and beat on medium speed until they are blended, about 30 seconds. Scrape the bowl.

5. Add the dry ingredients and mix on low speed for 15 seconds. Scrape the bowl.

6. Add the chocolate chips and blend until they are mixed in, 5 to 8 seconds.

7. Drop the dough by generously rounded tablespoonfuls (the equivalent of 3 level tablespoons) 2 inches apart onto the prepared cookie sheets.

8. Bake the cookies until the edges are dark golden and the center is light and slightly puffed up, 11 to 12 minutes. Remove the cookies from the oven and allow them to cool on the sheets. These are best eaten the same day they are baked.

Makes 24 large cookies

Note: This dough also works beautifully when it's refrigerated a minimum of 4 hours; it tends to produce a thicker, chewier cookie that is crisp around the edges.

Coconut Chocolate-Chip Cookies

*T*asting like a sweet shortbread, this cookie packs an extra punch of coconut and chocolate chips.

2¼ cups all-purpose flour
½ teaspoon baking soda
1 cup (2 sticks) unsalted butter, at room temperature
¾ cup sugar
1 teaspoon vanilla extract
1 large egg, at room temperature
1½ cups shredded coconut
1 cup semisweet chocolate chips

1. Preheat the oven to 325°F. Line several cookie sheets with parchment paper or grease them lightly with butter or vegetable oil.

2. Sift the flour and baking soda together into a small bowl and set aside.

3. Using an electric mixer on medium speed, cream the butter, sugar, and vanilla together in a medium-size mixing bowl until light and fluffy, about 1½ minutes. Stop the mixer twice to scrape the bowl with a rubber spatula.

4. Add the egg and mix at medium speed until it is incorporated, about 15 seconds. Scrape the bowl.

5. Add the dry ingredients on low speed and mix until blended, 20 to 25 seconds.

6. Add the coconut and chocolate chips and blend until they are mixed in, about 10 seconds.

7. Drop the dough by heaping tablespoonfuls about 2 inches apart onto the prepared cookie sheets, then flatten them out with your fingers to about 2 inches in diameter.

8. Bake the cookies until they are crunchy to the touch and golden around the edges, 20 to 25 minutes. Allow them to cool on the cookie sheets.

Makes 36 cookies

Orange Pecan Chocolate-Chip Cookies

*O*ranges and chocolate are such an ideal match to me that I wonder why I don't come across tons of desserts combining them. Here the taste of orange is strong and the cookie is crunchy, so together they make a tangy variation on a classic chocolate-chip cookie theme.

2 cups all-purpose flour
1 tablespoon baking powder
½ teaspoon salt
10 tablespoons (1¼ sticks) unsalted butter, at room temperature
½ cup granulated sugar
1 cup (lightly packed) light brown sugar
1 tablespoon grated orange zest
1 teaspoon vanilla extract
2 large eggs, at room temperature
1½ cups semisweet chocolate chips
1½ cups chopped pecans

1. Preheat the oven to 350°F. Line several cookie sheets with parchment paper or lightly grease them with butter or vegetable oil.

2. Sift the flour, baking powder, and salt together into a small bowl and set aside.

3. Using an electric mixer on medium-high speed, cream the butter, both sugars, the orange zest, and vanilla together in a medium-size mixing bowl until light and fluffy, about 1½ minutes. Stop the mixer twice to scrape the bowl with a rubber spatula.

4. Add the eggs one at a time and beat on medium speed after each addition until the egg is incorporated, about 10 seconds. Scrape the bowl with a rubber spatula after each addition.

5. Add the dry ingredients and mix on low speed until almost blended. Scrape the bowl.

6. Add the chocolate chips and nuts and mix until blended, 5 to 8 seconds.

7. Drop the dough by slightly rounded tablespoonfuls about 2 inches apart onto the prepared cookie sheets. Flatten them with the palm of your hand.

8. Bake the cookies until they are golden in color, 15 to 16 minutes. Allow them to cool on the sheets. They will get crunchier as they sit.

Makes 48 cookies

Soho Globs

The first time I was introduced to a glob at the Soho Charcuterie (a popular nouvelle American restaurant in the 1980s) in New York, I was outraged at the price. Two dollars indeed, I fumed until I bit into one and immediately went back for two more. Globs are the ideal combination of a bittersweet chocolate flavor and a chewy consistency, all studded with pecans and chocolate chips—kind of cookie-dom's answer to the brownie. And then there's the name. No wonder I became a believer.

INGREDIENTS

5 ounces semisweet chocolate
3 ounces unsweetened chocolate
6 tablespoons (¾ stick) unsalted butter, at room temperature
⅓ cup all-purpose flour
1 teaspoon baking powder
¼ teaspoon salt
2 large eggs, at room temperature
2 teaspoons vanilla extract
1 tablespoon instant espresso powder
¾ cup sugar
¾ cup semisweet chocolate chips
⅓ cup chopped pecans
⅓ cup chopped walnuts

1. Preheat the oven to 325°F. Line several cookie sheets with parchment paper or grease them lightly with butter or vegetable oil.

2. Melt the 8 ounces semisweet and unsweetened chocolate and the butter in the top of a double boiler placed over simmering water. Allow it to cool slightly.

3. Sift the flour, baking powder, and salt together into a small bowl and set aside.

4. Using an electric mixer on medium speed, beat the eggs, vanilla, and espresso powder in a medium-size mixing bowl until they are mixed together, about 10 seconds.

5. Add the sugar to the egg mixture and blend it all until thick, about 1 minute. Scrape the bowl.

6. Add the melted chocolate and blend 1 minute more. Scrape the bowl.

7. Add the flour mixture on low speed and mix until blended, 10 seconds. Fold in the chocolate chips and nuts by hand or with the mixer on low speed.

8. Drop the dough by generously rounded tablespoonfuls about 2 inches apart onto the prepared cookie sheets.

9. Bake the cookies until they rise slightly and form a thin crust, about 13 minutes. Immediately remove the cookies from the cookie sheets and place them on a rack to cool.

Makes 20 cookies

Big Jakes

A dark moist cookie studded with white chocolate that causes my son Jake's face to light up with joy and coats his entire lower face with chocolate.

I N G R E D I E N T S

> 1 recipe Soho Globs omitting the chocolate chips and nuts (recipe precedes)
> ¾ cup white chocolate chips or chopped white chocolate

Prepare the recipe as directed substituting the white chocolate for the chips and nuts.

Makes 20 cookies

Peanut Butter Cookies

H ere is Rosie's version of the classic peanut butter cookie. On the first day, they're chewy in the center and crunchy around the edge, but if there are any left over for day two, you'll find that they'll get crisper throughout.

I N G R E D I E N T S

> 1½ cups plus 2 tablespoons all-purpose flour
> ½ teaspoon baking soda
> ¼ teaspoon salt
> 8 tablespoons (1 stick) unsalted butter, at room temperature
> ½ cup plus 2 tablespoons peanut butter, creamy or crunchy
> ½ cup plus 1 teaspoon granulated sugar
> ½ cup plus 1 teaspoon (lightly packed) light brown sugar
> ½ teaspoon vanilla extract
> 1 large egg, at room temperature

1. Sift the flour, baking soda, and salt into a small bowl and set aside.

2. Using an electric mixer on medium speed, cream the butter, peanut butter, both sugars, and the vanilla together in a medium-size mixing bowl until light and fluffy, about 1½ minutes. Stop the mixer twice to scrape the bowl with a rubber spatula.

3. Add the egg and beat on medium speed until blended, about 1 minute. Scrape the bowl.

4. Add the dry ingredients to the peanut butter mixture and mix on low speed until blended, about 15 seconds. Scrape the bowl and mix several seconds more.

5. Place the dough in a small covered bowl and refrigerate it for several hours or overnight.

6. Fifteen minutes before baking, preheat the oven to 350°F. Line several cookie sheets with parchment paper or grease them lightly with butter or vegetable oil.

7. Measure out heaping tablespoonfuls of the dough and roll them into balls with your hands. Place the balls 2 inches apart on the prepared cookie sheets. Bake the cookies until they are dark gold around the edges and slightly puffy and light in the center, about 15 minutes. Allow the cookies to cool on the cookie sheets.

Makes 18 large cookies

Sunken Kisses

*I*n my household, baking these little peanut butter cookies is an occasion because I put my kids in charge of unwrapping the Hershey's Chocolate Kisses and placing one carefully in the middle of each cookie. You've never seen such concentration. By unanimous decision, though, the making doesn't hold a candle to the eating.

INGREDIENTS

1¾ cups all-purpose flour
1 teaspoon baking soda
¼ teaspoon salt
8 tablespoons (1 stick) unsalted butter, at room temperature
¾ cup (lightly packed) light brown sugar
¾ cup granulated sugar
½ cup peanut butter, smooth or crunchy
1 teaspoon vanilla extract
1 large egg, at room temperature
48 Hershey's Chocolate Kisses, removed from their wrappers

1. Preheat the oven to 375°F. Line 2 cookie sheets with parchment paper or grease them lightly with butter or vegetable oil.

2. Sift the flour, baking soda, and salt together into a small bowl and set aside.

3. Using an electric mixer on medium speed, cream the butter, brown sugar, ¼ cup of the granulated sugar, the peanut butter, and vanilla in a medium-size mixing bowl until light and fluffy, 2 to 3 minutes. Stop the mixer twice to scrape the bowl with a rubber spatula.

4. Add the egg and blend on medium speed until it is almost incorporated, about 10 seconds. Scrape the bowl.

5. Add the dry ingredients on low speed and blend 15 seconds. Stop the mixer to scrape the bowl and paddle, then blend until the dough is smooth, about 5 seconds more.

6. Measure out 48 rounded teaspoonfuls of the dough and roll them into balls with your hands.

7. Dip one side of each ball in the remaining ½ cup granulated sugar (optional) and place them 2 inches apart and sugar side up on the prepared cookie sheets.

8. Bake the cookies until they are light gold, 8 to 10 minutes. Remove the sheets from the oven. Immediately top each cookie with a Chocolate Kiss, wide side down, and press it firmly in the center of the cookie to imbed the kiss.

9. Carefully remove the cookies from the sheets and place them on a plate or cooling rack.

Makes 48 cookies

Ginger-snappers

I don't know if the "snap" in gingersnaps refers to the crispness of the cookie or the bite of the ginger, but I do know that Nabisco gingersnaps were a staple in our household when I was growing up. My mother loved to eat two or three at bedtime, dunking them into a glass of milk until they became soft, and giving me a bite of her treat. These ginger cookies don't snap when you break them—they're soft and chewy—but their ginger taste is distinctive.

INGREDIENTS

2½ cups all-purpose flour
2 teaspoons baking soda
½ teaspoon salt
2 teaspoons ground cinnamon
1 tablespoon plus 2 teaspoons ground ginger
12 tablespoons (1½ sticks) unsalted butter, at room temperature
1 cup (firmly packed) dark brown sugar
1 large egg, at room temperature
¼ cup unsulphured molasses
1 tablespoon grated lemon zest
¼ cup granulated sugar

1. Preheat the oven to 350°F. Line several cookie sheets with parchment paper or lightly grease them with butter or vegetable oil.

2. Sift the flour, baking soda, salt, cinnamon, and ginger together into a small bowl and set aside.

3. Using an electric mixer on medium-high speed, cream the butter and brown sugar in a medium-size mixing bowl until light and fluffy, 2 minutes. Stop the mixer twice to scrape the bowl with a rubber spatula.

4. Add the egg and beat on medium speed until blended, about 10 seconds. Scrape the bowl with the spatula.

5. Add the molasses and lemon zest and beat until blended, 10 seconds.

6. Fold in half the dry ingredients by hand using several broad strokes of the spatula, then fold in the remaining half. Mix on low speed until blended, about 20 seconds.

7. Measure out rounded tablespoonfuls of the dough and roll them into balls with your hands.

8. Roll the balls in the granulated sugar and place them 2 inches apart on the prepared cookie sheets.

9. Bake the cookies just until the edges are lightly golden and the center is puffy, about 12 minutes. Do not overbake them or they will become hard. Remove the cookies carefully from the sheets with a pancake spatula. Place them on a rack to cool.

Makes 26 cookies

Oatmeal Lace Cookies

*T*his cookie is very sweet like those caramels orthodontists outlawed because they stuck in your braces but which you snuck anyway because who could resist. Delicate and crisp, they're particularly good as an accent to ice cream.

INGREDIENTS

> *2 tablespoons all-purpose flour*
> *1 cup rolled oats*
> *1 teaspoon ground cinnamon*
> *8 tablespoons (1 stick) butter, cut into 8 pieces*
> *¾ cup (lightly packed) light brown sugar*
> *2 tablespoons water*
> *1 large egg, at room temperature*
> *1 teaspoon vanilla extract*
> *¼ cup finely chopped walnuts*

1. Preheat the oven to 350°F. Line several cookie sheets with parchment paper or lightly grease them with butter or vegetable oil. Have ready a large bowl of ice water.

2. Combine the flour, oats, and cinnamon in a small bowl and set aside.

3. Place the butter, brown sugar, and 2 tablespoons water in a medium-size saucepan; heat over low heat until the butter is melted, about 2 minutes. Increase the heat to medium-high and allow the mixture to come to a full boil. Boil for 1 minute.

4. Place the saucepan slightly into the bowl of ice water and whisk constantly for about 3 minutes to cool the mixture.

5. Transfer the mixture to a medium-size bowl, stir in the egg and vanilla rapidly with a whisk, then stir in the flour mixture and the nuts with a wooden spoon.

6. Place the mixing bowl slightly into the bowl filled with ice water and allow the dough to thicken slightly (don't stir), about 4 minutes.

7. Drop the dough by level teaspoonfuls about 2 inches apart onto the prepared cookie sheets.

8. Bake until the cookies are golden with darker edges, 10 to 12 minutes. Allow the cookies to cool on the sheets for 30 to 40 minutes, then remove them carefully with a spatula. Eat them that day or store them in an airtight container. These cookies are best eaten the day they're baked because they tend to lose their crispness.

Makes 24 cookies

Crispy Orange-Oatmeal Wafers

*D*elicate and crispy, this cookie is particularly nice as a garnish for ice cream.

INGREDIENTS

3/4 cup all-purpose flour
1/2 teaspoon baking soda
1/2 teaspoon salt
8 tablespoons (1 stick) butter, at room temperature
1/2 cup granulated sugar
1/2 cup (lightly packed) light brown sugar
1/2 teaspoon vanilla extract
1 tablespoon grated orange zest
1 large egg, at room temperature
1 1/2 cups rolled oats

1. Preheat the oven to 400°F. Line several cookie sheets with parchment paper or lightly grease them with butter or vegetable oil.

2. Sift the flour, baking soda, and salt together into a small bowl and set aside.

3. Using an electric mixer on medium speed, cream the butter, both sugars, the vanilla, and orange zest together in a medium-size bowl until light and fluffy, about 1½ minutes. Stop the mixer twice to scrape the bowl with a rubber spatula.

4. Add the egg and mix on medium-low speed to incorporate it, about 20 seconds.

5. Add the dry ingredients and mix on medium-low speed for 10 seconds. Scrape the bowl, then mix until blended, about 5 seconds more. Scrape the bowl.

6. Add the oats and mix for several seconds on low speed to blend them in.

7. Drop the dough by rounded tea-spoonfuls about 2 inches apart onto the prepared cookie sheets.

8. Bake the cookies until crisp and lightly golden with darker golden edges, about 8 minutes. Allow the cookies to cool on the sheets.

Makes 50 cookies

Chocolate Meringue Drops

I'm a sucker for these elegant-ly simple and not-so-little treats. This recipe produces a meringue that's crusty outside, chewy inside, and sweet every inch of the way.

INGREDIENTS

4 large egg whites, at room temperature
⅛ teaspoon salt
1¼ cups sugar
1 teaspoon vanilla extract
½ cup semisweet chocolate chips

1. Preheat the oven to 300°F. Lightly grease several cookie sheets with butter. Sprinkle flour over the sheets and shake to distribute the flour. Then turn the sheets upside down over the sink to knock off any excess flour.

2. Using an electric mixer on medium-low speed, beat the egg whites with the salt in a medium-size mixing bowl until frothy, about 40 seconds. Gradually add the sugar, then raise the mixer speed to high and add the va-nilla. Beat the mixture for 50 seconds, stop to scrape the bowl with a rubber spatula, then continue beating until the mixture forms very stiff peaks, 60 to 75 seconds longer. Then gently fold in the chocolate chips with the rubber spatula.

3. Drop the mixture by slightly rounded teaspoonfuls about 1 inch apart onto the prepared cookie sheets.

4. Bake the cookies until they turn a very light beige, 25 to 30 minutes. Cool the cookies on the cookie sheets.

Makes 75 cookies

Chocolate Macaroons

*T*he recipe for these cookies comes from the archives of Leah Winograd, erstwhile caterer of bar mitzvahs, baker extraordinaire and mother of my partner Eliot. Bored with the usual Passover fare, she substitutes these for the occasion, though I like to make them year-round. They have a thin outer crust and a chewy inside.

I N G R E D I E N T S

4 ounces semisweet chocolate
2 ounces unsweetened chocolate
2 large egg whites
1/2 cup sugar
1 teaspoon vanilla extract
2 cups shredded coconut

1. Preheat the oven to 375°F. Line a cookie sheet with parchment paper, or grease it lightly with butter or vegetable oil.

2. Melt both chocolates in the top of a double boiler placed over simmering water, then cool the chocolate to tepid.

3. Beat the egg whites in a medium-size mixing bowl with an electric mixer on medium-high speed until frothy, about 30 seconds.

4. Gradually add the sugar and continue beating until the mixture is the consistency of marshmallow fluff, about 30 seconds more. Blend in the vanilla, then fold in the melted chocolate, then the coconut.

5. Drop rounded tablespoonfuls of the dough about 1½ inches apart onto the prepared cookie sheet.

6. Bake the cookies until a light crust forms on the outside, about 13 minutes. Cool on the cookie sheet or remove the cookies to a cooling rack.

Makes 12 cookies

Hermits

*T*here's lots of disagreement about the attributes of a good hermit—the cookie, that is. I'm a strong advocate of something dark, spicy, and chewy, which is what you'll find in this recipe. Although these cookies are basically made from a drop cookie batter, I make them in freeform strips, then cut them after baking. It is important to store these cookies in an airtight container to preserve their chewiness.

INGREDIENTS

COOKIES

2 cups plus 1 tablespoon all-purpose flour
2 teaspoons baking soda
¼ teaspoon salt
1¾ teaspoons ground cinnamon
2 teaspoons ground ginger
1¾ teaspoons ground cloves
9 tablespoons (1 stick plus 1 tablespoon) unsalted butter, at room temperature
1 cup (lightly packed) light brown sugar
1 large egg, at room temperature
¼ cup unsulphured molasses
¾ cup raisins

GLAZE

1½ cups plus 3 tablespoons confectioner's sugar
2 tablespoons plus 2½ teaspoons milk
½ teaspoon grated lemon or orange zest

1. Preheat the oven to 375°F. Line a cookie sheet with parchment paper or leave it ungreased.

2. Sift the flour, baking soda, salt, cinnamon, ginger, and cloves together into a small bowl and set aside.

3. Using an electric mixer on medium speed, cream the butter and sugar together in a medium-size mixing bowl until light and fluffy, about 1½ minutes. Stop the mixer twice to scrape the bowl with a rubber spatula.

4. Add the egg and mix on medium speed until blended, 20 to 30 seconds. Scrape the bowl.

5. Add the molasses and mix until blended.

6. Add the dry ingredients and the raisins and mix on medium speed until the dough comes together, about 1 minute.

7. Divide the dough in half. Shape each half into a log 1½ inches in diameter by 12 inches long. Arrange the logs on the prepared cookie sheet, leaving at least 3 to 4 inches between them.

8. Bake the logs until they are golden but still very soft to the touch and puffy in the center, 17 to 18 minutes. (The dough cracks during baking and it will still seem slightly raw on the inside even when the logs are done.) The logs flatten out and lengthen as they bake.

9. Cool the logs on the sheet. Cut into 2-inch-wide slices when cool. Each log makes 7 cookies.

10. Prepare the glaze: Place all the ingredients in a small bowl and stir them vigorously with a whisk until blended.

11. Drizzle the glaze over the strips or use a pastry brush to paint the surface of the strips with the glaze. Allow the glaze to harden before eating or storing the cookies.

Makes 14 cookies

Nutballs

By tradition, these cookies are a staple at Mexican weddings, and I like to serve them around the winter holidays, which goes to show, I guess, that they melt in your mouth in any climate and on any occasion.

INGREDIENTS

8 tablespoons (1 stick) unsalted butter, at room temperature
2 tablespoons granulated sugar
1 teaspoon vanilla extract
1 cup all-purpose flour, sifted
1 cup walnuts, finely chopped
1 cup confectioner's sugar, sifted

1. Preheat the oven to 300°F. Line 2 cookie sheets with parchment paper or leave them ungreased.

2. Using an electric mixer on medium speed, cream the butter, granulated sugar, and vanilla until light and fluffy, 1½ to 2 minutes. Stop the mixer once or twice to scrape the bowl with a rubber spatula.

3. Add the flour and mix on low speed until it is blended in, about 45 seconds. Scrape the bowl once or twice during mixing.

4. Add the nuts and mix until well blended, about 10 seconds.

5. Measure out generously rounded teaspoonfuls of dough and roll them into balls with your hands. Place these balls about 2 inches apart on the prepared cookie sheets.

6. Bake the cookies until they just begin to turn golden, about 30 minutes. To test for doneness, remove one cookie from the sheet and cut it in half. There should be no doughy strip in the center.

7. Roll the cookies in the confectioner's sugar while they are still hot, then cool on the cookie sheets. Serve them when they have cooled.

Makes 35 cookies

Mandelbrot

It wasn't until I went to college that I began to learn about some of the delicacies of my Jewish heritage, and mandelbrot was one of them. At that time, my roommate Michelle Menzies introduced me to this zwieback-like cookie that her grandmother had taught her to make. It's more or less the Jewish counterpart to Italian anise biscuits, but without the anise and with a generous helping of nuts.

INGREDIENTS

3 cups all-purpose flour
2 teaspoons baking powder
¾ teaspoon salt
½ cup quick-cooking oatmeal
*1 cup (2 sticks) unsalted butter,
    at room temperature*
1¼ cups sugar
2 teaspoons vanilla extract
1 tablespoon fresh lemon juice
3 large eggs, at room temperature
*1 cup almonds, walnuts, or pecans,
    finely chopped*
1 tablespoon ground cinnamon

1. Preheat the oven to 350°F. Line 2 cookie sheets with parchment paper or lightly grease them with butter or vegetable oil.

2. Sift the flour, baking powder, and salt together in a medium-size bowl; stir in the oatmeal and set aside.

3. Using an electric mixer on medium-high speed, cream the butter, 1 cup of the sugar, the vanilla, and lemon juice together in a medium-size mixing bowl until light and fluffy, 2 to 2½ minutes. Stop the machine twice during the mixing to scrape the bowl with a rubber spatula.

4. Add the eggs one at a time on medium speed, mixing until each egg is partially incorporated, about 5 sec-

onds. Scrape the bowl after each addition. After the last egg has been added, beat the mixture on high speed for several seconds.

5. Mix in half the dry ingredients by hand with the rubber spatula, then blend with the electric mixer on low speed for several seconds. Add the remaining dry ingredients and mix on low speed until the dough is smooth, about 5 seconds. Add the nuts with a few more turns of the mixer.

6. Divide the dough into quarters. Using floured hands, lay one-quarter of the dough lengthwise on a prepared cookie sheet, molding it into a cylindrical strip 8½ inches in length by 2 inches in diameter. Place it a couple of inches from the edge of the pan. Form a second strip on that sheet 3 inches from the first strip, then place 2 more strips on the other cookie sheet in the same fashion.

7. Mix the remaining ¼ cup sugar with the cinnamon. Sprinkle the cinnamon sugar generously over each strip.

8. Bake the dough strips until firm to the touch and lightly golden, about 20 to 25 minutes.

9. Remove the sheets from the oven, but leave the oven on. Cut each strip into ¾-inch-thick slices and arrange all the slices on the sheets about ½ inch apart. Bake until crisp and golden, about 15 minutes. Cool the cookies on the sheets.

Makes 48 cookies

Lemon Cake Cookies

*T*hese cookies took so many tries to perfect that they almost got named Those Damn Lemon Cookies. I knew exactly what I wanted — something half-way between a sponge cake and a pound cake with a distinctive flavor — but there were times when I thought I'd have better luck finding it by advertising in the personals. Patience brought success, and here is a soft, moist cookie, wearing a most fetching lemon glaze.

INGREDIENTS

COOKIES
2½ cups plus 1 tablespoon cake flour
    (see Note)
¾ teaspoon baking powder
¾ teaspoon baking soda
½ teaspoon salt
9 tablespoons (1 stick plus 1
    tablespoon) butter, at room
    temperature
1 cup plus 2 tablespoons sugar
1 tablespoon grated lemon zest
2 large egg yolks, at room temperature
1 whole large egg, at room
    temperature
1¼ cups sour cream, at room
    temperature

GLAZE
6 tablespoons (¾ stick) unsalted butter
1½ cups confectioner's sugar
3 tablespoons fresh lemon juice

1. Preheat the oven to 375°F. Line several cookie sheets with parchment paper or lightly grease them with butter or vegetable oil.

2. Sift the flour, baking powder, baking soda, and salt together into a small bowl and set aside.

3. Using an electric mixer on medium speed, cream the butter, sugar, and lemon zest in a medium-size bowl until light and fluffy, about 2 minutes. Scrape the bowl.

4. Add the egg yolks and mix on medium speed until blended, about 10 seconds. Scrape the bowl, then add the whole egg and mix until blended, 10 seconds more.

5. Add the sour cream and mix on medium-low speed until blended, about 8 seconds.

6. Fold in the dry ingredients by hand, then turn the mixer on low speed for 5 seconds. Scrape the bowl with the rubber spatula and mix on low until the batter is smooth and velvety, 10 seconds. Give the batter a stir or two with the spatula.

7. Drop the batter by large rounded tablespoonfuls about 2 inches apart onto the prepared cookie sheets.

8. Bake until the cookies puff up, are firm to the touch, and just begin to turn golden, about 12 minutes. Remove the cookies from the sheets with a spatula and place them on a cooling rack. Allow them to cool completely.

9. Meanwhile prepare the glaze: Melt the butter in a small pan over low heat. Place the sugar in a medium-size bowl. Add the butter and lemon juice to the sugar and beat vigorously with a whisk until the mixture is smooth and creamy.

10. Once the cookies have cooled, dip the entire rounded top of each into the glaze. Place the cookies on the cookie sheets and allow them to sit until the glaze hardens, several hours. (If it is a humid day, refrigerate them in order to speed the process.)

Makes 36 cookies

Note: Although cake flour gives these cookies a superior texture, you may substitute 2 cups plus 3 tablespoons all-purpose flour for it.

Butter-Glazed Nutmeg Mounds

*T*hese are soft, cakelike cookies, flavored with nutmeg and topped with an old-fashioned buttery glaze. I like them even better several hours after they're made when the flavors come into their own and the consistency is softer and moister. Stored in an airtight container, they last a while—assuming you can resist raiding the cookie jar for that long.

INGREDIENTS

COOKIES
2¾ cups cake flour (see Note)
¾ teaspoon baking soda
¾ teaspoon baking powder
1 tablespoon plus 1 teaspoon ground nutmeg
½ teaspoon salt
9 tablespoons (1 stick plus 1 tablespoon) unsalted butter, at room temperature
1½ cups (lightly packed) light brown sugar
2 teaspoons vanilla extract
2 large egg yolks, at room temperature
1 whole large egg, at room temperature
1 cup sour cream, at room temperature

GLAZE
6 tablespoons (¾ stick) unsalted butter
1½ cups confectioner's sugar
1 teaspoon vanilla extract
3 tablespoons hot water

1. Preheat the oven to 375°F. Line several cookie sheets with parchment paper or lightly grease them with vegetable oil or butter.

2. Sift the flour, baking soda, baking powder, nutmeg, and salt together into a small bowl and set aside.

3. Using an electric mixer on medium-high speed, cream the butter, brown sugar, and vanilla together in a medium-size bowl until light and fluffy, about 2 minutes. Stop the mixer twice to scrape the bowl with a rubber spatula. Scrape the bowl a third time before going on to the next step.

4. Add the egg yolks and blend on medium speed for about 10 seconds. Scrape the bowl then add the whole egg and mix until blended, about 10 seconds. Scrape the bowl again.

5. Add the sour cream and mix on medium-low speed until well blended, about 10 seconds. Scrape the bowl.

6. Fold in the dry ingredients by hand, then turn the mixer on low speed and mix about 5 seconds. Scrape the bowl with the spatula and mix on low until the batter is smooth and velvety, 10 seconds. Give the batter a stir or two with the spatula.

7. Drop the batter by heaping table-spoonfuls about 2 inches apart onto the prepared cookie sheets.

8. Bake the cookies until they are just golden in color and firm to the touch, but not crusty, about 12 minutes. Using a metal spatula, carefully lift the cookies from the sheet and place them on a rack to cool.

9. While the cookies are cooling, prepare the glaze: Melt the butter in a small frying pan over medium-low heat until golden in color, 3 minutes.

10. Place the confectioner's sugar in a small bowl, add the butter, vanilla,

and hot water, and beat vigorously with a whisk until the mixture is smooth and creamy.

11. When the cookies have cooled, dip the rounded top of each into the glaze. Place the cookies on the cookie sheets and allow them to sit until the glaze hardens, several hours. (If it is a humid day, refrigerate them in order to speed the process.)

Makes 36 cookies

Note: Although cake flour gives these cookies a superior texture, you may substitute 2½ cups all-purpose flour for it.

Maya Pies

I confess that before my anti-preservative days, I was a fan of Devil Dogs and I recall with fondness their velvety texture and the contrast of those chocolate buns with the sweet cream filling. Even when I gave up eating chemicals, I didn't want to give up Devil Dogs completely, so I came up with a version, named after my daughter Maya, made from wholesome ingredients, which I like to think is just as good as our childhood memories. Their texture improves on the second day, so store them in an airtight container overnight.

INGREDIENTS

COOKIES
4 ounces unsweetened chocolate
14 tablespoons all-purpose flour
6 tablespoons cake flour
1 teaspoon baking powder
½ teaspoon baking soda
10 tablespoons (1¼ sticks) unsalted
    butter, at room temperature
½ teaspoon vegetable oil
1 cup granulated sugar
3 large eggs, at room temperature
½ cup plus 1 tablespoon milk, at room
    temperature
3 tablespoons sour cream, at room
    temperature

FILLING
½ cup milk
1½ tablespoons all-purpose flour
1¾ cups confectioner's sugar
12 tablespoons (1½ sticks) unsalted
    butter, at room temperature
½ teaspoon vanilla extract

1. Preheat the oven to 375°F and line 2 cookie sheets with cooking parchment or grease them lightly with butter or vegetable oil.

2. Melt the chocolate in the top of a double boiler placed over simmering water. Set it aside.

3. Sift both flours, the baking powder, and baking soda together into a small bowl and set aside.

4. Using an electric mixer on medium-high speed, cream the butter, oil, and granulated sugar together in a medium-size mixing bowl until light and fluffy, about 2 minutes. Stop the mixer once or twice to scrape the bowl with a rubber spatula.

5. Add the eggs one at a time and blend on medium speed for 10 seconds after each addition, scraping the bowl with the rubber spatula each time.

6. Add the milk and sour cream and beat on medium speed until blended, about 5 seconds, then on high speed for 3 seconds more. The mixture will not appear smooth.

7. Fold in the chocolate with the spatula until the batter is uniform in color.

8. Fold the dry ingredients in by hand with 6 or 7 broad strokes of the spatula, then mix on low speed until the batter is velvety, about 10 seconds, stopping once to scrape the bowl with the rubber spatula. Finish mixing by hand.

9. Drop the batter by rounded tablespoonfuls 2 inches apart onto the prepared cookie sheets. Bake the cookies until they have risen, spring back to the touch, and a tester inserted in the center of a cookie comes out dry, about 10 minutes.

10. Carefully lift the cookies from the sheets with a metal spatula and place them on a cooling rack.

11. While the cookies are cooling prepare the filling: Mix the milk and flour in a medium-size saucepan over low heat. Cook, stirring constantly, until a paste is formed, 2 to 3 minutes. Transfer the paste to a mixing bowl and allow it to cool for about 20 minutes in the refrigerator.

12. Add the confectioner's sugar, butter, and vanilla to the cooled paste, then beat it with the paddle attachment of an electric mixer on medium speed for 1 minute, then on high speed until light and fluffy, 3 to 4 minutes more.

13. When the cookies are completely cool, turn half the cookies upside down, spread each with a rounded tablespoon of filling, and top them with the remaining cookies. Store the cookies in an airtight container and eat them the next day. They will continue to soften overnight.

Makes 13 double cookies

Pecan Crunchies

7 hese crunchy, melt-in-your-mouth cookies are perfect for any occasion, and an all-time favorite at Rosie's.

INGREDIENTS

2 cups all-purpose flour
3/4 teaspoon salt
1 cup pecan pieces
1 cup plus 2 tablespoons (2 1/4 sticks) unsalted butter, at room temperature
1/3 cup (lightly packed) light brown sugar
3/4 cup plus 3 tablespoons granulated sugar

1. Sift the flour and salt together into a small bowl and set aside.

2. Grind the pecans in a food processor until they are finely chopped but not powdery, about 30 seconds. Set them aside.

3. Using an electric mixer on medium speed, cream the butter, brown sugar, and 1/4 cup plus 3 tablespoons of the granulated sugar in a medium-size mixing bowl until the ingredients are light and fluffy, about 2 minutes. Scrape the bowl with a rubber spatula.

4. Add the dry ingredients and the pecans and beat on medium-low speed for 20 seconds. Scrape the bowl, then beat until the flour and nuts are completely incorporated, about 15 seconds.

5. Spread a 2-foot length of waxed paper on a work surface. With floured fingers, shape the dough into a rough log about 18 to 20 inches in length along the length of one side of the paper. Roll the log in the waxed paper and twist the ends like a hard candy wrapper. Refrigerate the dough for 2 hours. You can cut the log in half in order to fit it in the refrigerator.

6. Remove the log from the refrigerator and, with the dough still in the waxed paper, gently roll it back and forth on the work surface to round the log.

7. Place the log back in the refrigerator for several more hours.

8. Preheat the oven to 300°F. Line 2 cookie sheets with parchment or leave them ungreased.

9. Place the log on the counter, unwrap it, and cut the log into ⅓-inch-thick slices.

10. Dip one side of each cookie in the remaining ½ cup granulated sugar and place it sugar side up an inch apart on the cookie sheets.

11. Bake the cookies until they are firm to the touch and slightly golden, about 25 minutes. Be careful not to underbake these cookies, which alters the texture significantly. To test for doneness, remove one cookie from the sheet and cut it in half. There should be no doughy strip in the center. Cool on the cookie sheets.

Makes 48 cookies

Black and Whites

*7*his is a crunchy cookie with alternating strips of vanilla and chocolate doughs. They are wonderful with tea, coffee, or milk and last forever if stored in an airtight container.

INGREDIENTS

½ cup semisweet chocolate chips
2 ounces unsweetened chocolate
1¼ cups sifted all-purpose flour
¾ teaspoon baking powder
1 cup (2 sticks) unsalted butter, at room temperature
1 cup sugar
1½ teaspoons vanilla extract
1 large egg, at room temperature

1. Line a 9 × 5 × 3-inch loaf pan with waxed paper that overhangs the long sides.

2. Melt both chocolates in a double boiler placed over simmering water. Allow the chocolate to cool.

3. Sift the flour and baking powder together into a small bowl and set aside.

4. Using an electric mixer on medium speed, cream the butter, sugar, and vanilla in a medium-size mixing bowl until light and fluffy, about 2 minutes. Stop the mixer once or twice to scrape the bowl with a rubber spatula.

5. Add the egg to the butter mixture and mix on high speed for several seconds. Scrape the bowl and mix the ingredients on medium speed until they are blended, 5 to 8 seconds.

6. Add the dry ingredients and blend on medium speed until incorporated, 5 to 8 seconds.

7. Take one-third of the dough (a scant cup) and place it in a small bowl.

8. Add the melted chocolate to the remaining two-thirds of the dough and mix until the dough is uniform in color, about 5 seconds.

9. Press half the chocolate dough (a generous cup) over the bottom of the loaf pan. Smooth the surface of the dough as much as possible.

10. Press the vanilla dough over the chocolate dough. Smooth the surface as much as possible.

11. Cover the vanilla dough with the remaining chocolate dough and cover the top with a piece of waxed paper.

Refrigerate the dough overnight.

12. The next day preheat the oven to 375°F. Line several cookie sheets with parchment paper, or lightly grease them with butter or vegetable oil.

13. Lift the chilled dough out of the pan using the overhanging pieces of waxed paper. Remove the waxed paper and cut the dough lengthwise in half into two 9 × 2½-inch strips.

14. Cut each strip crosswise into slices ¼ inch thick. Place the slices 1 inch apart on the prepared cookie sheets.

15. Bake the cookies until the vanilla strips are lightly golden, 12 to 15 minutes. They must be watched very carefully during the last 5 minutes of baking so that they don't burn.

16. Lift the paper from the sheets and place it on a counter or remove the individual cookies with a spatula and allow them to cool on a rack.

Makes 72 cookies

Butterscotch-Cinnamon Icebox Cookies

*T*he brown sugar combined with the butter gives these cookies their distinctive flavor, and the walnuts give them their crunch.

I N G R E D I E N T S

2 cups all-purpose flour
¾ teaspoon salt
1 cup (2 sticks) unsalted butter,
    at room temperature
½ cup plus 3 tablespoons (lightly
    packed) dark brown sugar
2 teaspoons vanilla extract
2½ teaspoons ground cinnamon
½ cup chopped pecans, walnuts,
    or almonds
2 tablespoons granulated sugar

1. Sift the flour and salt together into a small bowl and set aside.

2. Using an electric mixer on medium speed, cream the butter, brown sugar, vanilla, and 1½ teaspoons of the cinnamon together in a medium-size mixing bowl until light and fluffy, 2½ to 3 minutes. Stop the mixer once or twice to scrape the bowl with a rubber spatula.

3. Add the dry ingredients and mix on low speed until the mixture is fluffy again, about 45 seconds. Scrape the bowl.

4. Add the nuts and mix on low speed just until they are incorporated, several seconds.

5. Place a 2-foot length of waxed paper on a work surface. Shape the dough into a rough log 18 to 20 inches long along the length of one side of the paper. Roll the dough up in the waxed paper and twist the ends like a hard candy wrapper. Refrigerate the dough for 2 hours.

6. Remove the log from the refrigerator. Using your hands, roll the wrapped dough gently back and forth on the work surface to smooth out the cylinder. Refrigerate for 4 to 6 hours or overnight.

7. Fifteen minutes before baking, preheat the oven to 275°F. Line several cookie sheets with parchment paper, or leave them ungreased.

8. Remove the log from the refrigerator, unroll it, and cut cookie slices that are a generous ⅓ inch thick.

9. Mix the granulated sugar with the remaining 1 teaspoon cinnamon. Dip one side of each cookie in the cinnamon sugar and place the cookies sugar side up an inch apart on the prepared cookie sheets.

10. Bake the cookies until they are

golden, about 40 minutes. To test for doneness, remove one cookie from the oven and cut it in half. There should be no doughy strip in the center. Cool the cookies on the sheets.

Makes 50 to 60 cookies

Very Short Shortbread Cookies
(for people of all heights)

I treasure this recipe, which was introduced into my parents' home by my Swedish nanny, Inga. I loved to watch her rub the butter and flour together with a skill that seemed so innate I doubted I would ever master it. To my pleasure, it turned out to be an easy and quick process, so even though you can use a food processor for this recipe, I like to make it by hand in honor of Inga (who was, by the way, very tall).

INGREDIENTS

2½ cups all-purpose flour
½ cup sugar
½ teaspoon salt
1 cup (2 sticks) unsalted butter, slightly cool

1. Preheat the oven to 300°F. Line several cookie sheets with parchment paper or leave them ungreased.

2. Sift the flour, sugar, and salt together in a large bowl.

3. Cut the butter into about 32 pieces and distribute them throughout the flour mixture. Rub the pieces into the mixture with your fingers and continue to work the mixture with your hands until all the ingredients hold together and form a dough, 4 to 5 minutes.

4. Measure out generously rounded teaspoonfuls of the dough and roll them into balls with your hands. Place the balls 1½ inches apart on the prepared cookie sheets. Use the prongs of a fork to flatten the cookies to ¼ inch thick by making crisscross indentations on the top.

5. Bake the cookies until they are lightly golden in the center and a bit darker around the edges, 30 to 35 minutes. Cool the cookies on the sheets, then store them in an airtight container.

Makes 48 cookies

Noah Bedoahs

*O*ne of my favorites, these are mounds of shortbread with chocolate chips and walnuts. They bake low and long to achieve a wonderfully crunchy texture.

INGREDIENTS

1¾ cups plus 2 tablespoons all-purpose flour
½ teaspoon baking powder
¼ teaspoon salt
1 cup (2 sticks) unsalted butter, at room temperature
½ cup sugar
¾ cup semisweet chocolate chips
½ cup chopped walnuts or pecans

1. Preheat the oven to 275°F. Line 2 cookie sheets with parchment paper or leave them ungreased.

2. Sift the flour, baking powder, and salt together into a small bowl and set aside.

3. Using an electric mixer on medium speed, cream the butter and sugar together in a medium-size mixing bowl until light and fluffy, about 1½ minutes. Stop the mixer to scrape the bowl several times with a rubber spatula.

4. Add the dry ingredients on low speed and continue to blend for 10 seconds. Increase the speed to medium-high and beat until fluffy, 2 to 2½ minutes. Scrape the bowl.

5. Add the chocolate chips and nuts with several turns of the mixer, then complete the mixing by hand with a wooden spoon.

6. Measure out generously rounded tablespoonfuls of dough and roll them into balls with your hands.

7. Place the balls 1½ inches apart on the cookie sheets, and press them down lightly to form a flat bottom.

8. Bake the cookies until they are crunchy and golden, about 1 hour. To test for doneness, remove one cookie from the sheet and cut it in half. There should be no doughy strip in the center. Allow the cookies to cool on a rack.

Makes 15 cookies

Chocolate-Dipped Pecan Logs

*T*his shortbread cookie is chock-full of nuts and then dipped in bittersweet chocolate.

INGREDIENTS

1 cup (2 sticks) unsalted butter,
    at room temperature
1/2 cup plus 2 tablespoons sugar
2 teaspoons vanilla extract
2 1/2 cups all-purpose flour
1/2 teaspoon salt
1/2 cup coarsely chopped pecans
6 ounces bittersweet chocolate

1. Preheat the oven to 325°F. Line 2 cookie sheets with parchment paper or leave them ungreased.

2. Using an electric mixer on medium speed, cream the butter, sugar, and vanilla in a medium-size mixing bowl until light and fluffy, about 1 1/2 minutes. Stop the mixer once or twice to scrape the bowl with a rubber spatula.

3. Add the flour and salt and blend on medium speed about 1 minute. Scrape the bowl and add the nuts with several more turns of the mixer.

4. Measure out slightly rounded tablespoonfuls of dough and shape them into little logs 2 1/2 inches long. Place the logs a minimum of 1 1/2 inches apart on the prepared cookie sheets. Flatten them slightly with your palm so that they are about 1 1/2 inches wide.

5. Bake the cookies until they are lightly golden, about 30 to 35 minutes. Cool on the cookie sheets.

6. When the cookies have cooled, melt the chocolate in the top of a double boiler placed over simmering water.

7. Pour the melted chocolate into a small deep bowl and dip half of each cookie into the chocolate, using the rim of the bowl to scrape any excess chocolate off the bottom of the cookie.

8. As they are dipped, place the cookies on a large sheet of waxed paper and allow them to set until the chocolate hardens, several hours. If it is a humid day, refrigerate them in order to speed the process.

Makes 36 cookies

Rosie's Butter Cookies

*T*his butter cookie with its dollop of jam in the middle echoes something in nearly everyone's past: a grandmother or aunt who served them when you visited, a neighborhood bakery that sold them by the pound, or a roommate's relative who sent them during exam week, bless all their hearts. With this classic recipe, you can carry on the tradition. Do not devour these cookies when they're hot (hard as it may be to resist) because the jam can burn the roof of your mouth.

INGREDIENTS

2¼ *cups all-purpose flour*
¼ *teaspoon baking powder*
¼ *teaspoon salt*
1 *cup (2 sticks) unsalted butter,*
    at room temperature
½ *cup sugar*
½ *cup raspberry preserves with seeds*

1. Sift the flour, baking powder, and salt together into a small bowl and set aside.

2. Using an electric mixer on medium-high speed, cream the butter and sugar together in a medium-size mixing bowl until light and fluffy, about 2 minutes. Stop the mixer twice to scrape the bowl with a rubber spatula.

3. Add the dry ingredients and mix on low speed for several seconds. Scrape the bowl, then turn the mixer to high speed and beat until the batter is light and fluffy, about 1 minute.

4. Refrigerate the batter in plastic wrap or a covered container for 3 hours.

5. Fifteen minutes before baking, preheat the oven to 275°F. Line 2 cookie sheets with parchment paper or leave them ungreased.

6. Measure out rounded teaspoonfuls of dough and roll them into balls with your hands.

7. Place the balls about 1½ inches apart on the prepared cookie sheets. Then make a firm indentation in the center of each cookie with your thumb or index finger.

8. Bake the cookies until lightly golden, 25 to 30 minutes. Remove the sheet from the oven and increase the heat to 325°F.

9. Place ½ teaspoon jam in the center of each cookie and return the sheet to the oven.

10. Bake the cookies just until the jam melts and spreads, about 10 minutes. Allow the cookies to cool on the sheets before eating.

Makes 48 cookies

Ruby Gems

*T*hese were among my favorite cookies when I was a kid because the jam center seemed like a special reward. And then there was that yummy mustache of confectioner's sugar that I could lick off when I was done.

INGREDIENTS

1 large egg yolk, at room temperature
1 teaspoon vanilla extract
3 cups all-purpose flour
⅔ cup granulated sugar
¼ teaspoon salt
1 cup plus 1 tablespoon (2 sticks plus 1 tablespoon) unsalted butter, very cold, cut into about 16 pieces
Apricot or raspberry preserves
1 cup confectioner's sugar

1. Using a fork, stir the egg yolk and vanilla together in a small cup.

2. Process the flour, granulated sugar, and salt in a food processor for about 10 seconds.

3. Add the butter and process the mixture until it resembles coarse meal, 20 to 30 seconds.

4. With the machine running, add the yolk mixture through the feed tube and process for 5 seconds. Scrape the bowl, then process until the liquid is evenly absorbed, about 10 seconds.

5. Remove the dough and place it on a work surface. Work the dough with your hands just until you can form it into a mass. Divide the dough in half and shape it into 2 thick disks. Wrap each disk in plastic wrap. Refrigerate the dough several hours or overnight.

6. When you're ready to prepare the cookies, preheat the oven to 350°F. Lightly grease several cookie sheets with vegetable oil or butter. Remove the dough from the refrigerator and allow it to soften slightly.

7. Place each piece of dough between 2 new pieces of plastic wrap or waxed paper and roll it out ⅛ inch thick (see page 165 for rolling technique).

8. Remove the top piece of plastic wrap and, using a 2-inch round cookie cutter, cut out approximately 22 circles from each half. Make small holes in the center of half the circles with a smooth bottle cap or a small cookie cutter. Place the circles about ¾ inch apart on the prepared cookie sheets. Gather up the dough scraps and reroll the dough to make as many more cookies as possible.

9. Bake the cookies until the edges just begin to turn golden, about 15 minutes. Remove them from the oven and cool on the sheets.

10. Place ½ teaspoon preserves in the center of each cookie without a hole. Sprinkle confectioner's sugar over the ones with holes and place them on top of the jammed cookies so that the jam forms a perfect little glob in the middle.

Makes at least 22 cookies

Rugalah

I first tasted rugalah at
Ebinger's Bakery in Queens
when I was 10 years old and became an instant convert, so much
so that the memory lingered for
years after Ebinger's closed. Much
later, I came up with my own
recipe for this Russian tea pastry.
I use the same rich cream cheese
dough filled with preserves and
nuts that I remember from my
Ebinger's days, and I've yet to
meet anyone who doesn't end up
feeling the same way I do about
it. These pastries look lovely piled
high in a natural basket lined
with a crocheted doily. The dough
is very moist and difficult to work
with, so put on your patience
cap and work very slowly and
methodically.

I N G R E D I E N T S

DOUGH
1 cup all-purpose flour
½ teaspoon salt
8 tablespoons (1 stick) unsalted butter,
*   at room temperature*
9 ounces cream cheese,
*   at room temperature*

FILLING
¾ cup apricot preserves
2 tablespoons sugar
1 teaspoon ground cinnamon
¼ cup chopped pecans
*   or walnuts*
½ cup golden raisins

GLAZE
1 large egg

1. Sift the flour and salt into a small
bowl and set aside.

2. Using an electric mixer on medium speed, cream the butter and
cream cheese together in a medium-
size mixing bowl until light and fluffy,
1½ to 2 minutes. Stop the mixer once
or twice to scrape the bowl with a
rubber spatula.

3. Add the dry ingredients and mix
until blended, about 20 seconds, stopping the mixer once to scrape the
bowl.

4. Shape the dough into 2 equal
thick rectangles, wrap each in plastic
wrap, and freeze them for 2 hours.

5. Remove 1 dough rectangle from
the freezer and roll it out between 2
pieces of plastic wrap into a rectangle
about 19 × 8 inches (see page 165 for
rolling technique). It may be necessary to refrigerate the dough for 30
minutes during the rolling process,
because it will become a bit sticky.
Once rolled, refrigerate the dough for
30 minutes. While it is resting, remove
the second rectangle from the freezer
and roll it out the same way you did
the first.

6. To fill the dough, unwrap one
rectangle and place it on plastic wrap
on your work surface. Spread half the
preserves evenly over the rectangle,
leaving uncovered a ½-inch strip along
the length of one side.

7. Mix the cinnamon and sugar together. Sprinkle half the cinnamon sugar, nuts, and raisins over the preserves.

8. Loosen the edge of the dough that is covered with jam with a knife or spatula and roll it toward the uncovered edge like a jelly roll, peeling off the plastic wrap as you roll. The seam should be on the underside. Wrap the roll in plastic and refrigerate it. Repeat the process with the other dough rectangle. Keep the filled rolls refrigerated for 2 hours.

9. Fifteen minutes before baking, preheat the oven to 375°F. Line 2 cookie sheets with parchment paper or lightly grease them with butter or vegetable oil.

10. For the glaze, lightly beat the egg with a fork. Use a pastry brush to apply the glaze to the outside of the roll. Using a thin, sharp knife, carefully cut the rolls into pieces about 1¼ inches long.

11. Place the rugalah about 1 inch apart on the prepared cookie sheets.

12. Bake the rugalah until golden, about 25 minutes. (Some of the jam will ooze out and start to darken.) Use a spatula to remove the rugalah from the pan immediately and place them on a rack to cool. When they are cool, place them in an airtight container for a day before serving so that the taste and consistency have a chance to settle.

Makes 30 pieces

Maya's Pocketbooks

*W*hen I was young, our cook, Martha, always had a little dough left over when she made her fabulous fruit pies. She'd give it to me to make what I called pocketbooks, which I filled with jam, baked, and got to eat way before the pie was done. These miniature turnovers are the latter day version of my early creations.

INGREDIENTS

2½ cups all-purpose flour, sifted
3 tablespoons sugar
¾ teaspoon salt
1 cup (2 sticks) cold unsalted butter, cut into 16 pieces
3 large egg yolks
2 tablespoons ice water
About 1 cup fruit preserves (the thicker the better)

1. Place the flour, sugar, and salt in a food processor and process for about 6 seconds.

2. Add the butter to the flour mixture and process until all the ingredients are blended, 10 to 15 seconds.

3. Whisk the egg yolks and ice water

together. While the machine is running, pour the yolks through the feed tube, and pulse 15 times, then process until the dough comes together, 5 seconds more.

4. Remove the dough from the machine and knead it with 6 or 7 turns. Shape the dough into 2 thick disks, wrap each in plastic, and refrigerate at least 1 hour.

5. Preheat the oven to 400°F. Line several cookie sheets with parchment paper or lightly grease them with butter or vegetable oil.

6. Roll out each piece of dough between 2 pieces of plastic wrap or waxed paper $\frac{1}{8}$ inch thick (see page 165 for rolling technique). Using a

$2\frac{3}{4}$-inch round cookie cutter, cut out 20 round cookies from each piece. (On a humid day, it may be necessary to refrigerate the rolled-out dough for 15 minutes before cutting.)

7. Place 1 level teaspoon of fruit preserves on half of one side of each circle and fold the other side over. Seal the seams by pinching the edges together. Make a fork prick in the center of each pocketbook. Place the pocketbooks about 1 inch apart on the prepared cookie sheets.

8. Bake the pocketbooks until they are golden, about 12 minutes. Cool on a rack before serving.

Makes 40 pocketbooks

CHAPTER FOUR

Harvard

Squares

Not so long ago I read that somebody who pays attention to such things found that Americans ate over two billion brownies in one year, which comes to about nine per person. Right there I began to get suspicious. I mean, only nine?

After the brownie counters finished, the market researchers had their say and announced that men eat more brownies than women, particularly in the 13-to-34 and 45-to-54 age groups. (Females peak in brownie consumption between the ages of two and five, probably because at that age, they haven't yet been taught to worry about which part of their body will be wearing the calories.) The researchers went on to determine that southerners prefer homemade brownies, while northerners eat ready-made ones, and everyone eats more brownies on Fridays and Sundays than the rest of the week. Brownies are a hot item these days, they concluded, because they're "the ultimate comfort food, like mashed potatoes."

Now I could have saved all these people a lot of trouble, since I've known since early childhood that brownies are one of life's basic necessities. Moreover, I kept on consuming them well past the age of five, and my innocence wasn't shattered until I went away to college and had to wean myself from my mother's brownies. In desperation, I tried a Duncan Hines extra-fudgy mix, adding more chocolate and butter to make sure it was robust enough, and, to no one's surprise but my own, it was not what I had in mind.

Unwilling to go through life without a really good brownie to my name, I said good-bye to mixes and shortcuts and began experimenting with variations on my mother's recipe. I spent many hours — particularly around exam time — searching for something appropriate to my maturing taste buds: something deeply chocolate, sufficiently chewy and sweet enough to give me that brownie rush, but not anything gloppy or so saccharine that it made my teeth itch afterwards. In short, I was on a quest for the essential brownie. Many fiascoes later, I came up with the version I use to this day, the brownie that in many ways defines Rosie's.

The Bar Scene

It might have been possible to stop at brownies when Rosie's first opened, but I had a hankering for other kinds of bars and squares and figured other people would too. So early on, I added Congo Bars, Boom Booms, Honeypots, and later Walnut Dream Bars, Dagwoods, and Lemon Cream Cheese Squares.

In 1976 Rosie's and its brownies got a boost from an American original named C. P. Luongo, who strolled into my store one day to announce that he was writing a book called *America's Best*—restaurants, hotels, trains, ice cream, you know the sort of compendium. I remember being impressed that he had figured out how to make a living from such an enjoyable pastime, and I liked him even better when he proclaimed our brownies the best in the country. Other awards followed: so many Best of Boston citations from *Boston Magazine* that they put us in their Hall of Fame, a vote from *Chocolatier* magazine for our brownie as one of their all-time best, requests from *Gourmet* for recipes.

Then we got our strangest vote of confidence when a teacher friend who was carrying a book bag full of her students' final papers and a batch of Chocolate Orgasms (Rosie's luscious fudge-frosted brownies) was robbed on her way home. Two days later, the bag was returned to her with everything intact except the Chocolate Orgasms which were nowhere to be found.

To what do I attribute this tiny piece of immortality? I think it's true that brownies and their counterparts are an accessible indulgence and a comfort food, though that label sounds more like Cream of Wheat to me. They remind us of childhood, allow us to be self-indulgent in reasonable proportions, and are easy to make, highly portable, and more American than apple pie. Most important, they taste good.

Still, I balk at the suggestion that brownies and other pastry bars are only for kids. When I serve them as dessert at grown-up dinner parties, I receive only praise. I come across them for sale at fancy food shops from coast to coast. And if my customers are any indication, it's not just southern men of a certain age eating them on Sundays.

Belly Up to the Bar

*W*hen it comes to baking bars and squares, the only rule that applies is that they're relatively easy and quick to make—something you *can* whip up without planning and keep around for a snack. Beyond that, each recipe works differently to produce a distinctive taste and texture, though they fall into three basic categories.

Brownielike Bars

These include Chocolate Orgasms and Dagwoods, bars that contain many of the same ingredients as cakes but are proportionately different. As a rule, they contain less flour and no liquid, depending on eggs for moisture instead.

Preparing the Pan: Grease a baking pan lightly with butter or vegetable oil. If you want to remove a batch uncut from the pan, line the bottom with baking parchment.

Baking: The oven is usually set to 325°F but some recipes call for 350°F. Bake on the center rack of the oven.

Unlike cakes, you can vary the baking time of these bars slightly to produce different textures and still get good results. As the bars bake, a crust forms over the surface, so if you want chewy bars, you have to catch them when the crust is still paper thin. When the center is almost level with the sides, insert a cake tester in the middle and if it comes out dry or with moist crumbs, but no syrupy batter, remove the pan from the oven. The center will drop as it cools, and the texture will be chewy. For airier and cakier bars, allow the batter to bake longer — until the center has risen slightly and formed a slightly thicker crust. Keep in mind that this principle doesn't apply to baking cakes, even when you bake them in a flat pan like bars.

Cutting: You can cut these bars warm or cool using a thin, sharp knife. If the bars are completely cool, try dipping the knife in hot water before each cut to make it easier.

Storing: Stored in an airtight container, these bars will stay moist without refrigeration for about three days, but the chewier the bar, the longer its shelf life. When refrigerated, the bars will last for a week or two, and they freeze very well.

Shortbread Bars

Shortbread bars, such as Lemon Cream Cheese Squares, Dutch Butter Bars, Honeypots, or Walnut Dream Bars, are made either from a simple shortbread batter or by adding a topping to a pre-baked shortbread base.

Preparing the Pan: It's not absolutely necessary to grease the pans because shortbread contains enough butter to keep it from sticking, but I like to be on the safe side and do it anyway.

Spreading the Batter in the Pan: If the batter is extremely fluffy or sticky, I find it helps to dip my fingertips in flour before gently spreading the shortbread over the bottom of the pan.

Glazing the Base: When the recipe calls for a liquid topping, I glaze the base before baking it. Pour an egg white directly on the top of the batter, tilt the pan from side to side to make sure the surface is covered, then spill the excess egg white into the sink. As the base bakes, the egg white hardens and forms a thin crust to keep the base from absorbing the liquid.

Baking: I've found that the shortbread that is golden in color is the most flavorful, so I bake the base of these bars at 350°F until it turns light gold. I then chill it before adding the topping to make sure the base stays crunchy.

Cutting: These cut best when they've cooled some. Sugary bars with gooey centers, such as Walnut Dream Bars or Pecan Bars, should be cut as soon as they cool; if you wait too long, the top caramelizes and is hard to cut. Use a cleaver or sturdy knife.

Shortbread bars with soft toppings, such as Whitecaps and Tart Lemon Squares, can be cut later, but it's best to use a thin knife that has been dipped in hot water and wiped dry before each cut. The heat melts the topping just enough for the knife to glide through.

Bars made of one layer of shortbread, such as Dutch Butter Bars, should be cut when they're still hot, so the dough doesn't crack. Bars with a bottom and top crust, such as Jam Sandwiches and Linzer Bars, can be cut after they've cooled, but need a knife run around the sides of the pan while they're still hot so that the jam filling doesn't stick to the pan.

Storing: Keep bars with soft toppings in airtight containers in the refrigerator or freezer. All other shortbread bars can be stored at room temperature or in the fridge for several days.

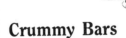

Crummy Bars

My one entry in this category is Apple Crumb Bars. These bars consist of two layers of crumbs with a filling in between. They tend to be more fragile than other bars, so if they're to be eaten by hand, I serve them cold because they're sturdier that way.

Preparing the Pan: Grease the pan lightly with butter or vegetable oil.

Baking: The temperature varies from 350°F to 425°F, depending on the recipe.

Cutting: These bars are cut best with a thin knife when they've cooled, but run a knife around the edge of the pan while they're still hot to prevent the filling from sticking.

Storing: Keep these bars in an airtight container in the refrigerator. They'll last for a week and can be frozen as well. Unfrosted bars that get soggy can be rebaked briefly in a cool oven (300°F) to restore their crispness.

Serving

*T*he spirit of bars comes a lot from how you cut them up and serve them. In hearty squares, they make a good afternoon or TV-watching snack, and when cut into dainty finger food, they turn into an elegant dessert suitable for any party. For the latter, I cut each bar into three or four pieces, depending on its richness, and arrange the pieces symmetrically on a small, doily-covered platter. If you're serving more than one kind of bar, use the differences in color, texture, and shape to create a pattern. I've found that people love bite-size pieces because that allows them to sample and enjoy without having to face up to just how much they've consumed.

I have to confess that bars are my favorite kind of dessert to make, although, saying that, I feel like the parent who hastens to protest that she loves all her children equally. Still there's something so dependable about a good brownie. Newsletters and conventions for chocolate lovers may come and go, but I believe that fudge brownies are here to stay. I take great comfort in knowing that when everything else in life is a mess, I can still bake a batch of Congo Bars in half an hour.

Rosie's Award-Winning Brownies

*G*rowing up, there was nothing I craved more than a good brownie. It took me years to come up with my own version—fudgy, but not too sweet. Countless all-nighters slaving over a hot mixing bowl and all those inches on my thighs proved to be worth it, though, when it was named Best Brownie in America.

INGREDIENTS

3½ ounces unsweetened chocolate
12 tablespoons (1½ sticks) unsalted butter, at room temperature
1½ cups sugar
¾ teaspoon vanilla extract
3 large eggs, at room temperature
¾ cup plus 2 tablespoons all-purpose flour
½ cup plus 2 tablespoons chopped walnuts

1. Preheat the oven to 350°F. Lightly grease an 8-inch square pan with butter or vegetable oil.

2. Melt the chocolate and butter in the top of a double boiler placed over simmering water. Cool the mixture for 5 minutes.

3. Place the sugar in a medium-size mixing bowl and pour in the chocolate mixture. Using an electric mixer on medium speed, mix until blended, about 25 seconds. Scrape the bowl with a rubber spatula.

4. Add the vanilla. With the mixer on medium-low speed, add the eggs one at a time, blending after each addition until the yolk is broken and dispersed, about 10 seconds. Scrape the bowl after the last egg and blend until velvety, about 15 more seconds.

5. Add the flour on low speed and mix for 20 seconds; finish the mixing by hand, being certain to mix in any flour at the bottom of the bowl. Stir in ½ cup of the nuts.

6. Spread the batter evenly in the prepared pan and sprinkle the remaining 2 tablespoons of nuts over the top.

7. Bake the brownies on the center oven rack until a thin crust forms on top and a tester inserted in the center comes out with a moist crumb, 25 to 30 minutes.

8. Remove the pan from the oven and place it on a rack to cool for 1 hour before cutting the brownies. Serve the next day (it takes a day for the flavor to set) and don't forget the tall glass of milk.

Makes 9 to 12 brownies

Chocolate Orgasms

*O*kay, Daddy, now you can admit you were wrong — this is a great name. After all, it has become Rosie's most famous dessert. Although people of all ages come to my store and eat big versions of this bar, when I make them at home, I like to cut them into small squares, top each one with a whole walnut or raspberry, and arrange them on a paper lace doily. They are also wonderful served in a small bowl with vanilla, chocolate chip, coffee, or mint ice cream.

INGREDIENTS

1 recipe Rosie's Award-Winning Brownies (nuts are optional; page 135)
1½ ounces unsweetened chocolate
¼ cup evaporated milk
⅓ cup sugar

1. Prepare the brownies and allow them to cool completely. Don't cut them yet.

2. To prepare the frosting, melt the chocolate in the top of a double boiler placed over simmering water.

3. Pour the evaporated milk into an electric blender and add the sugar and the melted chocolate. Blend the frosting on medium-low speed until it thickens, about 50 seconds (the sound of the machine will change when this process occurs).

4. Using a frosting spatula, spread the frosting evenly over the surface of the cooled brownies and allow them to sit for 1 hour before cutting.

Makes 36 small brownies

Boom Booms

I won't tell you what these were named after — those of us who were around for Rosie's beginnings will guard that secret — but I will tell you that they are a wonderful combination of a dark fudge brownie marbled with a sweet cream cheese mixture. They are beautiful to look at as well.

INGREDIENTS

1 recipe Rosie's Award-Winning Brownies, batter without nuts (page 135)
8 ounces cream cheese, chilled
1½ teaspoons all-purpose flour
5 tablespoons sugar
1 large egg, at room temperature
¼ teaspoon vanilla extract

1. Preheat the oven to 325°F. Lightly grease an 8-inch square pan with butter or vegetable oil.

2. Prepare the brownie batter, omitting the nuts, and set aside.

3. For the cream cheese filling, place all the remaining ingredients in a food processor and process until blended, about 45 seconds. Set aside.

4. Spread about two-thirds of the brownie batter in the prepared pan. Spread the cream cheese filling over the brownie batter. Using a spoon, scoop the remaining brownie batter over the filling in nine equal mounds arranged in rows of threes so that there is some space between them.

5. Run a chopstick or the handle of a wooden spoon back and forth the length of the pan, making parallel lines about 1½ inches apart, then do the same thing in the other direction as if making a grid. This will marbleize the two mixtures. Shake the pan gently back and forth to level the batter.

6. Bake the bars on the center oven rack until a tester inserted in the center comes out clean or with some moist crumbs, about 45 minutes. Allow the brownies to cool for 1 hour before cutting.

Makes 9 to 12 brownies

Mint Brownies

*T*he flavor of mint and chocolate combine beautifully in this bar without losing their integrity.

INGREDIENTS

1 recipe Rosie's Award-Winning Brownies without nuts or Extra Extra Fudgy Brownies without nuts (page 135 or 138)

MINT BUTTERCREAM
1 cup confectioner's sugar
4 tablespoons (½ stick) unsalted butter, at room temperature
2 teaspoons peppermint extract

GLAZE
4 ounces bittersweet chocolate
2 teaspoons light corn syrup

1. Prepare the desired brownies and allow them to cool completely (you can place the pan in the refrigerator or freezer to speed up the process).

2. To prepare the buttercream, using an electric mixer on high speed, cream the sugar, butter, and extract until white and fluffy, 2 to 2½ minutes.

3. Spread the buttercream evenly over the cooled brownie cake and freeze for 1 hour.

4. After the hour is up, melt the chocolate for the glaze in the top of a double boiler placed over simmering water. Remove the pan from the water and stir the corn syrup into the melted chocolate.

5. Allow the glaze to cool to the point where it is no longer hot but is still loose and spreadable. Using a frosting spatula, spread the glaze over the buttercream. Immediately place the pan in the refrigerator and allow the chocolate to harden for about 30 minutes.

6. Cut the brownies with a thin, sharp knife that has been dipped in hot water and dried before each cut.

Makes 16 brownies

Extra Extra Fudgy Brownies

A brownie made for fudge fanatics. These are the ones to make if your chocolate level is about a quart low.

INGREDIENTS

1½ ounces semisweet chocolate
2½ ounces unsweetened chocolate
8 tablespoons (1 stick) unsalted butter
1 cup plus 2 tablespoons sugar
3 large eggs
7 tablespoons all-purpose flour
½ cup plus 2 tablespoons chopped walnuts

1. Preheat the oven to 325°F. Lightly grease an 8-inch square pan with butter or vegetable oil.

2. Melt both chocolates and the butter in the top of a double boiler placed over simmering water. Cool the mixture for 5 minutes.

3. Place the sugar in a medium-size mixing bowl and pour in the chocolate mixture. Using an electric mixer on medium speed, mix until blended, about 25 seconds. Scrape the bowl with a rubber spatula.

4. With the mixer on medium-low speed, add the eggs one at a time, blending after each addition until the yolk is broken and dispersed, about 10 seconds. Scrape the bowl after the last egg and blend until velvety, about 15 seconds more.

5. Add the flour on low speed and mix for 20 seconds; finish the mixing by hand, being certain to mix in any flour at the bottom of the bowl. Stir in ½ cup of the nuts.

6. Spread the batter evenly in the prepared pan and sprinkle the remaining 2 tablespoons nuts over the top.

7. Bake the brownies on the center oven rack until a tester inserted in the center comes out with a moist crumb, about 25 minutes. Allow the brownies to cool for 1 hour before cutting.

Makes 9 to 12 brownies

D D's

These brownies ought to be served with a D D alert because they are decidedly a Deadly Dessert. They're dark, dense, delicious and *de rigueur* for chocolate lovers. The recipe requires a strong upper arm for folding in the egg whites, but other than that, it's a cinch.

INGREDIENTS

12 ounces semisweet chocolate
4 ounces unsweetened chocolate
1 cup (2 sticks) unsalted butter
9 large eggs, separated, at room temperature
1 cup plus 2 tablespoons sugar
Strawberry or raspberry jam for serving (optional)
½ recipe Whipped Cream (page 86) for serving (optional)

1. Melt both chocolates and the butter in the top of a double boiler placed over simmering water. Allow the mixture to cool until it is only slightly warm.

2. Preheat the oven to 325°F. Lightly grease a 13 × 9-inch pan with butter or vegetable oil.

3. Using an electric mixer on medium speed, beat the egg yolks and ¾ cup plus 2 tablespoons sugar in a medium-size mixing bowl until thick and pale, about 2 minutes. Stop the mixer once or twice to scrape the bowl with a rubber spatula.

4. With the mixer on medium-low speed, add the chocolate mixture and mix until the batter is uniform in color, about 10 seconds. Scrape the bowl, then mix for several seconds more.

5. In another mixing bowl, whip the egg whites on medium-high speed until frothy, about 30 seconds. Gradually add the remaining ¼ cup sugar and continue beating the whites to soft peaks, 45 seconds more.

6. Stir one-third of the whites into the batter to loosen it, then fold the remaining whites into the mixture carefully by hand, using a rubber spatula. Pour the batter evenly into the prepared pan.

7. Bake the brownies on the center oven rack until the top has risen and set and a tester inserted in the center comes out clean, about 40 minutes.

8. Place the pan on a rack to cool for 1 hour before cutting. Cut the brownies into bars and serve them as they are or spread a thin layer of strawberry or raspberry jam over the surface of the bars and cover that with a layer of whipped cream.

Makes 12 to 16 brownies

Chunky Chocolate Bars

*7*he name really says it all because what makes these bars unusual is their texture. They're something like what a Cadbury's fruit-and-nut bar would be if it could be a brownie: mouthfuls of chocolate with raisins and walnuts in every bite. Although they taste good as soon as they've cooled, they hold together better and crumble less if you wait a day to eat them. Give it a try.

INGREDIENTS

3 ounces unsweetened chocolate
8 tablespoons (1 stick) unsalted butter, at room temperature
1 cup sugar
1 teaspoon vanilla extract
2 large eggs, at room temperature
½ cup all-purpose flour
½ cup chopped walnuts
¼ cup chopped dates
½ cup raisins

1. Melt the chocolate in the top of a double boiler over simmering water. Cool slightly.

2. Preheat the oven to 350°F. Lightly grease an 8-inch square pan with butter or vegetable oil.

3. Using an electric mixer on medium speed, cream the butter, sugar, and vanilla in a medium-size mixing bowl until light and fluffy, 2 to 3 minutes. Stop the mixer to scrape the bowl twice with a rubber spatula.

4. Add the chocolate and mix on medium speed until blended, about 8 seconds. Scrape the bowl.

5. Add the eggs and blend the mixture on high speed for 3 seconds. Scrape the bowl, then mix on medium speed until the eggs are blended in, about 15 seconds. The batter will not be smooth.

6. On low speed, add the flour and mix until it is almost incorporated. Scrape the bowl. Add the nuts, dates, and raisins and mix until blended, about 5 seconds. Spread the batter evenly in the prepared pan.

7. Bake the bars on the center oven rack until a tester inserted in the center comes out clean, about 35 minutes. Place the pan on a rack to cool completely before cutting.

Makes 12 to 16 bars

White Chocolate Brownies

*B*uttery and chewy, this bar is an uncommon alternative to its counterpart, the fudge brownie.

INGREDIENTS

- *8 tablespoons (1 stick) unsalted butter*
- *4 ounces white chocolate*
- *2 large eggs, at room temperature*
- *1/2 teaspoon salt*
- *1 cup sugar*
- *1 teaspoon vanilla extract*
- *1 cup all-purpose flour*

1. Preheat the oven to 325°F. Lightly grease an 11 × 7-inch baking pan with butter or vegetable oil.

2. Melt the butter in the top of a double boiler placed over simmering water. When the butter has melted, add the chocolate and melt.

3. Using an electric mixer on medium-high speed, beat the eggs and salt in a medium-size mixing bowl until frothy, about 30 seconds. Gradually add the sugar and continue beating until the eggs are thick and pale, about 1½ minutes. Scrape the bowl with a rubber spatula.

4. Add the chocolate mixture and the vanilla and mix on medium-low speed until blended, about 5 seconds. Scrape the bowl.

5. Mix in the flour on low speed until blended, scraping the bowl with the rubber spatula once during blending. Pour the batter evenly into the prepared pan.

6. Bake the brownies on the center oven rack until a tester inserted in the center comes out clean, about 40 minutes. Allow the brownies to cool on a rack for 1 hour before cutting.

Makes 12 brownies

Dagwoods

*I*n my humble opinion, it's texture and thickness that makes this the perfect butterscotch brownie. The recipe came from my mother-in-law, Barbara, who insisted that you had to mix it by hand with a wooden spoon. Old-fashioned superstition, I scoffed, pulling out my Kitchen-Aid and setting to work. Barbara was right, of course. You can make these brownies with a machine, but they come out differently and not nearly as good. So, chastised, I now make them by hand, and I've found that it's just as quick and easy.

INGREDIENTS

1¼ cups all-purpose flour
1½ cups (lightly packed) light brown
    sugar
1½ teaspoon baking powder
⅛ teaspoon salt
2 large eggs, at room temperature
10 tablespoons (about 9½ tablespoons
    cold) melted unsalted butter
2 teaspoons vanilla extract
½ cup chopped walnuts

1. Preheat the oven to 350°F. Lightly grease an 8-inch square pan with butter or vegetable oil.

2. Blend the flour, sugar, baking powder, and salt in a medium-size bowl with a wooden spoon.

3. In another medium-size bowl, beat the eggs with a whisk until blended. Whisk in the melted butter and the vanilla.

4. Make a well in the center of the dry ingredients and pour the wet ingredients into the well. Using the wooden spoon, stir until the mixture is blended.

5. Add the nuts with a few broad strokes. Spread the batter evenly in the prepared pan.

6. Bake the bars on the center oven rack until golden and a tester inserted in the center comes out clean or with moist crumbs, 35 to 40 minutes. Place the pan on a rack to cool for 1 hour before cutting.

Makes 9 to 12 bars

Congo Bars

*T*he Congo Bar is a chewy butterscotch brownie full of chocolate chips and nuts. I have no idea where the name came from, but regardless of its roots, this was one of Rosie's first products and it remains a perennial favorite.

INGREDIENTS

1⅓ cups all-purpose flour
1½ teaspoons baking soda
½ teaspoon salt
9 tablespoons (1 stick plus
    1 tablespoon) unsalted butter,
    at room temperature
1¾ cups (lightly packed) light brown
    sugar
1¼ teaspoons vanilla extract
2 large eggs, at room temperature
1 cup semisweet chocolate chips
½ cup chopped walnuts

1. Preheat the oven to 350°F. Lightly grease a 13 × 9-inch baking pan with butter or vegetable oil.

2. Blend the flour, baking soda, and salt in a small bowl with a wooden spoon. Set aside.

3. Using an electric mixer on medium speed, cream the butter, sugar, and vanilla in a medium-size bowl until light and fluffy, about 2 minutes. Stop the mixer once or twice to scrape the bowl with a rubber spatula.

4. Add the eggs and mix on high speed for 3 seconds, then on medium speed until blended, about 5 more seconds.

5. Add the flour mixture and mix on low speed until almost blended, 8 to 10 seconds. Stop the mixer once to scrape the bowl.

6. Add the chocolate chips and nuts and mix on low speed for 5 seconds. Finish the mixing by hand with a wooden spoon. Spread the batter evenly in the prepared pan.

7. Bake the bars on the center oven rack until the top has formed a rich golden crust and dropped below the level of the darker golden outer edges, 30 minutes. These bars cannot be tested by inserting a tester because they remain very gooey inside. Cool for 30 minutes in the pan placed on a rack before cutting. They are best eaten the first day. Leftovers must be stored in an airtight container in the refrigerator.

Makes 12 bars

Jayne Mansfields

*M*y heroes have always been actresses. The other little girls were panting over Rock Hudson and Ricky Nelson while I was hanging pictures of Marilyn Monroe and Jayne Mansfield all over my walls. These are for you Jayne—blond, cakey, sweet, with an occasional chocolate chip.

INGREDIENTS

- *1½ cups plus 2 tablespoons cake flour*
- *¼ teaspoon baking powder*
- *⅛ teaspoon baking soda*
- *½ teaspoon salt*
- *12 tablespoons (1½ sticks) unsalted butter, at room temperature*
- *1½ cups (lightly packed) light brown sugar*
- *2 teaspoons vanilla extract*
- *3 large eggs, at room temperature*
- *¾ cup semisweet chocolate chips*

1. Preheat the oven to 350°F. Lightly grease an 11 × 7-inch baking pan with butter.

2. Sift the flour, baking powder, baking soda, and salt together into a small bowl and set aside.

3. Using an electric mixer on medium speed, cream the butter, sugar, and vanilla in a medium-size mixing bowl until light and fluffy, about 1½ minutes. Scrape the bowl with a rubber spatula.

4. Add the eggs one at a time and beat on medium speed after each addition until partially blended, 5 seconds. Scrape the bowl, then beat until the batter is blended, 20 seconds more.

5. With the mixer on low, add the dry ingredients and beat until almost blended, about 15 seconds. Scrape the bowl.

6. Add the chips and mix on low speed until they are blended in, about 5 seconds. Stir the batter several times with a rubber spatula. Spread the batter evenly in the prepared pan.

7. Bake the bars on the center oven rack until the top has risen and set, and is golden in color, 26 to 28 minutes. (The top won't spring back when touched; a depression remains.) Allow the bars to cool for 1 hour on a rack before cutting.

Makes 12 bars

Peanut-Butter Chocolate-Chip Bars

*Y*ou start with a blond brownie, add peanut butter and a generous helping of chocolate chips, and, if my son and his neighborhood cohorts are any indication, you've got the perfect treat. (My older acquaintances are fond of them too.) The precise flour measurements are a must.

INGREDIENTS

- 1⅓ cups plus 1 tablespoon plus 1 teaspoon all-purpose flour
- 2 teaspoons baking powder
- ⅛ teaspoon baking soda
- ¼ teaspoon salt
- 8 tablespoons (1 stick) unsalted butter, at room temperature
- ½ cup commercial smooth peanut butter
- ½ cup granulated sugar
- ½ cup plus 2 tablespoons (lightly packed) light brown sugar
- 1 teaspoon vanilla extract
- 2 large eggs, at room temperature
- 1 cup semisweet chocolate chips

1. Preheat the oven to 350°F. Lightly grease an 11 × 7-inch baking pan with butter or vegetable oil.

2. Sift the flour, baking powder, baking soda, and salt together into a medium-size mixing bowl and set aside.

3. Using an electric mixer on medium-high speed, cream the butter, peanut butter, both sugars, and the vanilla until light and fluffy, about 1½ minutes. Stop the mixer to scrape the bowl with a rubber spatula.

4. Add the eggs one at a time and beat on medium speed until partially blended after each addition, about 10 seconds. After the last addition, beat until blended, about 30 seconds, stopping the mixer twice to scrape the bowl.

5. Add the dry ingredients to the batter and mix with a spatula until the flour is absorbed. Then mix on low speed until blended, 7 to 10 seconds. Scrape the bowl, especially the bottom.

6. Add the chocolate chips and blend for several seconds. Scrape the bowl. Spread the batter evenly in the prepared pan.

7. Bake the bars on the center oven rack until the edges are deep golden and the center is lightly golden and slightly puffy, 25 to 30 minutes. The center will drop when the bars are taken out of the oven, creating a chewy texture. Cut the bars into squares after they have cooled a bit on the rack.

Makes 12 bars

Orange Birthday Cake Bars

*7*his pound-cake-like bar doesn't really fit into any of the categories in this chapter. But it is an easy-to-handle and not overly sweet bar. It's great for 1- to 2-year-old birthday parties. as well as a delicious treat for grown-ups.

INGREDIENTS

CAKE
2¼ cups cake flour
1 teaspoon baking soda
½ teaspoon salt
1 cup (2 sticks) unsalted butter, at room temperature
3 ounces cream cheese, at room temperature
1¾ cups granulated sugar
2 teaspoons vanilla extract
1 tablespoon grated orange zest
4 large eggs, at room temperature

GLAZE
1 cup sifted confectioner's sugar
4 tablespoons (½ stick) unsalted butter, melted
3 tablespoons fresh orange juice
1 teaspoon fresh lemon juice
Pinch of salt

1. Preheat the oven to 350°F. Lightly grease a 15 × 10-inch jelly-roll pan with butter or vegetable oil.

2. For the cake, sift the flour, baking soda, and salt together in a small bowl and set aside.

3. Using an electric mixer on medium-high speed, cream the butter, cream cheese, granulated sugar, vanilla, and orange zest together in a medium-size mixing bowl until light and fluffy, about 2 minutes. Stop the mixer once or twice to scrape the bowl with a rubber spatula.

4. Add the eggs one at a time and beat on medium-low speed until each yolk is partially blended, 10 seconds. Scrape the bowl after each addition.

5. Fold in half the dry ingredients with the rubber spatula until partially incorporated, then turn the mixer to low and blend for several seconds. Repeat with the remaining dry ingredients, blending for 10 seconds with the electric mixer. Finish the mixing by hand with a few broad strokes of the spatula. Spread the batter evenly in the prepared pan.

6. Bake until the cake is lightly golden, springs back to the touch, and a tester inserted in the center comes out clean, 20 to 25 minutes. Allow the cake to cool completely on a rack while preparing the glaze.

7. Place all the ingredients for the glaze in a small bowl and stir vigorously with a whisk until blended.

8. Pour the glaze over the cake and spread it evenly with a frosting spatula. Allow the glaze to harden, 3 to 4 hours before serving.

Makes 24 bars

Brownie Shortbread

I've added a layer of brownie to the top of a crunchy shortbread for those days when you can't decide which you prefer.

INGREDIENTS

BASE
1 cup all-purpose flour
¼ cup sugar
8 tablespoons (1 stick) unsalted butter, at room temperature, cut into 8 pieces

TOPPING
3 ounces unsweetened chocolate
8 tablespoons (1 stick) unsalted butter
2 large eggs, at room temperature
¾ cup sugar
½ teaspoon baking powder

1. Preheat the oven to 350°F. Lightly grease an 11 × 7-inch baking pan with butter.

2. For the base, process the flour and sugar in a food processor about 15 seconds. Add the butter and process until the dough comes together, 20 to 30 seconds.

3. Pat the dough gently over the bottom of the prepared pan. Bake on the center oven rack until it is lightly golden, about 20 minutes. Place the base in the refrigerator for 15 minutes to cool completely. Keep the oven on.

4. Meanwhile prepare the topping: Melt the chocolate and butter in the top of a double boiler over simmering water. Cool slightly.

5. Beat the eggs, sugar, and baking powder together in a medium-size bowl with a whisk. Add the chocolate mixture and stir vigorously with the whisk until the batter is blended.

Spread the chocolate mixture evenly over the base.

6. Bake the bars until the top rises and forms a very thin crust, about 20 minutes. The center will drop as it cools. (A tester inserted in the middle may come out with a fudgy, crumbly batter on it, but it should not be liquidy.) Cool completely on a rack. Cut the shortbread with a thin knife.

Makes 12 bars

Honeypots

*T*hese sweet, crunchy, buttery bars were part of my original Babycakes repertoire. My good friend Karen McCarthy was my partner then, and we rewarded ourselves for spending endless hours over hot stoves and not-so-hot accounts with a Honeypot apiece at the end of the day. It was usually too late for anyone else to be around, which is a good thing because we'd close our eyes and moan loudly from sheer pleasure.

INGREDIENTS

BASE
1 cup all-purpose flour
½ cup confectioner's sugar
8 tablespoons (1 stick) unsalted
    butter, at room temperature,
    cut into 8 pieces
1 egg white for glazing

TOPPING
6 tablespoons (¾ stick) unsalted butter
½ cup (lightly packed) light brown
    sugar
½ cup honey
1¼ cups chopped walnuts
¼ cup heavy (whipping) cream
1 teaspoon vanilla extract

1. Preheat the oven to 350°F. Lightly grease an 8-inch square pan with butter.

2. For the base, process the flour and confectioner's sugar in a food processor for 20 seconds. Add the butter and process until the dough comes together, 20 to 30 seconds.

3. Pat the dough gently over the bottom of the prepared pan and glaze it with the egg white: Pour the egg white on the dough and tip the pan from side to side so that the white spreads over the surface. Pour off the excess.

4. Bake the base on the center oven rack until golden, about 25 minutes. Place the base in the refrigerator for 15 minutes to cool completely. Keep the oven on.

5. Meanwhile prepare the topping: Combine the butter, brown sugar, and honey in a medium-size saucepan. Heat, stirring the mixture with a wooden spoon, over medium-low heat until it begins to boil. Boil without stirring for 5 minutes.

6. While the mixture is boiling, put the nuts in a medium-size bowl; add the cream and the vanilla and stir to combine.

7. Add the boiled honey mixture to the nuts mixture and stir the ingredients together. Pour the topping evenly over the cooled base.

8. Bake the bars on the center oven rack until the entire surface is bubbling, about 25 minutes.

9. Place the pan on a cooling rack and cool for 1 hour. Then run a sharp knife around the sides of the pan and let cool completely. Cut into bars with a cleaver or very strong knife.

Makes 16 bars

Cherry Cheesecake Bars

A luscious layer of cheesecake studded with cherries or berries atop a crunchy shortbread crust.

INGREDIENTS

BASE
1 cup all-purpose flour
3 tablespoons confectioner's sugar
7 tablespoons unsalted butter, at room temperature, cut into 7 pieces
½ teaspoon vanilla extract
1 egg white for glazing

TOPPING
½ cup drained canned pitted sour cherries or fresh blueberries
8 ounces cream cheese, at room temperature
1 cup sour cream, at room temperature
7 tablespoons granulated sugar
2 large egg yolks
1 teaspoon vanilla extract
2 teaspoons all-purpose flour

1. Preheat the oven to 350°F. Lightly grease an 8-inch square baking pan with butter.

2. For the base, process the flour and confectioner's sugar in a food processor for several seconds. Add the butter and vanilla and process until the dough comes together, 20 to 30 seconds.

3. Pat the dough gently over the bottom of the prepared pan and about 1½ inches up the sides. Glaze it with the egg white: Pour the egg white on the dough and tip the pan from side to side so that the white spreads over the surface. Pour off the excess.

4. Bake the base on the center oven rack until lightly golden, about 30 minutes. Place the base in the refrigerator for 15 minutes to cool completely. Keep the oven on.

5. Meanwhile prepare the topping: Wrap the cherries in paper towels to absorb any liquid.

6. Place the remaining topping ingredients in a food processor and process until blended, about 15 seconds.

7. Pour the topping evenly over the base, then arrange the cherries or blueberries evenly on the topping.

8. Bake the bars on the center oven rack until set, about 1 hour. Allow them to cool completely, then refrigerate overnight.

9. The next day cut the bars with a sharp knife that is dipped in hot water and wiped dry before each cut. Allow the bars to warm to room temperature before serving.

Makes 12 bars

Lemon Cream Cheese Squares

I think of these squares as portable cheesecake for, like the best of that genre, they're rich and tart. Of course, from the baker's viewpoint, they're much easier than making cheesecake, especially with their shortbread crust and relatively short baking time.

INGREDIENTS

BASE
1 cup all-purpose flour
¼ cup confectioner's sugar
8 tablespoons (1 stick) unsalted butter, at room temperature, cut into 8 pieces
1 egg white for glazing

TOPPING
10 ounces cream cheese, at room temperature
½ cup plus 1 tablespoon granulated sugar
2 teaspoons grated lemon zest
¼ cup plus 1 tablespoon sour cream, at room temperature
6 tablespoons fresh lemon juice
2 large eggs, at room temperature
1 teaspoon vanilla extract

1. Preheat the oven to 350°F. Lightly grease an 8-inch square baking pan with butter.

2. For the base, process the flour and confectioner's sugar in a food processor for several seconds. Add the butter and process until the dough comes together, 20 to 30 seconds.

3. Pat the dough gently over the bottom of the prepared pan and about 1 inch up the sides. Glaze it with the egg white: Pour the egg white on the dough and tip the pan from side to side so that the white spreads over the surface. Pour off the excess.

4. Bake the base on the center oven rack until golden, about 25 minutes. Place the base in the refrigerator for 15 minutes to cool completely. Keep the oven on.

5. Meanwhile prepare the topping: Using an electric mixer on medium-high speed, cream the cream cheese, granulated sugar, and lemon zest together in a medium-size bowl until light and fluffy, 2 to 3 minutes. Stop the mixer once or twice to scrape the bowl with a rubber spatula.

6. Add the sour cream and lemon juice and beat the mixture on medium-high speed until smooth, about 1 minute. Scrape the bowl.

7. Add the eggs and vanilla and beat on medium-high speed until smooth and creamy, about 10 seconds. Spread the topping evenly over the base.

8. Bake the bars on the center oven rack until the top is slightly golden and a tester inserted in the center comes out dry, about 1 hour. If the topping bubbles up during baking, prick the bubbles with a toothpick or a thin knife.

9. Allow the bars to cool completely on a rack. Cut them with the point of a thin sharp knife that is dipped in hot water and wiped dry before each cut.

Makes 12 to 16 bars

Pecan Bars

*I*f you like pecan pie, you'll love this portable version: a crunchy, buttery crust with a gooey nut topping.

I N G R E D I E N T S

BASE
1¼ cups all-purpose flour
½ cup plus 2 tablespoons confectioner's sugar
10 tablespoons (1¼ sticks) unsalted butter, at room temperature, cut into 10 pieces
1 egg white for glazing

TOPPING

½ cup (lightly packed) light brown
    sugar
½ cup granulated sugar
10 tablespoons dark corn syrup
2 large eggs, at room temperature
¼ teaspoon vanilla extract
Pinch of salt
3 tablespoons unsalted butter, melted
1½ cups chopped pecans

1. Preheat the oven to 350°F. Lightly grease a 9-inch square pan with butter or vegetable oil.

2. For the base, process the flour and confectioner's sugar in a food processor for several seconds. Add the butter and process until the dough comes together, 20 to 30 seconds.

3. Pat the dough gently over the bottom of the prepared pan and push it ½ inch up the sides with your thumb. Glaze it with the egg white: Pour the egg white on the dough and tip the pan from side to side to spread the white over the surface. Pour off the excess.

4. Bake the base on the center oven rack until lightly golden, about 30 minutes. Place the base in the refrigerator for 15 minutes to cool completely. Keep the oven on.

5. Meanwhile prepare the topping: Gently whisk together both sugars, the corn syrup, eggs, vanilla, and salt in a medium-size bowl until blended.

6. Stir in the melted butter, then the nuts. Pour the topping evenly over the base.

7. Bake the bars until the topping is set and forms a crust, about 50 minutes.

8. Allow the bars to cool for 15 minutes on a rack, then run a sharp knife around the sides of the pan. Cool the bars completely and cut into squares. A cleaver or very firm knife works best.

Makes 16 bars

Walnut Dream Bars

*T*his is a bar that refuses to compromise. It's sweet, chewy, full of butter, nuts, and coconut, and it rapidly attained cult status among Rosie's customers. Be forewarned, though: a small bite goes a long way. These bars can be stored forever in an airtight container in your fridge.

INGREDIENTS

BASE

1 cup all-purpose flour
½ cup plus 1 tablespoon (lightly
    packed) light brown sugar
8 tablespoons (1 stick) unsalted
    butter, at room temperature,
    cut into 8 pieces

TOPPING

1 cup (lightly packed) light brown
    sugar
¼ cup plus 3 tablespoons dark
    corn syrup
2 teaspoons vanilla extract
2 tablespoons unsalted butter, melted
1½ tablespoons all-purpose flour
2 large eggs, at room temperature
1 cup coarsely chopped walnuts
½ cup shredded coconut

1. Preheat the oven to 350°F. Lightly grease an 11 × 7-inch baking pan with butter or vegetable oil.

2. For the base, process the flour and sugar in a food processor for several seconds. Add the butter and process until the dough comes together, 20 to 30 seconds.

3. Pat the dough gently over the bottom of the prepared pan.

4. Bake the base on the center oven rack until golden around the edges, 10 to 12 minutes. Place the base in the refrigerator for 15 minutes to cool completely. Keep the oven on.

5. Meanwhile prepare the topping: Using a hand-held whisk, beat the sugar, corn syrup, vanilla, butter, flour, and eggs in a medium-size bowl until blended.

6. Stir in the walnuts and coconut with a rubber spatula. Spread the topping evenly over the base.

7. Bake the bars on the center oven rack until the top is golden and set, about 25 minutes. Allow them to cool completely before cutting.

Makes 16 bars

Tart Lemon Squares

I wanted to devise a lemon square recipe, so I decided to research the topic. And where else do you go for research but the library? All those lemon squares with degrees didn't add up to much, though. They were too sweet, and I was looking for something tart enough to make my lips pucker, so I had to come up with a recipe of my own. To contrast with the lemon topping, I added a sweet and crunchy shortbread base. I usually serve these squares with fresh or thawed frozen raspberries to add color and a dollop of whipped cream to cut the lemon. Of course, they're great just the way they are.

INGREDIENTS

BASE
1 cup all-purpose flour
1/4 cup confectioner's sugar
8 tablespoons (1 stick) unsalted butter, at room temperature, cut into 8 pieces
1 egg white for glazing

TOPPING
2 large eggs, at room temperature
1 cup granulated sugar
2 tablespoons all-purpose flour
1 1/2 tablespoons grated lemon zest
1/2 teaspoon baking soda
3 tablespoons fresh lemon juice
Confectioner's sugar for sprinkling

1. Preheat the oven to 350°F. Lightly grease an 8-inch square baking pan with butter.

2. For the base, process the flour and confectioner's sugar in a food processor for several seconds. Add the butter and process until the dough comes together, 20 to 30 seconds.

3. Press the dough gently and evenly over the bottom of the prepared pan. Glaze it with the egg white: Pour the egg white on the dough and tip the pan from side to side so that the white spreads over the surface. Pour out the excess.

4. Bake the base on the center oven rack until lightly golden, about 25 minutes. Place the base in the refrigerator for 15 minutes to cool completely. Keep the oven on.

5. Meanwhile prepare the topping: Gently whisk the eggs in a medium-size bowl until lightly mixed. Add the remaining topping ingredients and continue to whisk gently until they are blended.

6. Pour the topping evenly over the base. Bake the bars until the top is set and golden, about 25 minutes. Allow the lemon squares to cool completely.

7. Sprinkle the surface with confectioner's sugar and cut into squares with a sharp knife that is dipped in hot water and wiped dry before each cut. If you plan to keep the bars for longer than a day, put them in an airtight container and refrigerate or freeze them to preserve the crispness of the base.

Makes 9 to 12 bars

Rhubarb Bars

*7*his is one of my all-time favorite desserts; it's fruity, tart, sweet, crunchy, and buttery all in one dessert, and that's pretty exciting.

I N G R E D I E N T S

BASE
1 cup all-purpose flour
5 tablespoons confectioner's sugar
8 tablespoons (1 stick) unsalted butter, at room temperature, cut into 8 pieces
1 egg white for glazing

TOPPING
1 large egg, at room temperature
3/4 cup granulated sugar
2 1/2 tablespoons all-purpose flour
1/4 teaspoon salt
3 cups sliced (1/4 inch thick) rhubarb

1. Preheat the oven to 350°F. Lightly grease an 8-inch square baking pan with butter.

2. Process the flour and confectioner's sugar in a food processor for several seconds. Add the butter and process until the dough comes together, 20 to 30 seconds.

3. Pat the dough gently over the bottom of the prepared pan. Glaze it with the egg white: Pour the egg white over the dough and tip the pan from side to side so that the white spreads over the surface. Pour out the excess.

4. Bake the base on the center oven rack until golden, about 25 minutes. Place the base in the refrigerator for 15 minutes to cool completely. Keep the oven on.

5. Meanwhile prepare the topping: In a large bowl stir the egg, granulated sugar, flour, and salt together with a whisk. Add the rhubarb and toss.

6. Spread the rhubarb mixture evenly over the base.

7. Bake the bars on the center oven rack until set and lightly golden, about 50 minutes. Cool completely before cutting.

Makes 9 to 12 bars

Whitecaps

*T*hese bars look to me like whitecaps on a stormy sea, which is how they got their name. Nothing stormy about their taste, though: They're a sweet, buttery shortbread topped with jam and meringue. Lemon juice added to the jam enhances the contrast of flavors.

I N G R E D I E N T S

BASE
1 1/2 cups all-purpose flour
3/4 cup confectioner's sugar
12 tablespoons (1 1/2 sticks) unsalted butter, at room temperature, cut into 12 pieces

TOPPING
4 large egg whites, at room temperature
1/2 cup plus 1 teaspoon granulated sugar
3/4 cup raspberry or apricot preserves
2 teaspoons fresh lemon juice
Generous 1/2 cup shredded coconut

1. Preheat the oven to 350°F. Lightly grease a 13 × 9-inch baking pan with butter or vegetable oil.

2. For the base, process the flour and confectioner's sugar in a food processor for several seconds. Add the butter and process until the dough comes together, 20 to 30 seconds.

3. Pat the dough gently over the bottom of the prepared pan.

4. Bake on the center oven rack until golden in color, 25 to 30 minutes. Place the base in the refrigerator for 15 minutes to cool completely. Keep the oven on.

5. Meanwhile prepare the topping: Beat the egg whites in a medium-size mixing bowl with an electric mixer on medium-high speed until frothy, about 50 seconds. Gradually add the granulated sugar and continue beating until the whites resemble Marshmallow Fluff, about 30 seconds.

6. Remove the base from the freezer. Stir the preserves and lemon juice together and spread the mixture evenly over the surface.

7. Using a frosting spatula, spread the egg whites over the jam and make small peaks on the surface to form the whitecaps. Sprinkle the coconut over these whitecaps.

8. Bake the bars on the center oven rack until the peaks and coconut are golden, 15 to 20 minutes. Rotate the pan after 10 minutes.

9. Remove the pan from the oven and allow it to cool for 1 hour. Cut the bars with the tip of a sharp knife that is dipped in hot water and wiped dry before each cut.

Makes 24 bars

Jam Sandwiches

*N*o, these won't do in your child's lunchbox along with a handful of carrot sticks, but they are a great after-school treat. They consist of two delicate, buttery bars sandwiched together with raspberry or apricot preserves, kind of a high-class Pop Tart.

I N G R E D I E N T S

1¼ cups all-purpose flour
¼ cup plus 1 tablespoon granulated sugar
10 tablespoons (1¼ sticks) unsalted butter, chilled, cut into 8 to 10 pieces
1 egg white for glazing
½ cup raspberry, strawberry, or apricot preserves
Confectioner's sugar for sprinkling

1. Preheat the oven to 350°F. Have ready an 8-inch square baking pan.

2. Process the flour and granulated sugar in a food processor for 10 seconds. Add the butter and process until the dough comes together, 20 seconds.

3. Divide the dough in half. Cover one half with plastic and place it in the refrigerator. Pat the other half of the dough gently over the bottom of the prepared pan. Glaze it with egg white: Pour the egg white on the dough and tip the pan from side to side so that the white spreads over the surface. Pour off the excess.

4. Bake the base on the center oven rack until golden brown, 15 to 20 minutes. When the base is baked, place it in the refrigerator for 15 minutes to cool completely. Keep the oven on.

5. Spread the preserves evenly over the base.

6. Roll out the remaining half of the dough between two pieces of plastic wrap to an 8-inch square. Peel the top piece of plastic from the dough and flip the dough over the jam. Press the dough gently into the sides of the pan to seal the edges. Gently peel the remaining piece of plastic from the dough and remove any excess dough that has climbed up the sides of the pan. Prick the top crust in four or five places with the tip of a sharp knife.

7. Bake the bars on the center oven rack until the top turns golden, 30 to 35 minutes.

8. Remove the pan from the oven and place it on a cooling rack to cool completely. Cut the bars and store them in an airtight container. Serve them the next day when the flavor has settled. I like to sprinkle confectioner's sugar over the top.

Makes 16 bars

Linzer Bars

*7*hese bars boast the same unbeatable combination of spice-and-nut base and raspberry jam as a Linzertorte, but they're much quicker and easier to make. They can be just as elegantly served cut into small pieces and sprinkled with confectioner's sugar.

INGREDIENTS

DOUGH
11 tablespoons (1 stick plus
*   3 tablespoons) unsalted butter,*
*   at room temperature*
2 cups confectioner's sugar, sifted
1 teaspoon ground cinnamon
Grated zest of 1 small lemon
1 whole large egg, at room temperature
1 large egg white, at room temperature
1¹/₃ cups all-purpose flour
1 cup ground almonds

FILLING
¾ cup raspberry preserves

TOPPING
1 egg white for glazing
3 tablespoons crushed, slivered, or
   chopped almonds

1. For the dough, using an electric mixer on low speed, cream the butter, sugar, cinnamon, and lemon zest together in a medium-size mixing bowl until just mixed. Scrape the bowl with a rubber spatula, then mix on medium speed until smooth, 2 to 3 minutes more. Stop the mixer once or twice to scrape the bowl.

2. Add the egg and egg white and mix on medium speed until incorporated, about 10 seconds. Scrape the bowl.

3. Blend in the flour and almonds with the mixer on low speed until they are incorporated, 5 to 8 seconds.

4. Divide the dough in half. Wrap each piece in plastic wrap and refrigerate it for at least 4 hours.

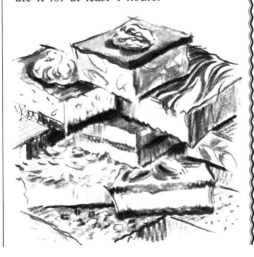

5. Fifteen minutes before you're ready to prepare the bars, preheat the oven to 350°F. Lightly grease a 9-inch square baking pan with butter or vegetable oil.

6. Gently press half the dough over the bottom of the prepared pan. Bake on the center oven rack until lightly golden but not hard, about 25 minutes. Place the base in the refrigerator for 15 minutes to cool completely. Keep the oven on.

7. Meanwhile prepare the top: Place the second half of the dough between two pieces of plastic wrap and, with your fingers and the palms of your hands, flatten it into a square slightly larger than the pan or roll it out with a rolling pin.

8. When the base is cool, spread the preserves evenly over it, leaving a ¼-inch border on all sides.

9. Peel the top piece of plastic from the remaining dough and flip the dough over the jam. Press the dough into the sides of the pan to seal the edges. Gently peel the remaining piece of plastic from the dough and remove any excess dough that has climbed up the sides of the pan.

10. For the topping, glaze the top of the dough with the egg white: Pour the egg white on the dough and tip the pan from side to side so that the white spreads over the surfaces. Pour off the excess. Sprinkle the almonds over the top.

11. Bake the bars on the center oven rack until the top is golden and firm, about 40 minutes.

12. Put the pan on a rack and cool for 10 minutes. Run a frosting spatula or knife around the sides of the pan. The bars cut best when completely cool.

Makes 16 to 20 bars

Dutch Butter Bars

*W*hen I decided that my kids were old enough to begin collecting taste memories, these bars were among the first treats I offered them. They seemed like a good transitional food since they taste like rich zwieback: not too much sugar but nice and buttery. That makes them appropriate for adults, too, at all hours of the day and night, when they want just a little sweet but a lot of flavor.

INGREDIENTS

1¼ cups plus 2 tablespoons all-purpose flour
Pinch of salt
1 cup (2 sticks) unsalted butter, at room temperature
¾ cup plus 2 teaspoons sugar
2 teaspoons vanilla extract
1 large egg, lightly beaten with a fork, at room temperature
¼ teaspoon ground cinnamon
1 egg white for glazing

1. Preheat the oven to 350°F. Have ready an 8-inch square baking pan.

2. Sift the flour and salt together into a medium-size mixing bowl and set aside.

3. Using an electric mixer on medium speed, cream the butter, ¾ cup of the sugar, and the vanilla in a medium-size mixing bowl until light and fluffy, about 2 minutes. Stop the mixer once or twice to scrape the bowl with a rubber spatula.

4. Add the egg and beat on medium speed until the egg is incorporated, about 10 seconds. Scrape the bowl.

5. Add the dry ingredients on medium-low speed and mix for 10 seconds. Scrape the bowl and mix until the flour is incorporated, about 5 more seconds. Pat the dough evenly over the bottom of the pan.

6. Mix the remaining sugar with the cinnamon. Glaze the dough with the egg white: Pour the egg white on the dough and tip the pan from side to side so that the white spreads over the surface. Pour off the excess. Sprinkle the cinnamon sugar over the top.

7. Bake the bars on the center oven rack until firm to the touch and golden in color, about 30 minutes. Remove the pan from the oven.

8. Reduce the oven heat to 250°F. Have ready a cookie sheet.

9. Cut the bars into 4-inch squares with the tip of a sharp knife. Allow the bars to sit for 15 minutes.

10. Remove the bars from the pan with a pancake spatula and place them an inch apart on the cookie sheet.

11. Bake the bars until they are crisp and golden around the edges, about 1 hour.

12. Cool the bars completely on a rack, then store them in an airtight container. Their flavor improves with time.

Makes 16 bars

Apple Crumb Bars

*W*ith a tart apple filling wedged between two layers of a crumb mixture, these bars can be served warm with whipped cream or vanilla ice cream, or cooled and simply eaten out of hand.

INGREDIENTS

FILLING
3½ cups peeled, sliced (³/8 inch thick) apples (3 to 4 medium, preferably McIntosh)
7 tablespoons apple cider or juice, or as needed
2 tablespoons fresh lemon juice
¾ teaspoon ground cinnamon
¼ teaspoon salt
2 teaspoons cornstarch

CRUMB LAYERS
½ cup plus 2 tablespoons all-purpose flour
¼ cup (lightly packed) light brown sugar
2 tablespoons granulated sugar
¾ cup quick-cooking oatmeal
⅛ teaspoon salt
5 tablespoons unsalted butter, chilled, cut into 5 pieces

1. In a small saucepan, simmer the apples, 3 tablespoons of the cider, the lemon juice, cinnamon, and salt over medium heat just until the apples lose their crispness, 3 to 4 minutes. (The time will vary depending on the type of apple and the season.)

2. Drain any juice (this, too, will vary depending on the type of apple) into a measuring cup and add enough of the remaining cider to measure ¼ cup. Transfer the apples to a small bowl.

3. Dissolve the cornstarch in the cider, then pour this mixture into the small saucepan. Cook, stirring constantly, over medium-low heat until thickened, 2 to 3 minutes. Pour this mixture over the apples and toss to coat. Refrigerate while you prepare the crumb layers.

4. Preheat the oven to 425°F. Lightly grease an 8-inch square baking pan with butter.

5. Place the flour, both sugars, the oatmeal, and salt in a food processor and pulse briefly 5 times.

6. Add the butter and pulse 8 to 10 times until it is incorporated evenly. Pat half the crumb mixture firmly over the bottom of the prepared pan.

7. When the apple mixture has cooled, cut the apple slices into ½-inch pieces. Spread the apple mixture carefully over the base and sprinkle the remaining crumbs over the top.

8. Bake the bars on the center oven rack until the crumbs are golden and the apple mixture is bubbling along the sides of the pan, about 25 minutes.

9. Cool the bars completely on a rack, then place them in the refrigerator to chill before cutting. Store the bars in an airtight container in the refrigerator.

Makes 9 to 12 bars

CHAPTER FIVE

Cutie
Pies

Plus Tarts and Baked Fruit Desserts

ifling through the archives of useless information I keep, I came across a bunch of clippings and quotes about pies, and all I could think was that pies couldn't have been made to symbolize more if Hallmark cards and Madison Avenue had collaborated in the cause.

To wit, from a 1950 Betty Crocker cookbook: "Pies had become distinctively American, as glamorous and exciting as this thrilling new nation!" Next, the whimsy of Donald Robert Perry Marquis: "I love you as New Englanders love pie." (He's the guy who created Archy and Mehitabel, and I figure anyone who can make a cockroach lovable deserves attention.) Finally, there's the Norman Rockwell drawing of an aproned grandmother taking a steaming pie from the oven to bestow upon her family.

Talk about conditioning! I mean the poor woman who didn't dedicate her life to creating the perfect pie for those she loved would be condemned as a crummy mother and a questionable American.

Normally I'd assume that Madison Avenue was responsible for the packaging, but, blessedly, pies have been around longer than advertising. The first women arriving in America from Europe hollowed out pumpkins and squashes, filled them with milk, and baked them as a treat. When summer brought fruits and progress brought a little extra time, these women added crusts. Later, frontier women baked as many as twenty-one pies each week, which doesn't even leave a day off for good behavior. So much for progress.

But then pie making has traditionally been a test of a woman's mettle. My friend Martha swears that her Hungarian-born grandmother wasn't officially betrothed until she could make strudel pastry delicate enough to see through.

Much as I like to think that we've come a long way, pie baking still seems to be a womanly activity, and I'm not sure I object to that. Pies reflect the pleasures of pampering yourself and the people you're baking for, making them a kind of currency of generosity. On top of that, they can be sophisticated and elegant, which, to my mind, makes them something women can be proud to claim.

I think of the fifties as the golden age of pie, as well as diners, movie detectives, and truck stops. I have fond memories of a Horn and Hardart Automat in

New York with its slices of pie tucked neatly behind rows of glass windows. It looked like a wall of post office boxes, only Automat windows seldom disappointed when you slipped your nickel in the slot, opened the door, and reached inside.

I first tasted coconut cream pie at an Automat, but before that we made pies from the beach plums and blackberries growing in the dunes at Fire Island, and afterwards (in the sixties, I confess), I fell in thrall to Crucheon's Fudge Pie in Berkeley.

To that list of favorites, I'd now add tarts. Though close relatives to pies, they haven't played a big part in the American dessert scene until recently when we became smitten with anything European. But since nothing marks our country so much as its ability to absorb, tarts are now on their way to being as American as Michael Jackson.

Four and Twenty Blackbirds

*A*ll of which leads to my main point: You can put nearly anything in a pie or tart. I think that's one of the reasons they're tied to the seasons more than other desserts. Some pie ingredients are good only at certain times of the year, and our bodies and palates seem to have atavistic cravings for different tastes, textures, and densities depending on the weather. So we eat dried fruit, nut, or chocolate pies with solid winter meals; rhubarb, strawberry, or chiffon pies when spring brings the first fruits; berry, peach, or cream pies as light summer treats; and all the largess of the harvest — apple and pumpkin pies — in the fall.

Fear of Flaking

*M*artha with the Hungarian grandmother and strudel dowry likes to say she's going to write an Anxiety Cookbook that chronicles all the things that can go wrong with a recipe. None of those soothing or rah-rah cookbooks for her; she doesn't trust them. Frankly, I don't think she'll ever get around to it (the prospect makes her too anxious), but if she does I intend to contribute a chapter about the affliction that keeps perfectly capable cooks from approaching the simplest pie. I call it "crustophobia," and I'm convinced that one day someone will discover an obscure monograph of Freud's entitled something like "Flake and Taboo" or "Civilization and Its Dishcontents."

I'm an expert on this because I'm a former sufferer, having spent years trying to make the entirely beautiful pie crust. Then, dear reader, I made two discoveries that changed my pie-baking career: First, I began using a food processor, and secondly, I came to understand that there's no such thing as an ugly pie crust — imperfections are what gives pies distinction. At that point, I relaxed, and pie crust became, well, as easy as pie.

The End-of-Anxiety Pie Crusts

*7*he recipes in this book use the following four kinds of crusts, which are reliable and easy to prepare when you follow my step-by-step methods:

1. **Basic Pie Crust** made with flour, butter, water, and sometimes sugar.

2. **Basic Pastry Crust** or **Pâte Sucrée** made with flour, butter, eggs, sugar, and sometimes water or milk.

3. **Basic Shortbread Crust** made with flour, butter, and sugar only (no liquid or eggs).

4. **Crumb Crust** (the easiest) made with butter, crushed cookies, and sometimes nuts, grated chocolate, coconut, etc.

Basic Pie and Pastry Crusts

These crusts can be mixed in a food processor or by hand. I find the machine method reliable and easy, so I've put it first. But some people believe that when you make a crust by hand, you get a greater feel for the texture of the dough, so you may prefer that technique. For both methods, make sure that your butter is cold when you start.

Mixing with a Food Processor

1. Place the dry ingredients (such as flour, salt, and sugar) in a food processor and process for 20 seconds.

2. Mix all liquid ingredients (such as water and egg) together in a cup and add an ice cube to chill them.

3. Cut the butter into 8 pieces per stick and distribute them evenly on top of the dry ingredients. Then process for 15 to 20 seconds or until the mixture resembles coarse meal.

4. Remove the ice cube from the liquid and add the liquid in a steady stream to the butter mixture while the food processor is running. Process just until it is distributed throughout the dough and the dough holds together. To test, pinch a piece the size of a marble between your thumb and forefinger; if it doesn't stick together, add more liquid.

Mixing by Hand

1. Sift the dry ingredients into a large mixing bowl or place them directly in the bowl and stir them around with a whisk.

2. Mix all liquid ingredients together in a cup and add an ice cube.

3. Cut the butter into 8 pieces per stick and distribute them evenly over the dry ingredients. Use both thumbs and forefingers to rub the butter into the flour mixture or cut it in with a pastry cutter. Continue until the mixture resembles coarse meal.

4. Remove the ice cube from the liquid and sprinkle the liquid over the dry ingredients while tossing them with a fork to distribute the moisture. When the dough can be gathered into a ball, it should be worked no longer.

Rolling the Dough

1. When the dough is the right consistency, gather it into a mass with your hands and place it on a lightly floured surface. Knead it several times with the heel of your palm so that it holds together.

2. Form the dough into a chubby disk (if the recipe requires a top crust also, make two disks). Wrap each disk in plastic and chill it for 1 hour. Doughs that contain sugar, such as Pie Crust 2, often can be rolled out right away.

3. When the dough is chilled, place it between two large (18 to 20 inches long) pieces of plastic wrap or waxed paper, and roll it out with a rolling pin. (It may be necessary to overlap pieces of plastic wrap or waxed paper to make them large enough.) Roll evenly, always beginning each roll at the center. Roll the pin outward, each time in a different direction. Lift the rolling pin after each roll. Don't roll the pin back and forth.

4. After you've rolled once in each direction, peel the top piece of plastic off the dough, then place it back. Flip the dough over and do the same thing on the second side. This keeps the dough from sticking to the wrap, giving it more room to expand.

5. Continue to roll the dough out, peeling off the plastic and putting it back again until it is ⅛ inch thick and at least 2 inches larger than your pie pan. Don't expect a perfect circle or beautiful edges. They're neither likely nor necessary.

6. Remove the top piece of plastic. Fold the crust in half, with the plastic on the inside, and lay the straight folded edge along the center of the pan. Unfold the crust to cover the pan, but leave the plastic wrap on.

Alternatively, lay the crust over your arm, plastic side against your skin. Gently lower the crust into the plate, using your hand as a guide.

7. Press the crust gently into the pan and smooth it with your fingers, taking special care at the corners of the pan and the flutes if the pan has them. Do not stretch the dough by hand because stretched dough shrinks

Problems with Pie Dough

❖

The pie crust recipes in this book are quite elastic and there really shouldn't be any problems with them if you follow the directions carefully. But if for some reason the dough cracks when being rolled, lift up the plastic wrap and pinch the dough together with your fingers, or cut off a little strip from another section and place it over the crack. Place the plastic wrap over the dough and roll right over the crack.

If you should pull up a chunk of dough when you remove the plastic wrap, leaving a hole, scrape the dough off the wrap, place it on the hole, and use your fingers to pinch it back in place. Then cover the dough with a fresh piece of plastic wrap and roll over the hole. This can happen when the dough gets too warm, so it's best to then slide your dough onto a plate or platter and refrigerate it for 15 to 20 minutes before proceeding.

Butter vs. Shortening

— ❖ —

Although many people think that crusts made with shortening are flakier, I think this is true only when they've just been baked. As soon as a shortening crust cools and sits for a while, it loses its crispness and it always lacks the extraordinary flavor of butter. If butter crusts are made correctly, they are wonderfully flaky and crisp and rich in taste.

during baking. When the crust is patted into place, peel off the remaining piece of plastic.

8. If you are making a single-crust pie, trim the excess dough and rough edges evenly with scissors and finish the edge decoratively. For a two-crust pie, trim the bottom crust so that it just overlaps the edge of the pan by about ¼ inch; you can make a finished edge when you cover the pie with the top crust (see Decorative Edges on page 170).

9. If you've put the crust in a tart pan, roll a rolling pin across the top of the pan to cut off any excess dough. You can press some of the extra into the sides of the tart shell to make them thicker and stronger.

10. Refrigerate all pie and tart shells for at least 30 minutes if they are to be prebaked.

Upper Crusts

Roll out the top crust in the same way you roll out the bottom one, between two pieces of plastic wrap or waxed paper until it is ⅛ inch thick and 2 inches larger than your pie pan. Peel off the top piece of plastic and flip the dough onto the pie filling. Peel off the second piece of plastic. Trim the edge of the dough ¾ inch larger than the bottom crust and tuck the edge of the top crust under the edge of the bottom crust all around. Make several little slits in the top crust with the point of a sharp knife so that steam can escape while the pie bakes.

To Prebake a Pie Crust

If you have two pie pans of the same size, I suggest the following simple method. It is a good technique for savory crusts, such as Basic Pie Crust 1, which contains no sugar, because it prevents the dough from shrinking, leaving you with a nice tall crust.

1. Lightly grease a pie pan with butter. Carefully fit a pie crust into the pan, then refrigerate it for at least 30 minutes.

2. Once chilled, cover the crust with a piece of baking parchment and stack the second pan into the first.

3. Flip both pans and bake the crust upside down between the two pans in a preheated 400°F oven for about 15 minutes.

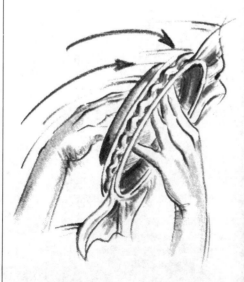

4. Remove the top pan and continue baking until the bottom of the crust is golden (about 5 minutes more). Take it out of the oven and replace the top pan.

5. Turn the whole thing right-side-up so that what was the top pan contains the crust, and carefully remove the pan that is now on top as well as the parchment.

6. If you're going to fill this crust and bake it again, cut this baking time to about 15 minutes total (12 minutes in the double pan, then 3 minutes in the single). Remove the crust when it is very lightly golden.

A Baking Alternative or Baking a Pie Crust That Contains Sugar

1. Fit a pie crust into a pan and refrigerate it for at least 30 minutes.

2. Remove the crust from the refrigerator and prick the bottom and sides in several places with a fork.

3. Line the crust with baking parchment or aluminum foil that has been greased on the underside. Fill it with rice, beans, or pie weights (little metal bean-shaped weights available at kitchen stores).

4. Bake the crust in a preheated 400°F oven until the edge is golden and the sides seem firm enough to support themselves, about 15 minutes.

5. Remove the weights and parchment very carefully so as not to disturb the crust, and continue to bake it until it is golden brown on the inside bottom, about 5 minutes. If it puffs during baking, prick it with a fork to let the steam escape. Crusts that will be baked a second time need only 2 to 3 minutes more baking time once the weights have been removed.

6. Allow the crust to cool completely before filling. If you bake the crust again after it is filled, cover the rim with aluminum foil before you put it in the oven to keep it from burning.

Basic Shortbread Crust

Since this is an eggless crust, you don't have to worry about overbeating. That means you can make it in a food processor or with an electric mixer without anxiety.

Using an Electric Mixer

1. Have the butter at room temperature.

2. Cream the butter and sugar (and vanilla) with the mixer at medium to medium-high speed until light and fluffy, 1½ minutes.

3. Add the dry ingredients with the mixer at low speed, then beat at medium speed until the dough becomes light and fluffy again. This time varies a lot depending on the proportions of ingredients but is usually about 2 minutes.

4. Gather the dough into a ball with your hands.

5. Dip your fingertips in flour so that the dough doesn't stick to them and pat the dough gently into a pie plate. Glaze with egg white (page 133) if the base will be covered with a wet filling after prebaking.

6. Prebake the crust at 300°F without using pie weights until it is a rich golden color, 40 to 45 minutes. Shortbread rises more than flaky dough and it needs to cook slowly to create a crunchy texture and a buttery flavor.

7. Allow the crust to cool before adding the filling.

Using a Food Processor

1. Place the dry ingredients in a food processor and process for 20 seconds.

2. Add the butter (cold or at room temperature) and process until the dough comes together (1½ to 2 minutes for cold butter, 30 to 40 seconds for butter at room temperature). Then follow steps 4 through 7, preceding.

Crumb Crusts

1. Put the crumbs, sugar, grated chocolate, nuts, or whatever the recipe calls for in a medium-size bowl and stir them together with a wooden spoon.

2. Melt the butter and pour it into the bowl with the crumbs. Toss the mixture with two forks or your fingers until the butter is fully distributed.

3. Pat the crumbs firmly over the bottom and up the sides of a pie pan to form a crust.

4. Bake it in a preheated 375°F oven until it is crisp and golden, about 10 minutes.

5. Allow the crust to cool completely before filling it so that it stays crunchy, and avoid pouring hot fillings into crumb crusts because they penetrate the crust easily and make it soggy.

Decorative Edges for Pies and Tarts

A pretty edge is a must for a well-turned-out pie or tart. As with anything to do with pastry, once you get it, it's as easy as — well, you know.

Forked Edge

Fold the overlapping dough under the crust at the rim of the pan to make a thick edge. Press the back of a fork into it all around, making a pattern with the tines. Dip the fork in flour before you use it and dip it again whenever it begins to stick.

Fluted Edge

Fold the overlapping dough under the crust at the rim of the pan to make a thick edge. Make flutes (tiny waves around the edge of the crust) with a gentle pinching motion: with the thumb and index finger of one hand, push the outer edge of the crust inward while, at the same time, the index finger of the other hand pushes the inner edge of the crust outward between the other two fingers. For a fancier version, dip a fork in flour and press with its back instead of your index finger.

Rope Edge

Fold the overlapping edge of the crust under the rim of the pan to make a thick edge. Pinch a small piece of the dough between your thumb and the first knuckle of your index finger, angling your hand slightly. Repeat this pinching motion around the edge of the crust, putting your index finger in the depression your thumb has just made.

Lattice Top

1. Roll out dough to about 9 inches wide and 2 inches longer than the diameter of your pie. The dough should never be thicker than 1/8 inch. With a sharp knife, cut about 10 strips 3/4 inch wide.

2. Lay half of the strips across the top of the pie or tart, spacing them equally and parallel to each other.

3. To weave the lattice, start at the outer edge and fold every other strip halfway back on itself. Lay one of the remaining strips across those on the pie that aren't folded back. Unfold the others over the new strip, and fold back the ones that haven't originally been folded back. Add a second strip parallel to the first and continue weaving until half the pie is done. Repeat this process on the other side of the pie.

4. Brush the underside of the strips with milk at the point where they meet the bottom crust and press down gently with your finger to make sure they adhere.

Fruit Fillings

*C*onquering crust is half the battle, but like books and their covers, what you put inside a pie matters too. I'm a longtime fan of fresh fruit pies and tarts and classic desserts like brown bettys. Each fruit has its own characteristics, though, so you'll need to take a few variables into consideration when you're shopping and baking.

I've found that because most fruit is naturally sweet, it's unnecessary to add a lot of sugar. Then, too, tart fruit provides a contrast to a sweet crumb topping or pastry crust. Lemon juice, lemon zest, and cinnamon work well to enhance a fruit's flavor, and I sometimes mix orange and lemon juice for the liquid to pour over the fruit. But in all pies and tarts, it's important to let the taste of the fruit come through, so whatever I add, I add it sparingly.

Apples

The best apple for baking is a firm apple because it holds its shape as it cooks. In the fall

when apples are at their best, I recommend McIntosh, Cortlands, and Granny Smiths; you can put any combination of these together in a pie. After apple season, though, most of the Cortlands and McIntoshes you find have been stored and become soft, so I suggest baking with Granny Smith for the rest of the year. Keep in mind that Granny Smiths are tart apples and may require more sugar than the Cortlands.

I add apple cider or orange juice as well as lemon juice to the apples because, as the liquid boils, it cooks the apples more evenly. The kind of apple you use dictates how much liquid you need. Obviously, the crisper the apple, the more liquid required. For instance, if a pie made exclusively with Granny Smiths requires ¼ cup liquid, one made with juicier apples might need only a tablespoon or two or none at all. The recipes in this chapter specify how much liquid to add, but you may need to experiment to find the right amount for the apples available to you. Keep in mind that soft apples and too much liquid will make your pie a mushy one.

Peaches, Pears, Plums, Nectarines, and Other Soft Fruits

Soft fruits appear in the stores at various stages of ripeness, so various, in fact, that it's hard to make any generalizations about them. When they're very ripe, they need no additional juice, other than fresh lemon juice for flavor, but with less ripe fruit, you can add any juice to the filling to get the proper consistency.

For the times when you can't find soft fruit that's ripe, rather than turn to the frozen food section for a Mrs. Smith's pie, try peeling and slicing a pie's worth (6 to 8 cups) of the too-hard fruit into ½-inch slices and simmering them with ½ cup of orange or apple juice in a covered saucepan. Toss the slices occasionally just until they lose their hardness, 3 to 5 minutes, then use the fruit and the juice as the recipe requires.

Thickening

I thicken my fruit fillings with cornstarch to produce a transparent and slightly viscous juice. The juicier the fruit, the more cornstarch you need, but too little is always better than too much. As a rule of thumb, use 1½ tablespoons cornstarch for every 6 cups fruit.

Baking Temperatures for Fruit Pies

*P*reheat the oven to 450°F 20 minutes before you put your pie in. Bake the pie in the center of the oven for 15 minutes at this temperature. Reduce the heat to 350°F and bake it for 45 to 60 minutes (if the top crust is getting too dark, cover it loosely with a piece of aluminum foil

Fruit for Tarts

— ❖ —

Fruit fillings for tarts need to be firmer than fruit fillings for pies because you remove the tarts from their pans for serving. To ensure that the tart will hold together, I often cook the filling a little with a thickener before I pour it into the crust so that the liquid doesn't make the crust soggy.

while it bakes) until the fruit starts to bubble. You'll be able to tell when this bubbling happens with any kind of top because the juice will ooze out of the crumb topping or through the slits of a top crust. I put a baking sheet on the bottom rack of the oven or directly under the pie to catch drips, which also works as a test for doneness: When the drips look thick, the pie is done or close to it. Let your pies cool on a rack and serve them when they are still warm.

Mousse-, Custard-, and Chiffon- Filled Pies

*W*ith the exception of the Vanilla Custard Tart, these fillings are always placed in fully baked pie or tart shells. For a discussion of the techniques involved, refer to the instructions in The Old Smoothies chapter.

Storing

*Y*ou can keep any leftover fruit pie overnight under a glass dome or covered with plastic wrap. Chiffon, mousse, custard, and cream pies must all be stored in the refrigerator, but it's best to take them out of the fridge an hour before you serve them so that the flavor isn't blunted.

To keep leftover pieces of these delicate pies looking fresh, "bubble" them with plastic wrap by inserting toothpicks around the edge of the pie and a few in the center, then lowering a generous piece of plastic wrap over the toothpicks and tucking it carefully under the edge of the pie dish. This bubble keeps the pie from drying out or changing color and its top from getting mushed.

Basic Pie Crust 1

A classic recipe, flaky and buttery. Remember, pastry, especially one made from butter, is easier to prepare if the kitchen is cool rather than warm.

INGREDIENTS

SINGLE CRUST FOR A 9-INCH PIE
(standard or deep dish)
1½ cups all-purpose flour
¼ teaspoon salt
9 tablespoons (1 stick plus 1 tablespoon) unsalted butter, chilled, cut into 9 pieces
3 tablespoons ice water

DOUBLE CRUST
2¼ cups all-purpose flour
½ teaspoon salt
13½ tablespoons (1 stick plus 5½ tablespoons) unsalted butter, chilled, cut into 14 pieces
4½ tablespoons ice water

1. Process the flour and salt in a food processor for 20 seconds. (Or whisk them together by hand in a large mixing bowl.)

2. Distribute the butter evenly over the flour and process until the mixture resembles coarse meal, 15 to 20 seconds. (Or rub the butter into the flour with your fingertips or cut it in with a pastry blender.)

3. With the food processor running, pour the ice water in a steady stream through the feed tube and process just until the dough comes together. (Or sprinkle the water over the mixture while tossing with a fork.)

4. Knead the dough for several turns on a lightly floured surface to bring it together.

5. Shape the dough into a thick disk (or 2 disks for a double crust), wrap in plastic, and refrigerate at least 1 hour.

6. To roll out the dough, place the chilled dough between 2 pieces of plastic wrap or waxed paper and roll it out to a circle 2 inches bigger than the size of the pie pan (see page 165 for rolling directions).

7. Fit the dough into a 9-inch pie plate and trim the edges (see page 170 for decorative edges). Keep the crust in the refrigerator until ready to fill. If prebaking the crust, refrigerate it for at least 30 minutes before baking. (See page 167 for baking directions.)

Makes one or two 9- or 10-inch crusts

Basic Pie Crust 2

*T*his crust is slightly sweeter than Basic Pie Crust 1 and has a texture that is somewhat more crunchy than flaky.

INGREDIENTS

SINGLE CRUST FOR A 9-INCH PIE
(standard or deep dish)
1½ cups all-purpose flour
2 tablespoons sugar
12 tablespoons (1½ sticks) unsalted
*   butter, chilled, cut into 12 pieces*
2 tablespoons ice water

DOUBLE CRUST
2¼ cups all-purpose flour
3 tablespoons sugar
1 cup plus 2 tablespoons (2¼ sticks)
*   unsalted butter, chilled, cut into*
*   18 pieces*
3 tablespoons ice water

1. Process the flour and sugar in a food processor for 20 seconds. (Or whisk them together by hand in a large mixing bowl.)

2. Distribute the butter evenly over the flour and process until the mixture resembles coarse meal, 15 to 20 seconds. (Or rub the butter into the flour with your fingertips or cut it in with a pastry blender.)

3. With the food processor running, pour the ice water in a steady stream through the feed tube and process just until the dough comes together. (Or sprinkle the water over the mixture while tossing with a fork.)

4. Knead the dough for several turns on a lightly floured surface to bring it together.

5. Shape the dough into a thick disk (or 2 disks for a double crust), wrap in plastic, and refrigerate at least 1 hour.

6. To roll out the dough, place the chilled dough between 2 pieces of plastic wrap or waxed paper and roll it out to a circle 2 inches bigger than the size of the pie pan (see page 165 for rolling directions).

7. Fit the dough into a 9-inch pie plate and trim the edges (see page 170 for decorative edges). Keep the crust in the refrigerator until ready to fill. If prebaking the crust, refrigerate it for at least 30 minutes before baking. (See page 167 for prebaking directions.)

Makes one or two 9- or 10-inch crusts

Basic Tart Crust

*T*his is a sturdy and tasty crust that is dependable and easy to make.

INGREDIENTS

**SINGLE CRUST FOR
    A 9- OR 10-INCH TART**
1 cup all-purpose flour
2½ tablespoons sugar
⅛ teaspoon salt
6 tablespoons (¾ stick) unsalted
    butter, chilled, cut into 6 pieces
1 tablespoon cold water
1 large egg yolk

DOUBLE CRUST
2 cups all-purpose flour
5 tablespoons sugar
¼ teaspoon salt
12 tablespoons (1½ sticks) unsalted
    butter, chilled, cut into 12 pieces
2 tablespoons cold water
2 large egg yolks

1. Process the flour, sugar, and salt in a food processor for 20 seconds. (Or whisk them together by hand in a large mixing bowl.)

2. Distribute the butter evenly over the flour and process until the mixture resembles coarse meal, 15 to 20 seconds. (Or rub the butter into the flour with your fingertips or cut it in with a pastry blender.)

3. Whisk together the cold water and egg yolk. With the food processor running, pour the egg mixture in a steady stream through the feed tube and process just until the dough comes together, 20 to 30 seconds. (Or sprinkle the egg mixture over the flour mixture while tossing with a fork.)

4. Knead the dough for several turns on a lightly floured surface to bring it together.

5. Shape the dough into a thick disk (or 2 disks for a double crust), wrap in plastic, and refrigerate or roll it out right away.

6. To roll out the dough, place the dough between 2 pieces of plastic wrap or waxed paper and roll it out to a circle 2 inches bigger than the size of the tart pan (see page 165 for rolling directions).

7. Fit the dough into a 9- or 10-inch tart pan and trim the edge by rolling over the top of the pan with a rolling pin. Keep the crust in the refrigerator until ready to fill. If prebaking the crust, refrigerate it for at least 30 minutes before baking. (See page 167 for prebaking directions.)

Makes one or two 9- or 10-inch crusts

Shortbread Tart Crust

A wonderfully crunchy crust with a buttery flavor. I use it for the Chocolate Berry Tart and The Meatless Mince Tart. It bakes at a lower temperature so that its texture is crisp throughout.

INGREDIENTS

SINGLE CRUST FOR A 9- OR 10-INCH TART

9½ tablespoons (1 stick plus 1½ tablespoons) unsalted butter, at room temperature
5 tablespoons confectioner's sugar
1 teaspoon vanilla extract
1 cup plus 3 tablespoons all-purpose flour

DOUBLE CRUST

1 cup (2 sticks) unsalted butter, at room temperature
½ cup confectioner's sugar
1½ teaspoons vanilla extract
2 cups all-purpose flour

1. Using an electric mixer on medium-high speed, cream the butter, sugar, and vanilla in a medium-size mixing bowl until light and fluffy, about 1½ minutes. (For food processor instructions, see page 164.)

2. Add the flour on low speed, then increase the speed to medium and beat until the mixture is light and fluffy again, about 2 minutes.

3. Gather the dough into a ball. With floured fingertips, press the dough gently over the bottom and up the sides of a 9- or 10-inch tart pan or pie plate.

4. Preheat the oven to 300°F.

5. Place the pan on the center oven rack and bake until a rich, golden color, 40 to 45 minutes.

6. Allow the crust to cool completely on a rack before filling.

Makes one or two 9- or 10-inch crusts

Cookie Crumb Crust

A crunchy butter crust that takes on the flavor of the cookie that it's made with. Plain wafer cookies work best.

INGREDIENTS

1¼ cups cookie crumbs from any plain crunchy cookie, such as vanilla wafers, chocolate wafers, or graham crackers
3 tablespoons sugar
6 tablespoons (¾ stick) unsalted butter, melted

1. Stir the cookie crumbs and sugar together in a small bowl. Add the melted butter and toss with two forks or your fingers until the butter is evenly distributed.

2. Pat the crumbs firmly over the bottom and up the sides of a 9- or 10-inch pie plate.

3. Preheat the oven to 375°F.

4. Place the pie plate on the center oven rack and bake until the crust is crisp and golden, 8 minutes.

5. Allow the crust to cool completely on a rack before filling.

Makes one 9- or 10-inch crust

All-American Apple Pie

*7*he apple: wedding gift for the Greek gods, instrument of Sir Isaac Newton's enlightenment, proof of William Tell's loyalty, fertility symbol in medieval times, talisman against homesickness for the American colonists, raison d'être for Johnny Appleseed, one-time gift of choice for a favorite grade-school teacher, and last, but not least, an apple a day keeps the doctor away. It's stood for practically everything at one time or another, although, interestingly, not for Adam and Eve's newfound knowledge (the Bible doesn't identify the fruit they ate). If you'd like to play your part in posterity, try this version of the classic apple pie — not too sweet, but pleasantly spicy, and contained in a buttery crust.

INGREDIENTS

1 double-crust recipe Basic Pie Crust 1 or 2 (page 175 or 176), rolled out
6 to 8 Granny Smith apples, peeled, cored, and cut into 3⁄8-inch-thick slices (8 cups)
3⁄4 cup sugar
1 teaspoon ground cinnamon
1⁄2 teaspoon ground nutmeg
1⁄4 teaspoon salt
1⁄4 cup apple cider, apple juice, or orange juice
2 tablespoons fresh lemon juice
1 1⁄2 tablespoons cornstarch
1 tablespoon unsalted butter
1 large egg mixed with 2 tablespoons water or milk for glazing

1. Place 1 crust in the pie plate. Refrigerate both the top and bottom crusts.

2. Preheat the oven to 450°F.

3. Place the apple slices in a large bowl with all the remaining ingredients except the butter and egg glaze. Toss them together with your hands to coat the apples evenly.

4. Scoop the apples into the bottom crust and dot the mixture with small pieces of the butter. Cover the apples with the top crust. Seal and trim the edge.

5. Make a pretty edge; cut 3 to 4 slits in the top crust; and using a pastry brush, brush the top with the egg glaze.

6. Bake the pie on the center oven rack for 15 minutes. Reduce the temperature to 350°F and continue baking until the top of the pie is golden and the filling is bubbling, about 1 hour 10 minutes longer. If the top crust is getting too dark, cover it with a piece of aluminum foil and continue to bake.

7. Remove the pie from the oven and cool it on a rack. Serve with vanilla ice cream.

Makes 8 to 12 servings

Sour Cream Apple Pie

I'm as much for apple pie as any mother or baseball fan, but I have to admit that this one gilds the lily just a bit. Because of its extra richness, it's important that you use tart, crisp apples. I like Granny Smith. I think of this as a harvest pie—with a little something extra on the top.

INGREDIENTS

1 single-crust recipe Basic Pie Crust 1 or 2 (page 175 or 176), rolled out

APPLE FILLING
3 to 4 tart apples, peeled, cored, and cut into ¼-inch-thick slices (4 cups)
¼ cup (½ stick) unsalted butter, melted
½ cup (lightly packed) light brown sugar
2 tablespoons fresh lemon juice
1 teaspoon grated lemon zest
¼ cup golden raisins
1 tablespoon all-purpose flour

SOUR CREAM TOPPING
1¼ cups sour cream
2 large eggs
½ cup granulated sugar
1 teaspoon vanilla extract

SUGAR NUT TOPPING
¾ cup chopped pecans
2 tablespoons unsalted butter, melted
¼ cup (lightly packed) light brown sugar

1. Place the pie crust in the pie plate and refrigerate it until ready to use.

2. Preheat the oven to 375°F.

3. Toss the apples with the melted butter in a large bowl. Add the brown sugar, lemon juice, lemon zest, raisins, and flour; stir to coat the apple slices.

4. Scoop the apples into the crust.

5. Bake the pie on the center oven rack for 30 minutes.

6. Meanwhile whisk together in a medium-size bowl the sour cream, eggs, granulated sugar, and vanilla for the topping.

7. After the pie has baked for 30 minutes, pour the sour cream mixture over the apples. Continue baking until the topping is set, 30 to 35 minutes.

8. Meanwhile make the sugar nut topping by tossing the pecans, melted butter, and brown sugar in a small bowl with a wooden spoon.

9. Crumble the topping over the pie (it will not cover the whole surface) and continue baking until the topping bubbles, about 10 minutes. Don't worry if the sour cream topping rises up; it will fall when you take it out of the oven.

10. Remove the pie from the oven and cool it on a rack.

Makes 8 to 10 servings

Apple Tart

*H*ere is a basic, two-crust tart with simple flavors and little sugar beyond the natural sweetness of the fruit. For that reason, it's nice with a dusting of confectioner's sugar on top, and it works well as the ending to a heavy or light meal.

INGREDIENTS

1 double-crust recipe Basic Tart Crust (page 176), rolled out; top crust refrigerated, bottom crust lightly baked in 9-inch tart pan (page 167)
4 tablespoons (1/2 stick) unsalted butter
1/4 cup granulated sugar
1/8 teaspoon salt
4 large apples, peeled, cored, and cut into 1/4-inch-thick slices (4 generous cups)
1 large egg mixed with 2 tablespoons water or milk for glazing
Confectioner's sugar for sprinkling

1. Make the tart crust.

2. Preheat the oven to 425°F.

3. Heat the butter, granulated sugar, and salt in a medium-size skillet over medium heat until the mixture starts to caramelize, about 3 minutes. Add the apples and sauté them just until they have lost their crispness. This will vary considerably depending on the apples.

4. Spread the apples evenly in the baked tart shell. Paint the edge of the shell with a bit of egg glaze.

5. Remove the top crust from the refrigerator, peel off the top piece of plastic, and flip the dough over on top of the tart. Peel off the second piece of plastic wrap and use your index finger to press the dough onto the edge of the crust, allowing the excess to drop off.

6. Cut 3 or 4 slits in the top crust.

Bake the tart on the center oven rack until the top is golden, 30 to 35 minutes.

7. Remove the tart from the oven and allow it to cool. Sprinkle the tart with confectioner's sugar before serving.

Makes 8 to 10 servings

Apple-Cranberry Tart

*7*he union of apples and cranberries produces a tart filling which is set in a sturdy crust. Keep in mind that unless you want to end up with an applesauce tart, you need to use crisp apples, such as Granny Smith or Macouns. If you can't get hold of hard apples, adjust the recipe by simmering the filling for only 1 minute before putting it in the tart.

INGREDIENTS

1 single-crust recipe Basic Tart Crust (page 176), lightly baked in 9-inch tart pan (page 167)

3 to 4 crisp apples (Granny Smiths or Macouns work best), peeled, cored, and cut into ¾-inch cubes (3 cups)

½ cup (lightly packed) light brown sugar

1 tablespoon grated orange zest

¼ teaspoon salt

1 teaspoon cornstarch

⅓ cup fresh orange juice

2 cups fresh cranberries, rinsed and picked clean for stems

TOPPING

½ cup chopped walnuts or pecans

½ cup plus 3 tablespoons (lightly packed) light brown sugar

¾ cup plus 2 tablespoons all-purpose flour

½ cup quick-cooking oatmeal

½ teaspoon ground cinnamon

8 tablespoons (1 stick) unsalted butter, melted

1. Make the tart crust and cool the baked shell.

2. Preheat the oven to 400°F.

3. Place the apples in a medium-size saucepan with the sugar, orange zest, and salt and toss to coat using a wooden spoon.

4. Dissolve the cornstarch in the orange juice and add it to the apples. Cover the pan and simmer the apples over medium-low heat just until they begin to lose their crispness, about 3 minutes. Stir them once after 1½ minutes.

5. Stir the cranberries into the apples, cover the pan, and bring the mixture to a simmer again. Cook just until the cranberries have softened slightly, about 2 minutes. Transfer the mixture to a bowl and refrigerate it while you prepare the topping.

6. For the topping, place the nuts, brown sugar, flour, oatmeal, and cinnamon in the food processor and process for 5 seconds. Or place all the ingredients except the butter in a large mixing bowl and toss them together with your hands or a large spoon.

7. If you used a food processor, transfer the mixture to a large mixing bowl. Add the melted butter and mix thoroughly with your hands or a large spoon.

8. Scoop the apple mixture into the tart shell and top with the nut crumb mixture.

9. Bake the tart on the center oven rack until the topping is a rich golden brown, 15 to 20 minutes. Drop a piece of aluminum foil lightly over the topping (do not mold or seal it) and continue baking the tart until the filling is bubbling, 25 to 30 minutes longer.

10. Remove the tart from the oven and allow it to cool for an hour or two before serving.

Makes 10 to 12 servings

Sour Cherry Tart

The Boston Globe claims that George Washington would have named this the best cherry pie in town if it had been around when he slept here. Prepare to pucker along with George; those sour cherries mean business.

INGREDIENTS

1 double-crust recipe Basic Tart Crust (page 176)
1 cup cherry juice (from canned sour cherries if using, see below) or 1 cup fresh orange juice (if using fresh sour cherries)
1 tablespoon plus 1½ teaspoons cornstarch
½ cup plus 3 tablespoons (lightly packed) light brown sugar
1 teaspoon ground cinnamon
Scant ¼ teaspoon ground mace
1½ teaspoons grated orange zest
⅛ teaspoon salt
4 cups drained canned sour cherries (save the juice), or 4 cups pitted fresh sour cherries
2 tablespoons dry bread crumbs
1 large egg mixed with 2 tablespoons water or milk for glazing

1. Make the tart crust. Roll out the bottom crust in a circle and line a 9-inch tart pan with it. Roll out the top crust as for a lattice (see page 171). Refrigerate both the bottom and top crusts.

2. Preheat the oven to 400°F.

3. Combine ⅓ cup of the cherry or orange juice with the cornstarch in a small bowl and set aside.

4. Combine the remaining ⅔ cup juice, the sugar, cinnamon, mace, orange zest, and salt in a small saucepan and bring it to a boil over medium-low heat.

5. Pour the cornstarch mixture slowly into the boiling juice while stirring vigorously with a whisk. Reduce the heat to low and bring the mixture to a boil again. Boil until it thickens, about 5 minutes.

6. Pour this syrup over the cherries in a medium-size bowl and toss to coat.

7. Remove the pie plate from the refrigerator and distribute the bread crumbs evenly over the bottom of the tart crust. Pour in the cherry filling and spread it evenly.

8. Cut the top crust into lattice strips and arrange the strips over the filling (see page 171). Brush the lattice and outer edges of the tart with the egg glaze.

9. Place the tart pan on a cookie sheet (to catch any drippings) and bake on the lower oven rack until the crust is golden, about 45 minutes.

10. Remove the tart from the oven and cool it on a rack for 1 hour. Then push the bottom of the tart pan up

slightly to loosen it from the pan before the syrup has the chance to harden over the edges. Cool the tart for 4 to 5 more hours before serving. Serve with whipped cream or vanilla ice cream.

Makes 10 to 12 servings

Blueberry-Plum Crumb Pie

A sumptuous summer pie with a tart filling and a sweet (but not too sweet) crunchy topping. Vanilla ice cream is a must.

INGREDIENTS

1 single-crust recipe Basic Pie Crust 1 or 2 (page 175 or 176), fully baked (page 167)

CRUMB TOPPING
6 tablespoons (lightly packed) light brown sugar
¾ cup plus 2 tablespoons all-purpose flour
½ cup quick-cooking oatmeal
¼ teaspoon ground cinnamon
½ cup ground almonds or walnuts
8 tablespoons (1 stick) unsalted butter, melted

FILLING

3 cups fresh blueberries, rinsed, stemmed, and patted dry

7 to 8 red plums, not too ripe, pitted and cut into ¾-inch-thick slices (3 cups)

6 to 8 tablespoons granulated sugar

¼ teaspoon grated orange zest

1 tablespoon plus 1 teaspoon cornstarch

2 tablespoons fresh orange juice

1. Make the pie crust and cool the baked shell.

2. Preheat the oven to 400°F.

3. For the topping, mix the sugar, flour, oatmeal, cinnamon, and nuts in a medium-size bowl. Pour in the melted butter and stir with a wooden spoon until it is fully incorporated. Set aside.

4. For the filling, place the fruit, granulated sugar, and orange zest in a large mixing bowl.

5. Dissolve the cornstarch in the orange juice and pour it over the fruit. Toss the mixture with your hands or a large spoon.

6. Scoop the fruit into the pie shell. Use your hands to distribute the topping evenly over the fruit. Cover the edge of the crust with aluminum foil.

7. Place the pie on a cookie sheet on the center oven rack. Bake for 20 minutes. Reduce the heat to 350°F and continue baking until the pie juices are bubbling and begin to drip onto the cookie sheet, about 1 hour longer.

8. Remove the pie from the oven and carefully remove the foil. Cool the pie on a rack for several hours before serving.

Makes 8 to 12 servings

Peach Crumb Pie

A classic dessert that pays homage to one of the world's greatest fruits.

INGREDIENTS

1 single-crust recipe Basic Pie Crust 1 or 2 (page 175 or 176), fully baked (page 167)

TOPPING

1 cup plus 2 tablespoons all-purpose flour

½ cup plus 2 tablespoons (lightly packed) light brown sugar

1 teaspoon ground cinnamon

¼ teaspoon salt

10 tablespoons (1 stick plus 2 tablespoons) unsalted butter, chilled, cut into 10 pieces

FILLING

6 to 7 peaches, peeled, pitted, and cut into ¾-inch-thick slices (7 cups)

⅓ to ½ cup granulated sugar

½ teaspoon ground cinnamon

¼ teaspoon salt

1 tablespoon plus 1 teaspoon cornstarch

3 tablespoons fresh lemon juice

2 tablespoons fresh orange juice

1. Make the pie crust and cool the baked shell.

2. Preheat the oven to 400°F.

3. For the topping, place the flour, brown sugar, cinnamon, and salt in a food processor and process for several seconds to mix. Add the butter and pulse until the butter is completely mixed in and the topping forms large moist clumps. Set aside.

4. Place the peaches, granulated sugar, cinnamon, and salt in a large bowl.

5. Dissolve the cornstarch in the lemon and orange juices and pour it over the fruit. Toss the mixture with your hands or a large spoon. Scoop the fruit into the pie shell and set aside.

6. Use your hands to distribute the topping evenly over the fruit. Cover the edge of the crust with aluminum foil.

7. Place the pie on a cookie sheet on the center oven rack. Bake for 20 minutes. Reduce the heat to 350°F and continue baking until the pie juices are bubbling and begin to drip onto the cookie sheet, about 1 hour longer.

8. Remove the pie from the oven and carefully remove the foil. Cool the pie on a rack for several hours before serving.

Makes 8 to 12 servings

Nectarine Synergy

*T*his dessert made its debut at a farewell dinner party for the Hamiltons, our erstwhile neighbors from England. "So what do you think?" I asked. "Fabulous," someone said, then someone else mentioned "synergy," and we were so amused by the concept that the name stuck.

CRUST
1½ cups all-purpose flour
1 cup granulated sugar
½ teaspoon ground cinnamon
¼ teaspoon baking powder
8 tablespoons (1 stick) unsalted butter, at room temperature, cut into 8 pieces

TOPPING
¾ cup all-purpose flour
½ cup quick-cooking oatmeal
¾ of 1 slice white bread, cut in cubes
¾ cup (lightly packed) light brown sugar
8 tablespoons (1 stick) unsalted butter, chilled, cut into 8 pieces

FILLING
7 to 8 ripe nectarines, peeled, pitted, and cut into ½-inch-thick slices (8 cups)
6 tablespoons granulated sugar
2 tablespoons cornstarch
¾ teaspoon salt
1 teaspoon ground cinnamon
3 tablespoons fresh lemon juice

1. Preheat the oven to 400°F. Lightly grease a 9-inch square baking pan with butter or vegetable oil. Line a cookie sheet with aluminum foil.

2. For the crust, place the flour, granulated sugar, cinnamon, and baking powder in a food processor and process for 10 seconds. Add the butter and process until the mixture resembles coarse meal.

3. Gather the dough into a ball. With floured fingertips, press the dough gently over the bottom and 1½ inches up the sides of the prepared pan.

4. Place the pan on the center oven rack and bake the crust until it is golden in color, 12 to 15 minutes. Let it cool. Leave the oven on.

5. Place the prepared cookie sheet on the center oven rack.

6. While the crust cools, prepare the topping: Process the flour, oatmeal, bread, and brown sugar in a food processor for 30 seconds.

7. Add the butter; process until the mixture resembles coarse meal. Set aside.

8. For the filling, place all the filling ingredients in a large bowl and toss them together with your hands.

9. Scoop the fruit mixture into the crust and sprinkle the topping over it.

10. Reduce the oven temperature to 375°F and place the pan on the cookie sheet.

11. Bake until the top is light gold and crispy and the juices are bubbling, about 1½ hours.

12. Open the oven door, turn the temperature to broil, and allow the topping to broil for 2 to 3 minutes until it turns a deep gold. (If your broiler is separate, remove the Synergy from the oven and place it under the broiler.) You'll need to watch it so that it doesn't burn!

13. Allow the Synergy to cool a little on a rack. Serve it warm.

Makes 9 servings

Meatless Mince Tart for Christmas

*7*his tart has a real mincemeat taste even though it has no suet. Its buttery crust holds a sweet-tart mixture of dried fruit laced with brandy, and it tastes good warm or at room temperature topped with whipped cream. I like to serve it at on a large silver platter surrounded by greens and cranberries.

INGREDIENTS

CRUST

1½ cups all-purpose flour
6 tablespoons confectioner's sugar
12 tablespoons (1½ sticks) unsalted
    butter, chilled, cut into 16 pieces
2 teaspoons vanilla extract

FILLING

3 large apples (Granny Smiths
    preferably), peeled, cored, and
    cut into ½-inch cubes (4½ cups)
3 tablespoons fresh orange juice
1 tablespoon grated orange zest
½ cup (lightly packed) light brown
    sugar
½ cup raisins (golden or dark)
½ cup chopped dried apricots
¼ teaspoon salt
Slightly rounded ¼ teaspoon ground
    cinnamon
Slightly rounded ¼ teaspoon ground
    nutmeg
Slightly rounded ¼ teaspoon ground
    cloves
½ cup chopped walnuts or pecans
1½ teaspoons vanilla extract
2 tablespoons brandy

1 large egg mixed with 2 tablespoons
    water or milk for glazing

1. For the crust, process the flour and confectioner's sugar in a food processor for 20 seconds. Distribute the butter evenly over the flour mixture, add the vanilla, and process until the dough comes together, 1½ to 2 minutes.

2. Divide the dough in half. Wrap each piece in plastic wrap and chill for 1 hour.

3. Preheat the oven to 350°F.

4. Prepare the filling: Combine the apples, orange juice and zest, brown sugar, raisins, apricots, salt, and spices in a medium-size saucepan. Cover and simmer over low heat for 25 to 30 minutes.

5. Uncover the pan and simmer until the liquid evaporates. Stir the nuts, vanilla, and brandy into the apple mixture and let cool.

6. Remove one of the dough halves from the refrigerator and roll it out ¼ inch thick between two pieces of plastic wrap. Peel off the top piece of plastic, flip the dough into a 9-inch tart pan, and press it in lightly. Remove the remaining plastic and spread the filling evenly in the tart shell.

7. Roll out the top crust ¼ inch thick and slightly larger than the pan between two pieces of plastic wrap.

8. Brush the edge of the filled tart shell with a little of the glaze. Remove the top piece of plastic from the top crust and flip the crust over onto the filling. Remove the remaining plastic and use your index finger to press the top crust into the bottom crust, pinching off any excess dough.

9. Make several slits in the top crust with the tip of a sharp knife. Brush the top with the egg glaze.

10. Place the tart pan on a rack in the oven that is just below the center. Bake until the tart is a golden color, about 45 minutes.

11. Remove the tart from the oven and cool it completely on a rack.

Makes 12 to 16 servings

Lemon- Raisin Pie

I met my husband's parents for the first time at a Thanksgiving dinner at their home in Indianapolis, and I didn't expect much. I don't mean of them, of course, but of any Thanksgiving that differed from the traditions I had grown up with and considered the last word on holiday indulgence. But my mother-in-law, Barbara, managed to surprise, impress, and delight me by serving four or five desserts at one sitting. This pie was my favorite. It's sweet, tart, and crunchy all at once, and also deceptive because it's much richer than it appears. So server beware: Small wedges are advised.

INGREDIENTS

1 single-crust recipe Basic Pie Crust 1 or 2 (page 175 or 176), lightly baked (page 167)

1¼ cups golden raisins
1 tablespoon grated lemon zest
½ cup fresh lemon juice
⅔ cup chopped walnuts
8 tablespoons (1 stick) unsalted butter, at room temperature
⅓ cup granulated sugar
⅓ cup (lightly packed) light brown sugar
¾ teaspoon ground cinnamon
¼ teaspoon salt
3 large eggs, at room temperature

1. Make the pie crust and cool the baked shell.

2. Preheat the oven to 350°F.

3. In a small bowl soak the raisins and lemon zest in the lemon juice for 10 minutes. Add the nuts.

4. Using an electric mixer on medium-high speed, cream the butter, both sugars, the cinnamon, and salt in a medium-size mixing bowl until light and fluffy, 2 to 3 minutes. Stop the mixer to scrape the bowl once or twice with a rubber spatula.

5. Add the eggs and beat on medium speed, stopping to scrape the sides of the bowl, until well mixed, about 8 seconds. The mixture will look curdled until it heats up in the baking.

6. Stir in the raisin mixture with a wooden spoon and pour the filling into the crust.

7. Bake the pie on the center oven rack until the top is set and light golden at the center and darker golden around the edges, 35 to 40 minutes. It will feel somewhat spongy to the touch.

8. Allow the pie to cool completely on a rack before serving.

Makes 8 to 12 servings

Pecan Pie

*T*ake a butter crust, fill it with pecans and syrupy caramel, make sure the flavor is sweet, and you've got a classic pie, unimpeded by any extraneous flavors.

I N G R E D I E N T S

1 single-crust recipe Basic Pie Crust 1 or 2 (page 175 or 176), rolled out
1 cup sugar
1½ cups plus 2 tablespoons dark corn syrup
7 tablespoons unsalted butter, cut into large pieces
⅛ teaspoon salt
4 large eggs, lightly beaten with a fork, at room temperature
½ teaspoon vanilla extract
1½ cups pecan halves

1. Place the pie crust in the pie plate and refrigerate it until ready to use.

2. Preheat the oven to 350°F.

3. Heat the sugar and corn syrup in a small saucepan over low heat, stirring occasionally, until the sugar is dissolved, about 5 minutes. Transfer the mixture to a medium-size bowl.

4. Stir in the butter and the salt and allow the mixture to cool for 8 to 10 minutes, stirring occasionally.

5. Add the eggs and vanilla to the cooled sugar mixture while beating constantly with a whisk. Stir in the pecans. Pour the filling into the pie shell.

6. Bake the pie on the center oven rack until the top is fully risen, set, and crisp to the touch, 50 to 55 minutes. The surface will be covered with little cracks that will settle.

7. Remove the pie from the oven and cool it on a rack. Serve the following day with ice cream or whipped cream.

Makes 12 to 16 servings

Chocolate-Bourbon Pecan Pie

*F*udgy, delicious, and studded with pecans, this pie is a show-stopper.

INGREDIENTS

1 single-crust recipe Basic Pie Crust 1 or 2 (page 175 or 176), rolled out
4 ounces unsweetened chocolate
1 cup sugar
1 cup dark corn syrup
4 tablespoons (½ stick) unsalted butter, at room temperature
¼ teaspoon salt
4 large eggs, at room temperature
¼ cup bourbon
1 teaspoon vanilla extract
1½ cups pecan halves

1. Place the pie crust in the pie plate and refrigerate it until ready to use.

2. Preheat the oven to 350°F.

3. Melt the chocolate in the top of a double boiler placed over simmering water. Set aside.

4. Heat the sugar and the corn syrup in a small saucepan over low heat, stirring occasionally, until the sugar is dissolved, about 5 minutes. Transfer the mixture to a medium-size bowl.

5. Stir in the butter and salt and allow the mixture to cool for 8 to 10 minutes, stirring occasionally.

6. Add the eggs and the bourbon to the cooled sugar mixture while beating constantly with a whisk.

7. Add the chocolate and vanilla and whisk vigorously until blended. Stir in the pecans. Pour the filling into the pie shell.

8. Bake the pie on the center oven rack until the top is risen, set, and crisp to the touch, 55 to 60 minutes. The surface will be covered with little cracks that will settle.

9. Remove the pie from the oven and cool it completely on a rack.

Makes 12 to 16 servings

Sweet-Potato Pecan Pie

*C*olumbus discovered the sweet potato along with America, and until about 1775, when the English talked about potatoes that was what they meant. Pecans are even more the province of our country, since they originally grew only in the American South. Even without such an impeccable pedigree, this would be the perfect southern dessert, although I'm a fan of it for those long northern winters.

INGREDIENTS

1 single-crust recipe Basic Pie Crust 1 or 2 (page 175 or 176), lightly baked in deep-dish pie plate (page 167)

FILLING
1¼ pounds sweet potatoes (about 2 large)
8 tablespoons (1 stick) unsalted butter, melted
¾ cup (lightly packed) dark brown sugar
2 large eggs, lightly beaten with a fork, at room temperature
1½ tablespoons fresh lemon juice
1 teaspoon grated lemon zest
¼ cup light cream or half-and-half
¼ teaspoon salt

TOPPING
¾ cup granulated sugar
¾ cup dark corn syrup
2 large eggs
1½ tablespoons unsalted butter, melted
2 teaspoons vanilla extract
Pinch of salt
Pinch of ground cinnamon
¾ cup pecan halves

1. Make the pie crust and cool the baked shell.

2. Preheat the oven to 450°F.

3. Bake the potatoes in the oven until they are soft, about 50 minutes. Reduce the oven temperature to 375°F.

4. Scoop the potatoes out of their skins into a medium-size bowl, add the remaining filling ingredients, and stir vigorously with a whisk until smooth and well blended. (This can also be done with an electric mixer on medium speed.) Set aside.

5. Put all the topping ingredients except the pecans in a medium-size bowl and stir them together with a wooden spoon. Then stir in the pecans.

6. Scoop the sweet potato filling into the pie shell, spread it evenly, and spread the topping over it. Cover the edge of the crust with aluminum foil.

7. Bake the pie on the center oven rack until the top rises and sets and is a rich golden color, about 1 hour.

8. Remove the pie from the oven and carefully remove the foil. Cool the pie on a rack and serve it while it is still warm.

Makes 8 to 12 servings

Deep-Dish Pumpkin Pie

*P*umpkins are one of the foods Americans can claim as all their own, since Europeans never laid eyes on them before the time of Columbus, and even after that they were pretty slow in figuring out what to do with this fleshy squash. Good old Yankee ingenuity came up with this ideal fall and winter dessert.

1 single-crust recipe Basic Pie Crust 1 or 2 (page 175 or 176), lightly baked in deep-dish pie plate (page 167)
1³/₄ cups (15-ounce can) pumpkin purée
¹/₂ cup plus 3 tablespoons (lightly packed) dark brown sugar
1¹/₂ teaspoons ground cinnamon
1 teaspoon ground nutmeg
¹/₂ teaspoon ground cloves
1¹/₂ teaspoons ground ginger
¹/₄ teaspoon salt
3 tablespoons molasses
1¹/₄ cups evaporated milk
3 large eggs
1 recipe Whipped Cream (page 86) for serving

1. Make the pie crust and cool the baked shell.

2. Preheat the oven to 375°F.

3. Place the pumpkin, brown sugar, spices, and salt in a large mixing bowl and blend with a whisk.

4. Add the molasses, milk, and the eggs; stir vigorously with the whisk until smooth.

5. Pour the filling into the pie shell. Cover the edge of the crust with aluminum foil.

6. Bake the pie on the center oven rack until the top is shiny and set and a tester inserted in the center comes out clean, about 1 hour.

7. Remove the pie from the oven and carefully remove the foil. Cool the pie on a rack. Serve the pie warm, cold, or at room temperature with a dollop of whipped cream.

Makes 10 to 12 servings

Florida Lime Pie

*T*his southern favorite used to take its name from a kind of lime found in the Florida Keys, which turns the color of your average lime inside out — that is, the green is on the inside and the yellow is outside. Key limes are almost impossible to get now, but do use fresh limes for a true flavor.

INGREDIENTS

1 recipe Cookie Crumb Crust
    made with graham crackers
    (page 178), baked

FILLING
1 can (14 ounces) sweetened
    condensed milk
1/2 cup plus 2 tablespoons fresh lime
    juice (5 to 6 limes)
2 large eggs
2 tablespoons grated lime zest
Dash of salt

TOPPING
8 ounces sour cream
1/4 cup sugar
1/8 teaspoon salt

Lime zest for garnish

1. Make the crumb crust and cool the baked shell.

2. Preheat the oven to 350°F.

3. Place all the filling ingredients in a medium-size mixing bowl and stir them with a whisk until they are completely mixed. Pour the filling into the pie shell.

4. Bake the pie on the center oven rack until it begins to set, 10 minutes. Remove the pie from the oven and increase the heat to 425°F.

5. Whisk the topping ingredients together in a small bowl and spread the topping over the pie.

6. Bake the pie for 5 minutes more. The topping will be loose when you remove the pie, but it will set as it cools. Cool on a rack, then chill the pie for 6 hours before serving.

7. With a vegetable peeler or citrus zester, shave strands of zest from a whole lime around the edge of the pie for garnish.

Makes 8 to 12 servings

Lemon Meringue Pie

As American as Mom playing baseball. I see Lemon Meringue Pie as a creature of the roadside diner, a special treat for the weary truck driver or, better yet, the handsome stranger who pulls into town and wins the heart of the good-natured waitress. Have you seen this movie too?

INGREDIENTS

**1 single-crust recipe Basic Pie Crust 1
or 2 (page 175 or 176), fully
baked (page 167), or 1 recipe
Cookie Crumb Crust made with
graham crackers (page 178), baked**

FILLING
6 tablespoons cornstarch
1½ cups water
¾ cup plus 2 tablespoons sugar
**¾ cup fresh lemon juice
    (about 3 lemons)**
3 large egg yolks
3 tablespoons unsalted butter
1½ teaspoons grated lemon zest

MERINGUE TOPPING
5 large egg whites, at room temperature
½ cup sugar
½ teaspoon cream of tartar

1. Make the pie crust and cool the baked shell.

2. Dissolve the cornstarch in the water in a medium-size saucepan. Add the sugar and cook the mixture over low heat, whisking constantly until it thickens, about 5 minutes.

3. Add the lemon juice and egg yolks and simmer, stirring occasionally, so the egg yolks cook, 3 minutes.

4. Strain the custard into a medium-size bowl and stir in the butter and lemon zest. Allow it to cool for 10 to 15 minutes, stirring occasionally with a wooden spoon.

5. Pour the custard into the pie crust. Place it in the refrigerator and allow it to set for 4 to 6 hours.

6. Preheat the oven to 350°F.

7. For the meringue, using an electric mixer on medium speed, beat the egg whites in a medium-size mixing bowl until frothy, about 50 seconds.

8. Gradually add the sugar and cream of tartar on medium speed. Increase the speed to medium-high and beat 15 seconds. Then increase the speed to high and beat until the meringue is shiny and holds stiff peaks, about 90 seconds more.

9. Use a rubber spatula to scoop and spread the meringue over the pie. Use the back of a metal spoon to make little peaks.

10. Cover the edge of the crust with aluminum foil. Bake the pie on the center oven rack until the tips and ridges are golden, about 15 minutes.

11. Remove the pie from the oven and carefully remove the foil. Allow the pie to cool on a rack for 1 hour, then refrigerate it for at least another hour before serving. Cut the pie with the tip of a thin sharp knife that has been dipped in hot water and wiped dry before each cut.

Makes 8 to 10 servings

Note: Water tends to form when meringue is baked on a water-based custard. If this occurs, after you have removed the first slice, tip the pan over the sink and pour off any excess liquid.

Banana Custard Pie

7his is a custard pie in the true sense of the word: It's richer than Croesus, smooth and creamy, layered with bananas, and topped with whipped cream.

INGREDIENTS

*1 single-crust recipe Basic Pie Crust 1
or 2 (page 175 or 176), fully
baked (page 167)*

2¼ cups milk

½ cup sugar

¼ teaspoon salt

¼ cup cornstarch

3 large egg yolks

*3 tablespoons unsalted butter,
at room temperature, cut into
3 pieces*

1 teaspoon vanilla extract

3 ripe bananas

2 tablespoons fresh lemon juice

*1½ cups Whipped Cream (page 86)
for topping*

1. Make the pie crust and cool the baked shell.

2. Scald 2 cups of the milk with the sugar and salt in a heavy medium-size saucepan over low heat. Stir occasionally to dissolve the sugar.

3. Dissolve the cornstarch in the remaining ¼ cup milk in a small bowl. Whisk in the egg yolks.

4. Whisk the egg mixture into the scalded milk. Cook, whisking constantly, over low heat until it thickens and bubbles, about 3 minutes, then cook for 1 minute more. The custard should form loose mounds when dropped from a spoon back into the pan.

5. Remove the custard from the heat and stir in the butter and vanilla. Transfer the custard to a small bowl and cool for 15 minutes, gently stirring it several times to allow the steam to escape. Place a piece of plastic wrap directly on the surface of the custard and puncture the wrap in several places with the tip of a knife. Cool for 30 minutes in the refrigerator.

6. While the custard is cooling, cut the bananas into ¼-inch-thick slices and toss them with the lemon juice to prevent them from turning brown.

7. Spread half the custard in the pie shell with a spatula and cover it with a layer of bananas. Spread the remaining custard carefully over the bananas and arrange the remaining bananas on top. Spread the whipped cream over the bananas.

8. Chill the pie for at least 2 hours before serving.

Makes 8 to 12 servings

Coconut Custard Pie

I love anything with coconut in it, so this pie is one of my long-time favorites. It starts with a simple butter crust, which I fill with thick, coconut-rich pudding, then top with meringue.

INGREDIENTS

1 single-crust recipe Basic Pie Crust 1 or 2 (page 175 or 176), fully baked (page 167)

FILLING
1½ cups heavy (whipping) cream
1¼ cups milk
¾ cup sugar
6 tablespoons cornstarch
2 large egg yolks
1 teaspoon vanilla extract
2 cups shredded coconut

MERINGUE TOPPING
5 large egg whites, at room temperature
½ cup sugar
½ teaspoon cream of tartar

1. Make the pie crust and cool the baked shell.

2. Scald the cream and ½ cup of the milk with the sugar in a heavy medium-size saucepan over low heat. Stir occasionally to dissolve the sugar.

3. Dissolve the cornstarch in the remaining ¾ cup milk. Whisk in the egg yolks.

4. Gradually add ½ cup of the hot cream mixture to the yolks while whisking vigorously. Whisk this mixture into the remaining scalded cream. Cook, whisking constantly, over low heat until it thickens, 5 to 6 minutes. Cook, continuing to whisk, 20 to 30 seconds more. The custard should form loose mounds when dropped from a spoon back into the pan.

5. Remove the custard from the heat and stir in the vanilla. Transfer the custard to a medium-size bowl and cool for 15 minutes, gently stirring it several times to allow the steam to escape.

6. Stir all but 3 tablespoons of the coconut into the custard. Place a piece of plastic wrap directly on the surface of the custard and puncture the wrap in several places with the tip of a knife. Cool for 1 hour at room temperature.

7. Preheat the oven to 350°F.

8. Scoop the custard into the pie shell and use a spatula to spread it evenly.

9. For the meringue, using an electric mixer on medium speed, beat the egg whites in a medium-size bowl until frothy, about 50 seconds.

10. Gradually add the sugar and cream of tartar on medium speed.

Increase the speed to medium-high and beat 15 seconds. Then increase the speed to high and beat until the meringue is shiny and holds stiff peaks, about 90 seconds more.

11. Use a rubber spatula to scoop and spread the meringue over the pie. Use the back of a metal spoon to make little peaks. Sprinkle the remaining coconut over the top.

12. Bake the pie on the center oven rack until the coconut and the meringue peaks are golden, about 15 minutes.

13. Cool for 15 minutes, then refrigerate the pie for 1 hour before serving.

Makes 8 to 10 servings

Vanilla Custard Tart

*U*nlike most custard tarts, this one is covered with a crust, combining the flavor of buttery dough and vanilla. It's delicious sprinkled with confectioner's sugar and served with sliced berries that have been tossed with sugar.

INGREDIENTS

1 double-crust recipe Basic Tart Crust (page 176), rolled out; top crust refrigerated, bottom crust lightly baked in 9-inch tart pan (page 167)

2 cups heavy (whipping) cream
2 cups milk
½ cup sugar
6 tablespoons cornstarch
8 large egg yolks
1 tablespoon vanilla extract
1 large egg mixed with 2 tablespoons water or milk for glazing

1. Make the tart crust and cool the baked shell.

2. Scald the cream and 1½ cups of the milk with the sugar in a heavy medium-size saucepan over low heat. Stir occasionally to dissolve the sugar.

3. Dissolve the cornstarch in the remaining ½ cup milk in a medium-size bowl. Vigorously whisk in the egg yolks.

4. Gradually add ½ cup of the hot cream mixture to the yolks while whisking vigorously. Whisk this mixture into the remaining scalded cream. Cook, whisking constantly, over low heat until it thickens, about 4 minutes, then cook for 1 minute more.

5. Remove the custard from the heat and stir in the vanilla. Transfer the custard to a ceramic bowl and cool for 15 minutes, gently stirring it several times to allow the steam to escape. Place a piece of plastic wrap directly on the surface of the custard and puncture the wrap in several places with the tip of a knife. Refrigerate for 15 minutes.

6. Preheat the oven to 350° F.

7. Scoop the custard into the tart shell and use a spatula to spread it evenly.

8. Brush the egg glaze along the edge of the shell. Lay the top crust over the custard and press along the edge with your thumb to seal the two crusts. Make a pretty edge; cut 3 to 4 small slits in the top crust; brush the top with the egg glaze.

9. Bake the tart on the center oven rack until the crust is golden, about 1 hour. Allow the tart to cool completely on a rack before serving.

Makes 8 to 12 servings

Raspberry Chiffon Pie

*U*nlike most chiffons, this pie has a very strong and tart raspberry flavor. It makes a good dessert for the warm summer months.

1. Make the pie crust and cool the baked shell.

2. For the filling, combine the raspberries and 4 tablespoons of the sugar in a small bowl and let stand for 30 minutes.

3. Process the raspberry mixture in a food processor to a purée, 20 seconds. Transfer the purée to a large bowl.

4. Sprinkle the gelatin over the orange juice in a cup or small bowl and let stand at least 2 minutes to soften.

5. Using an electric mixer on medium-high speed or a hand-held whisk, beat the cream in a small mixing bowl to firm but not dry peaks. Set aside.

6. Place the cup of gelatin in a larger bowl filled half-way with hot water and stir. When the gelatin has liquified, stir it into the raspberry purée.

7. Stir the salt into the lemon juice and add this mixture to the purée as well. Let the raspberry purée stand until slightly thickened, about 3 minutes.

8. Meanwhile, using an electric mixer on medium-high speed, beat the egg whites until frothy, about 15 seconds. Gradually add the remaining 3 tablespoons sugar and beat to soft peaks, 15 to 30 seconds more.

9. Fold the whipped cream into the purée, then fold in the egg whites. Pour this chiffon into the crust. Allow it to set for 6 hours in the refrigerator.

10. Before serving, top the pie with whipped cream and crown it with the fresh raspberries.

Makes 8 to 10 servings

Chocolate Chiffon Pie

*B*efore I started Rosie's, I thought that chiffon pies all came out of boxes of Jell-O brand instant something. Then I learned about homemade chiffon, and scales fell from my eyes. This pie calls for a vanilla cookie crust, but you can substitute a chocolate cookie crust if you prefer.

I N G R E D I E N T S

1 recipe Cookie Crumb Crust made with vanilla wafers (page 178), baked, or 1 single-crust recipe Basic Pie Crust 1 or 2 (page 175 or 176), fully baked (page 167)
2 ounces unsweetened chocolate
1 tablespoon instant coffee or espresso powder
3 tablespoons cold water
2¼ teaspoons unflavored gelatin
6 tablespoons boiling water
3 large eggs, separated
9 tablespoons sugar
1½ teaspoons vanilla extract
¾ cup heavy (whipping) cream, chilled
½ recipe Whipped Cream (page 86) for topping
½ ounce unsweetened chocolate for shaving

1. Make the pie crust and cool the baked shell.

2. Melt the chocolate in the top of a double boiler placed over simmering water. Transfer it to a large bowl and set aside.

3. Dissolve the instant coffee in the cold water. Then sprinkle the gelatin over the coffee and let stand at least 2 minutes to soften.

4. Pour the boiling water into the chocolate and stir with a wooden spoon until the mixture is smooth.

5. Add the gelatin mixture to the chocolate mixture and stir quickly until it dissolves.

6. Lightly beat the egg yolks together with a fork, then quickly add them along with 5 tablespoons of the sugar and the vanilla to the hot chocolate mixture and mix until smooth.

7. Beat the heavy cream in a small bowl on high speed until stiff.

8. Place the bowl with the chocolate mixture slightly into a bowl of ice water and whisk constantly until the mixture begins to thicken, 2 to 4 minutes.

9. Beat the egg whites in a medium-size bowl on medium-high speed until frothy, about 30 seconds. Gradually add the remaining 4 tablespoons sugar and continue beating until the whites are stiff but not dry, 60 seconds more. Immediately fold in the whipped cream.

10. Pour this chiffon into the crust. Refrigerate immediately and allow it to set for 6 hours.

11. Before serving, spread the whipped cream topping over the pie so that the outside edges of the chiffon are visible. Cover the cream with chocolate shavings (page 33). Eat within 1 day of making.

Makes 8 to 12 servings

Chocolate Mousse Pie in a Toasted Pecan Crust

A rich, dark mousse encased in a sweet nut crust that's glazed with semisweet chocolate.

INGREDIENTS

CRUST
2 cups chopped pecans
1/2 cup (lightly packed) light brown sugar
5 tablespoons unsalted butter, melted
3/4 cup semisweet chocolate chips

FILLING
4 ounces semisweet chocolate
2 ounces unsweetened chocolate
1 teaspoon instant coffee powder
4 large eggs, at room temperature
1/2 teaspoon vanilla extract
1 1/2 cups heavy (whipping) cream, chilled

1/2 ounce unsweetened chocolate for shaving

1. Preheat the oven to 375° F.

2. Toast the pecans on a cookie sheet until they are golden in color, about 5 minutes.

3. Place the nuts, sugar, and butter in a medium-size bowl and toss with a fork or your hands. Pat the mixture evenly over the bottom and up the sides of a 9-inch pie plate.

4. Bake the crust on the center oven rack until the butter and sugar begin to caramelize, 8 to 10 minutes.

5. Distribute the chocolate chips evenly over the crust, return it to the oven, and bake until the chips are softened, 1 to 1½ minutes. Remove the crust from the oven and spread the chips over the bottom and sides with a frosting spatula. Refrigerate the crust while you prepare the filling.

6. For the filling, melt both chocolates with the coffee in the top of a double boiler placed over simmering water. Then vigorously whisk in the eggs and vanilla until the mixture is smooth. Transfer this mixture to a medium-size bowl and cool for at least 5 minutes.

7. Using an electric mixer on medium-high speed, beat the cream until it forms firm peaks. Fold two-thirds of the cream into the chocolate mixture and spread the mousse in the crust.

8. Refrigerate the pie until ready to serve, 6 to 8 hours. Store the remain-ing whipped cream in a small bowl covered with plastic.

9. Before serving, spoon the cream onto the center of the pie and spread it, leaving a 1½-inch border free. Cover the cream with chocolate shavings (page 33).

Makes 10 servings

Crucheon's Fudge Pie

*W*hen I was a student at Berkeley, I was a regular at a little restaurant called Crucheon's, mostly because it had desserts I was prepared to die for. It seems appropriate that a fudge pie would be one of my college experiences because fudge first caught on about 150 years ago at women's colleges, where students made it as an excuse to stay up late and talk. I didn't need an excuse. I kept working on this recipe until I was able to create the dark, chocolaty filling in its butter crust. I dedicate the results to Crucheon's. Serve each slice with whipped cream.

INGREDIENTS

1 single-crust recipe Basic Pie Crust
  1 or 2 (page 175 or 176), lightly
  baked (page 167)
4 ounces unsweetened chocolate
8 tablespoons (1 stick) unsalted butter
3 large eggs, at room temperature
1 cup plus 2 tablespoons sugar
1/2 recipe Whipped Cream (page 86)
  for topping

1. Make the pie crust and cool the baked shell.

2. Preheat the oven to 375°F.

3. Melt the chocolate and butter in the top of a double boiler placed over simmering water. Cool until the mixture is tepid.

4. Using an electric mixer on medium speed, beat the eggs and sugar in a medium-size mixing bowl until the mixture is thick and light yellow, about 80 seconds.

5. Add the chocolate mixture and mix on medium speed until blended, about 30 seconds. Scrape the bottom and sides of the bowl with a rubber spatula and mix for 15 seconds more.

6. Cover the edge of the pie crust with a strip of aluminum foil so that it won't burn and pour the filling in.

7. Bake the pie on the center oven rack until the filling is set and forms a crust and a tester inserted in the center comes out with moist crumbs, 35 to 40 minutes. Remove the foil from the crust after 30 minutes of baking.

8. Serve the pie warm with whipped cream.

Makes 8 to 12 servings

Chocolate Berry Tart

I don't remember when I first tasted chocolate fondue, although I do remember someone ordering it for me and saying, "This'll knock your socks off." An understatement. I think of this pie as a less messy version of that fondue, and I'd like to propose a toast to the marriage of two of the world's most distinguished tastes—fresh berries and rich chocolate. May they thrive and prosper.

INGREDIENTS

1 single-crust recipe Shortbread Tart
   Crust (page 177), fully baked
   in 9-inch tart pan (page 167)

FILLING

1 ounce unsweetened chocolate,
   cut into 4 pieces
½ cup plus 2 tablespoons semisweet
   chocolate chips
¼ cup plus 2 tablespoons milk
½ cup plus 2 tablespoons heavy
   (whipping) cream
1½ large egg yolks (see Note),
   at room temperature
1 teaspoon vanilla extract
½ teaspoon instant espresso powder

TOPPING

⅓ cup heavy (whipping) cream, chilled
1 pint ripe strawberries, rinsed and
   hulled, or raspberries (not
   necessary to rinse)

1. Make the tart crust and cool the
baked shell.

2. Chop both the chocolates to fine
flakes in a food processor, about 20
seconds.

3. Heat the milk and cream in a
small saucepan over low heat just to
boiling, about 5 minutes. Remove it
from the heat.

4. Add the egg yolks, vanilla, and
espresso powder to the chocolate and
process about 8 seconds.

5. With the processor running, pour
the hot cream and milk through the
feed tube and process until the chocolate is melted. Scrape the bowl with

a rubber spatula
and process several
more seconds.

6. Let the mixture
cool to lukewarm,
10 to 15 minutes,
then spread it in the
tart shell.

7. Chill the tart at least 4
hours in the refrigerator.

8. Before serving, whip the cream
(for topping) until it forms firm peaks
and spread it over the surface of the
tart, starting at the center. Distribute
the berries evenly over the cream.

Makes 8 to 12 servings

Note: Crack the second egg yolk into
your palm. Use a knife to gently cut
through the center of the yolk, then
slide one half of the yolk into a cup
along with the first whole yolk. Put
the extra half yolk in a container in
the refrigerator and scramble it into
your kids' eggs the
next morning.

Chocolate-Crusted Peanut Butter Pie

$\mathcal{S}$ tart with a crust so deliciously crunchy that it would make a great candy bar, fill it with the flavor of peanut butter and the lightness of whipped cream cheese, and you've got yourself a dessert that's dangerous to have around the house.

INGREDIENTS

CRUST
2 cups coarsely chopped unsalted dry-roasted peanuts
1/4 cup granulated sugar
4 tablespoons (1/2 stick) unsalted butter, melted
3/4 cup semisweet chocolate chips

FILLING
8 ounces cream cheese, at room temperature
1/2 cup plus 2 tablespoons peanut butter (smooth or crunchy)
3/4 cup plus 2 tablespoons confectioner's sugar
1/2 cup milk
1 cup heavy (whipping) cream, chilled

1/2 ounce unsweetened chocolate for shaving

1. Preheat the oven to 375°F.

2. Place all the ingredients for the crust in a large bowl and toss them together with your hands or a wooden spoon.

3. Pat the mixture firmly into a 9-inch pie plate with your fingers, pushing it as far up the sides of the pan as possible.

4. Place the crust on the center oven rack and bake for 10 minutes. Place it in the freezer to cool completely, 15 minutes.

5. For the filling, using an electric mixer on medium speed, cream the cream cheese, peanut butter, and confectioner's sugar together in a medium-size mixing bowl until light and fluffy, about 1½ minutes. Scrape the bowl with a rubber spatula.

6. With the mixer on low speed, gradually add the milk and mix until it is incorporated, 10 seconds. Scrape the bowl and mix several seconds more.

7. Whip the cream in another mixing bowl to soft peaks and fold it into the peanut butter mixture.

8. Scoop the filling into the pie shell and freeze the pie for at least 6 hours.

9. Two hours before serving, move the pie from the freezer to the refrigerator. Shave chocolate over the top right before serving.

Makes 8 to 10 servings

Lemon Cream-Cheese Pie

*M*y version of a cream-cheese pie has quite a tart filling to enhance the variety of flavors. I've added a sour cream topping and graham cracker crust.

INGREDIENTS

1 recipe Cookie Crumb Crust
  made with graham crackers
  (page 178), baked

FILLING
9 ounces cream cheese, at room
  temperature
$\frac{1}{2}$ cup sugar
$1\frac{1}{2}$ teaspoons grated lemon zest
$\frac{1}{2}$ cup sour cream, at room
  temperature
1 large egg, at room temperature
5 tablespoons fresh lemon juice
1 teaspoon vanilla extract
2 tablespoons all-purpose flour

TOPPING
1 cup sour cream, at room temperature
3 tablespoons sugar
1 pint fresh raspberries or rinsed and
  hulled strawberries

1. Make the crumb crust and cool the baked shell.

2. Preheat the oven to 325°F.

3. Using an electric mixer on medium speed, cream the cream cheese, sugar, and lemon zest in a medium-size mixing bowl until light and fluffy, about 1 minute. Scrape the bowl halfway through and at the end.

4. Add the sour cream and mix on medium-low speed until the mixture is smooth, about 30 seconds. Scrape the bowl.

5. Beat in the egg, lemon juice, and vanilla on medium speed until blended, 30 to 45 seconds. Scrape the bowl.

6. Add the flour and mix just until blended, about 8 seconds. Pour the filling into the crust.

7. Bake the pie on the center oven rack until the top is rounded and springs back to the touch, 45 to 50 minutes. (A tester inserted in the center will not come out dry.) Small cracks may form on the surface.

8. Allow the pie to cool on a rack for 20 minutes.

9. Meanwhile, prepare the topping: Stir the sour cream and sugar together, and spread it over the cream-cheese filling. Return the pie to the oven for 5 minutes.

10. Allow the pie to cool to room temperature, then refrigerate it for 4 hours. Cover the top with whole fresh raspberries before serving.

Makes 8 to 12 servings

Strawberry Cream-Cheese Tart

Strawberries and cream have probably been keeping company since the first cow wandered into a berry patch. So herewith is my contribution to that excellent combination: a crunchy, buttery tart shell holding a sweet cream-cheese filling topped with whole strawberries. It's an elegant version of the classic New York cheesecake, and I like to display it on a cake pedestal for full effect.

INGREDIENTS

1 single-crust recipe Basic Tart Crust (page 176), lightly baked in 9-inch tart pan (page 167)

12½ ounces cream cheese (1½ large packages plus 1 tablespoon), at room temperature

¼ cup sour cream, at room temperature

½ cup sugar

¼ cup fresh lemon juice

2 large eggs, at room temperature

1 to 2 pints fresh strawberries, rinsed and hulled

½ cup strawberry or red currant jelly

1. Make the tart crust and cool the baked shell.

2. Preheat the oven to 350°F.

3. Cream the cream cheese, sour cream, sugar, and lemon juice in a food processor until thoroughly blended, about 30 seconds. Scrape the bottom and sides of the bowl with a rubber spatula.

4. Add the eggs and process for 10 seconds. Pour the filling into the tart shell.

5. Bake the tart on the center oven rack until the filling rises in the center and a toothpick inserted in the center comes out clean, about 40 minutes.

6. Cool the tart on a rack at least 2 hours. Top the tart with the strawberries arranged in concentric circles.

7. Heat the jelly in the top of a double boiler placed over simmering water until liquified. Glaze the berries by brushing the jelly over them with a pastry brush. Let the glaze set for 15 minutes. Serve the tart at room temperature.

Makes 8 to 10 servings

Linzertorte

*O*riginally from Vienna, the Linzertorte has become an extremely popular dessert in America. This beautiful lattice-topped tart is made from cookie dough rich in the flavor of ground almonds and fragrant spices. Layered between the crusts is a filling of raspberry preserves.

INGREDIENTS

CRUST
8 ounces almonds
1 cup (2 sticks) unsalted butter, at room temperature
3/4 cup sugar
1/4 teaspoon salt
1 teaspoon ground cinnamon
1/4 teaspoon ground cloves
1 teaspoon grated lemon zest
1 teaspoon grated orange zest
1 large egg
2 teaspoons vanilla extract
1 1/2 cups all-purpose flour
1 tablespoon unsweetened cocoa powder

FILLING
1 1/4 cups raspberry preserves (18-ounce jar)
2 teaspoons fresh lemon juice

1/4 cup finely chopped almonds for sprinkling

1. Preheat the oven to 400°F. Lightly grease an 11-inch tart pan with butter.

2. For the crust, process the almonds in a food processor until finely chopped, about 15 seconds. Set aside.

3. Using an electric mixer on medium speed, blend the butter, sugar, salt, spices, and citrus zests together in a medium-size mixing bowl just until the butter is incorporated, 15 to 20 seconds. Stop once to scrape the bowl with a rubber spatula.

4. Whisk the egg in a small bowl until blended; add 2 tablespoons of the egg to the butter mixture. Set aside the remaining egg for the glaze. Add the vanilla to the butter mixture and mix until they are incorporated, about 15 seconds. Scrape the bowl.

5. With the mixer on high speed, add the flour and the cocoa and beat just until blended, about 15 seconds. Scrape the bowl. Add the almonds on low speed and mix until blended.

6. Remove the dough from the mixing bowl and work it a bit with your hands so that it holds together. Break off about one-third of the dough, cover it with plastic wrap, and refrigerate it.

7. Press the remaining dough evenly over the bottom and up the sides of the prepared tart pan with your fingers. Wrap a strip of aluminum foil around the top edge of the pan and fold it over the very top of the crust to keep it from burning.

8. Bake the tart shell on the center oven rack until the dough loses its sheen and is golden, about 15 minutes. Cool the tart shell on a rack. Turn off the oven.

9. While the tart shell is baking and cooling, remove the dough from the refrigerator and place it between two pieces of plastic wrap or waxed paper. Roll it out to a rectangle about 12×8 inches. Slip this dough, still sandwiched between the plastic, onto a platter or cookie sheet and refrigerate it for 2 hours.

10. After 2 hours, preheat the oven to 400°F.

11. Remove the foil from the tart shell and set the foil aside.

12. For the filling, stir the raspberry preserves and lemon juice together in a small bowl. Spread the mixture evenly over the bottom of the baked tart shell.

13. Remove the chilled dough from the refrigerator and prepare the lattice. Peel off the top piece of plastic wrap and cut the dough lengthwise into 9 strips about ¾ inch wide.

14. Using a frosting spatula, carefully remove the first 4 strips from the paper one at a time and place them across the top of the tart. Pinch the edges of the strips down onto the top of the baked edge and save any extra dough. Then place the next 5 strips at right angles to the first 4 across the tart. Use the scraps to fill in the spaces along the edges of the crust between the lattice strips.

15. For the glaze, brush the remaining egg over the lattice strips with a pastry brush. Sprinkle the crushed almonds over the entire surface of the tart.

16. Replace the foil around the top edge of the tart and place the tart on the center rack of the oven. Bake it until the top is shiny and golden and the jam is bubbling, about 30 minutes.

17. Remove the tart from the oven and allow it to cool completely on a rack.

Makes 12 to 16 servings

Almond Raspberry Tartlets

*F*or these miniature tarts, I fill a butter crust with an almond paste mixture and accent it with raspberry preserves.

INGREDIENTS

*1 single-crust recipe Basic Tart Crust
    (page 176), dough refrigerated
    but not rolled out*
2½ ounces almond paste
5 tablespoons sugar
1 large egg, at room temperature
*1 tablespoon plus 1 teaspoon
    all-purpose flour*
2 teaspoons melted unsalted butter
¼ teaspoon salt
2 to 3 tablespoons raspberry preserves

1. Preheat the oven to 425°F. Have
ready 2 mini-muffin tins (twelve 1¾-
inch cups per pan).

2. Pinch off 24 rounded tablespoons
of the tart dough and press them into
the cups with your fingers so that
the dough forms a rim about ⅛ inch
above the top of the pan. The shells
should be about ³⁄₁₆ inch thick. (There
will be dough left over. This can be
wrapped and frozen for future use.)
Refrigerate the shells for 15 minutes.

3. Bake the shells on the center oven
rack until golden, about 10 minutes.
Cool on a rack. Reduce the heat to
350°F.

4. While the shells are baking, beat
all the remaining ingredients except
the raspberry jam in a small mixing
bowl with an electric mixer on
medium-high speed until thoroughly
mixed, about 1½ minutes.

5. Place ¼ teaspoon raspberry jam in
the bottom of each tart shell, then
spoon a rounded teaspoon of almond
filling over the jam.

6. Bake the tartlets until the tops are
golden and a tester inserted in the
center comes out dry, about 15 minutes. Cool for 2 hours before removing
the tartlets from the pans.

Makes 24 tartlets

Apple Brown Betty

*A*mong the important ques-
tions that will go unan-
swered in this book are who was
Betty and how did her name get
attached to this crumble, which
isn't particularly brown. It's
something you'll want to ponder,
no doubt, as you work your way
through its scrumptious pecan
crumb topping to the apples underneath. You may also find yourself pondering whether you even
need the apples with a crust this
good. Serve Apple Brown Betty
with vanilla or other favorite ice
cream.

FILLING

5 to 6 medium-size Granny Smith
 apples, peeled, cored, and cut into
 ³/₈-inch-thick slices (7¹/₂ cups)
5 tablespoons granulated sugar

TOPPING

²/₃ cup all-purpose flour
²/₃ cup (lightly packed) light brown
 sugar
²/₃ cup finely chopped pecans
¹/₂ teaspoon ground cinnamon
5 tablespoons plus 1 teaspoon (¹/₃ cup)
 unsalted butter, at room temperature, cut into 5 pieces

1. Preheat the oven to 350°F. Generously grease an 8-inch square baking
pan with butter.

2. Place half the apple slices in the
prepared pan and sprinkle them with
the granulated sugar. Layer the remaining apples over the sugar.

3. For the topping, place the flour,
brown sugar, nuts, and cinnamon in a
large bowl and stir them together with
a wooden spoon. Work the butter into
the mixture with your fingertips until
it is evenly distributed. Spread the
topping evenly over the apples.

4. Bake the betty on the center oven
rack until the topping is crunchy and
golden and the apples are bubbling,
55 to 60 minutes. Serve hot.

Makes 9 servings

Caramel Apple Casserole

*E*ven my cousin Kate Dooley,
who ingests 750 milligrams
of lecithin every day instead of
other fats, couldn't resist this
dessert. I felt a little guilty about
tempting her when I made it
with the Vermont apples we had
picked that day—but not very
guilty because even virtuous
people need an occasional treat
to remind them of how virtuous
they're being.

PASTRY

3 cups all-purpose flour
3 tablespoons granulated sugar
¹/₂ teaspoon salt
1 cup (2 sticks) unsalted butter,
 chilled, cut into 16 pieces
3 large egg yolks, at room temperature
2 tablespoons ice water

APPLE FILLING

5 medium-large apples, peeled, cored,
 and cut into ¹/₄-inch-thick slices
 (6 cups)
1 cup (lightly packed) light brown sugar
2 tablespoons fresh lemon juice
¹/₄ teaspoon salt

CARAMEL

8 tablespoons (1 stick) unsalted butter
¹/₂ cup granulated sugar

1. Preheat the oven to 375°F. Grease a 2-quart soufflé dish with butter.

2. To make the pastry, process the flour, granulated sugar, and salt in a food processor for 20 seconds. Add the butter and process until the dough resembles coarse meal, about 30 seconds.

3. Stir the egg yolks and water together in a cup. With the processor running, pour this mixture through the feed tube and process until the dough comes together, 35 seconds.

4. Remove the dough from the processor and knead it for several turns. Divide the dough into quarters and shape each piece into a thick round disk.

5. Roll each disk ⅛ inch thick between 2 pieces of plastic wrap (see page 165 for rolling instructions). Trim each disk to fit the soufflé dish. Stack the pancakes on a plate with plastic wrap between each layer and place them in the refrigerator while you prepare the filling.

6. Place all the ingredients for the filling in a large bowl and toss to evenly coat the apples. Set aside.

7. For the caramel, melt the butter in a small saucepan and stir in the granulated sugar. Bring the mixture to a boil over medium heat, then simmer for 2 minutes.

8. Pour two-thirds of the caramel into the prepared dish. Fit one pastry circle in the bottom over the caramel.

9. Place a third of the apple mixture (2 cups) over the pastry and top with a second pastry circle. Add another third of the apples, top with the third pastry circle, then the remaining apples and the fourth pastry circle.

10. Pour the remaining caramel over the top and spread evenly with a frosting spatula.

11. Cover the top of the dish with aluminum foil and pierce the foil in several places with the tip of a knife.

12. Place the dish on the center oven rack and put a cookie sheet on the rack below to catch any drips. Bake the casserole for 30 minutes. Remove the foil and continue baking until the top is golden and the apple mixture is bubbling, 30 to 35 minutes longer.

13. Remove the dish from the oven and cool on a rack. Serve warm or at room temperature.

Makes 8 servings

CHAPTER SIX

The Old
Smoothies

The recipes in this chapter have the odd distinction of being defined mostly by what they aren't: no flour, crust or icing, neither pie nor cake, square nor cookie. What's left over are custards, puddings, and chilled and whipped confections, the foods of childhood and old age. They're soothing and I like to think of them as a kind of culinary tribute to the roundness of life.

That leaves five other ages of man, and when I was growing up, we spent those eating Jell-O. Remember Jell-O? The dessert there's always room for, the thing you could count on finding at family restaurants, the only salad you'd eat and only then if your mother mixed it up with canned fruit and those little marshmallows that look like pussy willows? (My mother would never forgive me if I didn't note that marshmallow ne'er touched Jell-O in her kitchen, but I ate enough at friends' houses to know all about this concoction.)

It's likely that Jell-O is one of those things you put away with childhood and, with all due respect, that's probably for the best. But sophisticated as our palates may now be, that slithery, creamy texture, that flavor bursting onto our tongues almost as an afterthought provide the same familiar pleasure whether we're eating pudding, Bavarian, or crème brûlée—which are, after all, only fancy versions of the shimmery food we grew up on.

Apparently, food smoothness is a universal craving because puddings and custards show up in cooking almost everywhere in the world. Try out this richness on your tongue: mousse, charlotte, chiffon, coeur à la crème, tiramisù, baked Alaska, Persian cream, blancmange, blote kage, tapioca, meringue, weinschaum, zerde, zabaglione. And that's not even counting the wonderful names the English have for their puddings, like Poor Knights of Windsor and Grateful Pudding and, my favorite, Kiss-Me-Quick.

Now if you have a list of names a mile long for a single food, that says something about where it stands in your pantheon of pleasures, and, in fact, the British use "pudding" to signify all dessert. The children of my former neighbors would politely ask me what's for pudding when I invited them over for a meal, and it took me months to admit my cross-cultural clumsiness and ask their mother what they were talking about.

To me, pudding is custard, a fancier version of Beechnut baby food, though lighter and richer. I think of puddings and other chilled creations as the most seasonal of desserts (with the possible exception of pies before frozen fruit became passable). Chills and whips are the ideal dessert in the sultry summer months when you crave something sweet, but not ponderous. Others, such as Indian or bread pudding, are creatures of the autumn harvest months, and chocolate and butterscotch puddings are to me what sacrifices to the gods were for the ancients when the winter dark made them fear the sun would never return.

Pudding It all Together

*T*hese desserts are perhaps the most delicate of all to make because they demand precision and seldom allow for a middle ground. They don't usually take too long, though, and you'll find that once you're familiar with a few basic recipes, whole worlds of mousses, crèmes, and trifles will open to you. I've divided the recipes in this chapter into three categories in order to explain some of the preparation techniques.

Stove-Top Puddings

For puddings that contain liquid, sugar, cornstarch, and eggs, it is usually best to dissolve the cornstarch in a portion of the liquid and to stir in the eggs with a whisk. The remaining liquid should be heated with the sugar in a heavy saucepan over medium-low heat just to the boiling point. Then give the cornstarch mixture a final stir (it tends to settle as it sits) and add it in a stream to the boiling mixture while stirring vigorously with a whisk. The mixture is then brought to a second boil while stirring constantly and usually boiled for 10 to 30 seconds more to ensure proper thickening. It is essential for cornstarch to be brought to a boil in order for it to "clear," that is to lose its chalky taste and become less cloudy in appearance.

After the pudding has cooked, pour it into a large bowl. Let it sit for 10 minutes, stirring occasionally with a wooden spoon. Then cover the surface of the custard with plastic wrap that has been punctured several times with a knife or skewer to release steam and refrigerate.

Curdled eggs are the biggest problem that can occur with these puddings. If this starts to happen, you can do one of two things. Either pour the mixture immediately from the pot into a cool bowl and stir it vigorously with a whisk (you can strain it to check for evidence of cooked eggs), or pour the mixture into a blender and blend on medium-high speed for 5 to 10 seconds until it's smooth. The second process is more reliable for making your pudding smooth, but it also tends to loosen it.

Baked Custards

These desserts, which include such delights as Noodle Kugel, Pumpkin Caramel, and Baked Chocolate Custard, occasionally call for some stove-top cooking, but regardless of preliminaries, they're all baked in a large baking dish or individual ramekins after the ingredients have been stirred together in a mixing bowl.

I bake my custards in a water bath, which allows them to cook more evenly and gently. To make a water bath, put the custard dish or dishes in a shallow pan on the center rack of the oven, and pour enough hot water into the pan to come about two-thirds of the way up the sides of the custard baking dish.

For more delicate puddings, such as Chocolate Almond Custard, Peaches 'n' Cream Custard, and Baked Chocolate Custard, I find that individual ramekins allow the custard to bake more evenly than a large baking dish. Hearty puddings, such as the bread puddings, Noodle Kugel, and Indian Pudding, can be baked in large dishes with no problem.

Test if baked puddings are done by inserting a tester close to the center but not directly in it. If it comes out clean, the pudding is done. The center will continue to cook after the custard comes out of the oven. Remove the custard from the water bath as soon as it leaves the oven and allow it to cool to room temperature before refrigerating.

Mousses and Gelatin Desserts

Mousses are soft and creamy, sometimes frothy desserts which derive their lightness from egg whites and/or whipped cream. A classic chocolate mousse is made by folding whipped cream and/or beaten egg whites gently into a mixture of egg yolks and melted chocolate. I loosen the chocolate mixture by stirring in one-third of the egg whites with a whisk first, then completing the folding process with a rubber spatula.

Fruit mousses and chiffons are made by mixing fruit with juice and sometimes egg yolks, then adding gelatin to thicken the mixture slightly before folding in whipped cream and/or beaten egg whites.

Gelatin, if used properly, is a great enhancer, but too much of it can make a dessert tough and rubbery. I've found that most recipes call for too much. The chocolate in chocolate mousses gives them enough firmness, so they seldom require gelatin, though you can use it in conjunction with whipped cream or beaten egg whites. You can also use it with sour cream, heavy cream, cream cheese, or fruit juice for other desserts, such as fruit mousses, which need the gelatin to help them set so that they don't separate.

Before folding egg whites or whipped cream into a mixture that contains gelatin, let the gelatin mixture set enough first so that it forms a very loose mound when dropped from a spoon.

To unmold a gelatin dessert, moisten a chilled plate slightly and have it ready. Then run the point of a knife around the edge of the mold, turn it upside down over the plate, and put a hot, damp cloth over the bottom of the mold for several seconds. Shake it lightly to loosen the dessert onto the plate.

Pudding on the Ritz

*7*he desserts in this chapter vary greatly from hearty winter fare to the light, fruity gossamers that make a perfect end to a summer meal. Of the latter, fruit mousses and Bavarians are particularly lovely accented with fruit sauces. I like to serve each portion on a dessert plate and surround it with a pool of sauce that contrasts in both color and taste. Several slices of kiwi or whole strawberries make an attractive garnish. Add a couple of butter cookies on the side!

Bread pudding, Indian pudding, chocolate mousse, and traditional puddings, such as Daddy's Oedipal Chocolate Pudding and Butterscotch Pudding, are stick-to-your-rib sweets and are best served piled generously in a dessert bowl with whipped cream and in some cases a heavier bourbon or vanilla sauce.

The beauty of nearly all these desserts is the ease and speed with which they're made. Because so many of them call for ingredients you're likely to have around the house, you can literally whip up a little something at a moment's notice. And all that froth and shimmer make them look more impressive and less filling than they have a right to. Up until not so long ago, fancy restaurants would serve anything before they would use the word "pudding" on a dessert menu. It sounded so — heaven forbid — family style. But now they've learned what smart cooks knew all along — the proof is in the pudding.

Daddy's Oedipal Chocolate Pudding

*M*y father, the champion dessert eater, has never been much of a dessert maker, but this pudding is all his own. For those who prefer their comfort food on the rich, indulgent side, this one's for you!

INGREDIENTS

3 ounces unsweetened chocolate
1½ cups heavy (whipping) cream
2¼ cups milk
½ cup plus 2 tablespoons sugar
¼ cup cornstarch
2 large egg yolks
2 tablespoons unsalted butter,
*   cut into 2 pieces*
1 recipe Whipped Cream (page 86)
*   for serving*

1. Melt the chocolate in the top of a double boiler placed over simmering water.

2. Pour the cream, 1½ cups milk, and the sugar into a large saucepan. Heat over medium heat, stirring twice during this time, until scalded, about 5 minutes.

3. Meanwhile, in a medium-size bowl, dissolve the cornstarch in the remaining ¾ cup milk. Then whisk in the egg yolks.

4. Whisk the melted chocolate vigorously into the scalded mixture. Cover and heat over very low heat to blend, about 2 minutes. Uncover the saucepan and whisk again vigorously until the mixture is uniform in color and all specks of chocolate have disappeared.

5. Raise the heat to medium-low. Remove about 1 cup of the chocolate mixture from the pan and pour it in a stream into the egg yolk mixture while mixing vigorously with a whisk. (If the mixture should curdle, place it in a blender and blend it on low speed until smooth, 5 to 10 seconds.)

6. Bring the chocolate mixture remaining in the saucepan just to the boiling point and add the egg yolk mixture to it in a stream while mixing vigorously with a whisk. Mix constantly until the mixture thickens and forms loose mounds when dropped from the whisk back into the pan, 30 seconds.

7. Strain the pudding into a medium-size bowl and gently fold in the butter until it is completely incorporated.

8. Allow the pudding to sit for 5 minutes, stirring it gently several times to release steam. Puncture a piece of plastic wrap in several places with a knife or skewer. Lay it directly on the surface of the pudding. Leave the pudding at room temperature for 10 minutes. Then lift the plastic wrap and stir the pudding gently again.

9. Place the plastic wrap back on the surface of the pudding and refrigerate the pudding until chilled, 4 to 6 hours. Serve piled in a bowl topped with whipped cream.

Makes 8 to 10 servings

Butterscotch Pudding

*I*t must have been sometime during my high school years that I indulged myself almost daily with butterscotch pudding. This is an especially creamy version of that adolescent pleasure.

INGREDIENTS

2 cups milk
1 cup heavy (whipping) cream
1 cup plus 2 tablespoons (lightly packed) dark brown sugar
⅛ teaspoon salt
¼ cup plus 2 teaspoons cornstarch
2 large egg yolks, at room temperature
3 tablespoons unsalted butter, cut into 3 pieces
1½ teaspoons vanilla extract

1. Pour 1¼ cups of the milk, the cream, sugar, and salt in a heavy

medium-size saucepan. Heat over medium heat, stirring twice during this time, until scalded, about 5 minutes.

2. In a small bowl, dissolve the cornstarch in the remaining ¾ cup milk. Whisk in the egg yolks.

3. Remove about 1 cup of the cream mixture from the pan and pour it in a stream into the egg yolk mixture while mixing vigorously with a whisk. (If the mixture should curdle, place it in a blender and blend it on low speed until smooth, 5 to 10 seconds.)

4. Bring the cream mixture remaining in the saucepan just to the boiling point over medium-low heat. Then add the egg mixture in a stream while stirring vigorously with the whisk. Cook, stirring constantly, over low heat until the mixture thickens and forms loose mounds when dropped from the whisk back into the pan, 1½ minutes.

5. Strain the pudding into a medium-size bowl and gently fold in the butter and vanilla until they are completely incorporated. Allow the pudding to cool for 10 minutes, stirring it gently several times to release the steam. Puncture a piece of plastic wrap in several places with a knife or skewer. Lay it directly on the surface of the pudding. Refrigerate the pudding for at least 6 hours before serving.

Makes 4 to 6 servings

Creamy Stove-Top Rice Pudding

(for Eliot)

*T*his recipe took a lot of attempts to perfect, for it had a penchant for curdling. The method that I came up with, to my relief, is foolproof. The custard is cooked first so that if it curdles it can be put in the blender and made smooth again before adding the rice. Eliot, my business partner, is such a devotee of my rice pudding that he would drive miles to my house to eat it each time I tested the recipe.

INGREDIENTS

1¾ cups plus 2 tablespoons water
½ cup plus 3 tablespoons long-grain
    white rice
½ teaspoon salt
2 tablespoons unsalted
    butter
½ cup raisins
1 cup milk
1 cup heavy (whipping) cream
4 large eggs
7 tablespoons sugar
1 teaspoon ground nutmeg
1½ teaspoons vanilla
    extract

1. Bring the water, rice, and salt to a simmer in an uncovered, medium-size saucepan over medium-high heat. Cover the pan and simmer over low heat until the rice is tender, about 15 minutes. The water should be completely absorbed by the rice.

2. Remove the pan from the heat and stir in the butter and the raisins. Cover the pan and allow the rice to sit while you prepare the custard.

3. In a heavy large saucepan, vigorously whisk the milk, cream, eggs, sugar, and nutmeg until well blended.

4. Cook the mixture over low heat, whisking constantly, until it is thick enough to coat the back of a wooden spoon, 10 to 15 minutes. (The time may vary considerably depending on the pan and the stove.) Immediately remove the pan from the heat, stir in the vanilla, and then add the rice by large spoonfuls, stirring gently after each addition. (If the pudding should curdle before adding the rice, place it in a blender and blend on low speed until smooth, 5 to 10 seconds. Then pour the custard into a large bowl and add the rice.)

5. Allow the pudding to sit for 30 minutes, then cover and refrigerate until ready to serve. It can be served warm or cold.

Makes 8 servings

Chocolate Almond Custard

*L*ight and delicate, this custard is topped with a brownielike meringue.

INGREDIENTS

CUSTARD
2¹/₂ cups milk
¹/₂ cup heavy (whipping) cream
¹/₄ cup sugar
3 tablespoons cornstarch
Pinch of salt
2 large egg yolks,
  at room temperature
1 teaspoon almond extract

TOPPING
1¹/₄ ounces unsweetened chocolate,
  chopped
3 tablespoons heavy (whipping) cream
2 large egg whites,
  at room temperature
2 tablespoons sugar

1. Preheat the oven to 325°F. Lightly grease 6 ramekins with butter.

2. For the custard, scald 2 cups of the milk and the cream in a heavy medium-size saucepan over medium-low heat.

3. In a small bowl, combine the remaining ¹/₂ cup milk, the sugar, cornstarch, and salt and stir until the cornstarch is dissolved.

4. Stir the cornstarch mixture into the scalded milk and cook, stirring constantly, over medium-low heat until it boils, about 6 minutes. Remove the pan from the heat.

5. Gently stir the egg yolks with a fork in a small bowl. Gradually add one-third of the hot milk mixture to the yolks while whisking vigorously. Pour this mixture back into the remaining milk mixture, stirring constantly. Bring the custard to a boil while stirring constantly over medium-low heat and boil for 2 minutes.

6. Remove the pan from the heat and stir in the almond extract.

7. Fill each prepared ramekin two-thirds full with the custard.

8. Prepare the topping: Melt the chocolate with the cream in the top of a double boiler over simmering water. Mix it with a spoon, then pour it into a medium-size bowl.

9. Beat the egg whites with an electric mixer on high speed until frothy, about 30 seconds. Gradually add the sugar and continue beating the whites to form soft peaks, 30 seconds. Stir one-third of the whites into the chocolate rapidly with a whisk, then fold in the rest of the whites with a rubber spatula. The chocolate will be quite stiff, making the folding process somewhat difficult.

10. Top each cup of custard with 2 heaping tablespoonsful of the chocolate mixture.

11. Place the cups in a shallow baking pan on the center oven rack. Pour enough hot water into the baking pan to come two-thirds of the way up the sides of the ramekins.

12. Bake until the custard is loosely set and a tester inserted close to but not in the center comes out dry, about 45 minutes.

13. Remove the ramekins from the water bath; the custard will set further as it cools. Serve at room temperature.

Makes 6 servings

Baked Chocolate Custard

A dense, dark custard, this is great served hot or cold with whipped cream on top.

2 cups heavy (whipping) cream
¾ cup milk
1 cup semisweet chocolate chips
½ ounce unsweetened chocolate, cut into 4 pieces
6 large egg yolks, at room temperature
2 teaspoons vanilla extract
1 recipe Whipped Cream (page 86) for serving

1. Preheat the oven to 325°F. Lightly grease 6 ramekins with butter.

2. Combine the cream, milk, and both chocolates in the top of a double boiler. Heat over simmering water, whisking occasionally, until the chocolate is melted, 8 to 12 minutes. Then stir the mixture very briskly with the whisk until any specks or strands of chocolate are dissolved and the liquid is uniformly brown. Turn off the heat.

3. Using the whisk attachment of an electric mixer on medium-high speed, beat the egg yolks in a medium-size mixing bowl until thick and pale in color, 3 to 4 minutes.

4. Gradually add the chocolate mixture to the egg yolks, stirring rapidly with a whisk. Blend in the vanilla.

5. Pour the mixture through a sieve or strainer into the prepared ramekins. Place the ramekins in a shallow baking pan on the center oven rack. Pour in enough hot water to come two-thirds of the way up the sides of the ramekins.

6. Bake the puddings until a tester

inserted close to but not in the center comes out dry, about 1 hour 20 minutes.

7. Remove the ramekins from the water bath and serve warm or cold with whipped cream.

Makes 6 servings

Peaches 'n' Cream Custard

A rich and flavorful baked custard topped with fresh peaches that have been lightly sautéed in bourbon. It is best to prepare the topping right before serving. If you prepare it earlier, heat it slightly before spooning it over the custard.

I N G R E D I E N T S

CUSTARD
2¼ cups milk
¾ cup heavy (whipping) cream
1 cup plus 2 tablespoons (lightly packed) light brown sugar
5 large egg yolks
3 large eggs
2¼ teaspoons grated lemon zest
1¼ teaspoons vanilla extract
½ teaspoon salt
¾ teaspoon ground cinnamon

TOPPING
4 medium-size peaches, pitted and cut (with peel) into ½-inch-thick slices (about 4 cups)
2 tablespoons (lightly packed) light brown sugar
3 tablespoons fresh orange juice
Pinch of salt
2 tablespoons plus 2 teaspoons bourbon

1. Preheat the oven to 350°F. Lightly grease 8 ramekins with butter.

2. Place all the ingredients for the custard in a large bowl and stir vigorously with a whisk until completely blended.

3. Pour the custard mixture into the ramekins. Place them in a shallow baking pan on the center oven rack. Pour enough hot water into the baking pan to come two-thirds of the way up the sides of the ramekins.

4. Bake the custard until it is loosely set and a tester inserted close to but not in the center comes out clean, about 35 minutes.

5. Allow the custard to cool to room temperature, then cover with plastic wrap if you plan to refrigerate it. The custard should be at room temperature when served.

6. To prepare the topping, place the peaches, sugar, orange juice, and salt in a medium-size skillet. Bring to a simmer over medium-high heat; simmer until most of the liquid is absorbed but the peaches still hold their shape, 2 to 3 minutes.

7. Remove the skillet from the heat, add the bourbon, and toss gently.

8. Spoon the peaches on top of each custard and serve.

Makes 8 servings

Pumpkin Caramel Custard

*T*his smooth custard with a mild taste of pumpkin and a caramel glaze makes a nice surprise at the end of a winter holiday meal.

I N G R E D I E N T S

PUDDING
4 whole large eggs
3 large egg yolks
1½ teaspoons vanilla extract
2 cups milk
⅔ cup sugar
*1 tablespoon plus 1 teaspoon
    ground ginger*
1 teaspoon ground nutmeg
1 teaspoon ground cinnamon
1 teaspoon ground allspice
⅛ teaspoon ground cloves
½ teaspoon salt
½ cup canned pumpkin purée

CARAMEL
½ cup sugar
2 tablespoons water

1. Preheat the oven to 350°F. Arrange an oven rack just below the center. Grease a 6-cup soufflé dish with butter.

2. For the pudding, vigorously whisk the eggs, egg yolks, and vanilla in a large mixing bowl until blended. Set aside.

3. Place the milk, sugar, spices, and salt in a medium-size saucepan and set aside.

4. Place the sugar and water for the caramel in another medium-size saucepan and heat to boiling over medium heat without stirring. As soon as it boils, swirl the pan and continue swirling over the heat until the mixture turns a rich amber, 4 to 5 minutes.

5. Remove the caramel from the heat and immediately pour it into the prepared soufflé dish. Tilt the dish from side to side to evenly coat the bottom. Place the dish in a shallow baking pan. Pour enough hot water in the baking pan to come two-thirds of the way up the side of the soufflé dish. Set aside.

6. Bring the milk mixture just to a boil over medium heat. While whisking vigorously, pour the milk mixture in a thin stream into the egg mixture. Strain the mixture into a large bowl and whisk in the pumpkin, blending thoroughly so that there are no lumps.

7. Pour the pumpkin mixture into the soufflé dish and place it, with the baking pan, in the oven. Reduce the heat to 325°F and bake the custard until it is firm and a tester inserted close to but not in the center comes out clean, about 1¼ hours.

8. Remove the dish from the water bath. Cool the custard on a rack, then refrigerate it for 4 to 6 hours or overnight.

9. To serve, run a thin knife around the sides of the dish. Invert a serving dish on the soufflé dish and flip the custard carefully onto the serving dish.

Makes 8 servings

Truffle Soufflé

*I*n a book of recipes notable for their richness, this one probably takes the cake. It's loaded with butter and chocolate, and although it's flourless, you can slice it into pieces like a cake. But it works better scooped out like a pudding.

INGREDIENTS

4 ounces unsweetened chocolate, chopped

4 ounces semisweet chocolate, chopped, or ⅔ cup chocolate chips

1 cup sugar

2 teaspoons instant espresso powder

½ cup boiling water

4 large eggs, separated

2 teaspoons vanilla extract

1 cup (2 sticks) unsalted butter, melted and cooled to tepid

1 recipe Whipped Cream (page 86) for serving

1. Preheat the oven to 300°F. Lightly grease a 6- to 8-cup soufflé dish with butter.

2. Place both chocolates, ¾ cup of the sugar, and the espresso in a large bowl. Add the boiling water and stir until the chocolate melts. Cool the mixture to tepid.

3. Whisk the egg yolks and the vanilla together in a small bowl. Add the butter and whisk until the mixture is silky and smooth, about 10 seconds.

4. Using an electric mixer on medium-high speed, whip the egg whites in a medium-size mixing bowl until frothy, about 30 seconds. Gradually add the remaining sugar and continue beating until the whites form firm peaks, 1 minute.

5. Add the egg yolk mixture to the chocolate mixture and stir, then fold in the egg whites.

6. Pour the soufflé batter into the prepared dish and place the dish in a shallow baking pan on the center oven rack. Pour enough hot water into the baking dish to come two-thirds of the way up the sides of the soufflé dish.

7. Bake the soufflé until the top rises up and cracks, about 1½ hours. (A tester inserted in the center will not come out dry. When checking for doneness, be sure to open and close the oven carefully.) Turn the oven off and allow the soufflé to set for 1 hour in the water bath, in the oven. Serve the soufflé hot or warm, garnished with whipped cream.

Makes 6 to 8 servings

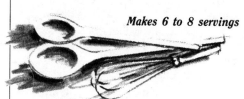

Chocolate Bread Pudding

*C*ertainly not your average bread pudding, this is more of a rich chocolate dessert with bread in it. It is great served hot or cold with whipped cream or vanilla ice cream. I like to use challah, which makes it a bit more special, but croissants or buttered French baguettes work well too.

INGREDIENTS

1½ cups milk
1¾ cups plus 2 tablespoons heavy (whipping) cream
6 tablespoons sugar
1½ cups semisweet chocolate chips
⅛ teaspoon salt
3 large eggs, lightly beaten with a fork
3 cups cubed (1-inch) challah, 3 croissants cut into ½-inch cubes (3 cups), or ⅓ French baguette, split lengthwise, generously buttered, and cut into ½-inch cubes (3 cups)

1. Heat the milk, cream, sugar, chocolate chips, and salt in a medium-size saucepan over low heat, whisking occasionally, until the chocolate is completely melted and all the chocolate specks are gone, 3 to 4 minutes. Remove the pan from the heat.

2. Briskly whisk in the eggs.

3. Place the cut-up bread in a large bowl and pour the chocolate mixture over the bread. Toss, then refrigerate the pudding for 2 to 3 hours, tossing the mixture occasionally with a large spoon to make sure all the bread is soaked. You can pull a few pieces apart with your fingers to check.

4. Fifteen minutes before baking, preheat the oven to 350°F. Generously grease a 6- or 8-cup soufflé dish with butter.

5. Scoop the pudding into the prepared dish. Bake on the center oven rack until the top is crisp, about 40 minutes. Then lay a piece of aluminum foil loosely over the surface of the pudding and bake until the pudding is set and a tester inserted close to but not in the center comes out dry, 30 minutes more. Cool slightly before serving.

Makes 8 to 10 servings

Bourbon Bread Pudding

7 his dessert melts in your mouth from its crunchy topping down through its custard filling, with or without the sauce. You can make it with crusty French bread, but I think that croissants make it extra special. Serve it warm on the first day and right out of the refrigerator thereafter.

1 cup heavy (whipping) cream
1 cup whole milk
4 large eggs
1 teaspoon vanilla extract
¼ cup bourbon
½ cup plus 2 tablespoons sugar
¼ teaspoon ground nutmeg
¼ teaspoon salt
3 to 4 croissants, cut into ½-inch cubes (4 cups), or ⅓ to ½ French baguette, split lengthwise, generously buttered, and cut into ½-inch cubes (4 cups)
⅓ cup dark raisins
Bourbon Sauce (recipe follows; optional)

1. In a large bowl, vigorously whisk the cream, milk, eggs, vanilla, bourbon, ½ cup of the sugar, nutmeg, and salt until blended. Add the bread cubes and toss to ensure even saturation.

2. Refrigerate the pudding for at least 2 hours, tossing the mixture with a large spoon occasionally to make sure all the croissants are soaked. You can pull a few pieces apart with your fingers to check.

3. Fifteen minutes before baking, preheat the oven to 350°F. Grease an 8-inch square baking dish with butter. Scoop the pudding into the baking dish. Sprinkle the remaining 2 tablespoons sugar over the top of the pudding.

4. Bake the pudding on the center oven rack until the top is crisp and golden and has risen in the center, about 50 minutes.

5. Allow the pudding to cool 30 minutes before devouring or, if you wish, while you make the sauce.

Makes 8 servings

Bourbon Sauce

I N G R E D I E N T S

½ cup sugar
2 large egg yolks
5 tablespoons bourbon
4 tablespoons (½ stick) unsalted butter, cut into 4 pieces

1. Pour ¾ inch water in the bottom of a double boiler and bring it to a simmer over medium-low heat.

2. Place the sugar and egg yolks in the top of the double boiler (not yet over the simmering water) and stir vigorously with a whisk until light in color.

3. Whisk in the bourbon and place the top of the double boiler over the simmering water. Cook, whisking vigorously, until the mixture is hot and slightly thickened, 3 to 4 minutes.

4. Pour the mixture through a fine strainer into a small bowl, add the butter, and stir until it melts.

5. Serve the sauce warm over the bread pudding. If you prepare the sauce ahead of time, reheat it in a double boiler over hot water.

Makes ¾ cup

Apple Bread Pudding with Vanilla Sauce

A classic pudding accented with tart apple chunks and vanilla sauce.

I N G R E D I E N T S

1 cup heavy (whipping) cream
1 cup milk
2 whole large eggs
2 large egg yolks
⅓ cup (lightly packed) light brown sugar
¼ teaspoon salt
1 teaspoon vanilla extract
2¼ teaspoons ground cinnamon
3 to 4 croissants, cut into ½-inch cubes (4 cups), or ⅓ to ½ French baguette, split lengthwise, generously buttered, and cut into ½ inch cubes (4 cups)
2 cups cubed (½-inch) peeled tart apples (about 3), such as McIntosh or Granny Smith
⅓ cup golden raisins
1 tablespoon plus 1 teaspoon granulated sugar
Vanilla Sauce (recipe follows)

1. In a large mixing bowl, vigorously whisk the cream, milk, eggs, egg yolks, brown sugar, salt, vanilla, and ¼ teaspoon of the cinnamon until blended.

2. Add the croissant cubes, apples, and raisins, and toss several times with a large wooden spoon to ensure even saturation.

3. Refrigerate the pudding for at least 2 hours, tossing the mixture occasionally with the wooden spoon to make sure the bread is soaked. You can pull a few pieces apart with your fingers to check.

4. Fifteen minutes before baking, preheat the oven to 350°F. Grease an 8-inch square baking dish with butter. Scoop the pudding into the baking dish. Mix the granulated sugar and the remaining cinnamon together and sprinkle it over the bread pudding.

5. Place the baking dish in a shallow baking pan on the center oven rack and pour enough hot water into the larger pan to come two-thirds of the way up the sides of the pudding baking dish.

6. Bake the pudding until the top is golden and crisp and has risen in the center, about 50 minutes.

7. Remove the pudding from the water bath and allow it to cool for 30 minutes while you make the sauce.

Makes 8 servings

Vanilla Sauce

INGREDIENTS

½ cup plus 2 tablespoons heavy (whipping) cream
½ cup plus 2 tablespoons milk
¼ cup sugar
¼ teaspoon salt
1 tablespoon cornstarch
3 tablespoons unsalted butter, cut into 3 pieces
1½ teaspoons vanilla extract
½ teaspoon ground nutmeg

1. Scald the cream, all but ¼ cup of the milk, the sugar, and salt in a heavy medium-size saucepan over medium heat.

2. Dissolve the cornstarch in the remaining ¼ cup milk in a small cup. Stir it into the cream mixture.

3. Bring the mixture to a boil over low heat, whisking constantly. Continue boiling and whisking until the sauce thickens, about 3 minutes.

4. Remove the pan from the heat and stir in the butter, vanilla, and nutmeg. Allow the sauce to cool slightly before serving.

Makes 1¼ cups

Indian Pudding

*T*he Puritan women learned how to make this dark, spicy dessert from the Indians, and it has remained a New England favorite ever since, probably because it warms the cockles and sticks to the bones during those long winters. My partner Eliot can't get enough of it. He likes it served warm with vanilla ice cream or heavy cream spooned over the top, so this recipe is for him.

INGREDIENTS

2 cups milk
1 cup heavy (whipping) cream
½ cup yellow cornmeal
½ cup (lightly packed) light brown sugar
½ cup molasses
1 teaspoon salt
2 teaspoons ground cinnamon
¼ teaspoon ground nutmeg
¼ teaspoon ground cloves
¼ teaspoon ground ginger
4 large eggs
4 tablespoons (½ stick) unsalted butter, cut into 4 pieces

1. Preheat the oven to 325°F. Lightly grease a 6- or 8-cup soufflé dish with butter.

2. Scald the milk in a medium-size saucepan over medium-low heat.

3. While the milk is heating, pour the cream into a medium-size bowl and stir in the cornmeal, sugar, molasses, salt, and spices.

4. Add the cornmeal mixture to the scalded milk and cook, whisking constantly, over medium-low heat until the pudding has thickened to the consistency of syrup, about 5 minutes. Remove it from the heat.

5. Beat the eggs in a small bowl with a whisk. Add ½ cup of the hot cornmeal mixture to the eggs while whisking rapidly. Then vigorously whisk the egg mixture into the remaining cornmeal mixture. Add the butter and stir until it melts.

6. Pour the pudding into the prepared baking dish, and place the dish in a shallow baking pan on the center oven rack. Pour enough hot water into the larger pan to come two-thirds of the way up the sides of the pudding baking dish.

7. Bake the pudding until it is set and a tester inserted close to but not in the center comes out clean, about 1¼ hours.

8. Remove the pudding from the water bath and cool slightly. Serve the pudding warm.

Makes 10 servings

Noodle Kugel

*A*lthough this pudding traditionally accompanies a plate of brisket, I always find myself continuing to indulge in it long after the meat is gone. So I've sweetened the basic recipe and serve it as a dessert, warm or cold.

INGREDIENTS

8 ounces enriched broad egg noodles
2 cups sour cream
8 ounces whipped cream cheese
8 ounces small- or large-curd cottage cheese
½ cup plus 4 teaspoons sugar
2 teaspoons grated lemon zest
¼ teaspoon salt
4 large eggs
8 tablespoons (1 stick) unsalted butter, melted
¾ cup golden raisins
2 teaspoons ground cinnamon

1. Preheat the oven to 350°F. Lightly grease a 13 × 9-inch baking pan with butter.

2. Cook the noodles in a large pot of boiling water until tender but still slightly firm, about 7 minutes. Drain and set aside.

3. Place the sour cream, cream cheese, cottage cheese, ½ cup sugar, the lemon zest, and salt in a food processor and process until blended, about 20 seconds.

4. Add the eggs and butter and process until incorporated, about 5 seconds more.

5. Pour the cream cheese mixture over the noodles in a large bowl, add the raisins, and toss the pudding together with a large spoon.

6. Spread this kugel evenly into the prepared pan. Mix the remaining 4 teaspoons sugar and the cinnamon and sprinkle it over the top.

7. Bake the pudding on the center oven rack until the top is crisp, the center is firm and has risen, and a tester inserted in the center comes out dry, 45 to 50 minutes. Cool at least 30 minutes before serving.

Makes 10 to 12 servings

Chocolate Mousse

*T*hough it may verge on culinary cliché by now, I've found a good chocolate mousse to be one of the mainstays of dessert making. Part of the reason is that it's easy to make, but considered a major accomplishment — kind of like having mastered the soufflé.

This recipe imparts a no-nonsense, full-bodied taste from the first spoonful to the last.

INGREDIENTS

9 ounces semisweet chocolate

3 ounces unsweetened chocolate

2 large eggs, at room temperature

4 large eggs, separated, at room temperature

2 tablespoons rum, or 2 tablespoons strong brewed coffee, or 1 tablespoon each rum and coffee

1¼ cups heavy (whipping) cream, chilled

2 tablespoons sugar

1 recipe Whipped Cream (page 86) for serving

½ ounce unsweetened chocolate for shaving

1. Melt both chocolates in the top of a double boiler placed over simmering water.

2. Whisk the 2 whole eggs and 4 egg yolks together in a large bowl until blended. Whisk in the rum and/or coffee.

3. Add the chocolate to the whole egg mixture and whisk very vigorously so the eggs don't curdle. Cool just to room temperature.

4. Meanwhile, using an electric mixer on high speed, beat the cream in a medium-size mixing bowl, until soft peaks form, 1 minute. Chill in the refrigerator.

5. In a separate bowl, beat the egg whites until frothy, about 15 seconds.

Gradually add the sugar and continue beating until the whites form soft peaks, 30 seconds more.

6. Add one-third of the egg whites to the chocolate mixture and whisk to loosen the mixture, then fold in the rest of the whites. Fold in the cream.

7. Spoon the mousse into a 2-quart serving bowl or 8 individual dessert cups. Refrigerate immediately for at least 6 hours. Serve with whipped cream and chocolate shavings (see page 33). Eat within one day of making.

Makes 8 servings

Chocolate Cream-Cheese Mousse

*W*hen I realized that most of my chocolate desserts have a bittersweet flavor, I set out to find something that was pure sweetness, and this is it. The taste is like a Hershey's Kiss, and the texture like a dense mousse because of the cream cheese.

INGREDIENTS

MOUSSE

3 ounces semisweet chocolate
3 ounces unsweetened chocolate
8 ounces cream cheese, at room
*   temperature*
¾ cup sugar
3 large eggs, separated
1½ teaspoons vanilla extract
1½ cups heavy (whipping) cream,
*   chilled*

BOURBON CREAM

1 cup heavy (whipping) cream
2 tablespoons sugar
3 tablespoons bourbon

½ ounce semisweet or unsweetened
*   chocolate for shaving*

1. Melt both chocolates in the top of a double boiler over simmering water.

2. Process the cream cheese and ½ cup of the sugar in a food processor until smooth, about 10 seconds. Scrape the bowl with a rubber spatula.

3. Add the egg yolks and vanilla and process until smooth, about 5 seconds. Add the hot chocolate and process until the mixture is velvety, about 10 seconds. Transfer it to a large mixing bowl.

4. Using an electric mixer on high speed, whip the cream in a medium-size mixing bowl just until the peaks are firm, 1¼ minutes.

5. Whip the egg whites in a separate bowl on medium-high speed until frothy, 15 seconds. Gradually add the

remaining ¼ cup sugar and continue beating until the whites form soft peaks, 30 seconds more.

6. Whisk about one-third of the whites into the chocolate mixture to lighten it, then fold in the rest of the whites.

7. Fold in the whipped cream.

8. Pour the mousse into a 2-quart serving bowl and refrigerate at least 8 hours or overnight.

9. Just before serving, prepare the bourbon cream: Using an electric mixer on high speed, beat the cream, sugar, and bourbon in a medium-size bowl until soft peaks form, 1 minute.

10. Scoop out small portions of the mousse and serve each portion with a dollop of the bourbon cream. Shave chocolate over the cream (see page 33). Eat within one day of making.

*Makes 12 to
16 servings*

Coeur à la Crème

*T*his rich dessert is surprisingly delicate in taste, perhaps because it's not too sweet. It takes its name from the heart-shaped mold, and I find that it's a wonderful accompaniment to peeled and sliced peaches and plums, or fresh or frozen strawberries and raspberries. Toss the fruit with a bit of sugar before serving.

INGREDIENTS

1 cup small- or large-curd cottage cheese, at room temperature

8 ounces cream cheese, at room temperature

½ cup sour cream, at room temperature

½ cup heavy (whipping) cream, at room temperature

½ cup plus 2 tablespoons sugar

1. Line a 2-cup coeur à la crème mold with a double layer of cheesecloth that overhangs all sides and place the mold on a larger plate.

2. Process all the ingredients in a food processor until smooth, 20 to 30 seconds.

3. Use a rubber spatula to scoop the cream cheese mixture into the mold and smooth the surface. Fold the excess cheesecloth over the top and re-frigerate at least 8 hours or overnight.

4. To serve, unfold the cheesecloth. Invert a serving plate over the mold and flip the crème onto the plate. Gently remove the mold and the cheesecloth.

5. Serve small portions along with fruit, if desired.

Makes 8 servings

Orange Cream-Cheese Bavarian

*J*ust when you think your Thanksgiving menu will never change, along comes this Bavarian that mixes the flavors of orange and cranberry with the smooth richness of cream cheese, and *voilà!*—the perfect and unexpected dessert.

INGREDIENTS

BAVARIAN
¼ cup cold water
1 envelope unflavored gelatin
1 cup heavy (whipping) cream
8 ounces cream cheese
1 can (6 ounces) frozen orange juice
    concentrate
¼ cup sugar
1½ teaspoons vanilla extract
1 tablespoon fresh lemon
    juice

CRANBERRY SAUCE
1¾ cups cranberries
1½ cups fresh orange juice
5 tablespoons sugar
½ teaspoon grated orange zest

Fresh mint leaves and cranberries
    for garnish

1. Grease a 4-cup mold or bowl lightly with vegetable oil.

2. Put the water and gelatin in a food processor and process for 5 seconds.

3. Heat the cream just to the boiling point, then pour it into the food processor. Process to dissolve the gelatin, about 10 seconds.

4. Add the cream cheese, orange juice concentrate, sugar, vanilla, and lemon juice and process another 10 seconds.

5. Pour the mixture into the prepared mold and refrigerate until set, 3 to 4 hours.

6. Meanwhile prepare the sauce: Place the cranberries and ½ cup of the orange juice in a small saucepan. Simmer covered over medium heat until the berries crack and become soft, 2 to 3 minutes. Remove the pan from the heat and stir in the sugar and orange zest.

7. Pour the cranberry mixture and the remaining 1 cup juice into a food processor and process to a purée. Strain the purée into a small bowl and cover with plastic wrap until ready to serve.

8. To serve, remove the Bavarian from the mold (see page 217). Slice it and spoon the sauce around the slice on a small dessert plate. Garnish each plate with several mint leaves and whole cranberries.

Makes 12 servings

Smooth as Silk with Raspberry Sauce

A slippery smooth Bavarian with a hint of lemon, accented with a raspberry sauce.

INGREDIENTS

BAVARIAN

1½ teaspoons unflavored gelatin
½ cup water
1 cup light cream
½ cup plus 1 tablespoon sugar
1½ teaspoons grated lemon zest
1¼ teaspoons vanilla extract
1 cup sour cream

RASPBERRY SAUCE

2 pints fresh raspberries
⅓ to ½ cup sugar
2 tablespoons fresh lemon juice or
    orange juice

1 kiwi, cut into 6 slices, for garnish

1. Stir the gelatin into the water to soften in a small bowl. Set aside.

2. Place the cream and sugar in a medium-size saucepan over low heat, stirring frequently until the sugar is dissolved, 3 to 4 minutes.

3. Add the softened gelatin to the cream mixture and stir until it is dissolved. Remove the pan from the heat, stir in the lemon zest and the vanilla, and cool the mixture to room temperature.

4. When cool, add the sour cream and stir until completely blended. Pour the mixture into 6 dessert cups or wine glasses and refrigerate for 4 hours.

5. To make the sauce, purée the raspberries with the sugar in a food processor for about 10 seconds.

6. Strain the mixture into a small bowl, add the lemon or orange juice, and stir.

7. Just before serving, pour the sauce over each Bavarian. Garnish with a slice of kiwi.

Makes 6 servings

Rosie's BAKERY

CHOCOLATE-
P·A·C·K·E·D
JAM-FILLED
BUTTER-RICH
N O - H O L D S - B A R R E D
COOKIE
BOOK

IN PRAISE

OF COOKIES

There's no getting around it: I love cookies. We go back a long way, after all, since I first made their acquaintance by way of a zweiback that my mother stuck in my eager hands around the time I got my first tooth. I like to think it was more than mere instinct that led me to insert it directly into my mouth and gum away to my heart's content, knowing with baby certainty that here was a thing of glory.

Call it a knowledge bred in the bone, or maybe an omen that one day I would switch from living *for* cookies to making my living *from* cookies. It's a big burden to put on a little cookie, I know, but the memory of zweiback's combination of crunch and light sweetness came flooding back when I became a professional baker years later, and it stayed with me as I opened each Rosie's Bakery, reminding me that there are few things in this world more deeply satisfying than a really good cookie.

Armed with that first taste of happiness, I became a toddler with a mission. It was cookies I craved, and cookies I demanded. As soon as my first tooth was joined by a few others, I moved on to arrowroots. Now *there* was a cookie: crisp, buttery, dainty, decidedly more big-girl than zweiback. I sucked on the arrowroots too, but when I was ready to take real bites, I graduated to Lorna Doones, which even grown-ups ate.

Hot on the Cookie Trail

After that, whole worlds opened up to me, and with those limitless possibilities, nothing would do but to try them all. From the store: Oreos, Vienna Fingers, Nutter Butters, gingersnaps, the wafers (sugar and vanilla), Fig Newtons, animal crackers, windmills, and chocolate chips. And then there were the bar cookies: the brownies and butterscotch bars and dream bars and lemon bars and Congo bars. I reveled in them all, Nabisco's best and those homemade blue-ribbon winners.

Obviously I didn't arrive home from school each day to batches of cookies freshly pulled from the oven. My mother's not exactly the Norman Rockwell type, but that didn't matter. She knew a good cookie when she met one, and since cookies had carved out a place for themselves in my pantheon of essential foods, I made sure I got my fix in lots of other places.

In my childhood, midtown Manhattan wasn't what you'd call Girl Scout country, but some enterprising little girl always made her way up to our apartment each spring, bearing boxes of mint chocolate wafers and peanut butter sandwiches, which I urged my parents to buy in bulk and squirrel away for emergencies. (My kids do the same thing with me now, thinking that they're urging me too, but the truth is that I'd never skip a year of doing my part for Girl Scout cookie sales.)

Then there were the cookies you could buy by the pound at William Greenberg, a New York bakery that's still going strong. They were bite-size, many-shaped, and just sweet enough to please—a classier version of the bakery cookies that were standard fare at every bar mitzvah and wedding reception throughout the 1950s (although I confess to a lingering fondness for the pink and green checkered ones that were part of that mix).

Come high school, I made a daily stop at a bakery on my way home to get a half moon, those chubby cakelike rounds iced with half chocolate, half vanilla. And on weekends there were all those old favorites on the grocery store shelves. I could spend a half-hour, easy, deciding which kind to buy.

Any time was cookie time, but it was mostly at night that I indulged. You know—a little milk, a few cookies to soak it up, the perfect ending to the day. I could still go through a bag in a sitting today, if I hadn't reached this age of stunning self-restraint. Now, at the end of a meal I often crave just a taste of something sweet, and I've often thought that restaurants would do well to offer a cookie or two as an alternative to elaborate desserts. Hold the tiramisù, the kumquat–passion fruit coulis, the chocolate mocha devil's food mud pie. Just give me a couple of cookies on a plate, stately and elegant in their simplicity.

Of course, part of the pleasure of cookies is that they *can* be eaten in moderation and can be moderate in themselves. I know this goes against the prevailing morality, but let me throw caution to the winds and state unequivocally that the road to uncertain virtue is not paved with cookies. You can eat one butter-and-sugar-filled cookie— hey, even two or three—without condemning yourself to a lifetime of fat or ill-health. I'm of the belief that attending to your desires from time to time is a lot healthier than denial, anyway.

The Sweetest of Times

My soft spot for cookies isn't based just on taste. Rosie's Bakery—my work and my pleasure—came into being by way of a batch of sugar cookies I decorated for a long-ago Valentine's Day. Overdecorated might be a more accurate description: with feathers, sugar pearls, food coloring, and flowers, I really went to town. Opening a bakery was the last thing on my mind, but there it was, Valentine's Day, and cookies straight from the heart seemed the proper way to celebrate. It didn't hurt that they sold out at the galleries and the cake shop that stocked them, nor that customers clamored for more.

I figure that zweiback epiphany had something to do with it too, since there weren't a lot of other signs that I was destined to become a baker. I had never been one to play house or throw tea parties for my dolls, and until I began baking for public consumption, my repertoire consisted chiefly of a dynamite brownie recipe and an occasional birthday cake when no one else could be roped into making one. But I had always gravitated to food. I liked eating it, of course, but I also liked talking about it, looking at pictures of it, just being around it. Other people get that buzz, that all's-right-with-the-world feeling from books or ballparks, fast cars or frequent-flyer miles. For me, it's food—preferably of the sweet, bite-size variety.

So Rosie's began in 1974 with that batch of cookies, and before I knew it, I was officially in business in Harvard Square. In those days Cambridge, Massachusetts, wasn't like anyplace else. It's still not Main Street, U.S.A., but in the early 1970s there was such a sense of possibility—the air was positively perfumed with it. Graduate students were ferreting out the discovery that would change the world, revolutionaries were crafting the ideal society, teachers instructed in peace and harmony, feminists claimed their place in the sun, artists opened galleries, musicians serenaded on street corners, and everyone was writing the great American novel. All that ferment needed to be fed, and Rosie's Bakery was on the scene to feed mind, body, and soul.

In those early days, there was only me. I was up before sunrise to order the ingredients, prepare the batters, scoop the cookies, bake the pies, cut the brownies, frost the cakes, set up the bakery cases, sell the cookies, brownies, pies, and cakes, then wash the dishes and mop the floor before going home to catch four hours of sleep so I could begin all over the next morning. You have to like cookies an awful lot to keep that up, but I too was caught up in the free-floating optimism. I marvel a little, even now as I say it, but I learned how to be a baker by being one. I gathered and tested recipes, experimented with flavors and textures, tried different taste combinations. I was on the trail of something new, and I was having a great time! What sweeter way to greet the brave new world, I reasoned, than surrounded by chocolate chip cookies and sour cherry cream cheese brownies?

Food for All Ages

♥ ♥ ♥ ♥ ♥ ♥ ♥ ♥ ♥ ♥ ♥ ♥ ♥ ♥

Now—two decades, three stores, and millions of cookies and brownies later—Rosie's still meets the needs of the artists, teachers, revolutionaries, novelists, graduate students who have become professors, feminists who are also parents, and a host of other people who remember the '70s fondly, skeptically, or not at all. Cookies, it seems, are something we can all agree on.

As kids, we nosh on them. Then we learn to bake by making them when Mom or our teacher lets us add the chocolate chips and, in time, crack the eggs and mix the batter. Later on, we binge on them while we pull all-nighters at college, whip up a batch to impress our lovers, sell them at bake sales to raise money for worthy causes. Eventually we come full circle to teach our children how to make them, and finally we offer them joyfully to our beloved grandchildren.

Given all that, it's clear that cookies aren't just for kids. There's the occasional ambivalence: we tsk-tsk over those caught with their hand in the cookie jar or imply that we must tuck cookies away with our ballerina and firefighter dreams in order to be serious adults. But twenty years of chocolate chip cookies on Rosie's best-seller list have convinced me that the craving for cookies doesn't lessen with age.

The Collective Cookie Consciousness

♥ ♥ ♥ ♥ ♥ ♥ ♥ ♥ ♥ ♥ ♥ ♥ ♥ ♥

Cookies are part of a shared American experience, but we can't claim them all for ourselves. They've been delighting people all over the world for centuries: shortbread from Scotland; gingerbread from England (rumor has it that the first Queen Elizabeth invented the gingerbread man when she ordered her cooks to make little ginger cakes to imitate her courtiers); macaroons, éclairs, meringues, and other delectables from France; biscotti from Italy; kipfel from Austria; all manner of butter and spice cookies from the Netherlands, Germany, Scandinavia, Russia, and Greece.

Cookies seem to have made their debut in the south of France about 400 years ago. As the story goes, cooks tested the heat of their ovens by dropping little cakes onto hot pans; when they were baked, they were given to children as treats, presumably because they weren't fit food for grown-ups.

We know they were wrong, of course, but the childhood joy in cookies is certainly part of their appeal for me. I bake cookies because I want to pass on to my children the taste memories I treasure—the butter crunch of real shortbread, the rich ooze of good chocolate. Sharing food and the making

of it has always been a bond, tying generations together. I want to offer those resonant tastes to my customers too, which is another reason why I bake and the prime one behind my enthusiastic "yes!" when my editor asked if I would be interested in writing a cookie book.

I wasn't alone in my excitement. All I had to do was announce the project to my kids and their cookie reflex kicked in higher than a line of Rockettes. They're used to having a mother who's up to her elbows in desserts every day, but a seemingly endless supply of cookies just waiting to be tasted must have conjured up Charlie's chocolate factory *and* a convention of stove-happy grandmothers, all in their very own kitchen. On cookie-baking days (which became nearly every day while this book was in progress), their pleasure perfumed the air more strongly than any spice, until we all slept with visions of snickerdoodles dancing in our heads.

My husband, Richard, was happy too, since he and I are living proof of the old adage about the way to a man's heart. Richard was a customer in my Cambridge store when he fell in love . . . with my chocolate chip cookies. Sometime later, he decided to ask me out, and the rest, as they say, is history.

The neighbors didn't mind my cookie marathon, either, nor did my kids' teachers, their playmates, the parents who stopped by to pick them up, my friends, nor anyone staging a bake sale or reception during the past two

years. My freezer was stuffed with cookies of all manner, ensuring that there was never an occasion for which I was not prepared.

Though I was glad to be a community resource, preparing a cookbook is a serious and consuming enterprise. I was immersed in perfecting recipes and baking techniques, culling the best from all those that had crossed my path over the years. I wanted to create a cookbook that would provide the only recipes you'd ever need for old standbys while offering a generous heap of new possibilities as well. And I was determined to find ways to make baking cookies easy and enjoyable so that you too could be prepared for all occasions—and for some non-occasions as well. It's my hope that you'll use this gathering of cookies as a kind of workbook, one to be underlined, starred, and notated for repeated use and future reference. That's what a cookbook is meant to be, after all: a sharing of knowledge and a laying on of hands.

Which, of course, is a large part of the pleasure in baking and eating cookies—those sweet mouthfuls that are portable, palatable, individual, ornamental, neat to eat, and simple to make. All praise, and pass the cookie jar.

CHAPTER 1

RULES OF THE GAME

t is true that cookies are a large part of the essence of childhood. "Cookie" is one of the first words babies learn and among the top ten they continue to use long after their vocabularies have expanded. Cookies are rewards, sneak treats, even bribes, I confess. And when kids try their hand at cooking, chances are that cookies will be one of the first things they make. That's because you learn to cook first what you like to eat best.

But cookies don't lose their appeal when we grow up—why should they? Cookies can be as sophisticated as we want them to be. Even those childhood favorites can be baked in smaller sizes and displayed elegantly, can be dipped in imported chocolate, cut in fancy shapes, studded with hazelnuts, accented with liqueurs . . . or eaten just as they were in the old days. Cookies are a sweet that we never tire of.

Into the Mouths of Babes

♥ ♥ ♥ ♥ ♥ ♥ ♥ ♥ ♥ ♥ ♥ ♥ ♥ ♥ ♥

I love making cookies with my kids— with everybody's kids, in fact. Kids are great on quality control, and they're full of enthusiasm for the product—and usually for the process too, because it's wonderfully straightforward. I ask you: what could possibly cement the parent-child bond more solidly than a gob of cookie dough in common?

For me, a large part of the pleasure in baking cookies with kids comes in what they reveal about themselves as they contribute to the process. Before my children and I first made cookies together, I had perfect-mother fantasies that each of them would have their own kind of cookie, and I even named a few after them in encouragement. Then reality intervened. Now that they're old enough to help me bake when they want to, I spend much more time trying to keep everything even-steven than I do inventing toothsome new creations that they'll remember all their lives.

Still, each of the kids has carved out a role in the cookie baking process, though that happened more because of their personalities than because of my designs. My daughter, Maya, is meticulous by nature, so she's a natural at arranging the cookies. Her twin, Noah, is a sugar freak whose only goal in making cookies is to get as much batter into his mouth as possible. And their older brother, Jake, has reached the age of coolness, which means that he would never deign to take part in something so unhip as baking cookies. Funny, but coolness doesn't get in the way of his eating his share.

What you end up with when you bake with kids may look less than perfect, but with cookies, the making is so delectable and the eating is so satisfying that art is beside the point. Also, children aren't yet saddled with conventional wisdom about what a cookie *should* be, and more than once, the freedom of their imagination has given me ideas for new combinations. After all, if chocolate and cherries go together in ice cream, why not in cookies too? And why *can't* cheesecake come in bars or Boston cream pie in cookies?

But, enough about baking with children. Rest assured cookies can be baked successfully even when you bake them alone!

Doughs and Don'ts

♥ ♥ ♥ ♥ ♥ ♥ ♥ ♥ ♥ ♥ ♥ ♥ ♥ ♥ ♥ ♥

After that paean to unbridled creativity, it seems pedestrian to return to do's and don'ts. But return I do, because there are techniques and hints that will make your cookie baking smoother—or chunkier, crispier, or whatever you're aiming for. A read-through of this chapter will set you in good stead for tackling any of the recipes that follow.

Good Bakers Praise Their Tools

♥ ♥ ♥ ♥ ♥ ♥ ♥ ♥ ♥ ♥ ♥ ♥ ♥ ♥ ♥ ♥

I don't know if it will come as a relief or a disappointment to know that baking cookies doesn't require much equipment. Some cooks I know spend as much time in kitchen stores as in the kitchen, which I admit is an excellent form of procrastination and certainly a boon to the economy. For the rest of us, though, most of the recipes in this book can be made with the following basic items.

♥ An *electric mixer* with paddle and whisk attachments and two mixing bowls. I prefer a mixer mounted on a base because it leaves your hands free to do other things while the batter is mixing. But a sturdy hand-held mixer does the trick as well, although it may take slightly longer.

♥ A *food processor*. This nearly all-purpose machine is excellent for grinding the nuts and fruits many cookies call for and for mixing shortbread dough and pastry crusts. I find myself using it more and more in my baking and can't remember how we got along without it in the old days.

♥ Three good-quality *baking sheets*. These should be flat, with slightly rolled edges. Shiny heavy-gauge aluminum is good, and so is a nonstick surface such as Silverstone. Air-cushion pans may now be all the rage, but I'm not crazy about them. Cookies baked on them don't get enough heat, so drop cookies don't crisp enough around the edges, cakey cookies spread too much, and shortbreads take forever.

❤ Several *mixing bowls* of various sizes.

❤ A set of *measuring scoops* for dry ingredients. (Glass measuring cups aren't accurate here.)

❤ A set of *measuring spoons*.

❤ A set of *measuring cups* for liquids.

❤ Two sturdy *rubber spatulas* for scraping bowls and folding in ingredients.

❤ Two *whisks:* one small, one medium.

❤ A medium-size *sifter* or *strainer* for sifting dry ingredients.

❤ A *wooden spoon* for custard fillings.

❤ A *metal spatula* for lifting the baked cookies off the baking sheet.

❤ *Parchment paper,* an absolute must for lining baking sheets, as I'll explain later (see "The Well-Tempered Pan," page 11).

❤ A *timer* to alert you when the cookies are ready.

❤ Two or three *wire cooling racks*.

❤ Two small *microwave-safe* or *Pyrex dishes* for softening butter and cream cheese and melting chocolate.

❤ A *double boiler* for melting chocolate on the stove.

❤ Several good-quality air-tight plastic *containers* for storage.

❤ A *butter knife* or *small spatula* for frosting and filling cookies.

Getting the Goods

❤❤❤❤❤❤❤❤❤❤❤❤❤❤❤

I'm a great fan of experiments. On more than one occasion, that's how I've come up with a new or improved recipe or saved a less-than-stellar batch of cookies from oblivion. But when it comes to what goes into cookies, I become considerably less laissez-faire. The simple and commonsense truth is that good baking depends on good ingredients. That means that in most cases, the quality of your cookies will be in direct proportion to the quality of the ingredients you use.

Quality doesn't necessarily mean most expensive or hardest to find. In keeping with the trinity of cookiedom—convenience, availability, and yumminess—most of the ingredients in these recipes are available at your average grocery store and won't require you to leave an arm or leg in payment.

Flour

The recipes in this book usually call for either all-purpose or cake flour. I like to keep pre-sifted all-purpose flour on hand in case I'm feeling lazy and want to avoid extra steps. But because all flour settles as it sits, it's a good idea to sift even this flour along with the salt and leavening to make sure it's evenly incorporated.

Since cake flour is powdery and contains less gluten than all-purpose flour, it works better in certain cookies. But it *must* be sifted before or after it's measured or it will remain lumpy. When you sift it depends on the recipe. I'm told plain cake flour can be hard to find in some parts of the country, so if you run into that problem, you can substitute 1 cup minus 2 tablespoons of all-purpose flour for 1 cup of cake flour (you may find that you have to make some other adjustments too).

Formula:
1 cup – 2 tablespoons all-purpose flour=
1 cup cake flour

One note: Regular cake flour is *not* the same as self-rising cake flour. I had a call recently from a woman who had tried to make a couple of the cake recipes in *Rosie's All-Butter, Fresh Cream, Sugar-Packed, No-Holds-Barred*

Baking Book and had created Mt. Vesuvius in her oven. Her kids declared it more fun than their chemistry set, but she was somewhat less pleased. Still, she was curious about what had gone wrong, and so was I. After we talked for a while, she mentioned that she had used self-rising cake flour, and the case was solved. Self-rising cake flour already contains leavening, so by adding the leavening the recipes called for, she had seriously overloaded the equation.

Butter

Since we seem to be living in an age where everything goes under the microscope, it was just a matter of time, I suppose, before bookstore shelves would be filled with books explaining the cultural and political significance of what we put into our mouths. The first time I came face to face with this phenomenon, my reaction was to reach for the nearest cookie jar as solace. But as soon as I was fortified with a handful of gingersnaps, I felt a rush of kindred warmth. I mean, what else could all these books mean but that there's a ton of people out there as fervent about food and flavor as I am?

The books are mines of food factoids, which won't make a dot of difference in how your cookies come out, but may entertain you while you're snacking on them. It was from one of these books, for instance, that I learned that a Frenchman invented margarine (*mon dieu!*) and that margarine used to be outlawed in Canada and New Zealand.

Strong butter lobbies, I guess. That got me thinking about the news flashes we get almost weekly, one insisting that banning butter from our kitchens will make us live forever, the next bringing word that margarine isn't so hot for us either. The problem is that I really like butter. I don't think there is a substitute for it in baking, particularly as a flavor enhancer. So my solution—imperfect, but most things are—is to use butter in my cookies, but to eat fewer of them than I might have before all the dispatches from the fat front.

I use only unsalted butter for baking because it gives me more control over the saltiness of a recipe. Salt was originally added to butter as a preservative, anyway, so it's unnecessary in these refrigerated days.

The temperature of the butter plays a role in baking, so I indicate in each recipe whether it should be cold, cool, or at room temperature. Room temperature works well for recipes such as chocolate chip cookies that require you to cream the butter and sugar. Cookies prepared in a food processor, such as Almond Raspberry Sandwiches, call for cold butter because the particles formed during processing leave air pockets when they melt during baking and create a crunchy texture.

To bring cold butter to room temperature, use a microwave oven set to the right time and power (on mine, it's 15 seconds at medium power), taking care not to melt the butter. Or leave the butter out of the fridge overnight or for 4 to 6 hours before you plan to bake (the time required depends on the temperature of the room, obviously).

Finally, remember that melted butter measures slightly differently from solid butter, so you're well advised to measure the butter *after* it is melted.

Brown Sugar

Brown sugar is white sugar with a dark syrup added. For dark brown sugar, the syrup is molasses; for light brown, it may be a smaller dose of molasses or another kind of syrup. What goes by the name of brown sugar today is a pale imitation of the stuff our foremothers used, which was full of calcium, iron, and a few other useful minerals. It's heartening to find that sugar has some healthful properties because of its bad rap in you-can-never-be-too-thin circles.

Dark brown sugar is less refined than its light cousin and contains more moisture, so it weighs more. The two types are often interchangeable, but they produce somewhat different out-

253

comes: dark brown sugar tends to make a softer, moister cookie with a slightly sweeter taste.

Store brown sugar in an airtight container in the fridge or freezer to keep it from turning rock-hard. If this suggestion comes too late, you can soften brown sugar in the microwave.

Chocolate

If they asked me, I could write a book. Then again, maybe I have, since so many of the recipes in my first cookbook are chocolate-coated. I certainly have researched the stuff, believing first and foremost in mouth-on experimentation. I also collect chocolatiana, both by predilection and because once you become known for your chocolate obsession, the news comes in faster than an irate customer.

Chocolate has been around for a very long time. According to Aztec legend, the god of wisdom gave them the arts, the calendar, and chocolate. Not a bad legacy. Chocolate made its way to Spain and eventually to the rest of Europe (the French got hold of the recipe as part of the dowry of Louis XIII's Spanish bride), where it remained expensive and deliciously naughty for centuries. In England in the 17th century, a cup of chocolate cost nearly half its weight in gold and they say the English don't know the value of good food! Perhaps it's that aristocratic pedigree that accounts for competing claims of supremacy among chocolates, but what makes the difference is the amount of cocoa butter, which is what gives chocolate its richness.

I have always stood firmly behind Baker's chocolate. That's where chocolate began on our shores—with a doctor named James Baker, who opened North America's first chocolate mill about five miles from where Rosie's home store now stands. Even a force as strong as chocolate can't buck the tide of history, though, and the mills were turned into condos several years ago. When they took the towers down, the air was chocolate perfumed for weeks. My kind of town.

When you come across chocolate in a recipe here, keep in mind that there are several types of chocolate, not just many brands, and the differences among the types matter. When a recipe specifies white chocolate—or unsweetened, or semisweet, or bittersweet chocolate—another kind won't do. The

types vary in flavor and in sugar content, and that can alter the chemistry of the recipe and the texture of the cookie.

For glazes, ganaches, and chopped chunks in cookies, I often use imported chocolates, such as Valrhona and Lindt, to mention just a couple of excellent brands. You'll find these and their cohorts in gourmet shops, upscale markets, and some cookware stores, such as Williams-Sonoma.

But because roundness is all, I come back to where I began: You can't go wrong with Baker's. Its quality is consistently good, you can find it in any grocery store in any part of the country, and it won't break the bank to keep it on hand for those I-can't-believe-it's-raining-again-we're-all-going-stir-crazy-so-the-only-possible-response-is-to-bake-a-batch-of-brownies days.

Eggs

The recipes in this book use large eggs, simply because that's what I chose to test them with. If you substitute other sizes, be aware that this will affect the result, though not necessarily drastically.

Occasionally I call for half an egg or egg yolk. Believe me, I've done this not to torment my readers, but because after many trials, I've found that it's the only solution to maintaining the texture or moistness for a reasonable-size batch of cookies.

💙 *To halve an egg,* crack it into a small bowl and whisk it vigorously until the yellow and white are as integrated as possible. Better yet, use a small electric chopper/grinder to do the work; it will blend the egg perfectly. A stirred large egg measures ¼ cup, so half an egg equals 2 tablespoons of egg. When a recipe calls for half an egg, simply pour out that amount.

Formula:
½ large egg = 2 tablespoons stirred egg

💙 *To divide a yolk in half,* hold a raw egg over a small bowl and crack its shell gently around the middle with a knife. Carefully separate the halves of the shell, and slide the yolk into the palm of your hand as you let the white run through your fingers into the bowl. With a sharp knife, slowly, carefully slice through the yolk's center (you can do this easily without also slicing your hand) and push half of it into the batter.

Oats

Those of us bred in cold northern climes have long been devotees of the humble oat, probably because it grows where other grains won't and it sticks to the ribs come those cold northern winters. None of which has much to do with the current cachet of oats in climes of all kinds, which seems to have come about because they're a health food that tastes good. I'm glad about the health and the heartiness, but I use oats for their taste and consistency.

255

These recipes call for either quick or rolled oats or sometimes a mixture of the two. Quick oats are rolled oats chopped smaller. They tend to absorb more liquid, so it's a good idea to use the kind a recipe calls for. If you have only rolled oats and need quick ones, chop them up in a good processor by pulsing several times. (Don't pulse more or you'll have oat flour.) For obvious reasons, you can't make the smaller quick oats into larger rolled ones, so in a pinch use the quick oats, but be aware that you may have to make other adjustments along the way, such as increasing the amount of flour slightly.

Raisins and Nuts

Whenever possible, I like to buy nuts in bulk at the health-food store. In any case, I always opt for nuts that are not chopped; they maintain their taste and freshness better. Store all nuts in an airtight container in the fridge—they'll stay fresher longer. In the event that they get the least bit soggy, they can always be recrisped in a 300°F oven for about 10 minutes. Raisins must be stored in an airtight container, in or out of the refrigerator. If they become dried out over time, just soak them in hot water for 10 minutes, drain off the water, and pat them dry.

Spices and Flavorings

Whenever possible, spices and flavorings should be fresh. Spices lose their punch over time and need to be re-

placed periodically—some sources say as often as every six months, though that seems extreme to me. In the same vein, something like bottled lemon juice is a poor substitute for freshly squeezed, and there's really nothing equal to just-peeled lemon zest (the yellow layer of the rind).

You can cream a flavoring or spice in with the butter and sugar, or you can sift it into the flour. Opinions differ, and since I belong in neither camp, I'm very democratic in this book: I do it both ways to allow you to decide for yourself.

The Setup

♥ ♥ ♥ ♥ ♥ ♥ ♥ ♥ ♥ ♥ ♥ ♥ ♥ ♥ ♥

I recommend reading through a recipe in its entirety and gathering all the necessary ingredients ahead of time. In fact, I recommend this to myself whenever I bake, which results in my following the advice at least half the time. The other half, I'm likely to find that I'm completely out of something I need—or a couple of ounces short, which isn't much better. Then I'm stuck with abandoning the effort to schlepping to the convenience store at some ungodly hour, all the time cursing myself for this false economy of time.

By taking out ingredients before you start, you can ensure that they're at room temperature, which they should be unless a recipe specifies otherwise (with butter, for instance). The truly organized baker not only lines up her ingredients beforehand but also sets each one aside as she uses it, so she doesn't get confused about which have gone in and which have yet to go.

May all my readers be truly organized, tranquil, and efficient bakers. For the rest, like me, I recommend that you pay attention and, more to the point, try to bake when you can concentrate on what you're doing. You'll enjoy it more.

The Well-Tempered Pan

♥ ♥ ♥ ♥ ♥ ♥ ♥ ♥ ♥ ♥ ♥ ♥ ♥ ♥ ♥

As far as I'm concerned, parchment paper is right up there with the invention of the dishwasher. I always use it to bake cookies and I've started using it for baking bars as well—shortbreads, brownies, crumb bars, the whole gang. With parchment, cookies don't stick and bars slide right out of the pan. It's economical too, because you can reuse it several times: In most cases, a quick wipe with a paper towel will remove any leftover crumbs and allow you to use the sheet for your next batch of cookies—even if it's a different type. As a fallback when you don't have parchment paper, grease your baking sheet with a thin coating of vegetable oil. Avoid butter as a grease; it tends to burn quickly.

At the Tone, the Time and Temperature Will Be . . .

♥ ♥ ♥ ♥ ♥ ♥ ♥

Mixers, food processors, ovens, and the strength of mixing arms vary greatly from kitchen to kitchen, so oven temperatures and lengths of baking time will vary too. That means that the specifications I offer here should be used as guides, not gospel. You'll learn what adjustments you need to make the first time you try a recipe. You may also discover that every recipe you try takes more or less time in your oven than in mine, which will help you to adjust your settings or times accordingly for all the other recipes in the book.

♥ Make sure that your oven is thoroughly preheated before you bake. This isn't just one of those things cookbook writers say because they're supposed to. If you put the cookies in before your oven has reached the right temperature, you can't count on their coming out as you expect, and why make unnecessary trouble for yourself? Preheating to the correct temperature can take anywhere from 5 to 10 minutes, depending on the oven, so plan that much ahead.

♥ Cookies bake more evenly when you make them the same size and space them at regular intervals on the baking sheet. The recipe will often specify how much space to leave between them. Leave a similar distance from the edge of the sheet too.

♥ I prefer to bake one sheet of cookies at a time. I place the baking sheet on a rack in the center of the oven so the air can circulate around it, baking the cookies evenly at the designated temperature. If you're pressed for time, you can place two sheets on two racks arranged as close to the center of the oven as possible. About two thirds of the way through, switch the top and bottom sheets and rotate them back to front. (Be careful to move them gently.) The baking time will be slightly longer with two sheets than with one.

♥ Even though it takes up time, wait until the baking sheet has cooled before putting more dough on it, or the cookies will spread too much. And the baked cookies need to cool, too: each recipe notes how to cool them, since this varies with type. For instance, when a batch of tender cakelike cookies

is done, slide the sheet of parchment off the hot baking sheet onto the counter (or, using a spatula, carefully transfer each cookie onto a sheet of foil or waxed paper on the counter), and let them cool further. Other types—chocolate chips are a prime example—get a little extra crunch around the edges from sitting on the hot baking sheet, so they should be allowed to cool there. Lining the sheets with parchment gives you another advantage here. You can just lift the paper off the cookie sheet and slide all the cookies onto a cooling rack in one fell swoop.

A Storehouse of Freshness

Freezing Dough

With the exception of cakelike cookies, most cookie doughs freeze well for up to three weeks, and some stay fresh in the refrigerator for three or four days. Doughs for drop cookies, shortbreads, rolled cookies, and brownies that don't contain leavening all do well in the refrigerator. Doughs for cakelike cookies don't last in the fridge, however, because their leavening and liquid become active over time and affect the cookies' flavor and texture. Doughs containing oats or oatmeal can be frozen, but they become a little drier because the oatmeal soaks up the liquid. To compensate, when I come to

Cookie Jars

A while ago, my husband, Richard, picked up about a dozen antique cookie jars at a garage sale, and I used them as decorations in our stores, where they were part of the furnishings and drew only the occasional comment. Then about eight years ago, I began to have more and more conversations about them. It turns out that Andy Warhol collected cookie jars, along with tons of other things, and when they were auctioned off after his death, they brought in nearly a quarter of a million dollars! That signaled the start of cookie jars as hot collector's items. Hotter than the cookies they held. So hot, in fact, that there are now cookie jar newsletters, a cookie jar encyclopedia, and even a cookie jar museum (it's in Lemont, Illinois, south of Chicago).

I myself prefer what's inside, but I do understand the appeal of this wonderfully whimsical pottery. I don't go quite as far as the old Betty Crocker cookbook that suggests tinting your cookies to match the color scheme of your tea party, but I like to use cookie jars as part of the presentation. My favorites tend to be from the 1930s and '40s, the heyday of cookie jar creation at midwestern potteries. I'm particularly fond of the quirky animal jars—pigs, cats, mice, a wise old owl, not exactly the fauna you'd want in your kitchen under other circumstances. I also love the red-nosed clown we named Baldy because of his wisp of hair, my fat little Dutch boy, and a jaunty sailor all in blue. Every time I look at him, I want to wink and say, "Can I buy you a cookie, sailor?"

baking them, I sometimes add a bit of water to the dough, or I flatten the mounds after I drop them onto the baking sheet so they will spread better.

Keeping Cookies

Wait until your cookies are completely cool before you put them in a container. This has many advantages, the most important being that it keeps them from getting soggy. The most immediate, though, is that you and everyone who wanders into the kitchen can snack on them in the meantime. Clear plastic containers are best for storing cookies and bars. The plastic preserves freshness; the clarity lets you see what's inside.

For soft cookies that are glazed or frosted (Maple Softies, Boston Cream

Pies) and delicate drop cookies (Banana-Nut Chocolate Chunks, Cranberry Orange Oatmeals), use the widest container available and put parchment paper between the layers. It's not a good idea to pile these cookies more than two deep because they get squashed. Shortbread cookies, such as Peanut Shortbread, and hearty drop cookies, like Chocolate Chips, can be layered three or four times. Common sense should steer you through other quandaries.

Unless I plan to eat the cookies on baking day, I refrigerate or freeze them, even if they're on the menu for tomorrow. Freezing arrests things in time, so that if you take a newly baked cookie that has just cooled and freeze it, when you defrost it, it will come out as close to fresh as to make no difference. I don't recommend freezing baked goods for longer than two weeks, though. They tend to absorb a kind of freezer flavor or get freezer burn, a frost that forms in all freezers, frost-free or not.

When you're ready to eat frozen cookies, let them come to room temperature or pop them in the microwave on the correct setting (40 to 50 seconds on medium-high in mine). Or for those too impatient to wait for defrosting (need I note that this includes me?), there are always frozen chocolate chip cookie pops. Delicious!

Your second storage option is to put the cookies in a container in the fridge. Be sure to store cookies of simi-

lar textures together; if you mix crisp cookies with cakey ones, the softer ones will make the crisps go limp.

Option number three—leaving cookies sitting out at room temperature beyond the day they are baked—isn't often an option at all. Left to their own devices, some crisp cookies go soggy, chewy cookies dry out, and cakey cookies grow dry and heavy. (One exception to the rule is bar cookies containing fruit.) Cookie jars, enchanting as they are, don't protect cookies much from these forces of nature. Still, if you're like me and can't imagine a kitchen without one or two cookie jars on the counter, use them for crisp shortbread-type cookies, which will do just fine there for several days in most weather.

The Cookie's in the Mail

When people talk about E-mail, they leave me far behind, but I bow to no one when it comes to b-mail. For the uninitiated, that's bakery mail. I speak from experience when I say that the best way to ship baked goods is in a sturdy tin lined with plain or decorative cellophane. For gifts, line the tin with a doily, then fit a piece of cellophane over the bottom and up the sides, leaving several inches extra to tuck over the top. Put your firmest, sturdiest, least gooey things on the bottom, cover them with cellophane, arrange another layer of goodies, follow with more cellophane, and continue until the tin is full but not too tightly packed.

When I send something moist, like a brownie, I usually wrap it in plastic before I put it in the tin to keep it from sticking to anything else. If there's a gap somewhere, fill it with a crinkled piece of cellophane or tissue paper to keep things from shifting around. When all the pieces are fitted in securely, fold the excess cellophane over them to keep them snug. Close the tin and freeze it overnight.

Just before shipping, pack the tin in a heavy cardboard box that is large enough for the tin to be surrounded by Styrofoam peanuts. Popcorn (the real thing) works too as a cushion, should you happen to have some sitting around the house. Or swathe the tin in bubble wrap and pack it securely enough to keep it from moving around. If you still have extra room, wad up newspaper or parchment paper to stuff the shipping box.

Overnight mail is best, of course, but that can get expensive; two-day mail is usually fine.

Mail Order

The best cookies for mailing are crispy or crunchy through and through: shortbreads, biscottis, and any cookies whose centers are as crisp as their edges, such as Thin Crisp Chocochips or Pecan Crisps. They will be just as fresh when they arrive as when you shipped them. Cookies with chewy centers and crispy edges, such as Rosie's Oatmeal Cookies and Dark Brown Sugar Chocolate Chips can certainly be shipped, but they will be just a step below what they were when you sent them out—their edges will be a bit soggier and their centers a bit drier. Macaroons, such as Hazelnut Macaroons and Chocolate-Dipped Almond Macaroons, actually ship quite well because of their moist and chewy nature, which becomes only more so when stored in a container for a day or two.

I do not recommend shipping cakey cookies; they get too moist. Any cookie with a soft or gooey top or a custard center, like the Lemon Meringues or the Boston Cream Pies, should not be shipped at all (any cookie with custard or a custard-like filling should not be left at room temperature for more than a day, lest the eggs spoil).

Showing Off

❤ ❤ ❤ ❤ ❤ ❤ ❤ ❤ ❤ ❤ ❤ ❤ ❤ ❤ ❤

I think of cookies as the chameleons of pastries, since they can take on so many different appearances, depending on their size, shape, and presentation.

Is it elegance you want? Fan delicate, lacy cookies over a flowery antique dish.

Artistic plentitude? Create a mosaic using cookies of various shapes and sizes arranged in concentric circles, a checkerboard, or alternating rows or waves. Or give Motherwell and de Kooning a run for their money and try your hand at abstract expressionism.

Barbecue-hearty or picnic-casual more what you had in mind? Plump oatmeal cookies, stuffed with raisins and heaped to overflowing in a basket lined with a gingham cloth, ought to do the trick.

Or maybe what you're aiming for is a smorgasbord of the how-will-I-ever-choose-oh-I-guess-I'll-just-have-to-have-one-of-each variety. A pyramid of brownies and other bars, statuesque on a stoneware plate, is a good place to start. (As an aid to the decision making, you can cut the bars into smaller pieces, so it really is possible to taste everything.)

You can doll up a display of cookies with doilies, a starched white napkin folded to create a pocket, whole flowers, petals or buds, all manner of containers and pottery (I like to use platters of varying heights and sizes together), and table coverings of different colors and textures to create a backdrop. You can cast cookies as the star of your dinner table, as the pinnacle of a buffet, or as a complement for fruit, ice cream, or puddings.

There are limits, of course. I draw the line at floating cookies, wearable cookies, and any cookie too precious to eat. The purpose of display is to tantalize the senses, not torment them. So show off your cookies to their best advantage—then sit back and watch them disappear.

CHAPTER 2

KNOW YOUR DOUGH

The world, some say, can be divided into two kinds of people: those who feel the need to divide it into parts and those who don't. Baking books can also be divided into two kinds: those organized by baking methods and those organized by types of pastries. Most books fall into the first category, but never one to choose sides when I don't have to, I've organized this cookie book both ways.

The recipe chapters that make up the bulk of the book are designed around texture—how a cookie feels in your mouth or yields when you bite into it—since that's usually how we think about cookies. I mean, who sits down and says, "Gee, I'm really in the mood for a refrigerator cookie," or, "Couldn't you just sink your teeth into a rolled cookie right now?" Instead, when our taste buds tug at our neural circuits or hormones or whatever it is that sends feed-me messages to our brain, they say, "crunchy" or "melt on the tongue" or "make it sweet!" Gathering the recipes by texture should make it easier for you to find the right cookie for the right moment as well as a good mix of cookies for more elaborate baking projects.

Even those of us who don't care to divvy up the world need organizing principles from time to time, so I've ordered this how-to chapter along the more conventional line of baking techniques. Here you'll find mixing, baking, cutting, and storing tips for five categories of cookies: drop cookies, refrigerator cookies, rolled cookies, shortbreads, and bars.

Cookies are more forgiving than many other kinds of pastries, less fussy about the order you add the ingredients in, and flexible enough in their baking time and temperature to allow you to experiment to get the results you desire. It's only fairly recently, anyway, that recipes were carefully quantified and cooking was raised to a science governed by charts and rules. Before that, bakers worked by feel and by instructions passed down in appren-

ticeships and mothers' kitchens. I encourage you to do some of that too, finding the baking time, for instance, to give just the right crunch or butteriness that you seek in a specific cookie.

Even the most elaborate of systems has its limits, and you'll find some overlap of techniques and pointers among the categories. Conversely, some cookies and bars fit into a category only with a certain amount of prodding. Still, a read-through of this chapter and an occasional checking back will give you a good grounding for cookie baking of all kinds.

Drop Cookies

♥ ♥ ♥ ♥ ♥ ♥ ♥ ♥ ♥ ♥ ♥ ♥ ♥ ♥ ♥

The "drop" in drop cookies refers to the way they're made: by dropping scoops of dough (sometimes they're formed) onto the baking sheet. Drop cookies are kind of the five dwarfs of cookiedom: They can be chewy, crunchy, crispy, hearty, or cakey. This category is a large one. To make the appropriate instructions easier to find, I've divided drop cookies into three subcategories: chewy and crunchy drops, crispy drops, and cake-like drops.

Chewy and Crunchy Drops

Mixing: These are the most traditional drop cookies, including such favorite types as chocolate chip, oatmeal, and peanut butter. The method for mixing their dough is traditional, too: you cream the butter and sugar together, then add the eggs and, last, the dry ingredients.

Baking: Chewy drops and crunchy drops are essentially the same cookies, except for a difference in texture. Chewy cookies can be chewy through and through, as in Chocolate-Dipped Almond Macaroons and Hazelnut Macaroons; they can have chewy centers and a crunchy veneer, as with meringues; or they can have chewy centers and crunchy edges, as in many of the big drop cookies, like Rosie's

Oatmeal Cookies. Many of these cookies can also be baked until they are crunchy throughout. For instance, I like to make Noah's Chocolate Chocolatey Chocolate Chips and Pecan Oatmeal Chips that way. The beauty of this category is that you can control how chewy or crunchy your cookies are by how you form and bake them.

To get the soft centers that are the hallmark of chewy cookies, drop the batter in mounds onto a prepared baking sheet and bake the cookies at 375° to 400°F. Their edges will spread and become crunchier, but their centers will stay nice and soft. (The exception to this rule is the meringue, which is baked very slowly at a temperature as low as 200°F.) Remove chewy drop cookies from the oven when their edges are golden or crisp and their centers are a little lighter in color and still a bit puffy and tender.

Chilling the dough before you bake it is another way to get the center chewier than the edges. This works with all kinds of drop cookies, because chilling keeps the center set long into the baking process.

To create crunchier cookies, drop them onto the baking sheet as you would chewy drops, but then either press them flatter before baking so that the center doesn't puff up as they cook, or bake them a little longer. Sometimes you'll want to do both. Set the oven to 375° to 400°F, and bake the cookies long enough for the center to set and turn the same color and texture as the edges. Cooling these cookies on the baking sheet will make their bottom even crunchier, but they cool well on a rack too. Experiment with both methods to find the specifics that produce your ideal cookie.

Storing: These cookies are best eaten the first day. The crunchy edges become just a little less crunchy and the chewy centers just a little less chewy by the second day. However, as soon as you've decided that you just can't eat any more, you can place them in a plastic container in the freezer, where they'll hold for up to two weeks. When you're in the mood for a treat, remove a cookie (or three) from the freezer and bring it to room temperature or zap it in your microwave for between 30 to 50 seconds (depending on the size of the cookies) on medium-high power.

Crispy Drops

Mixing: Crispy drops, such as Orange Pecan Ginger Florentines and Fresh Ginger Crisps, take top honors for elegance and daintiness. They're the sort of sweet that Eloise might nibble when she goes down for tea at the Plaza's Palm Court. Or they're the lacelike creations in the shop windows of the Place de la Madeleine that would entice Eloise's French counterpart, the irrepressible Madeline, as she and her schoolmates march by in two straight lines. This category also includes heartier cookies, such as Thin Crisp Chocochips and Chocolate Chip Pecan Mounds, which I suspect would please Eloise and Madeline too, because for all their grown-up grandeur, these cookies are among the most basic, appealing to spunky kids as well as more reserved adults.

Baking: Crispy drop cookies usually contain less flour than other drop cookies, so their dough is wetter and spreads more during baking. But because most of these delicacies are baked at 350° to 400°F, the higher heat caramelizes the sugar and butter and prevents the cookie from running all over the baking sheet. Some recipes call for the sugar and butter mixture to be cooked over a burner first, to speed up the caramelizing process. Others require the butter to be creamed with the sugar. No overarching guidelines here; crisps are individualists, each demanding its own instructions.

Storing: Although like most cookies, crispy cookies are best the first day, they can be kept in an airtight container at room temperature for a couple of days. After that I like to store the container in the freezer, in order to maintain their requisite crispness.

Cakelike Drops

Mixing: These gems, which include Sacher Tortes and Maple Softies, are miniature cakes you can have all to yourself with no need to share or to be modest in the slice you cut. Cakey drop cookies are mixed the same way as cakes: butter and sugar creamed together, eggs added, then liquid mixed in before or alternately with dry ingredients.

Baking: What you want here is a moist cookie, so scoop a good amount of batter onto the baking sheet for each one. I recommend a heaping tablespoonful, or at least a generously rounded one. Drop the cookies 2 inches apart, and if need be, run your index finger gently around their circumference to make perfect rounds.

Bake these cookies between 375° and 400°F until they rise. Be vigilant to catch them when they have just set but haven't yet formed a crust. At the right doneness, the cookies will spring back when you touch them. Don't wait until a crust has formed, or the drops will be slightly overbaked and drier than is optimal.

Storing: These cookies are great the first day, but if you wish to save them, freeze them in an airtight container for up to two weeks. Be sure to defrost them thoroughly before scarfing.

Refrigerator Cookies

We used to call these icebox cookies, although I've never seen a real icebox in my life. I've heard stories about them, though. A friend's mother talks about dragging her red wooden wagon with its block of ice up a steep hill each week of her childhood, rushing against the heat to arrive home before the ice had melted away.

There's something appealing about that image, even if it was hard work, probably because it speaks of a friendlier time. I romanticize it, I'm sure, but for me just saying "icebox" evokes an era of neighbors chatting from their front stoops, waiting for the iceman to cometh, while kids play stickball and kick-the-can in the street until their mothers call them in to dinner and, half grumbling, half grateful, they comply.

"Refrigerator," on the other hand, sounds much more efficient, which is accurate when it comes to preparing these cookies. They are made from stiff dough that's formed into a log, chilled, sliced, and then baked. Some cooking column I read noted that refrigerator cookies are

convenient when you want to bake just a few cookies at a time. I have a little trouble imagining such a situation, but I suppose it's not inconceivable. Me, I damn the torpedoes and bake the whole batch in the following way.

Mixing and Molding: When the dough has been mixed, either with an electric mixer or in a food processor, mold it by hand into one or two logs. (You may need to dip your hands in flour to keep the dough from sticking.) Place the log along one edge of a piece of waxed paper or plastic wrap that is 3 to 4 inches longer than the log. Roll the log in the paper or wrap, and twist the ends like a hard-candy wrapper.

Chill the log for several hours. Then gently roll it back and forth on a countertop, using your palms and fingers, until it forms a smooth cylinder, or hit all four sides on the countertop to create corners and shape a rectangular loaf; the recipe will tell you which shape you want. Return the log to the fridge for several hours or overnight, or freeze it for up to two weeks. When you're ready to bake, slice the log into pieces as required by the recipe and place them 1½ inches apart on a baking sheet.

Baking: Refrigerator cookies usually bake at 300° to 350°F. As a rule of thumb, thicker cookies need the lower temperature so their centers bake evenly along with the edges. The cool temperature of the dough helps them retain their shape as they bake and also contributes to their crunchiness.

Test these cookies for doneness as you would shortbread; that is, take a cookie from the oven, break it in half, and check to make sure there's no doughy strip left in the center. (If there is, return them to the oven and continue to bake the cookies until they're crunchy through and through.)

Storing: Cool refrigerator cookies on the baking sheet or on a rack, and wait at least until they reach room temperature before digging in. Store refrigerator cookies at room temperature in an airtight plastic container for a day or two. I find that this often enhances their flavor. After that, store the container in the freezer for up to two weeks. Bring the cookies to room temperature before eating.

Rolled Cookies

❤ ❤ ❤ ❤ ❤ ❤ ❤ ❤ ❤ ❤ ❤ ❤ ❤ ❤ ❤

This is the category of cookies that fill the holiday issues of women's magazines and the days of the Supermom who haunts our best intentions. It's the favored child of Christmas givers and the more-creative-than-thou baker who seems to pluck delightful cookie shapes from thin air. Fortunately, it also includes simple-to-make favorites, such as Classic Sugar Cookies and Gingerbread People.

Rolled cookies start with a stiff dough that is rolled out flat and then cut into shapes. You can use heirloom cookie cutters passed down from generation to generation, fad-of-the-month cookie cutters bought at Woolworth's or a cake decorating store, or whatever you happen to have around the house that will cut dough. I usually use a thin-rimmed glass, which cuts perfect circles, but I don't want to be a killjoy. Cookie cutters can be a lot of fun, especially for holiday baking or for baking with kids.

Mixing and Cutting: You can make the dough for rolled cookies with an electric mixer or a food processor. Form the dough into slabs, place them between layers of plastic wrap, and use a rolling pin to roll them out evenly to the designated thickness, usually ¼ to ⅛ inch.

Some doughs are so rich with egg yolks or butter that they need to be

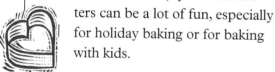

chilled after rolling so they won't be too sticky to cut easily. Just set the rolled-out dough, still sandwiched in the plastic wrap (and still on the cutting board if you like), on a refrigerator shelf for 1 to 2 hours.

When the dough is ready to be cut into shapes, dip the cookie cutter or glass in flour (to keep the dough from sticking) and cut out your cookies. Make sure you press down hard enough so that the edge of the cutter cuts totally through the dough. With your hand, gently pull the scraps away from the cookie. Then, using a spatula, carefully transfer the cookies from the cutting board to the baking sheet, placing them 1½ inches apart. Re-roll the scraps and cut out as many more cookies as possible, adding them to the rest.

Baking: Bake these cookies between 350° and 400°F until the centers are firm and the edges are just beginning to turn golden. They should be crisp through and through.

Storing: Rolled cookies are best cooled on the baking sheet, since they are too delicate to be moved when they're warm. They can be stored in cookie jars, as tradition dictates, or in your dependable airtight plastic container. If they're not gone in a day or two, refrigerate them in a plastic container to help maintain their crispness. After that, store the container in the freezer for up to two weeks. Bring the cookies to room temperature before eating.

Un-Rolling

For those who hate rolling dough, many of these doughs can also be shaped into logs and sliced like refrigerator cookies. Or you can form the dough into a mass, pinch off pieces, roll them into a ball with your hands, set them on a baking sheet, and press them flat with your hand or with the bottom of a glass. These cookies require a lower heat—325° to 350°F—because they will be thicker and need to bake more slowly.

Short-breads

Shortbread takes its name from all the butter or shortening used to give it both a rich and a pure taste. And rich it is. A very early recipe for something called Bath Shortbread required a pound of "flower," half a pound of butter, and a pound of sugar made into a paste with wine!

Shortbread has always been among my favorite cookies. I was introduced to it when my mother brought home those round tins decorated with a tartan and filled with wedges of Dundee shortbread. It was crunchy and buttery beyond belief! When I got old enough to think about what went into the food I liked, I wondered how something so simple could taste so good, and as I explored baking more, I came to appreciate how something so basic could take on so many variations. I read that Scottish business leaders feel sorely misunderstood by a world that recognizes them only for bagpipes and shortbread, and while the business-woman in me sympathizes, every other part of me yearns to reassure them that there are few forms of immortality more noble than a really fine piece of shortbread.

Mixing: Shortbreads are dense, solid cookies. They can be eggless, like Ginger Shortbread, or can contain whole eggs or yolks or whites, like Chocolate Orange Shortbread or Little Princesses. With the exception of spritzes and piped cookies, all kinds of shortbread can be made equally well with a food processor or an electric mixer. (For spritzes and piped cookies, you need to use the paddle attachment on an electric mixer to cream the butter and sugar to the right consistency for squeezing the dough from a tube.)

If you use an electric mixer, cream room-temperature butter with the sugar until the mixture is light and fluffy. Creaming the butter and sugar this way aerates the dough nicely, making for a wonderfully crunchy shortbread. Next, beat in the eggs, and add the dry ingredients at the end, beating only enough to incorporate them into the dough.

As an alternative, you can use a food processor and incorporate the butter at any temperature. Cool or cold butter will give you the requisite crunchiness because minute particles will remain and will melt in baking, leaving tiny air pockets that create a "short," or crunchy, texture. Blend the flour and sugar, add the butter, and process the dough until it resembles coarse cornmeal. With the processor running, add the eggs through the feed tube and process until they're incorporated and the dough just comes together. Sometimes a little hand kneading is necessary.

Whatever appliance you use, take care not to overbeat the dough after you've added the flour because beating can toughen dough that contains both eggs and flour.

Baking: Shortbread doughs can be rolled out, scooped, formed, or made into a log to be refrigerated and then cut. Each variety will call for a somewhat different baking time and temperature, but shortbreads bake best between 300° and 350°F; they can even bake as low as 275°F if you have the patience. Lower temperatures ensure that they bake evenly, with the center as crunchy as the edges.

To test for doneness, remove one cookie from the oven and cut or break it in half to make sure that there is no doughy strip in the center. (If there is, continue baking.) I prefer my shortbread slightly golden for the texture that

it gives and because butter is even more flavorful when it reaches this color.

Storing: Because of their crunchy nature, shortbread cookies store beautifully. Keep them in an airtight container at room temperature for two days if you plan to snack on them during that time. After that, store the container in the freezer for up to two weeks. Bring the cookies to room temperature before eating them. If you don't have sufficient freezer space, shortbread, unlike many other cookies, can be left at room temperature for up to a week.

Bar Cookies

❤ ❤ ❤ ❤ ❤ ❤ ❤ ❤ ❤ ❤ ❤ ❤ ❤ ❤ ❤

This category is so popular at Rosie's that I've often felt like breaking into a chorus of "Belly Up to the Bar, Boys." Certainly boys, girls, women, men, and the occasional puppy line up for them regularly, making brownies and fruit bars hard to keep in stock. I don't usually think of brownies and their ilk as cookies, but they're more that than anything else, and they fill a similar role as snacks and desserts.

Brownies are an American original, something I like to offer foreign visitors as part of their authentic American experience. But bar-type cookies show up in many other cultures, and I've found them to be particularly adaptable to flavors and ingredients

from all over, which has inspired me to come up with three kinds of linzer bars, White Chocolate Brownies with Macadamia Nuts, and all kinds of fruit bars, to note just a few.

In my mind, bars fall into three categories: brownie bars, which include such variations as Sour Cherry Cheesecake Brownies and Peanut Butter Topped Brownies; shortbread bars, such as Cranberry Walnut Squares and Chunky Pecan Shortbread; and pastry bars, which subdivide further into bars with crumb crusts (Dating Bars, Cranberry Crumb Bars); bars with fine crusts (Pucker-Your-Lips Apricot Linzer Bars); and sturdy-crusted linzer bars. A couple of bars (Carrot Cake Cream Cheese Bars and Poppyseed Coffee Cake Bars) don't fit into any of these categories. Their recipes will give specific instructions.

Brownie Bars

Mixing: These batters are usually made by one of two methods. The first requires creaming the butter and sugar together and then adding the eggs,

flour, and melted chocolate. The second requires you to melt the butter and chocolate together, and then to add the eggs and flour.

Baking: I bake most of my brownies between 325° and 350°F. Since I don't want too much of the aeration that higher temperatures bring, I use a lower heat to produce a fudgier, moister bar.

Most brownies are done when the center has risen and is no longer liquidy. You want to take the bars out of the oven when their center is less crusty and set than the edges. If the center has only a thin crust, it will drop slightly as it cools to create a fudgier bar. So to test for doneness, insert a cake tester in the center of the pan; remove the pan from the oven when the tester comes out dry or with moist crumbs but no syrupy batter.

Cutting: The bars can be cut 10 minutes after they come out of the oven or when they are room temperature. Use the point of a sharp, thin knife and perhaps a spatula or cake cutter to lift them out of the pan. For frosted or glazed brownie bars, dip the knife in hot water and wipe it dry before each cut.

Storing: Although there are those who would disagree, I think a brownie, like a cheesecake or a great stew, is better the second day. The texture settles to become more what it is meant to be, and the flavor seems to intensify and become more full-bodied. I always leave the bars, cut, in the pan overnight at room temperature. (Once they have completely cooled, I cover them with plastic wrap, but it's not absolutely necessary that first night.)

The following day, if there are leftovers after you've passed the brownies around, place them in an airtight container and refrigerate them for two to three days. (If the brownies are frosted, layer them with parchment or waxed paper between.) After that, any remains can be frozen for up to two weeks.

Shortbread Bars

Mixing: These cookies are made from a shortbread dough, which may or may not be finished off with a topping. Mix the dough with an electric mixer or a food processor, as explained in the section on shortbread cookies. Then spread it over the bottom of a prepared pan with your fingertips. If the dough is too sticky, dip your fingers in flour.

Sometimes the shortbread is glazed to keep a wet topping from sinking into the base. Glazing also works as decoration when there's no topping. There are two ways to glaze: You can separate an egg white into a dish or cup, then paint it over the surface of the unbaked dough with a pastry brush. Or you can drop an egg white directly onto the unbaked dough, tilt the pan from side to side until the white covers the entire surface, and then spill the excess into the sink.

Baking: I bake plain shortbread bars at 325°F, but I raise the temperature to 350°F for bars that will get a topping. Bake both kinds until they are light golden with slightly darker edges. Once shortbread bars are topped, the baking time will vary considerably from recipe to recipe.

Cutting: Plain shortbread bars should be cut with the point of a sharp, thin knife or a cleaver. Cut them when they're hot because once they cool, they're more likely to break.

Shortbread bars with sugary toppings—Tropical Macadamia Bars or Pecan Delight Bars, for example—should be cut when they've just reached room temperature. If they get too cool, the caramelized sugar around the edges becomes hard to cut through. A cleaver or heavy knife works well here (remove any goo after each cut).

Bars topped with fruit, such as Cranberry Walnut Squares, should be cut carefully at room temperature with the point of a sharp, thin knife.

Storing: Plain shortbread bars, such as Semolina Shortbread and Cinnamon Pecan Shortbread, should be stored, when cooled, in an airtight container at room temperature for two to three days. Their buttery flavor will become even more intense as they sit. After this, store them in the freezer for up to two weeks. Bring the bars to room temperature before eating.

Shortbread bars that are topped with fruit or cream cheese or gooey toppings have individual storing needs that are too numerous to note in a general way here. As with all the recipes in this book, the storing instructions for this type of bar are included within the recipe.

Pastry Bars with Crumb Crusts

Mixing: Crumb crusts generally consist of a combination of flour, sugars, melted butter, and sometimes oats or nuts. Toss the dry ingredients in a bowl or process them gently in a food processor, then add the melted butter. Next, cover the bottom of the baking pan with a portion of this mixture to form a base, and when the recipe specifies, prebake it. Spread the filling over the base and sprinkle the remaining crumb mixture over the top.

Baking: These bars are usually baked at 350° to 375°F until their top is golden and crunchy.

Cutting: Cut crumb-crust bars when they reach room temperature.

Storing: For the ultimate crunch of the crumb mixture, these bars are particularly delicious on the first day. After that, store them in an airtight container in the refrigerator for a few days. If the bars contain fruit, you can leave them in the pan, covered, for up to two days at room temperature or layer them in an airtight container with plastic wrap, parchment, or waxed paper between the layers, and refrigerate for up to four days. Fruit bars can also be frozen; however, dried fruit bars (apricot, date) remain crisper than fresh-fruit bars (apple) when defrosted. Follow the same storage procedure with bars with cream cheese, but keep them refrigerated for easy handling. All bar cookies should be brought to room temperature before eating.

Pastry Bars with Fine Crusts

Mixing: Bars in this category are made with pastry crusts that are either pressed into the bottom of the pan by hand or rolled out like a pie crust and then fitted into the pan. These bottom crusts may be prebaked. They are then filled with a fruit mixture and covered with the remaining dough or with a lattice of dough.

Baking: These bars are usually baked at 400°F so that the bottom and top crusts both become crisp. This high heat allows the crust beneath the fruit to get crisp or crunchy, depending on the recipe, rather than becoming soggy or remaining raw tasting.

Cutting: Cut these bars at room temperature.

Storing: Fine pastry bars that contain fruit are best eaten the first day, when you get the full experience of the contrast between the crispness of the dough and the moisture of the fruit. After day one, store them in an airtight container in the fridge. I don't like to freeze these bars. Like the crumb crust bars, they get soggy when defrosted.

Linzer Bars

Mixing: Linzer bars use their own type of crust made of flour, sugar, butter, eggs, spices, and lots of ground nuts, all of which can be creamed together in a mixer or a food processor. A portion of this dough is then pressed into the bottom of a pan and sometimes prebaked slightly. A jam or jam-and-fruit filling is spread over this base, and the remaining crust is rolled into strips and woven into a lattice over the filling.

Baking: For recipes that require prebaking the crust, I suggest doing so at 350°F until the crust is just firm to the touch, about 20 minutes. After they're assembled, return the bars to the oven and bake them at 350° to 375°F until the top is crisp and the filling is bubbling.

Cutting: Wait until these bars have cooled completely before you cut them.

Storing: Linzer bars are very durable and are as great on day two or three as on day one. For the first few days, store them, with parchment or waxed paper between the layers, in an airtight container. After that, put the container in the refrigerator or freezer, depending on how quickly you think you'll go through them.

CHAPTER 3

CHEWY

CRUNCHY

Noah's Chocolate Chocolatey Chocolate
Chips

Fudgie Wudgies

Pecan Chocolate Chips

Dark Brown Sugar Chocolate Chips

Chocolate Chunkers

Whole-Grain Earthy Chocolate Chips

Chocolate Chocolate Chip Meringues

Rosie's Oatmeal Cookies

Oatmeal Chocolate Chips

Pecan Oatmeal Chips

Chocolate Chocolate Chip Oatmeal Cookies

Cranberry Orange Oatmeal Cookies

Chocolate Peanut Butter Volcanoes

Banana-Nut Chocolate Chunks

Chocolate-Dipped Almond Macaroons

Chocolate-Coconut Scoops

Hazelnut Macaroons

Baker's Best Snickerdoodles

Classic Snickerdoodles

Apple 'n' Spice Drops

usually get into trouble when I make sweeping pronouncements, but I'll go out on a limb and proclaim this category of cookie America's sweetheart. It includes such basics as chocolate chip cookies, oatmeal and peanut butter cookies, snickerdoodles and macaroons.

While I've raided other cultures and climates for some of the ingredients, most of these cookies are quintessentially American—a fistful of good taste straight out of a Norman Rockwell kitchen—and so is what goes into them. Our southern states give the world its pecans, oatmeal probably came over with the Pilgrims, great New England fortunes were founded on molasses and rum (hermit cookies were created by Cape Cod bakers to outlast the long sea voyages of American clipper ships), and what else but American ingenuity would come up with something like peanut butter?

A large part of the widespread appeal of these cookies comes, I think, from their texture. There's something so reinforcing, so comforting and rewarding, about biting through a crunchy edge and encountering a moist, chewy center and often a further prize of raisins or nuts. There's a word used in Louisiana, *lagniappe,* that means an unexpected extra something. That's how I think of my chewy cookies.

These cookies are baked large and generous and tend to keep well, so when we imagine the perfect cookie jar filler, these chewies often come to mind. Even the names are straightforward, telling us that what we see is what we get. (I know, there's "snickerdoodles," and where that name came from is anybody's guess. But it's fun to say, so who cares?)

Most of the cookies in this chapter are made from sturdy doughs, so carefully regulated mixing isn't as important as in other baking. If you're the type of baker who needs to be anxious about something, concentrate on finding the right baking time and temperature to create the texture you want. Chewier cookies are dropped in mounds on the baking sheet and removed from the oven when their centers are a little less done than their edges. Crunchier cookies can be pressed flatter on the baking sheet and baked until their centers and edges are the same doneness. Play around to get precisely the chew and crunch that your little heart desires.

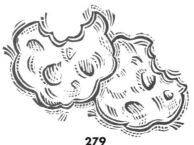

Noah's Chocolate Chocolatey Chocolate Chips

❤ ❤ ❤ ❤ ❤ ❤ ❤ ❤ ❤ ❤ *drop cookie*

C runchy edges, chewy centers, dark chocolatey chocolate cookies filled to bursting with chocolate chips, and claimed for his own by my son, Noah, whom I love more than chocolate itself.

INGREDIENTS

4 ounces unsweetened chocolate
2¼ cups all-purpose flour
1 teaspoon baking soda
½ teaspoon salt
1 cup (2 sticks) unsalted butter at room temperature
1¼ cups (lightly packed) light brown sugar
½ cup plus 2 tablespoons granulated sugar
2 large whole eggs
1 large egg yolk
8 ounces (1¼ cups) semisweet chocolate chips

1. Preheat the oven to 400°F. Line several baking sheets with parchment paper, or grease them lightly with vegetable oil.

2. Melt the unsweetened chocolate in the top of a double boiler placed over simmering water. Then remove it from the heat and let it cool slightly.

3. Sift the flour, baking soda, and salt together into a small bowl and set aside.

4. Using an electric mixer on medium speed, cream the butter and both sugars together in a medium-size bowl until light and fluffy, 1½ to 2 minutes. Stop the mixer twice during the process to scrape the bowl with a rubber spatula.

5. Add the eggs and egg yolk and beat on medium speed until they are blended, about 30 seconds. Scrape the bowl. Add the melted chocolate and blend until mixed, about 10 seconds, stopping the mixer once to scrape the bowl.

6. Add the flour mixture, and mix on low speed for 15 seconds.

7. Add the chocolate chips and blend until they are mixed in, 5 to 8 seconds.

8. Drop the dough by generously rounded tablespoons onto the prepared baking sheets, spacing them 2 inches apart.

9. Bake the cookies until the centers are puffed up and lightly cracked, but still soft, 12 to 13 minutes. Remove the cookies from the oven and allow them to cool on the sheets.

10. These are best eaten the same day they are baked. Otherwise, store them in an airtight container in the freezer for up to 2 weeks. Before eating, bring them to room temperature or heat them lightly in the microwave (50 seconds on medium-high power).

Makes 24 large cookies

Fudgie Wudgies

♥ ♥ ♥ ♥ ♥ ♥ ♥ ♥ ♥ *drop cookie*

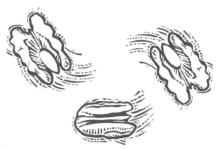

Named by my son Jake, this extra-fudgy, almost flourless, abounding-in-nuts-and-chips cookie is a dark—as dark can be—sensation. It's a chocoholic's dream, and not bad for the casual indulger too.

INGREDIENTS

6 ounces (1 cup) plus 4 ounces (¾ cup)
  semisweet chocolate chips
10 tablespoons (1¼ sticks)
  unsalted butter
6 tablespoons all-purpose flour
1 teaspoon baking powder
3 tablespoons unsweetened cocoa powder
⅛ teaspoon salt
2 large eggs
2 teaspoons pure vanilla extract
¾ cup sugar
½ cup chopped pecans or walnuts

1. Preheat the oven to 325°F. Line several baking sheets with parchment paper, or grease them lightly with vegetable oil.

2. Melt the 6 ounces of chocolate chips and the butter in the top of a double boiler placed over simmering water. Then remove the pan from the heat and allow to cool slightly.

3. Sift the flour, baking powder, cocoa, and salt together into a small bowl and set aside.

4. Using an electric mixer on medium speed, beat the eggs and vanilla in a medium-size mixing bowl until they are blended, about 10 seconds.

5. Add the sugar to the egg mixture and blend until the mixture is thick, about 1 minute. Scrape the bowl.

6. Add the melted chocolate and blend 1 minute more. Scrape the bowl.

7. Add the flour mixture on low speed and mix until blended, 10 seconds, scraping the bowl with a rubber spatula.

8. Add the remaining 4 ounces chocolate chips and the nuts, and blend until they are mixed in, 5 to 8 seconds.

9. Drop the dough by generously rounded tablespoons about 2 inches apart onto the prepared baking sheets.

10. Bake the cookies until they rise slightly and form a thin crust, 14 to 16 minutes. Immediately transfer the cookies from the baking sheets to wire racks to cool.

11. If you plan to snack on them the first day, place the cookies on a plate. After that, place the cookies in an airtight container and refrigerate for a day or two or store in the freezer for up to 2 weeks. Bring the cookies to room temperature before eating.

Makes 20 large cookies

Pecan Chocolate Chips

♥ ♥ ♥ ♥ ♥ ♥ ♥ ♥ ♥ *drop cookie*

In the baking biz, the big debate is nuts versus no nuts. Nearly everyone under age twelve falls firmly in the no-nuts camp, but those of us who have made it through adolescence are less predictable and depend more on mood. I, for one, consider the nutted chocolate chip cookie to be a valuable variation on the classic, and this is one of the best of its breed. It's chewy in the center, crunchy around the edges, and enhanced by the chomp of chopped pecans.

INGREDIENTS

2¼ cups plus 2 tablespoons all-purpose flour
2 teaspoons baking soda
1 teaspoon salt
1 cup (2 sticks) unsalted butter at room temperature
1 cup (lightly packed) light brown sugar
7 tablespoons granulated sugar
1 tablespoon pure vanilla extract
2 tablespoons light corn syrup
2 teaspoons water
2 large eggs
12 ounces (2 cups) semisweet chocolate chips
1½ cups chopped pecans

1. Preheat the oven to 400°F. Line several baking sheets with parchment paper, or grease them lightly with vegetable oil.

2. Sift the flour, baking soda, and salt together into a small bowl and set aside.

3. Using an electric mixer on medium speed, cream the butter, both sugars, and the vanilla together in a medium-size bowl until light and fluffy, 1½ to 2 minutes. Stop the mixer twice during the process to scrape the bowl with a rubber spatula. Then add the corn syrup and the water, and mix for several seconds.

4. Add the eggs and beat on medium speed until they are blended, about 30 seconds. Scrape the bowl.

5. Add the flour mixture and mix on low speed for 15 seconds. Scrape the bowl.

6. Add the chocolate chips and the nuts and blend until they are mixed in, 5 to 8 seconds.

7. Drop the dough by rounded tablespoonfuls 2 inches apart onto the prepared baking sheets.

8. Bake the cookies until the edges are dark golden and the centers are light and slightly puffed up, 11 to 12 minutes. Remove from the oven and allow them to cool on the sheets.

9. These are best eaten the same day they are baked. Otherwise, store them in an airtight container in the freezer for up to 2 weeks, and bring them to room temperature before eating.

Makes 40 cookies

Chips Off the Old Block

If you were to ask any group of people anywhere in this country what their favorite cookie was, the answer, hands down, would be chocolate chip. I know this for a fact because pollsters *have* asked people everywhere just that—though I'm always a little perplexed about what we're supposed to do with the information.

The chocolate chip—or Toll House cookie, as it was first known—has topped the American hit parade almost since the fateful day sixty-five years ago when Ruth Wakefield, proprietor of the Toll House Inn in Whitman, Massachusetts, stumbled onto the perfect *ménage à trois* of butter, sugar, and chocolate. That story has been told often: How Mrs. Wakefield set out to make an old colonial recipe called the Butter Drop Do. How she didn't have the nuts the recipe called for, so cut up a bar of semisweet chocolate, expecting it to melt evenly. How it didn't, but instead studded the cookies with luscious bits of soft chocolate. How a guest sampled the cookies and told a journalist friend in Boston about them. And how Nestle's bought out Mrs. Wakefield, created the chocolate chip, and put her recipe on the package for posterity.

Which goes to show that many an empire has been founded on a goof.

I'm grateful to Ruth Wakefield—who would want to live in a world devoid of chocolate chip cookies?—and also to Nestle's, who, I think, still make the best chocolate chips. I use no other for my cookies. You may decide otherwise, but whatever brand you use, make sure that they're real chocolate, not chocolate flavored.

Dark Brown Sugar Chocolate Chips

drop cookie

A bit deeper in color and flavor because it uses dark brown sugar, this cookie offers up the same beloved oomph as a classic chocolate chip cookie.

INGREDIENTS

2 cups plus 5 tablespoons all-purpose flour
1 teaspoon baking soda
1 teaspoon salt
1 cup (2 sticks) unsalted butter at room temperature
1¼ cups (lightly packed) dark brown sugar
½ cup granulated sugar
1½ teaspoons pure vanilla extract
2 large eggs
6 ounces (1 cup) semisweet chocolate chips
¾ cup chopped pecans
1¼ cups shredded sweetened coconut (optional)

1. Preheat the oven to 400°F. Line several baking sheets with parchment paper, or lightly grease them with vegetable oil.

2. Sift the flour, baking soda, and salt together into a small bowl and set aside.

3. Using an electric mixer on medium speed, cream the butter, both sugars, and vanilla together in a medium-size bowl until light and fluffy, 1½ to 2 minutes. Stop the mixer twice during the process to scrape the bowl with a rubber spatula.

4. Add the eggs and beat on medium speed until they are blended, about 30 seconds. Scrape the bowl.

5. Add the flour mixture and mix on low speed for 20 seconds. Scrape the bowl.

6. Add the chocolate chips and blend until they are mixed in, 5 to 8 seconds. Then add the nuts and coconut, if using, and mix until blended, 5 to 8 seconds more.

7. Drop the dough by heaping table-spoons 2 inches apart onto the pre-pared baking sheets.

8. Bake the cookies until the edges are dark golden and the centers are light and slightly puffed up, 9 to 11 minutes. Remove the cookies from the oven and allow them to cool on the sheets.

9. These are best eaten the same day they are baked. Otherwise, store them in an airtight container in the freezer for up to 2 weeks. Before eating, bring them to room temperature or heat them slightly in the microwave (50 seconds on medium-high power).

Makes 24 large cookies

Chocolate Chunkers

♥ ♥ ♥ ♥ ♥ ♥ ♥ ♥ ♥ ♥ *drop cookie*

Remember Chunky, the candy? Well, meet Chocolate Chunkers, the cookie. They're a craggy mountain stuffed full of chocolate chips, raisins, and pecans, then coated with a velvety chocolate ganache. For the kid in all of us.

INGREDIENTS

THE COOKIE
3½ ounces unsweetened chocolate
8 tablespoons (1 stick) unsalted butter
1 cup plus 2 tablespoons all-purpose flour
⅛ teaspoon baking powder
1¼ cups sugar
2 whole large eggs
1 large egg yolk
1 cup raisins
¾ cup chopped pecans
4 ounces (¾ cup) semisweet chocolate chips

THE GLAZE
½ cup heavy (whipping) cream
2 tablespoons sugar
*8 ounces bittersweet chocolate, chopped
    small*
1 tablespoon unsalted butter

1. Preheat the oven to 325°F. Line several baking sheets with parchment paper, or grease them lightly with vegetable oil.

2. Make the cookies: Melt the unsweetened chocolate and the butter in the top of a double boiler placed over simmering water. Remove the pan from the heat and allow to cool slightly.

3. Sift the flour and baking powder together into a small bowl and set aside.

4. Place the sugar in a medium-size mixing bowl, add the melted chocolate mixture, and blend for 10 seconds. Scrape the bowl with a rubber spatula.

5. Add the eggs and the yolk and mix until blended, 10 seconds, stopping the bowl once to scrape the sides with a rubber spatula.

6. Add the flour mixture on low speed and mix until blended, 10 seconds, stopping the mixer once to scrape the bowl.

7. Add the raisins and blend 5 seconds. Then add the nuts and chocolate chips, and blend several seconds more. Finish the mixing by hand.

8. Scoop heaping tablespoons of dough and form them into mounds with your hands. Arrange them 2 inches apart on the prepared baking sheets.

9. Bake the cookies until they form a thin crust, 20 to 25 minutes. Allow them to cool on the sheets.

10. Meanwhile, prepare the glaze: Place the cream and sugar in a small saucepan and bring to a boil, whisking occasionally. Remove from the heat immediately.

11. Add the chocolate and butter to the pan, cover, and let sit about 5 minutes until the chocolate melts.

12. Stir the mixture with a whisk until it is shiny and velvety.

13. Dip each cookie, upside down, in the glaze, coating the entire top. Place right side up on cooling racks or on a sheet of parchment to set for several hours.

14. Store the cookies in an airtight container, with parchment paper between the layers, for a couple of days in the refrigerator. After that, store them in the freezer for up to 2 weeks.

Makes 24 cookies

Whole-Grain Earthy Chocolate Chips

❤ ❤ ❤ ❤ ❤ ❤ ❤ ❤ ❤ ❤ ❤   *drop cookie*

Go on, sneak in a little healthiness. Your kids will never know. These cookies contain bran, wheat germ, and whole wheat flour, and they're still a hit in my house (though if my son Jake suspected that they have any nutritional value whatsoever, they'd never pass his lips again).

INGREDIENTS

2¼ cups plus 2 tablespoons whole wheat flour
1 teaspoon baking soda
1 teaspoon salt
¾ cup plus 2 tablespoons quick-cooking oats
2 tablespoons wheat bran (coarse or fine)
2 tablespoons toasted wheat germ
1 cup (2 sticks) unsalted butter at room temperature
1 cup (lightly packed) light brown sugar
½ cup granulated sugar
1½ teaspoons pure vanilla extract
2 large eggs
9 ounces (1½ cups) semisweet chocolate chips

1. Preheat the oven to 400°F. Line several baking sheets with parchment paper, or grease them lightly with vegetable oil.

2. Sift the flour, baking soda, and salt together into a small bowl and set aside.

3. Mix the oats, bran, and wheat germ together in another small bowl and set aside.

4. Using an electric mixer on medium speed, cream the butter, both sugars, and the vanilla together in a medium-size bowl until light and fluffy, 1½ to 2 minutes. Stop the mixer twice during the process to scrape the bowl with a rubber spatula.

5. Add the eggs and beat on medium speed until they are blended, about 30 seconds. Scrape the bowl.

6. Add the flour mixture and mix on low speed for 10 seconds. Scrape the bowl.

7. Add the oat mixture and mix on low speed for several seconds to blend.

8. Add the chocolate chips and blend until they are mixed in, 5 to 8 seconds.

9. Drop the dough by heaping table-spoons 2 inches apart onto the pre-pared baking sheets.

10. Bake the cookies until the edges are dark golden and the centers are light and slightly puffed up, 11 to 12 min-utes. Remove the cookies from the oven and allow them to cool on the sheets. These are best eaten the same day they are baked. Otherwise, store them in an airtight container in the freezer for up to 2 weeks, and bring them to room temperature before eating.

Makes about 26 cookies

Chocolate Chocolate Chip Meringues

❤ ❤ ❤ ❤ ❤ ❤ ❤ ❤ ❤ ❤ *drop cookie*

These are a low-fat sweet treat that both you and your kids will love. (Their only fat is in the cocoa and the chocolate chips, and that's not much.) You can determine how chewy their center is by varying the baking time.

INGREDIENTS

¼ cup unsweetened cocoa powder
¾ cup plus 2 tablespoons confectioners'
    sugar
3 large egg whites
¼ teaspoon cream of tartar
6 tablespoons granulated sugar
6 ounces (1 cup) semisweet chocolate chips

1. Line several baking sheets with parchment paper, or grease them lightly with vegetable oil and flour them.

2. Sift the cocoa and the confection-ers' sugar together into a small bowl.

3. Using an electric mixer on medium-low speed, beat the egg whites with the cream of tartar in a medium-size bowl until frothy, 30 to 40 seconds.

4. Gradually add the cocoa mixture and the granulated sugar to the egg whites. Then increase the mixer speed to medium-high and beat for 1 minute. Stop to scrape the bowl with a rubber spatula, increase the speed to high, and continue beating until the mixture forms stiff peaks, 60 to 75 seconds longer. Then gently fold in the choco-late chips with a rubber spatula.

5. Drop the mixture by generously rounded tablespoons onto the baking sheets, leaving 1½ inches between each of the cookies. Allow the cookies to set for 45 minutes.

6. Preheat the oven to 200°F.

7. Place the baking sheets in the oven, and bake for 1½ to 2 hours, depending on how chewy you like your meringue centers to be.

8. Cool the cookies for several minutes on the sheets; then run a spatula under each one and transfer them to cooling racks. Eat warm or at room temperature.

9. After the first day, place the cookies in an airtight plastic container with parchment paper between the layers, and store them for a couple of days at room temperature.

Makes 20 cookies

Rosie's Oatmeal Cookies

♥ ♥ ♥ ♥ ♥ ♥ ♥ ♥ ♥ ♥ *drop cookie*

This Rosie's staple—moist, chewy, and replete with golden raisins—didn't make it into my first book. Many of my customers were disappointed and pleaded with me to adapt the recipe for home use. Here it is: the perfect choice for easy baking, moist in the center and crunchy around the edges. Just guard against overbaking.

INGREDIENTS

¾ cup all-purpose flour
¾ teaspoon baking soda
¾ teaspoon ground cinnamon
½ teaspoon salt
8½ tablespoons (1 stick plus 1½ teaspoons) unsalted butter at room temperature
⅓ cup plus 2 tablespoons (lightly packed) light brown sugar
7 tablespoons granulated sugar
1 tablespoon plus 1 teaspoon molasses
2¼ teaspoons water
½ teaspoon pure vanilla extract
1 large egg
2 cups plus 1 tablespoon rolled oats
½ cup shredded sweetened coconut
½ cup plus 2 tablespoons golden raisins

1. Preheat the oven to 375°F. Line several baking sheets with parchment paper, or lightly grease them with vegetable oil.

2. Sift the flour, baking soda, cinnamon, and salt together into a small bowl and set aside.

3. Using an electric mixer on medium speed, cream the butter, both sugars, the molasses, water, and vanilla together in a medium-size bowl until light and fluffy, about 1½ minutes. Stop the mixer twice during the process to scrape the bowl with a rubber spatula.

4. Add the egg and mix on medium-low speed to incorporate it, about 20 seconds.

5. Add the flour mixture and mix on medium-low speed for 10 seconds.

Scrape the bowl, then mix until blended, about 5 seconds more. Scrape the bowl.

6. Add the oats and mix for several seconds on low speed to blend them in. Add the coconut and raisins and mix until blended.

7. Drop the dough by heaping tablespoons about 2 inches apart onto the prepared baking sheets.

8. Bake the cookies until they are golden around the edges and lighter in the center, 12 to 14 minutes. Cool them on the baking sheets.

9. If you plan to snack on them the first day, place the cookies on a plate or simply leave them on the baking sheet. After that, layer the cookies in an airtight container, using plastic wrap, parchment, or waxed paper between the layers, and store the container in the freezer for up to 2 weeks. Bring the cookies to room temperature before eating.

Makes 20 cookies

Oatmeal Chocolate Chips

♥ ♥ ♥ ♥ ♥ ♥ ♥ ♥ ♥ *drop cookie*

The perfect union of two classic cookies—more an oatmeal cookie with chocolate chips than a chocolate chip cookie with oats! Chewy in the center, crunchy around the edges, it's a hearty and delicious treat.

INGREDIENTS

1¼ cups all-purpose flour
6 tablespoons whole wheat flour
1 teaspoon baking soda
1 teaspoon salt
1¼ cups (2½ sticks) unsalted butter at
   room temperature
1¼ cups (lightly packed) light brown sugar
½ cup granulated sugar
2 teaspoons pure vanilla extract
2 large eggs
2 tablespoons milk
2¼ cups quick oats
8 ounces (1¼ cups) semisweet chocolate
   chips

1. Preheat the oven to 375°F. Line several baking sheets with parchment paper, or lightly grease them with vegetable oil.

2. Sift both flours, the baking soda, and salt together into a small bowl and set aside.

3. Using an electric mixer on medium-high speed, cream the butter, both sugars, and the vanilla together in a medium-size mixing bowl until light and fluffy, 1½ minutes. Stop the mixer twice during the process to scrape the bowl with a rubber spatula.

4. Add 1 egg and beat on medium speed for 10 seconds. Scrape the bowl and add the second egg and the milk. Beat on medium speed until blended, 10 seconds. Scrape the bowl.

5. Add the flour mixture and mix on low speed until almost blended. Once again, scrape the bowl.

6. Add the oats and blend on medium speed for 10 seconds. Scrape the bowl. Then add the chocolate chips and blend on low speed for 10 to 15 seconds, until incorporated.

7. Drop the cookies by generously rounded tablespoons 2 inches apart on the prepared baking sheets. Bake until the edges are golden and the centers are lighter in color and just set, 14 to 16 minutes. Cool them on the baking sheets.

8. Store the cookies in a plastic container at room temperature for 1 day. After that, store them in the freezer for up to 2 weeks. Bring them to room temperature before eating, or heat them in a microwave for 50 seconds on medium power.

Makes about 26 cookies

Pecan Oatmeal Chips

♥ ♥ ♥ ♥ ♥ ♥ ♥ ♥ ♥   *drop cookie*

I adapted these cookies from what was purportedly an original Neiman Marcus creation, and I must say that they're a good argument for department stores branching out into everything under the sun. The oats are ground into flour before you add them to the batter—neither chic nor expensive like the source of this recipe, they're downright earthy.

INGREDIENTS

1¼ cups rolled oats
1 cup all-purpose flour
¾ teaspoon baking soda
½ teaspoon salt
12 tablespoons (1½ sticks) unsalted butter
    at room temperature
½ cup (lightly packed) light brown sugar
½ cup granulated sugar
1½ teaspoons pure vanilla extract
1 large egg
6 ounces (1 cup) semisweet chocolate chips
½ cup chopped pecans

1. Preheat the oven to 375°F. Line several baking sheets with parchment paper, or grease them lightly with vegetable oil.

2. Process the oats in a food processor until they have the consistency of coarse flour. Set aside.

3. Sift the flour, baking soda, and salt together into a small bowl and set aside.

4. Using an electric mixer on medium speed, cream the butter, both sugars, and the vanilla together in a medium-size bowl until light and fluffy, 1 to 1½ minutes. Stop the mixer twice during the process to scrape the bowl with a rubber spatula.

5. Add the egg and beat on medium speed until blended, about 15 seconds. Scrape the bowl.

6. Add the flour mixture and mix on low speed for 15 seconds. Scrape the bowl. Add the oats and blend for 8 to 10 seconds.

7. Add the chocolate chips and pecans and blend until they are mixed in, 5 to 8 seconds.

8. Drop the dough by heaping tablespoons 2 inches apart onto the prepared cookie sheets.

9. Bake the cookies until the edges are dark golden and the centers are light and slightly puffed up, 12 to 14 minutes. Remove the cookies from the oven and allow them to cool on the sheets.

10. These are best eaten the same day they are baked. If you plan to snack on them the first day, place the cookies on a plate or simply leave them on the baking sheet. After that, layer the cookies in an airtight container, using plastic wrap, parchment, or waxed paper between the layers, and store the container in the freezer for up to 2 weeks. Bring the cookies to room temperature before eating.

Makes about 20 cookies

Chocolate Chocolate Chip Oatmeal Cookies

❤ ❤ ❤ ❤ ❤ ❤ ❤ ❤ ❤ *drop cookie*

A great combination of America's favorites, this is very much an oatmeal cookie, yet totally chocolatey at the same time.

INGREDIENTS

3½ ounces unsweetened chocolate
1 cup plus 6 tablespoons all-purpose flour
1 teaspoon baking soda
½ teaspoon salt
1 cup (2 sticks) unsalted butter at room temperature
1½ cups sugar
1 teaspoon pure vanilla extract
1 large egg
6 tablespoons milk
2½ cups quick-cooking oats
6 ounces (1 cup) semisweet chocolate chips

1. Preheat the oven to 350°F. Line several baking sheets with parchment paper, or grease them lightly with vegetable oil.

2. Melt the unsweetened chocolate in the top of a double boiler placed over simmering water. Remove the pan from the heat and allow to cool slightly.

3. Sift the flour, baking soda, and salt together into a small bowl and set aside.

4. Using an electric mixer on medium speed, cream the butter, sugar, and vanilla together in a medium-size bowl until light and fluffy, 1½ to 2 minutes. Stop the mixer twice during the process to scrape the bowl with a rubber spatula.

5. Add the egg and milk and beat on medium speed until blended, about 20 seconds. Scrape the bowl.

6. Add the flour mixture and blend on low speed for 15 seconds. Scrape the bowl. Add the oats and mix until blended, about 15 seconds. Scrape the bowl.

7. Add the melted chocolate and mix on medium speed until blended, 20 seconds. Scrape the bowl.

8. Add the chocolate chips and blend until they are mixed in, 5 to 8 seconds.

9. Drop the batter by heaping tablespoons 2 inches apart on the prepared baking sheets.

10. Bake the cookies until the centers have risen and just begun to set, about 17 minutes. Allow them to cool completely on the sheets.

11. Leave the cookies on the baking sheets or transfer them to a plate if you plan on snacking on them that day. Otherwise, store the cookies in an airtight container in the freezer for up to 2 weeks, and bring them to room temperature before eating.

Makes about 45 cookies

Cranberry Orange Oatmeal Cookies

♥ ♥ ♥ ♥ ♥ ♥ ♥ ♥ ♥ *drop cookie*

To my mind, the cranberry is most enticing when its tartness is surrounded by sweetness. So this cookie, with its chewy center and distinctive citrus-accented oatmeal taste, provides the perfect setting for the little ruby-red fruits. These cookies are best the day they're baked, especially when they've cooled just enough to put in your mouth without burning your tongue.

INGREDIENTS

¾ cup plus 2 tablespoons all-purpose flour
¾ teaspoon baking soda
¾ teaspoon salt
10 tablespoons (1¼ sticks) unsalted butter
   at room temperature
½ cup plus 1 tablespoon granulated sugar
5 tablespoons (lightly packed) light
   brown sugar
1 teaspoon fresh lemon juice
½ teaspoon pure vanilla extract
2 tablespoons grated orange zest
1 tablespoon grated lemon zest
2 large eggs
1¼ cups rolled oats
¾ cup chopped walnuts
1 cup whole cranberries

1. Preheat the oven to 375°F. Line several baking sheets with parchment paper, or lightly grease them with vegetable oil.

2. Sift the flour, baking soda, and salt together into a small bowl and set aside.

3. Using an electric mixer on medium speed, cream the butter, both sugars, lemon juice, vanilla, orange zest, and lemon zest together in a medium-size bowl until light and fluffy, about 1½ minutes. Stop the mixer twice during the process to scrape the bowl with a rubber spatula.

4. Add the eggs and mix on medium-low speed to incorporate, about 20 seconds.

5. Add the flour mixture and mix on medium-low speed for 10 seconds.

Scrape the bowl, then mix until blended, about 5 seconds more. Scrape the bowl.

6. Add the oats and mix for several seconds on low speed to blend them in. Fold in the nuts and then the cranberries by hand.

7. Drop the dough by heaping tablespoons about 2 inches apart onto the prepared baking sheets.

8. Bake the cookies until the edges are golden and the centers are still light and puffy, about 11 minutes. Allow them to cool on the sheets.

9. If you plan to snack on them the first day, place the cookies on a plate or simply leave them on the baking sheet. After that, layer the cookies in an airtight container, using plastic wrap, parchment, or waxed paper between the layers, and store the container in the freezer for up to 2 weeks. Bring the cookies to room temperature before eating.

Makes 36 cookies

Chocolate Peanut Butter Volcanoes

♥ ♥ ♥ ♥ ♥ ♥ ♥ ♥ *formed cookie*

With all due credit to George Washington Carver, I'm sure it was a kid who invented the peanut butter-chocolate combination. It certainly is a perfect one. The next time your kids (or you) are in the mood for a Reese's Peanut Butter Cup, bake a batch of these cookies instead. They're little peanut butter volcanoes erupting in soft chocolate lava.

INGREDIENTS

THE LAVA
3 ounces (½ cup) semisweet chocolate chips
½ ounce unsweetened chocolate
½ cup sweetened condensed milk
1½ teaspoons pure vanilla extract

THE COOKIE
1¾ cups all-purpose flour
¼ teaspoon plus ⅛ teaspoon baking soda
¼ teaspoon salt
11 tablespoons (1 stick plus 3 tablespoons)
    unsalted butter at room temperature
¾ cup smooth peanut butter
½ cup plus 1 tablespoon (lightly packed)
    light brown sugar
6 tablespoons granulated sugar
¾ teaspoon pure vanilla extract
1 large egg

1. Preheat the oven to 350°F. Line several baking sheets with parchment paper, or lightly grease them with vegetable oil.

2. Make the lava: Melt the chocolates together in the top of a double boiler placed over simmering water.

3. Combine the condensed milk and the vanilla in a medium-size bowl.

4. Using a whisk, stir the melted chocolate vigorously into the milk until the mixture is smooth and well blended. Set it aside.

5. Make the cookie dough: Sift the flour, baking soda, and salt together into a small bowl and set aside.

6. Using an electric mixer on medium speed, cream the butter, peanut butter, both sugars, and the vanilla together in a medium-size mixing bowl until light and fluffy, about 1½ minutes. Stop the mixer twice during the process to scrape the bowl with a rubber spatula.

7. Add the egg and beat on medium speed until blended, about 1 minute. Scrape the bowl.

8. Add the flour mixture and mix on low speed until blended, about 15 seconds. Scrape the bowl and mix several seconds more.

9. Measure out heaping tablespoons of the dough and roll them into balls with your hands. Place the balls 2 inches apart on the prepared baking sheets.

10. Using your thumb, press a deep hole into the center of each ball, and plop a heaping teaspoon of the lava mixture into the hole. Pinch the opening together just a little bit so the lava will not overflow, but so that it is still visible.

11. Bake the cookies until they are lightly golden, 16 to 18 minutes. Cool the cookies on the sheets or eat them while they're still warm for an extra-special treat.

12. Store the cookies in an airtight container in the refrigerator for 1 day. After that, store them in the freezer for up to 2 weeks. Bring them to room temperature before eating.

Makes 30 cookies

Banana-Nut Chocolate Chunks

❤ ❤ ❤ ❤ ❤ ❤ ❤ ❤ ❤ *drop cookie*

According to exhaustive surveys of monkeys in the zoo, when they get to scarf up a fallen ice cream cone, their favorite—hands and feet down—is Chunky Monkey, the dynamic flavor combo from Ben and Jerry's. So in homage to those ice cream artists and to sophisticated monkeys everywhere, I came up with this earthy oatmeal cookie, filled it with nutritious chunks of bananas and walnuts, and tossed in chocolate morsels just for the heck of it. Eat the cookies when they're warm so the chips are still squishy, then make a monkey of yourself as you squeal with delight.

INGREDIENTS

1 cup plus 3 tablespoons all-purpose flour
½ teaspoon baking soda
½ teaspoon baking powder
1 teaspoon salt
12 tablespoons (1½ sticks) unsalted butter at room temperature
½ cup plus 3 tablespoons (lightly packed) light brown sugar
5 tablespoons granulated sugar
1 tablespoon pure vanilla extract
2 large eggs
1 tablespoon milk
1¼ cups rolled oats
3 ounces (½ cup) plus 1 tablespoon semisweet chocolate chips
1 cup chopped walnuts or pecans
1½ cups chopped bananas

1. Preheat the oven to 400°F. Line several baking sheets with parchment paper, or lightly grease them with vegetable oil.

2. Sift the flour, baking soda, baking powder, and salt together into a small bowl and set aside.

3. Using an electric mixer on medium speed, cream the butter, both

295

sugars, and the vanilla together in a medium-size bowl until light and fluffy, about 1½ minutes. Stop the mixer twice during the process to scrape the bowl with a rubber spatula.

4. Add the eggs and mix on medium-low speed to incorporate, about 20 seconds. Scrape the bowl. Then add the milk and blend for several seconds.

5. Add the flour mixture and mix on medium-low speed for 10 seconds. Scrape the bowl. Then mix until blended, about 5 seconds more. Scrape the bowl again.

6. Add the oats and mix for several seconds on low speed to blend them in. Then add the chocolate chips and the nuts, and blend for several seconds.

7. Fold the banana pieces in by hand, stirring very gently with a rubber spatula.

8. Drop the dough by rounded tablespoons 2 inches apart on the prepared baking sheets.

9. Bake the cookies until the edges are golden and the centers are light and puffy and not quite set, 8 or 9 minutes.

10. Cool the cookies on the sheets and eat them soon after they cool. They are extremely fragile and cannot be stacked or stored easily.

Makes about 30 cookies

Chocolate-Dipped Almond Macaroons

❤ ❤ ❤ ❤ ❤ ❤ ❤ ❤ *formed cookie*

This cookie comes with a list of acknowledgments and thanks. First to Chagit Gluska of the Jerusalem Cafe, a kosher bakery in Flushing, New York. These macaroons are one of her to-die-for Jewish specialties. And second, to my cousins Roberta and Nathan for introducing me to the bakery and for buying me all manner of goodies from there to take back to Boston. For those of you who seldom find yourself in Flushing, all I can say is *essen* and enjoy.

INGREDIENTS

THE COOKIE
½ cup all-purpose flour
½ teaspoon plus ⅛ teaspoon baking powder
6 ounces (slightly rounded ¾ cup) almond paste (not marzipan)
½ cup plus 2 tablespoons sugar
1 teaspoon pure vanilla extract
2 large egg whites

THE GLAZE
5 ounces bittersweet chocolate

1. Sift the flour and baking powder together into a small bowl and set aside.

2. Cut the almond paste into 8 pieces and distribute them in the bowl of a food processor.

3. Add the sugar and vanilla, and process until the mixture resembles coarse meal, about 15 seconds. Distribute the flour mixture evenly over the almond mixture, and pulse 3 times to blend.

4. Pour the egg whites evenly over the almond mixture and pulse 4 or 5 times to incorporate. Scrape the bowl with a rubber spatula. Then pulse several more times, until the mixture just starts to form a sticky pastelike dough.

5. Scrape the contents of the work bowl into a small bowl, cover with plastic wrap, and refrigerate for 2 to 3 hours (or freeze for 1 to 1½ hours).

6. After that time, preheat the oven to 350°F. Line a baking sheet with parchment paper, or grease it lightly with vegetable oil.

7. Remove the dough from the refrigerator or freezer, and scoop out rounded tablespoons. Using your hands, roll them into balls and place them 2 inches apart on the prepared sheet. Press them down slightly with the palm of your hand.

8. Place the sheet on the middle rack of the oven and bake the cookies for 15 minutes. Then lower the heat to 300°F and bake until they are risen, slightly cracked, and lightly golden, 5 more minutes. Cool on the sheet for 1 hour.

9. Melt the bittersweet chocolate in the top of a double boiler placed over simmering water. Using a spatula, remove the cookies from the baking sheet. Dip half of each cookie in the chocolate.

10. Place the cookies back on the sheet and allow to set for 4 hours before eating (or place the sheet in the refrigerator for about 1 hour).

11. If you plan to snack on them the first day, place the cookies on a plate or simply leave them on the baking sheet. After that, layer the cookies in an airtight container, using plastic wrap, parchment, or waxed paper between the layers, and store the container in the refrigerator for a couple of days or in the freezer for up to 2 weeks. Bring the cookies to room temperature before eating.

Makes 12 cookies

Chocolate-Coconut Scoops

♥ ♥ ♥ ♥ ♥ ♥ ♥ ♥ ♥ *drop cookie*

Do you love Mounds Bars? Meet their cookie cousins: chewy, moist mounds of shredded coconut whose bottoms are dipped in bittersweet chocolate.

INGREDIENTS

THE COOKIE
1 cup sugar
4 large egg whites
6 tablespoons all-purpose flour
3 cups shredded sweetened
    coconut

THE GLAZE
6 ounces bittersweet chocolate
4 teaspoons vegetable oil

1. Preheat the oven to 350°F. Line one or two baking sheets with parchment paper.

2. Using a whisk, vigorously stir the sugar, egg whites, and flour together in a medium-size bowl. Then stir in the coconut.

3. Using a melon baller, or a mini cookie scoop, or a tablespoon, scoop mounds of the mixture onto the prepared baking sheets, placing them 2 inches apart. Bake until the edges and tops just begin to turn golden, about 12 minutes. Cool completely on the sheets.

4. When the cookies have cooled, prepare the glaze: Melt the chocolate in the top of a double boiler placed over simmering water. Stir in the oil.

5. Place the chocolate mixture in a small deep bowl, and dip the bottom of each coconut cookie in the glaze. Set them upside down (they will tip slightly) on a plate or rack, and refrigerate for 1 to 2 hours.

6. If you plan to snack on them the first day, place the cookies on a plate, if you haven't already done so. After that, layer the cookies in an airtight container, using plastic wrap, parchment, or waxed paper between the layers, and store the container in the refrigerator for a couple of days or in the freezer for up to 2 weeks. Bring the cookies to room temperature before eating.

Makes 14 scoops

Hazelnut Macaroons
❤ ❤ ❤ ❤ ❤ ❤ ❤ ❤ ❤   *drop cookie*

Welcome to the Hazelnut Era. Hazelnut mousse, hazelnut ganache, hazelnut coffee—you'd think the nut had never existed before ten years ago. Ever a child of my times, I offer the hazelnut macaroon as my contribution. It looks like a classic macaroon, and it's bursting forth with that ever-so-current flavor that we've come to love.

INGREDIENTS

2⅔ cups (14 ounces) hazelnuts, skins
    removed (see box)
5 large egg whites
2¼ cups sugar
7 tablespoons all-purpose flour

1. Place the nuts in a food processor and process to form a powder.

2. Combine the egg whites and the sugar in a medium-size mixing bowl and stir by hand with a wooden spoon until mixed, 10 seconds.

3. Add the flour and stir to mix. Then add the ground nuts and continue to mix by hand until blended, 10 seconds.

4. Refrigerate the dough, covered, for at least 2 hours.

5. Fifteen minutes before baking, preheat the oven to 350°F. Line several baking sheets with parchment paper. Lightly grease the paper with butter, then dust with flour.

6. Drop the dough by heaping table-spoons onto the prepared baking sheets, allowing 3 inches between cookies.

7. Bake the cookies until they are lightly golden, approximately 15 minutes.

8. While they are still warm, carefully remove the cookies from the sheets and place them on a rack to cool.

9. If you plan to snack on them the first day, place the cookies on a plate or simply leave them on the baking sheet. After that, layer the cookies in an air-tight container, using plastic wrap, parchment, or waxed paper between the layers, and store the container in the refrigerator for a couple of days or in the freezer for up to 2 weeks. Bring the cookies to room temperature before eating.

Makes 20 cookies

Skinning Hazelnuts

To remove the skin from un-blanched hazelnuts, toast the nuts on a baking sheet in a pre-heated 350°F oven for 5 minutes. Then immediately transfer the nuts (about a cupful at a time) onto a clean kitchen towel and lift all four corners to make a bundle. Using one hand to keep the bundle closed, use the other hand to squeeze and massage the nuts to loosen the skin, about 30 seconds. Then open the towel and place the nuts in a small bowl, making sure not to transfer the skins. (It will be impossible to remove all the skins from the nuts, but a good portion should come off.)

Baker's Best Snicker-doodles

♥ ♥ ♥ ♥ ♥ ♥ ♥ ♥ ♥ *drop cookie*

When my family tasted these classics at a street fair, they went wild. Those chewy centers, those crispy edges! I tracked down Michael Baker, proprietor of Baker's Best in Newton Highland, Massachusetts, and he was kind enough to share his recipe with me. You can play with the baking time to get the chewy-crisp combo just the way you want.

INGREDIENTS

3 cups all-purpose flour
1 tablespoon plus 1 teaspoon baking
*   powder*
½ teaspoon salt
2 teaspoons ground cinnamon
1½ cups plus 2 tablespoons sugar
1 cup (2 sticks) unsalted butter at room
*   temperature*
1 teaspoon pure vanilla extract
2 large eggs

1. Preheat the oven to 375°F. Line several baking sheets with parchment paper, or grease them lightly with vegetable oil.

2. Sift the flour, baking powder, and salt together into a small bowl and set aside.

3. Combine the cinnamon with the 2 tablespoons sugar in a small bowl. Stir together thoroughly, and pour into a plastic bag.

4. Using an electric mixer on medium speed, cream the butter, 1½ cups sugar, and vanilla together in a medium-size mixing bowl until light and fluffy, 1 minute. Stop the mixer once during the process to scrape the bowl with a rubber spatula, and scrape the bowl again at the end.

5. Add the eggs and beat on medium speed until they are blended, about 30 seconds. Scrape the bowl.

6. Add half of the flour mixture, and mix on low speed for 10 seconds.

Scrape the bowl. Add the remaining flour mixture and blend on low for 25 seconds, stopping the mixer twice to scrape the bowl.

7. Measure out generously rounded tablespoons of the dough, and roll them into balls with your hands.

8. Place 2 cookies at a time in the cinnamon/sugar mix and shake the bag to coat. Then place the balls 2 inches apart on the prepared baking sheets, and bake until the centers are risen and slightly cracked and the edges are crisp, 16 to 18 minutes. Cool the cookies on the baking sheets.

9. If you plan to snack on them the first day, place the cookies on a plate or simply leave them on the baking sheet. After that, layer the cookies in an airtight container, using plastic wrap, parchment, or waxed paper between the layers, and store the container in the freezer for up to 2 weeks. Bring the cookies to room temperature before eating.

Makes 30 cookies

Classic Snicker-doodles

❤ ❤ ❤ ❤ ❤ ❤ ❤ ❤ ❤ *drop cookie*

This is the classic sugar cookie baked to just the right chewiness. I think of it as a well-tailored sort of cookie: subtle, never showy, and *always* appropriate. It's perfect with a cup of tea or dunked into a glass of milk.

INGREDIENTS

THE COOKIE
3 cups all-purpose flour
1 teaspoon baking soda
½ teaspoon salt
1 teaspoon cream of tartar
Scant ½ teaspoon ground nutmeg
1 cup (2 sticks) unsalted butter at room
    temperature
1⅓ cups sugar
1½ teaspoons pure vanilla extract
2 large eggs

THE TOPPING
¼ cup sugar
¾ teaspoon ground cinnamon

1. Preheat the oven to 375°F. Line several baking sheets with parchment paper, or grease them lightly with vegetable oil.

2. Sift the flour, baking soda, salt, cream of tartar, and nutmeg together into a small bowl and set aside.

3. Using an electric mixer on medium speed, cream the butter, sugar, and vanilla together in a medium-size mixing bowl until light and fluffy, about 1½ minutes. Stop the mixer twice during the process to scrape the bowl with a rubber spatula.

4. Add the eggs one at a time, mixing at medium speed until each is incorpo-rated, about 30 seconds in all. Scrape the bowl.

5. Add the flour mixture on low speed and mix until blended, 20 to 25 seconds. Scrape the bowl and blend 10 seconds more.

6. Drop the dough by rounded table-spoons about 2 inches apart onto the prepared baking sheets. Stir the top-ping ingredients together, and sprinkle over the cookies.

7. Bake the cookies until they are firm and have small cracks on top, about 12 or 13 minutes. Transfer the cookies to wire racks to cool. As soon as they have completely cooled, store them in an airtight plastic container at room temperature for a day. After that, store the container in the freezer for up to 2 weeks.

Makes 30 cookies

Apple 'n' Spice Drops

❤ ❤ ❤ ❤ ❤ ❤ ❤ ❤ ❤ *drop cookie*

A perfect winter cookie with the texture of a traditional Toll House: crunchy edges, soft center. With its apple pie flavor, this is a wonderful treat with a tall glass of milk on a night when you want to feel warm and cozy.

INGREDIENTS

2 cups dried apples, chopped into ⅜-inch
pieces
½ cup apple juice or cider
2 cups plus 1 tablespoon all-purpose flour
1 teaspoon baking soda
¾ teaspoon salt
2½ teaspoons ground cinnamon
1½ teaspoons ground nutmeg
1 cup (2 sticks) unsalted butter, at room
temperature
1 cup plus 1 tablespoon (lightly packed)
light brown sugar
½ cup plus 2 tablespoons
granulated sugar
1 teaspoon pure vanilla extract
1 teaspoon grated lemon zest
2 large eggs
½ cup raisins
½ cup chopped walnuts

1. Place the apples and juice in a small saucepan over medium heat. Bring to a simmer, and simmer for 1 minute, tossing the apples lightly once or twice with a wooden spoon.

2. Drain the apples of any juice, and place them on a double sheet of paper towels. Roll them up in the paper towels, and squeeze out any excess juice. Unroll the towels and let the apples sit, uncovered, while you prepare the dough.

3. Preheat the oven to 425°F. Line several baking sheets with parchment paper, or grease them lightly with vegetable oil.

4. Sift the flour, baking soda, salt, and spices together into a small bowl and set aside.

5. Using an electric mixer on medium speed, cream the butter, both sugars, vanilla, and lemon zest together in a medium-size bowl until light and fluffy, 1½ to 2 minutes. Stop the mixer twice during the process to scrape the bowl with a rubber spatula.

6. Add the eggs and beat on medium speed until they are blended, about 30 seconds. Scrape the bowl.

7. Add the flour mixture and mix on low speed for 15 seconds. Scrape the bowl.

8. Add the apples, raisins, and walnuts, and blend until they are mixed in, 5 to 8 seconds.

9. Drop the dough by heaping tablespoons 2 inches apart onto the prepared baking sheets.

10. Bake the cookies until the edges are dark golden and the center is light and slightly puffed, 11 to 12 minutes. Remove the cookies from the oven and allow them to cool on the sheets.

11. These are best eaten the same day; they tend to get soggy over time because of the moisture in the apples. Leave them on a plate the first day, and then freeze any leftovers in an airtight container for up to 2 weeks.

Makes 28 to 30 cookies

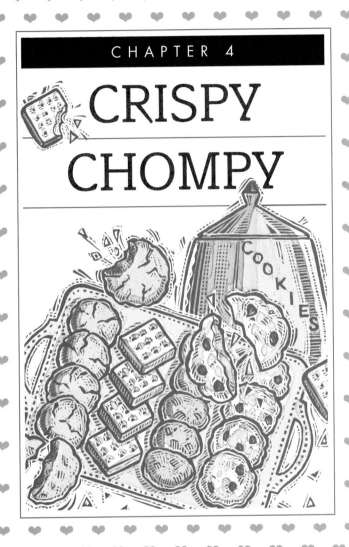

CHAPTER 4

CRISPY

CHOMPY

COOKIES

Crunchy Chocolate Chips
Thin Crisp Chocochips
Chocolate Chip Strips
Chocolate Chip Pecan Mounds
Hazelnut White Chocolate Chunk Cookies
Broken Brittle Crisps
Coconut Dainties
Fresh Ginger Crisps
Hazelnut Crisps
Glazed Lemon Cookies
Chinese Almond Cornmeal Wafers
Lovely Lemon Crisps
Orange Pecan Crisps
Pecan Crisps
Pecan Fingers
Très French Palmiers
Aunt Florence's Anise Biscotti
Low-Fat Almond Biscotti
Orange Walnut Mandelbrot
Chocolate Chocolate Chip Mandelbrot
Amy's Mandelbrot
Lemon Meringues
Golden Pecan Squares
Cappuccino Shortbread Sails
Chunky Chocolate Almond Shortbread
Chocolate Orange Shortbread
Chocolate-Glazed Chocolate Shortbread
Toasted Coconut Macadamia Shortbread
Chunky Pecan Shortbread
Peanut Butter Shortbread Cookies
Ginger Shortbread
Cornmeal Shortbread Cookies

This chapter encompasses the wonderful world of shortbreads, crisps, florentines, ground-nut cookies, and spritzes. Sounds a little like a cookie ride at Disneyland, doesn't it? Or better yet, something from Jane Austen: Under the watchful eye of a Shortbread, that guardian of standards, a sophisticated Florentine gossips behind her lace fan to a demure Spritz, who blushes prettily, while a gingery Crisp thumbs her nose at convention and marries well anyway.

From Disney to Austen, there's nothing like a classic shortbread cookie to win the heart of all age groups. Otherwise, crisps are pretty much the cookies of adulthood. Maybe that's because they have a certain refinement that gives them their character—and this particular character, I've found, is an acquired taste.

Though "crisp" and "chomp" are shared by all the cookies in this chapter, the texture is arrived at by different means for different cookies. Pecan cookies take their texture from their fleshy nuts, for instance, biscotti and mandelbrot are double-baked for crispness, and cookies like Cappuccino Shortbread Sails are rolled thin to achieve their crispy nature.

Shortbread, of course, depends on butter to give it its distinctive brisk texture, as do most of these cookies. That butter flavor also makes them seem to melt in your mouth—a mixed blessing, since they may disappear almost  too quickly. That's just as well because some of them may lose their crispness when left at room temperature for more than two days. Crispy cookies freeze beautifully, though, so you don't *have* to eat them all at once.

The crispier of these cookies can be fragile, so handle them carefully when removing them from the baking sheet, arranging them on a plate, and most especially, sending them through the mail.

Crunchy Chocolate Chips

❤ ❤ ❤ ❤ ❤ ❤ ❤ ❤ ❤ ❤ *drop cookie*

This cookie is for those of you who share my husband's view that a good chocolate chip cookie should be crunchy. They are great alone, and a real treat broken up as a topping over ice cream.

INGREDIENTS

1¾ cups all-purpose flour
¼ teaspoon baking soda
¼ teaspoon baking powder
½ teaspoon salt
13 tablespoons (1 stick plus 5 tablespoons)
    unsalted butter at room temperature
½ cup plus 2½ tablespoons (lightly
    packed) light brown sugar
5 tablespoons granulated sugar
1½ teaspoons pure vanilla extract
1 whole large egg
½ large egg yolk
4 ounces (¾ cup) semisweet chocolate chips

1. Preheat the oven to 400°F. Line several baking sheets with parchment paper, or grease them lightly with vegetable oil.

2. Sift the flour, baking soda, baking powder, and salt together into a small bowl and set aside.

3. Using an electric mixer on medium speed, cream the butter, both sugars, and the vanilla together in a medium-size bowl until light and fluffy, 1 minute. Stop the mixer once during the process to scrape the bowl with a rubber spatula.

4. Add the egg and yolk and beat on medium speed until they are blended, about 30 seconds. Scrape the bowl.

5. Add the flour mixture and mix on low speed for 15 seconds. Scrape the bowl.

6. Add the chocolate chips and blend until they are mixed in, 5 to 8 seconds.

7. Drop the dough by heaping teaspoons 2 inches apart on the prepared baking sheets.

8. Bake the cookies until they are firm and very light golden with darker golden edges, 15 minutes. Cool on the sheets.

9. Store the cookies in an airtight container at room temperature for a day or two if you think you will be snacking on them. After that, store the container in the freezer for up to 2 weeks. Bring the cookies to room temperature before eating.

Makes 48 cookies

Thin Crisp Chocochips

♥ ♥ ♥ ♥ ♥ ♥ ♥ ♥ ♥ *drop cookie*

Despite their dainty and elegant appearance, these waferlike cookies completely satisfy your chocolate chip cravings! They're lovely served as an accent with fruit, sorbet, or ice cream, or with a cup of tea in the afternoon.

INGREDIENTS

1½ cups all-purpose flour
¼ teaspoon baking powder
½ teaspoon salt
14 tablespoons (1¾ sticks) unsalted butter
    at room temperature
1 cup (lightly packed) light brown sugar
½ cup granulated sugar
1½ teaspoons pure vanilla extract
1 large egg
6 ounces (1 cup) semisweet chocolate
    chips

1. Preheat the oven to 400°F. Line several baking sheets with parchment paper, or grease them lightly with vegetable oil.

2. Sift the flour, baking powder, and salt together into a small bowl and set aside.

3. Using an electric mixer on medium speed, cream the butter, both sugars, and the vanilla together in a medium-size bowl until light and fluffy, 1 minute. Stop the mixer once during the process to scrape the bowl with a rubber spatula. Scrape the bowl again at the end.

4. Add the egg and beat on medium speed until blended, about 10 seconds. Scrape the bowl.

5. Add the flour mixture and mix on low speed for 15 seconds. Scrape the bowl.

6. Add the chocolate chips and blend until they are mixed in, 5 to 8 seconds.

7. Drop the cookies by rounded teaspoons 2 inches apart on the prepared baking sheets. Flatten each cookie to ¼ inch thickness.

8. Bake the cookies until they are firm and light golden with deep golden edges, about 12 minutes. Allow to cool on the sheets.

9. Store the cookies in an airtight container at room temperature for a day or two if you think you will be snacking on them. After that, store the container in the freezer for up to 2 weeks. Bring the cookies to room temperature before eating.

Makes 75 cookies

Chocolate Chip Strips

♥ ♥ ♥ ♥ ♥ ♥ ♥ ♥ *formed cookie*

You bake these strips and then cut them to the size you want. I cut them thin and dainty for tea, wide and hearty for teen-age appetites. They're flavorful and crunchy, like the little chocolate chip cookies I used to buy at William Greenberg Bakery in New York.

INGREDIENTS

1½ cups all-purpose flour
¼ teaspoon baking powder
½ teaspoon salt
14 tablespoons (1¾ sticks) unsalted butter
    at room temperature
½ cup plus 2 tablespoons (lightly packed)
    light brown sugar
6 tablespoons granulated sugar
1½ teaspoons pure vanilla extract
1 large egg
6 ounces (1 cup) semisweet chocolate chips

1. Preheat the oven to 400°F. Line two baking sheets with parchment paper, or grease them lightly with vegetable oil.

2. Sift the flour, baking powder, and salt together into a small bowl and set aside.

3. Using an electric mixer on medium speed, cream the butter, both sugars, and the vanilla together in a medium-size bowl until light and fluffy,

1 minute. Stop the mixer once during the process to scrape the bowl with a rubber spatula.

4. Add the egg and beat on medium speed until blended, about 10 seconds. Scrape the bowl.

5. Add the flour mixture and mix on low speed for 15 seconds. Scrape the bowl.

6. Add the chocolate chips and blend until they are mixed in, 5 to 8 seconds.

7. Form the dough into four equal strips 14 inches long. Place two strips of dough on each baking sheet, and using your hands, flatten each one to a width of 2½ inches. The strips should be 4 inches apart.

8. Bake until the strips are light golden with darker golden edges, about 16 minutes.

9. Remove the baking sheets from the oven, and immediately slice each strip crosswise into 14 slices for dainty cookies or 7 slices for hearty cookies. Let them cool on the sheets.

10. Store the cookies in an airtight container at room temperature for a day or two if you think you will be snacking on them. After that, store the container in the freezer for up to 2 weeks. Bring the cookies to room temperature before eating.

Makes 28 to 56 cookies, depending on how wide you slice them

Chocolate Chip Pecan Mounds

❤ ❤ ❤ ❤ ❤ ❤ ❤ ❤ ❤ *drop cookie*

This sturdy chocolate chip cookie is made with both whole wheat and white flour, which gives it a somewhat earthy texture. The recipe comes from Amy Nastasi, architect par excellence, designer of Rosie's stores, and mother of twins who are almost as cute as mine. . . . Well, all right, they're just as cute!

INGREDIENTS

1 cup whole wheat flour
2 cups all-purpose flour
1 teaspoon baking soda
1 teaspoon salt
1 cup (2 sticks) unsalted butter at room temperature
½ cup granulated sugar
1 cup (lightly packed) light brown sugar
1 teaspoon pure vanilla extract
2 extra large eggs
9 ounces (1½ cups) semisweet chocolate chips
1 cup chopped pecans (optional)

1. Preheat the oven to 375°F. Line several baking sheets with parchment paper, or grease them lightly with vegetable oil.

2. Sift both flours, the baking soda, and the salt together into a small bowl and set aside.

3. Using an electric mixer on medium speed, cream the butter, both sugars, and the vanilla together in a medium-size bowl until light and fluffy, about 1 minute.

4. Add the eggs and beat on medium speed until they are blended, about 30 seconds. Scrape the bowl.

5. Add the flour mixture and mix on low speed for 15 seconds. Scrape the bowl.

6. Add the chocolate chips and blend until they are mixed in, 5 to 8 seconds. Add the nuts, if using, and blend until smooth, 5 seconds more.

7. Drop the dough in ¼-cup mounds, spaced 2 inches apart, onto the prepared baking sheets.

8. Bake the cookies until the edges are a rich golden color and the top is lightly golden, risen, and slightly tender, 14 to 18 minutes, depending on desired chewiness. Remove the cookies from the oven and allow them to cool on the sheets.

9. If you plan to snack on them the first day (which is the best idea), place the cookies on a plate or simply leave them on the baking sheet. After that, layer the cookies in an airtight container, using plastic wrap, parchment, or waxed paper between the layers, and store the container in the freezer for up to 3 weeks. Bring the cookies to room temperature before eating.

Makes 20 cookies

Hazelnut White Chocolate Chunk Cookies

♥ ♥ ♥ ♥ ♥ ♥ ♥ ♥ ♥ ♥   *drop cookie*

Imagine peanut butter cookies with chunks of chocolate. Then imagine substituting hazelnuts for the peanuts and white chocolate for the chunks. Finally, imagine a cookie like none you've ever tasted, and now we're talking Hazelnut White Chocolate Chunks.

INGREDIENTS

1½ cups all-purpose flour
½ teaspoon baking soda
½ teaspoon salt
1¼ cups skinned toasted
    hazelnuts (see pages 53 and 89)
2 tablespoons unsalted butter, melted
7 tablespoons unsalted butter at room
    temperature
½ cup (lightly packed) light brown sugar
½ cup granulated sugar
1 teaspoon pure vanilla extract
1 large egg
6 ounces (1 cup) coarsely chopped white
    chocolate or whole white chocolate
    chips

1. Preheat the oven to 350°F. Line several baking sheets with parchment paper, or grease them lightly with vegetable oil.

2. Sift the flour, baking soda, and salt together into a small bowl and set aside.

3. Chop ½ cup of the hazelnuts coarsely and set aside.

4. Place the remaining ¾ cup hazelnuts and the 2 tablespoons melted butter in a food processor, and process until the mixture forms a crumbly paste, 30 seconds.

5. Using an electric mixer on medium speed, cream the butter, both sugars, and the vanilla together until blended, 30 seconds. Stop once during the process to scrape the bowl.

6. Add the hazelnut butter mixture and beat on medium speed for 10 seconds to blend. Scrape the bowl.

7. Add the egg and continue to beat on medium speed until blended, 10 seconds. Scrape the bowl.

8. Add the flour mixture and mix on low speed until almost blended, 20 seconds. Scrape the bowl. Then add the reserved chopped nuts and the white chocolate, and mix for 3 seconds. Finish the mixing by hand.

9. Drop the dough by generously rounded teaspoons about 2 inches apart onto the prepared baking sheets. Using the prongs of a fork, press each cookie down lightly, making a criss-cross pattern.

10. Bake the cookies until they are firm and lightly golden, 16 to 18 minutes. Cool them on the baking sheets.

11. If you plan to snack on them the first day, place the cookies on a plate or simply leave them on the baking sheet. After that, layer the cookies in an air-tight container, using plastic wrap, parchment, or waxed paper between the layers, and store the container in the freezer for up to 2 weeks. Bring the cookies to room temperature before eating.

Makes about 55 cookies

Broken Brittle Crisps

❤ ❤ ❤ ❤ ❤ ❤ ❤ ❤ ❤ *formed cookie*

Take a classic chocolate chip cookie, stud it with your choice of shattered Heath Bar or Skōr bar, and you've got yourself a treat. Although the chocolate coating on the candy melts into the cookie, the hard toffee remains intact once the cookie cools. A perfect candy/cookie combo.

INGREDIENTS

2 cups all-purpose flour
¼ teaspoon baking soda
1 teaspoon salt
1 cup (2 sticks) unsalted butter at room
    temperature
¾ cup (lightly packed) light brown sugar
¼ cup (lightly packed) dark brown sugar
½ cup granulated sugar
1½ teaspoons pure vanilla extract
1 large egg
4 ounces Heath or Skōr candy bars,
    chopped very coarsely and unevenly

1. Preheat the oven to 400°F. Line several baking sheets with parchment paper, or grease them lightly with vegetable oil.

2. Sift the flour, baking soda, and salt together into a small bowl and set aside.

3. Using an electric mixer on medium speed, cream the butter, three sugars, and the vanilla together in a medium-size bowl until light and fluffy, 1½ to 2 minutes. Stop the mixer twice during the process to scrape the bowl with a rubber spatula.

4. Add the egg and beat on medium speed until blended, about 10 seconds. Scrape the bowl.

5. Add the flour mixture and mix on low speed for 15 seconds. Scrape the bowl.

6. Add the candy and mix on low speed just enough to incorporate.

7. Measure out generously rounded teaspoons of the dough and roll them into balls with your hands.

8. Place the balls 2 inches apart on the prepared baking sheets, and then press each cookie down as thin as possible with your hand (dip your hand in flour for every other cookie).

9. Bake the cookies until they are golden with a deeper golden edge, 13 to 14 minutes. Cool the cookies on the sheets.

10. If you plan to snack on them the first day, place the cookies on a plate or simply leave them on the baking sheet. After that, layer the cookies in an airtight container, using plastic wrap, parchment, or waxed paper between the layers, and store the container in the freezer for up to 2 weeks. Bring the cookies to room temperature before eating.

Makes about 50 cookies

Coconut Dainties

❤ ❤ ❤ ❤ ❤ ❤ ❤ ❤ ❤ *formed cookie*

Melt-in-your-mouth coconut wafers—crisp, delicate, coated with confectioners' sugar. They came to me from Susan Allison of Healdsburg, California—they're an Allison family heirloom.

INGREDIENTS

2 cups plus 2 tablespoons cake flour
5 tablespoons granulated sugar
½ teaspoon salt
1 cup (2 sticks) unsalted butter, cold, cut into 16 pieces
½ teaspoon pure vanilla extract
1 teaspoon pure almond extract
2 cups shredded sweetened coconut
2 cups sifted confectioners' sugar for coating

1. Preheat the oven to 350°F. Line several baking sheets with parchment paper.

2. Place the flour, sugar, and salt in a food processor and process to blend, 5 seconds.

3. Scatter the butter over the flour mixture, and dribble the extracts over that. Process until the butter is blended and the dough is beginning to come together, 35 seconds. Scrape the sides and bottom of the bowl with a rubber spatula.

4. Add the coconut and pulse 7 or 8 times to blend.

5. Scoop out rounded teaspoons of the dough, and use your hands to form them into 2-inch-long logs about ¼ inch thick. Place the logs 2 inches apart on the prepared baking sheets, and flatten them with your hands so that they form an oval shape.

6. Bake the cookies until they are firm and golden around the edges,

15 to 18 minutes. Let them cool on the baking sheets.

7. Place the confectioners' sugar in a plastic bag or a bowl, and one by one drop the cookies in, tossing lightly to coat.

8. Store the cookies in an airtight container at room temperature for a day or two if you think you will be snacking on them. After that, store the container in the freezer for up to 2 weeks. Bring the cookies to room temperature before eating.

Makes about 50 cookies

Fresh Ginger Crisps

❤ ❤ ❤ ❤ ❤ ❤ ❤   *refrigerator cookie*

I'm willing to bet that these are the gingeriest cookies you'll ever taste—so gingery that you can see the strands of fresh ginger in each cookie, so gingery that the taste lingers on your tongue for a few minutes after you've eaten your last bite.

1 cup plus 5 tablespoons all-purpose
   flour
¼ teaspoon baking soda
¼ teaspoon salt
10 tablespoons (1¼ sticks) unsalted
   butter at room temperature
½ cup (lightly packed) light brown sugar
¼ teaspoon ground cinnamon
¼ teaspoon ground allspice
2 teaspoons grated lemon zest
¼ cup grated fresh ginger (use a hand
   grater)
¼ cup molasses

1. Sift the flour, baking soda, and salt together into a small bowl and set aside.

2. Using an electric mixer on medium speed, cream the butter, brown sugar, cinnamon, allspice, lemon zest, and ginger together in a medium-size bowl until light and fluffy, 2½ to 3 minutes. Stop the mixer once or twice during the process to scrape the bowl with a rubber spatula.

3. Add the molasses and mix on low speed for several seconds. Scrape the bowl.

4. Add the flour mixture and mix on low speed until the mixture is fluffy again, about 45 seconds. Scrape the bowl. Divide the dough in half.

5. Place a 15-inch length of waxed paper or plastic wrap on a work surface. Shape one portion of the dough into a rough log 10 to 11 inches long and place it along one long side of the paper. Roll the dough up in the paper, and twist the ends like a hard-candy wrapper. Repeat with the second portion of dough. Refrigerate the dough for 2 hours.

6. Remove the logs from the refrigerator. Using your hands, gently roll the wrapped dough back and forth on the work surface to smooth out the cylinder. Refrigerate for 4 to 6 hours or as long as overnight.

7. Fifteen minutes before baking preheat the oven to 350°F. Line several baking sheets with parchment paper, or leave them ungreased.

8. Remove the logs from the refrigerator, unwrap them, and cut them into ¼-inch-thick slices.

9. Place the cookies 1 inch apart on the prepared baking sheets. Bake until they are crisp and firm, golden in color with brown edges, 14 to 16 minutes. Cool them on the baking sheets.

10. Store the cookies in an airtight container at room temperature for a day or two if you think you will be snacking on them. After that, store the container in the freezer for up to 2 weeks. Bring the cookies to room temperature before eating.

Makes 40 cookies

Hazelnut Crisps

♥ ♥ ♥ ♥ ♥ ♥ ♥ ♥ ♥   *drop cookie*

Lacy ladylike cookies with a strong hazelnut flavor and enough crisp to keep them interesting.

INGREDIENTS

6 tablespoons all-purpose flour
½ teaspoon baking powder
¼ teaspoon salt
⅛ teaspoon ground cinnamon
½ cup granulated sugar
¼ cup (lightly packed) light brown sugar
7 tablespoons unsalted butter at room temperature, cut into 7 pieces
1 large egg white
1¼ cups skinned toasted hazelnuts (pages 53 and 89)

1. Preheat the oven to 375°F. Line several baking sheets with parchment paper, or grease them lightly with vegetable oil.

2. Place the flour, baking powder, salt, cinnamon, and both sugars in a food processor and process for 5 seconds.

3. Distribute the butter over the flour mixture and process until blended, 10 to 15 seconds. Scrape the bowl with a rubber spatula.

4. With the machine running, add the egg white through the feed tube and process to blend, several seconds. Scrape the bowl.

5. Add the hazelnuts and process until they are ground, 90 seconds. (The grind will be somewhat irregular.) Stop the mixer once during the process to scrape the bowl.

6. Drop the dough by rounded teaspoons 2 inches apart on the prepared baking sheets. Press them down lightly with the tip of a finger.

7. Bake the cookies until they have spread and are a rich golden color with deep golden edges, 12 to 14 minutes.

8. Remove the cookies from the oven and allow them to cool completely on the sheets.

9. If you plan to snack on them the first day, place the cookies on a plate or simply leave them on the baking sheet. After that, layer the cookies in an airtight container, using plastic wrap, parchment, or waxed paper between the layers, and store the container in the freezer for up to 2 weeks. Bring the cookies to room temperature before eating.

Makes 50 cookies

Glazed Lemon Cookies

❤ ❤ ❤ ❤ ❤ ❤ *refrigerator cookie*

I love the pure citrus taste of these cookies. They're strongly flavored with lemon and topped with a tart lemon glaze. They make a lovely dessert served with fresh berries, or offer them as part of a cookie platter along with Chocolate Snowballs and Pecan Crisps.

INGREDIENTS

THE COOKIE
2 cups plus 2 tablespoons cake flour
¼ teaspoon baking powder
½ teaspoon salt
1 tablespoon plus 1 teaspoon grated
     lemon zest
¾ cup confectioners' sugar
¼ cup granulated sugar
12 tablespoons (1½ sticks) unsalted butter,
     cold, cut into 12 pieces
1 teaspoon pure vanilla extract
2 tablespoons fresh lemon juice

THE GLAZE
6 tablespoons confectioners' sugar
2½ teaspoons heavy (whipping)
     cream
2 teaspoons fresh lemon juice

1. Combine the flour, baking powder, salt, lemon zest, and both sugars in a food processor and process for 10 seconds.

2. Scatter the butter over the flour mixture, and process for 45 seconds or until the dough just comes together. During this time, while the machine is running, add the vanilla and lemon juice through the feed tube.

3. Spread a 24-inch length of waxed paper on a work surface. With floured fingers, shape the dough into a rough log about 18 or 19 inches long, and place it along one long side of the paper. Roll the log up in the waxed paper and twist the ends like a hard-candy wrapper. Refrigerate the dough for 2 hours. (If necessary, cut the log in half and wrap it up in two packages in order to fit it in the refrigerator.)

4. Remove the dough from the refrigerator, and with it still in the waxed paper, gently roll it back and forth on the work surface to round the log.

5. Place the log back in the refrigerator and chill it for 2 to 3 more hours.

6. Preheat the oven to 325°F. Line two baking sheets with parchment paper, or leave them ungreased.

7. Unwrap the log and cut it into ⅜-inch-thick slices.

8. Place the cookies 2 inches apart on the prepared baking sheets, and bake until the centers are set and the edges are golden, 25 to 30 minutes.

9. Transfer the cookies to wire racks, and allow them to cool completely.

10. Meanwhile, prepare the glaze: Combine the ingredients in a small bowl, and stir vigorously with a whisk until smooth.

11. When the cookies are completely cool, drizzle the glaze randomly over the tops. If possible, place the racks in the refrigerator for the glaze to set, or leave them out for 2 to 3 hours so the glaze can harden.

12. If you plan to snack on them the first day, place the cookies on a plate. After that, layer the cookies in an air-tight container, using plastic wrap, parchment, or waxed paper between the layers, and store the container in the refrigerator for 2 days or in the freezer for up to 2 weeks. Bring the cookies to room temperature before eating.

Makes about 44 cookies

Chinese Almond Cornmeal Wafers

♥ ♥ ♥ ♥ ♥ ♥ ♥ ♥ ♥ ♥ *rolled cookie*

Beverly Jones, one of my two recipe testers, tells me that these cookies are of Chinese origin. Mimi

Santini-Ritt, my other recipe tester, insists that can't be. "Change the name immediately," she advised. "The Chinese don't eat cornmeal." My Solomonic decision was to do nothing, since I think the taste is more important than the name. In whatever culture, the addition of cornmeal to this sweet and buttery Chinese-style almond cookie was a wise move.

INGREDIENTS

THE COOKIE
1¼ cups all-purpose flour
1 cup yellow cornmeal
½ teaspoon salt
1 cup (2 sticks) unsalted butter at
    room temperature
½ cup (lightly packed) light brown
    sugar
¾ cup confectioners' sugar
½ teaspoon pure vanilla extract
1 cup finely chopped almonds

THE GLAZE
1 large egg
1 tablespoon water
1 cup sliced almonds

1. Place the flour, cornmeal, and salt in a small bowl and stir with a whisk.

2. Using an electric mixer on medium speed, cream the butter, both sugars, and the vanilla together in a medium-size mixing bowl until light and fluffy, 2 minutes. Stop the mixer three times during the process to scrape the bowl with a rubber spatula.

3. With the mixer on low, add the flour mixture and beat just until blended, 20 seconds. Scrape the bowl.

4. Add the almonds and blend on low speed for 5 seconds. Divide the dough in half. (If the dough is sticky, wrap each portion in plastic wrap and refrigerate for 1 hour before rolling.)

5. Preheat the oven to 350°F. Line several baking sheets with parchment paper, or leave them ungreased.

6. Place one portion of the dough between two pieces of plastic wrap and roll it out ⅛ inch thick.

7. Remove the top piece of plastic wrap, and using a 2¼- or 2½-inch round cookie cutter, cut out approximately 20 cookies. Place the cookies about ¾ inch apart on the prepared baking sheets. Gather up the dough scraps and reroll the dough to make as many cookies as possible. Repeat with the second portion of dough.

8. Prepare the glaze: In a small cup, stir the egg and water together with a small whisk or fork to blend. Brush glaze over each cookie with a pastry brush. Then arrange the almond slices in a circle around the edges of each cookie, and glaze gently once again to set the almonds.

9. Bake the cookies until they are a rich golden brown, about 16 minutes. Allow to cool on the sheets.

10. Store the cookies in an airtight container at room temperature for a day or two if you think you will be snacking on them. After that, store the container in the freezer for up to 2 weeks. Bring the cookies to room temperature before eating.

Makes about 48 cookies

Lovely Lemon Crisps

♥ ♥ ♥ ♥ ♥ ♥ ♥ *refrigerator cookie*

As a child I was always fond of thin crisp lemon wafers, delicate in texture yet pungent in flavor—like these. I like to dunk them in milk, but they're also lovely served with tea or as an accompaniment to sherbet.

I N G R E D I E N T S

1½ cups all-purpose flour
½ teaspoon baking powder
¼ teaspoon baking soda
¼ teaspoon salt
*10 tablespoons (1¼ sticks) unsalted butter
    at room temperature*
½ cup plus 3 tablespoons sugar
1 teaspoon pure vanilla extract
*1 tablespoon plus 1 teaspoon grated
    lemon zest*
¼ cup fresh lemon juice

1. Sift the flour, baking powder, baking soda, and salt together into a small bowl and set aside.

2. Using an electric mixer on medium speed, cream the butter, sugar, vanilla, and lemon zest together in a medium-size mixing bowl until light and fluffy, 45 seconds. Stop the mixer once during the process to scrape the bowl with a rubber spatula.

3. Add the lemon juice and mix on medium speed for 15 seconds.

4. Add the flour mixture and mix on low speed until the mixture is fluffy again, about 30 seconds. Scrape the bowl.

5. Place a 20-inch length of waxed paper or plastic wrap on a work surface. Shape the dough into a rough log about 18 inches long, and place it along one long side of the paper. Roll the dough up in the paper, and twist the ends like a hard-candy wrapper. Refrigerate the dough for 2 hours.

6. Remove the dough from the refrigerator, and using your hands, roll the wrapped dough gently back and forth on a work surface to smooth out the log. Refrigerate it for 4 to 6 hours or as long as 2 days.

7. Fifteen minutes before baking, preheat the oven to 350°F. Line several baking sheets with parchment paper. If you don't have parchment paper, leave the baking sheets ungreased.

8. Unwrap the dough and cut it into ¼-inch-thick slices. Place the cookies 1 inch apart on the baking sheets.

9. Bake the cookies until they are golden around the edges, 10 or 11 minutes. Allow them to cool on the baking sheets.

10. Store the cookies in an airtight container at room temperature for a day or two if you think you will be snacking on them. After that, store the container in the freezer for up to 2 weeks. Bring the cookies to room temperature before eating.

Makes 72 cookies

Orange Pecan Crisps

❤ ❤ ❤ ❤ ❤ ❤ ❤   *refrigerator cookie*

A wonderful wafer-like cookie bursting with the flavor of oranges and loaded with pecans. Adjust the amount of pecans in either direction according to your taste.

INGREDIENTS

2¼ cups all-purpose flour
¼ teaspoon baking soda
½ teaspoon salt
1 cup (2 sticks) unsalted butter at room
  temperature
½ cup (lightly packed) light brown sugar
½ cup granulated sugar
¼ cup grated orange zest
1 large egg
2 tablespoons frozen orange juice
  concentrate, thawed
1 cup chopped pecans

1. Sift the flour, baking soda, and salt together into a medium-size bowl and set aside.

2. Using an electric mixer on medium speed, cream the butter, both sugars, and the orange zest together in a medium-size mixing bowl until the ingredients are light and fluffy, about 1 minute. Scrape the bowl with a rubber spatula.

3. Add the egg and orange juice concentrate, and beat on medium speed until blended, 20 seconds. Scrape the bowl.

4. Add the flour mixture and beat on medium-low speed for 20 seconds. Scrape the bowl. Then add the nuts and beat until they are completely incorporated, about 15 seconds.

5. Spread a 13-inch length of waxed paper on a work surface. With floured fingers, shape the dough into a rough log about 12 inches long, and place it

319

along one long side of the paper. Roll the log in the waxed paper, and twist the ends like a hard-candy wrapper. Refrigerate the dough for 2 hours.

6. Remove the dough from the refrigerator, and using your hands, gently roll the dough back and forth on the work surface to round the log.

7. Refrigerate the dough for 4 hours, or up to 2 days.

8. Fifteen minutes before cooking, preheat the oven to 400°F. Line two baking sheets with parchment paper, or leave them ungreased.

9. Unwrap the dough and cut it into ⅛-inch-thick slices. Place the slices 2 inches apart on the baking sheets.

10. Bake the cookies until they are firm to the touch and golden around the edges, 7 to 8 minutes. (They should be crisp through and through when cooled.) Let them cool on the baking sheets.

11. Store the cookies in an airtight container at room temperature for a day or two if you think you will be snacking on them. After that, store the container in the freezer for up to 2 weeks. Bring the cookies to room temperature before eating.

Makes about 90 cookies

Pecan Crisps
♥ ♥ ♥ ♥ ♥ ♥ ♥ ♥ ♥ *drop cookie*

For the pecan purist. The wonderful nutty flavor of this crispy delight is enhanced only by butter and vanilla.

INGREDIENTS

2 cups plus 2 tablespoons all-purpose flour
1 teaspoon baking soda
1½ teaspoons salt
1¼ cups (2½ sticks) unsalted butter at room temperature
¾ cup plus 2 tablespoons granulated sugar
¾ cup plus 2 tablespoons (lightly packed) light brown sugar
2½ teaspoons pure vanilla extract
2 large eggs
2 cups coarsely chopped pecans

1. Preheat the oven to 400°F. Line several baking sheets with parchment paper, or grease them lightly with vegetable oil.

2. Sift the flour, baking soda, and salt together into a small bowl and set aside.

3. Using an electric mixer on medium speed, cream the butter, both sugars, and the vanilla together in a medium-size bowl until light and fluffy, 1 minute. Stop the mixer once during the process to scrape the bowl with a rubber spatula.

4. Add the eggs and beat on medium speed until they are blended, about 20 seconds. Scrape the bowl.

5. Add the flour mixture and mix on low speed for 15 seconds, stopping the mixer once to scrape the bowl.

6. Add the pecans and blend them in by hand with the rubber spatula.

7. Drop the dough by generously rounded teaspoons 2 inches apart onto the prepared baking sheets.

8. Bake the cookies until they are firm and light golden with darker golden edges, 10 to 12 minutes. Let them cool on the baking sheets; then remove them carefully with a spatula.

9. Store the cookies in an airtight container at room temperature for a day or two if you think you will be snacking on them. After that, store the container in the freezer for up to 2 weeks. Bring the cookies to room temperature before eating.

Makes about 30 cookies

Pecan Fingers

❤ ❤ ❤ ❤ ❤ ❤ ❤ ❤ *formed cookie*

This is a taste memory that's bred in the bone: Biting into these thin crispy cookies and being greeted with a browned-butter-pecan flavor brings back my childhood in the form of a Danish butter cookie that my mother used to buy at a sensational gourmet store called the Danish Bowl. I was always thrilled when she went there because it meant a dinner of lobster salad finished off with Pecan Fingers.

INGREDIENTS

THE COOKIE
1¼ cups all-purpose flour
¼ teaspoon baking powder
¼ teaspoon salt
12 tablespoons (1½ sticks) unsalted butter at room temperature
5 tablespoons (lightly packed) light brown sugar
5 tablespoons granulated sugar
2½ teaspoons pure vanilla extract
1 large egg (optional)

THE GLAZE
2 teaspoons milk
2 tablespoons granulated sugar
6 pecans, finely chopped

1. Sift the flour, baking powder, and salt together into a small bowl and set aside.

2. Using an electric mixer on medium speed, cream the butter, both sugars, and the vanilla in a medium-size mixing bowl until light and fluffy, 1 minute. Stop the mixer twice during the process to scrape the bowl with a rubber spatula.

3. Add the egg, if using, and mix at medium-high speed until blended, 15 seconds. Scrape the bowl.

4. Add the flour mixture and beat on medium-low speed until blended,

20 seconds, stopping the mixer once to scrape the bowl. Then scrape the bowl again at the end.

5. Divide the dough in half, wrap each half in plastic wrap, and refrigerate for 4 hours or as long as 2 days.

6. Fifteen minutes before cooking, preheat the oven to 300°F. Line two baking sheets with parchment paper, or grease them lightly with vegetable oil.

7. Using a frosting spatula or your fingertips repeatedly dipped in flour, spread each portion of the dough out on one of the baking sheets to form a rough rectangle ⅛ inch thick (the shape is not important).

8. To glaze, using a pastry brush, lightly brush each portion of dough with the milk. Then sprinkle each with the sugar and the chopped pecans.

9. Bake for 30 minutes. Then remove the baking sheets from the oven and cut the shortbreads into approximately 20 pieces each. Move the pieces ½ inch apart, and return the sheets to the oven. Bake until the cookies are a deep golden color, 15 to 20 minutes.

10. Allow the cookies to cool completely on the baking sheets before eating. These store beautifully in an airtight container for several days. After that, place the container in the freezer for up to 2 weeks.

Makes about 40 small fingers

Très French Palmiers

♥ ♥ ♥ ♥ ♥ ♥ ♥ ♥ ♥ *rolled cookie*

I confess that these elegant cookies look more like elephant ears than palm leaves to me, but I know better than to argue with French chefs. After all, who would want to eat an elephant's ear? These palmiers are made of a very buttery puff pastry that's swirled into concentric circles and baked to crunchy perfection. *Magnifique!* And just the right thing to accompany a *tisane*.

INGREDIENTS

THE DOUGH
1 cup (2 sticks) unsalted butter, cold
2 cups all-purpose flour
¼ teaspoon salt
½ cup heavy (whipping) cream, cold,
    plus 2 tablespoons if needed

THE FILLING
⅓ cup plus ¾ cup sugar
1½ teaspoons ground cinnamon

1. Melt ¼ cup (½ stick) of the butter in a microwave oven or in a small saucepan over low heat. Remove from the heat.

2. Cut the remaining butter into 12 pieces, and cut the 12 pieces in half. Place these chunks in the freezer for 5 minutes.

3. Place the flour and salt in a food processor and process for 5 seconds.

4. Distribute the butter over the flour mixture and pulse 5 or 6 times, just to break up the pieces.

5. Pour the ½ cup cream evenly over the flour-butter mixture. Pulse several times, until the crumbs appear to be evenly moist (the size of the butter chunks will stay fairly large and inconsistent, ranging from a grain of rice to a pea). Test for moistness: pinch some crumbs together. If the mixture holds together like pie dough, there is enough cream. If it doesn't, add 1 tablespoon of cream and pulse twice. Retest. If the dough is still not moist enough, add 1 more tablespoon of cream and pulse twice.

6. Place the (crumbly) dough on a work surface and gently mold it into a 4 × 12-inch rectangle.

7. Place the dough between two pieces of plastic wrap, and roll it out to form a 10 × 20-inch rectangle. Remove the top piece of plastic wrap.

8. Using a pastry brush, brush the yellow part of the melted butter (the milky solids will have sunk to the bottom) over the surface of the dough.

9. With the point of a sharp knife, lightly score the dough lengthwise in thirds. Take the right-hand third of the dough and fold it over the middle third. Then take the left-hand third and fold it over the double thickness. You will have a rectangle measuring about 3½ by 20 inches.

10. Beginning at one end of the length, using the plastic wrap to lift it, roll the dough up like a jelly roll, to form one big fat roll.

11. Place a piece of plastic wrap over this roll and using a rolling pin, roll out a 5-inch square. Cut the square in half, forming two rectangles, each 2½ x 5 inches. Wrap each rectangle in plastic wrap, and refrigerate for several hours or as long as overnight (no more than 48 hours).

12. Prepare the filling: Mix the ⅓ cup sugar and the cinnamon together in a small bowl and set aside. Remove one rectangle of dough from the refrigerator and unwrap it.

13. Sprinkle 1½ tablespoons of the remaining sugar on a large piece of plastic wrap, and place the dough on the plastic. Sprinkle another 1½ tablespoons sugar on top of the dough, cover it with a second piece of plastic, and roll it out, flipping the dough several times, to form a 6 × 12-inch rectangle.

14. Remove the top piece of plastic, sprinkle half of the cinnamon-sugar mixture over the dough, replace the plastic, and roll it out to form a 9 × 12-inch rectangle.

15. Remove the top plastic. Take the long sides of the rectangle and fold them toward the center so that the edges just meet. Then fold in half the long way, as if closing a book. You should have a 9 × 3-inch rectangle.

16. Sprinkle 1½ tablespoons sugar over the long rectangle, then flip it over and sprinkle 1½ tablespoons sugar over the other side.

17. Roll a rolling pin very gently over the length of the rectangle—just to seal it, not to flatten it. Wrap it in plastic wrap and chill for 1 hour.

18. Repeat steps 13 through 17 with the second rectangle.

19. When you are ready to bake the palmiers, preheat the oven to 350°F. Line several baking sheets with parchment paper.

20. Remove the dough from the refrigerator, and cut the rectangles into ⅓-inch-thick slices. Place them, cut side down, 1½ inches apart on the prepared baking sheets.

21. Bake until crisp in texture and deep golden in color, 18 to 21 minutes. Cool on the baking sheets.

22. Because of their incredibly flaky nature, these are best if eaten the first day. However, if storing is a must, place them in an airtight plastic container in the freezer for up to 2 weeks.

Makes 54 palmiers

Aunt Florence's Anise Biscotti

❤ ❤ ❤ ❤ ❤ ❤ ❤ ❤ *formed cookie*

Aunt Florence is ninety years old. She is the eldest of three sisters, all of whom are stellar cooks. For the sake of efficiency or maybe family feeling, each carved out her domain. Florence's is biscotti. For many years the recipe existed only in her mind, so her niece, Mary Susan DeLaura, petitioned her aunt to teach her the secret of the biscotti, which she wrote down and brought back to us. I can't believe a crunchier, more delicious biscotti exists. If you store biscotti correctly, in an airtight container at room temperature, they'll return the favor and last forever.

INGREDIENTS

2¾ cups plus 2 tablespoons all-purpose
   flour
3 teaspoons baking powder
¼ teaspoon salt
3 large eggs
¾ cup plus 2 teaspoons sugar
1 teaspoon anise flavoring
8 tablespoons (1 stick) unsalted butter,
   melted

1. Preheat the oven to 325°F. Line two baking sheets with parchment paper, or grease them lightly with vegetable oil.

Biscottibrot?

You say biscotti, I say mandelbrot. Time was when biscotti were one thing and mandelbrot another, and never the twain did meet. Nowadays they're acknowledged as essentially the same crunchy cookie, separated only by different names and pedigrees. I've long harbored the belief that Jews and Italians view the world in similar ways, and this congruence is just one more manifestation. Dip your mandelbrot in cappuccino or your biscotti in hot milk. The beauty of multiculturalism is that you don't have to choose.

2. Sift the flour, baking powder, and salt together into a small bowl and set aside.

3. Using an electric mixer on medium speed, beat the eggs in a medium-size bowl until foamy, 30 seconds. Add the sugar gradually, continuing to beat on medium speed until mixed, 30 seconds. Add the anise flavoring and the melted butter and beat until blended, 10 seconds.

4. With the mixer on low speed, add the flour mixture and mix only until blended, 20 seconds, stopping the mixer once to scrape the bowl with a rubber spatula.

5. Turn the dough out onto a work surface and divide it in half. Form a strip about 2½ inches wide and 12 inches long with one of the portions, and place it on one of the prepared baking sheets.

6. Form a second strip and place it on the second sheet.

7. Bake the dough strips until firm to the touch, 30 minutes. Remove the baking sheets from the oven and lower the oven temperature to 275°F. Allow the strips to cool for 10 minutes.

8. Using a serrated knife, cut each strip into ½-inch-thick slices. Arrange the slices, standing up, about ½ inch apart on the baking sheets. Bake until thoroughly crisp and lightly golden, about 30 minutes. Let the biscotti cool on the baking sheets.

9. Store in an airtight container at room temperature for up to 2 weeks.

Makes 48 cookies

Low-Fat Almond Biscotti

♥ ♥ ♥ ♥ ♥ ♥ ♥ ♥ *formed cookie*

If you like your biscotti hard and crunchy, this is the one for you. Just dunk them in some coffee or skim milk, and you've got yourself one scrumptious low-fat dessert.

INGREDIENTS

2 cups plus 2 tablespoons all-purpose flour
1 teaspoon baking powder
⅛ teaspoon baking soda
¼ teaspoon salt
2 large eggs at room temperature
2 large egg whites at room temperature
1 cup sugar
4 teaspoons pure almond extract
1 cup coarsely chopped almonds

1. Preheat the oven to 325°F. Line two baking sheets with parchment paper, or grease them lightly with vegetable oil.

2. Sift the flour, baking powder, baking soda, and salt together into a medium-size bowl and set aside.

3. Using an electric mixer on medium speed, beat the eggs, egg whites, sugar, and almond extract together until well blended, 20 seconds. Scrape the bowl with a rubber spatula.

4. Using the rubber spatula, mix in half the flour mixture by hand. Then blend with the electric mixer on low speed for several seconds. Add the remaining flour mixture and mix on low speed until the dough is smooth, about 5 seconds. Add the nuts with a few more turns of the mixer.

5. Turn the dough out onto a work surface and divide it in half. Form a strip about 2½ inches wide and 12 inches long with one of the portions, and place it on one of the prepared baking sheets.

6. Form a second strip and place it on the second sheet.

7. Bake the dough strips until firm to the touch and lightly golden, 20 to 25 minutes.

8. Remove the sheets from the oven and lower the oven temperature to 300°F. Let the strips cool for 10 minutes. Then, using a serrated knife, cut each strip into ½-inch-thick slices. Arrange the slices, standing up, about ½ inch apart on the baking sheets. Bake until crisp and very lightly golden, about 35 minutes.

9. Store in an airtight container at room temperature for up to 2 weeks.

Makes about 48 cookies

Orange Walnut Mandelbrot

❤ ❤ ❤ ❤ ❤ ❤ ❤ *formed cookie*

Although we usually think of mandelbrot as flavored with cinnamon and vanilla, it's actually a very versatile base for a variety of flavors—and there's no reason to ignore a great flavor like orange. Feel free to substitute chocolate chips for the nuts if you're in the mood for something

sweeter. For a fruitier experience, substitute dried cranberries.

INGREDIENTS

2 cups all-purpose flour
1 teaspoon baking powder
Pinch of baking soda
1 teaspoon salt
4 tablespoons (½ stick) unsalted butter at
   room temperature
¼ cup vegetable oil
¾ cup sugar
1 tablespoon pure vanilla extract
¼ cup grated orange zest
2 large eggs
½ cup plus 2 tablespoons chopped walnuts

1. Preheat the oven to 350°F. Line two baking sheets with parchment paper, or lightly grease them with vegetable oil.

2. Sift the flour, baking powder, baking soda, and salt together into a medium-size bowl.

3. Using an electric mixer on medium-high speed, cream the butter, oil, sugar, vanilla, and orange zest together in a medium-size mixing bowl until light and fluffy, 1 to 1½ minutes. Stop the machine twice during the process to scrape the bowl with a rubber spatula.

4. Add the eggs one at a time on medium speed, mixing until each egg is partially incorporated, about 5 seconds. Scrape the bowl after each addition.

5. Using the rubber spatula, mix in half the flour mixture by hand. Then blend with the electric mixer on low speed for several seconds. Add the remaining flour mixture and mix on low speed until the dough is smooth, about 5 seconds. Add the nuts with a few more turns of the mixer.

6. Turn the dough out onto a work surface and divide it in half (it will be somewhat sticky). Form a strip about 3 inches wide and 11 inches long with one of the portions, and place it on one of the prepared baking sheets.

7. Form a second strip and place it on the second sheet.

8. Bake the dough strips until firm to the touch and lightly golden, 20 to 25 minutes.

9. Remove the baking sheets from the oven and lower the oven temperature to 275°F. Let the strips cool for 10 minutes. Then, using a serrated knife, cut each strip into ½-inch-thick slices. Arrange the slices, standing up, about ½ inch apart on the sheets. Bake until crisp and golden, about 20 minutes.

10. Turn the oven off and leave the cookies in for 15 minutes more. Then remove them from the oven and let them cool on the baking sheets.

11. Store the cookies in an airtight container at room temperature or in the freezer for up to 2 weeks. Bring them to room temperature before eating.

Makes about 44 cookies

Chocolate Chocolate Chip Mandelbrot

❤ ❤ ❤ ❤ ❤ ❤ ❤ ❤ *formed cookie*

This is a brownie-like version of a traditional mandelbrot, noteworthy for its richness, density, and ever-so-chocolately chocolateness. Bake it for the designated length of time if you like your mandelbrot crunchy. For a fudgier texture, take it out of the oven a little sooner.

INGREDIENTS

4 ounces bittersweet chocolate

1 ounce unsweetened chocolate

1¼ cups all-purpose flour

1 teaspoon baking powder

¼ teaspoon salt

2 tablespoons grated orange zest, or
    1 teaspoon instant espresso or
    coffee powder

1 teaspoon pure vanilla extract

7 tablespoons unsalted butter at room
    temperature

5 tablespoons granulated sugar

¼ cup (lightly packed) light brown sugar

1 whole large egg

1 large egg yolk

3 ounces (½ cup) semisweet chocolate chips

THE GLAZE

2 ounces bittersweet or semisweet
    chocolate

2 teaspoons pure vegetable oil

1. Preheat the oven to 350°F. Line a baking sheet with parchment paper, or lightly grease it with vegetable oil.

2. Melt the bittersweet and unsweetened chocolate in the top of a double boiler placed over simmering water. Then let it cool to room temperature.

3. Sift the flour, baking powder, and salt together into a medium-size bowl. If you are using instant coffee, dissolve it in the vanilla.

4. Using an electric mixer on medium-high speed, cream the butter, both sugars, the vanilla, and the orange zest, if using, together in a medium-size mixing bowl until light and fluffy, 1 to 1½ minutes. Stop the machine twice during the process to scrape the bowl with a rubber spatula.

5. Add the egg and the egg yolk and mix on medium speed until blended, 10 seconds.

6. Add the melted chocolate with the mixer on medium-low speed and mix to blend, 10 seconds, stopping the mixer once to scrape the bowl.

7. Add the flour mixture with the mixer on low, and blend until almost incorporated, 10 seconds. Then add the chocolate chips and blend to mix, 5 more seconds.

8. Lay the dough on the prepared baking sheet, and mold it to form a cylindrical strip about 10 inches long and 3 inches wide.

9. Bake until firm to the touch, about 50 minutes.

10. Remove the sheet from the oven, and lower the oven temperature to 275°F.

11. Let the strip cool for 10 minutes. Then, using a serrated knife, cut the strip into ½-inch-thick slices. Arrange the slices, standing up, about ½ inch apart on the baking sheet. Bake until crunchy through and through, 20 minutes. Then turn off the oven and allow the cookies to sit in the oven for an additional 15 minutes. Remove the sheets from the oven and allow the cookies to cool on the sheets.

12. Meanwhile, prepare the glaze: Melt the chocolate in the top of a double boiler placed over simmering water. Using a whisk, stir in the oil and mix until smooth.

13. When the cookies have cooled, use a pastry brush to paint one side, or the top of the cookies with the chocolate glaze.

14. When the glaze has completely set, 3 hours, place the cookies in an airtight container, with parchment or waxed paper between the layers, and store it in a cool place or in the refrigerator for 2 to 3 days. (At room temperature, the glaze may discolor after several days.) After that, store the container in the freezer for up to 2 weeks. Bring to room temperature before eating.

Makes about 20 cookies

Amy's Mandelbrot

♥ ♥ ♥ ♥ ♥ ♥ ♥ ♥   *formed cookie*

After all the recipes for this book had been completed and the manuscript was actually in my editor's hands, I received this recipe in the mail from my old friend, Amy Etra, who lives in Los Angeles. Although I needed a brief respite from baking, the recipe was just too tempting—I tried it and loved it! The cookies are not too rich and so are great any time of the day. Thanks, Amy.

INGREDIENTS

1 cup water
½ cup raisins
3 cups all-purpose flour
2½ teaspoons baking powder
1 teaspoon salt
¾ cup vegetable oil
1 cup plus 1½ tablespoons sugar
2 teaspoons pure vanilla extract
1½ teaspoons lemon zest
1½ teaspoons orange zest
3 large eggs
½ cup chopped walnuts
1½ teaspoons ground cinnamon

1. Preheat the oven to 375°F. Line two baking sheets with parchment paper, or lightly grease them with vegetable oil.

2. Bring the water to a boil in a small saucepan. Turn off the heat, place the raisins in the pan, and cover while you prepare the dough.

3. Sift the flour, baking powder, and salt together in a medium-size bowl, and set aside.

4. Using an electric mixer on medium-high speed, cream the oil, 1 cup of the sugar, the vanilla, and both zests together in a medium-size bowl until light and fluffy, 30 to 45 seconds. Stop the machine once during the process to scrape the bowl with a rubber spatula.

5. Add the eggs one at a time on medium speed, mixing until each egg is partially incorporated, about 5 seconds. Scrape the bowl after each addition.

6. Add half the flour mixture to the egg mixture and blend with the mixer on medium speed for 10 to 15 seconds. Scrape the bowl with a rubber spatula. Then, add the remaining flour mixture and mix on medium speed until the dough is smooth, about 5 seconds.

7. Drain the raisins and pat dry with paper towels. Add the nuts and the raisins to the dough with a few more turns of the mixer.

8. Remove the dough from the bowl and divide it into quarters. Using floured hands, lay one-quarter of the dough lengthwise on a prepared baking sheet, molding it into a strip 2½ inches wide and 7 inches long. Make sure it sits about 2 inches from the edge of the pan. Form the remaining dough quarters into strips and place them on the pans, 2 inches from the edge and 3 inches from each other (there should be 2 strips on each pan).

9. Mix the remaining 1½ tablespoons sugar with the cinnamon. Sprinkle the cinnamon sugar generously over each strip.

10. Bake the dough strips until firm to the touch and lightly golden, 25 to 30 minutes.

11. Remove the sheets from the oven and lower the oven temperature to 350°F. Let the strips cool for 10 minutes. Then, using a serrated knife, cut each strip into ½-inch-thick slices. Arrange the slices, standing up, about ½ inch apart on the sheets. Bake until crisp and lightly golden, about 15 minutes. Remove the cookies from the oven and let them cool on the baking sheets.

12. Store the cookies in an airtight container at room temperature for up to 2 weeks. Otherwise, store the container in the freezer for up to 2 weeks. Bring them to room temperature before eating.

Makes 56 cookies

Lemon Meringues

❤ ❤ ❤ ❤ ❤ ❤ *refrigerator cookie*

Built of three parts—a crunchy shortbread cookie, a dollop of tart lemon curd, and a cap of airy meringue—this confection offers a contrast of flavors and textures with each bite. If you don't eat them all on the first day, you'll need to freeze them, since they wilt at room temperature.

INGREDIENTS

THE COOKIE

1½ cups sifted all-purpose flour
5 tablespoons confectioners' sugar
3 tablespoons granulated sugar
10 tablespoons (1¼ sticks)
  unsalted butter, cold,
  cut into 10 pieces
1 large egg yolk

THE CURD

¼ teaspoon unflavored gelatin powder
⅓ cup plus 1 tablespoon fresh lemon juice
4 large egg yolks
½ cup plus 1 tablespoon sugar
1 tablespoon unsalted butter

THE MERINGUE

4 large egg whites at room temperature
Pinch of salt
2 cups confectioners' sugar, sifted
¼ teaspoon pure vanilla extract

1. Prepare the cookie dough: Place the flour and both sugars in a food processor and process for 5 seconds.

2. Distribute the butter over the flour mixture and process until the mixture resembles coarse meal, about 20 seconds.

3. With the machine running, add the egg yolk through the feed tube and process for 5 seconds. Stop the machine, scrape the bowl, and process until the yolk has been absorbed and the dough is just coming together, 30 seconds.

4. Form the dough into two logs, each about 4½ inches long and 1½ inches in diameter. Wrap each log in plastic wrap and refrigerate.

5. Next, prepare the curd: In a small cup, stir the gelatin into the lemon juice until dissolved. Place the yolks and sugar in a small saucepan, and mix to blend.

6. Add the gelatin mixture to the yolk mixture and stir. Then cook this mixture over low heat, stirring constantly, until it just comes to a boil and starts to thicken, about 5 minutes.

7. Remove the pot from the heat, pour the mixture through a strainer into a small bowl, and stir in the butter. Place plastic wrap directly on the surface, and refrigerate both the curd and the cookie dough for 4 to 6 hours.

8. When you are ready to bake, preheat the oven to 375°F. Fit a pastry bag with a ¼-inch round tip, and place the bag, tip side down, in a tall glass. Line several baking sheets with parchment paper, or grease them lightly with vegetable oil.

9. Unwrap the logs of dough, and cut them into slices that are a generous ⅛ inch thick. Place them 1 inch apart on the prepared baking sheets. Bake until the edges are golden, 10 to 11 minutes.

10. While the cookies are baking, prepare the meringue: Place the egg whites in the top of a double boiler set over tepid water. Add the salt, and stir with a whisk until foamy but not stiff. Whisk in the confectioners' sugar, a teaspoon at a time. Then whisk in the vanilla.

11. Place the double boiler over low heat and continue to stir the meringue with the whisk until it thickens, about 8 minutes. (When it is ready, it will leave a thick trail when the whisk is lifted out of the mixture.) Fill the pastry bag with the meringue.

12. When the cookies have finished baking, remove them from the oven. Place a generous ½ teaspoon of the curd in the center of each cookie, and then pipe a mound of meringue over the curd. Return the cookies to the oven and bake until the meringue starts to turn golden, 8 or 9 minutes. Remove the cookies from the oven and allow them to cool on the baking sheets, or on wire racks for 4 hours. These cookies should be eaten on the same day they are baked.

Makes about 55 cookies

Golden Pecan Squares

❤ ❤ ❤ ❤ ❤ ❤ *refrigerator cookie*

The little bit of maple syrup in this primarily brown sugar shortbread enhances and enriches the flavor and combines perfectly with the pecans. It is a beautiful glazed square cookie, which on a dessert platter is a wonderful complement to all its round cookie cousins.

INGREDIENTS

THE COOKIE
1½ cups all-purpose flour
½ teaspoon salt
¼ teaspoon ground nutmeg
¼ teaspoon ground cinnamon
6 tablespoons (lightly packed) light brown
  sugar
2 tablespoons granulated sugar
11 tablespoons (1 stick plus 3 tablespoons)
  unsalted butter, cut in pieces
2 tablespoons maple syrup
½ cup chopped pecans

THE GLAZE
1 large egg yolk
1 teaspoon water
½ teaspoon ground cinnamon
2 tablespoons granulated sugar

1. Preheat the oven to 325°F. Line several baking sheets with parchment paper, or grease them lightly with vegetable oil.

2. Place the flour, salt, nutmeg, cinnamon, and both sugars in a food processor and process for 10 seconds.

3. Scatter the butter over the flour mixture and process until the mixture resembles coarse meal, 10 to 15 seconds.

4. Add the maple syrup and process just until the dough comes together, 45 seconds.

5. Break the dough apart with your hands. Then add the nuts and pulse 30 times to distribute.

6. Place a 16-inch length of waxed paper or plastic wrap on a work surface. Shape the dough into a rough log 12 inches long, and place it along one long side of the paper. Roll the dough up in the paper and twist the ends like a hard-candy wrapper. Refrigerate the dough for 1½ hours.

7. Remove the dough from the refrigerator. Slap each side of the log against a work surface to flatten it so the cookies will be square.

8. Refrigerate it again for 4 to 6 hours or as long as overnight.

9. Fifteen minutes before baking, preheat the oven to 350°F. Line several baking sheets with parchment paper, or leave them ungreased.

10. Prepare the glaze: Stir the egg yolk and the water together in a cup. Mix the cinnamon and sugar in another cup.

11. Remove the dough from the refrigerator, unwrap it, and cut it into ¼-inch-thick slices.

12. Place the cookies 1 inch apart on the baking sheets. Using a pastry brush, glaze each cookie with the yolk mixture and sprinkle with the cinnamon-sugar mix.

13. Bake the cookies on the center rack of the oven until they are a rich golden color and completely firm, 25 minutes. (To test for doneness, remove a cookie from the oven and cut it in half. There should be no doughy strip in the center.) Allow the cookies to cool on the sheets.

14. If you plan to snack on them the first day, place the cookies on a plate or simply leave them on the baking sheet. After that, layer the cookies in an airtight container, using plastic wrap, parchment, or waxed paper between the layers, and store the container in the freezer for up to 2 weeks. Bring the cookies to room temperature before eating.

Makes 48 cookies

Cappuccino Shortbread Sails

♥ ♥ ♥ ♥ ♥ ♥ ♥ ♥ *rolled cookie*

This is the way I trim my sails: I take triangular wedges of coffee-flavored shortbread and dip them in chocolate before coating them with nuts. They'd probably sink the boat, but what a way to go!

INGREDIENTS

THE COOKIE
2 tablespoons instant coffee powder
1¾ cups plus 2 tablespoons all-purpose flour
⅛ teaspoon baking powder
¾ teaspoon salt
6 tablespoons granulated sugar
3 tablespoons light brown sugar
1 teaspoon ground cinnamon
1 cup (2 sticks) unsalted butter, cold, cut into 1-inch chunks
1 tablespoon strong brewed coffee
¼ teaspoon pure vanilla extract

THE GLAZE
7 ounces bittersweet chocolate
1½ cups finely chopped toasted almonds (see box, facing page)

1. Place the instant coffee, flour, baking powder, salt, both sugars, and the cinnamon in a food processor and process for 5 seconds.

2. Distribute the butter over the flour mixture, and process until the mixture resembles coarse meal, 10 seconds.

3. With the processor running, pour the brewed coffee and vanilla through the feed tube and process just until the mixture comes together, 45 seconds. Stop the machine once during the mixing to scrape the bowl with a rubber spatula.

4. Place the dough between two pieces of plastic wrap, and roll it out to form a 10-inch square that is ⅜ inch thick. Slide this square onto a baking sheet and refrigerate it for 45 minutes.

5. Preheat the oven to 300°F. Line several baking sheets with parchment paper, or grease them lightly with vegetable oil.

6. Cut the dough into 25 squares, and then cut each square in half diagonally to make triangles.

7. Using a spatula, carefully transfer the triangles to the prepared baking sheets, leaving 1½ inches between each cookie. Bake the cookies until they are lightly golden and firm to the touch, 25 to 30 minutes. Transfer the cookies to a rack to cool.

8. Meanwhile, prepare the glaze: Melt the chocolate in the top of a double boiler placed over simmering water. Place the almonds in a small bowl. When the cookies have cooled, dip the base of each triangle about ¾ inch deep into the chocolate and then into the almonds. Set the cookies aside on parch-

Toasting Nuts

I t's best to chop nuts before toasting them to ensure a more even result. Place the chopped nuts on an ungreased baking sheet and place them in a preheated 350°F oven for 5 minutes. Open the oven door and toss the nuts by shaking the pan gently back and forth. Close the door and continue until the nuts give off a toasted aroma and are lightly golden, 3 to 5 minutes more.

ment paper, waxed paper, or aluminum foil, and allow them to set for several hours (slide the paper onto baking sheets and refrigerate them to speed up the process).

9. If you plan to snack on them the first day, place the cookies on a plate or simply leave them on the baking sheet. After that, layer the cookies in an airtight container, using plastic wrap, parchment, or waxed paper between the layers, and store the container in the freezer for up to 2 weeks. Bring the cookies to room temperature before eating.

Makes 50 cookies

Chunky Chocolate Almond Shortbread

❤ ❤ ❤ ❤ ❤ ❤ ❤ ❤   *formed cookie*

W andering the streets of SoHo, NYC, one day, I spotted a big log of almond shortbread studded with chopped chocolate sitting in a bakery window. It called out to me. Here is a mini version of that memory.

INGREDIENTS

1 cup plus 3 tablespoons all-purpose flour
¼ teaspoon baking powder
½ teaspoon salt
8 tablespoons (1 stick) unsalted butter at room temperature
½ cup (lightly packed) light brown sugar
¾ teaspoon pure vanilla extract
1 large egg white
½ cup ground almonds (from 1 scant cup whole almonds)
4 ounces coarsely chopped bittersweet chocolate
⅓ cup coarsely chopped almonds
¼ cup granulated sugar in a plastic bag

1. Preheat the oven to 325°F. Line several baking sheets with parchment paper, or leave them ungreased.

2. Sift the flour, baking powder, and salt together into a small bowl and set aside.

3. Using an electric mixer on medium speed, cream the butter, brown sugar, and vanilla in a medium-size mixing bowl until the ingredients are light and fluffy, about 1 minute. Scrape the sides of the bowl with a rubber spatula.

4. Add the egg white and mix until blended, 10 seconds.

5. Add the flour mixture and the ground almonds, and beat on medium-low speed for 20 seconds. Scrape the bowl.

6. Add the chocolate chunks and coarsely chopped almonds, and beat on low speed until incorporated, 10 seconds.

7. Measure out rounded teaspoons of the dough and roll them into balls with your hands.

8. Place each ball in the bag of sugar and toss to coat.

9. Place the balls 2 inches apart on the baking sheets. Using your hands or the bottom of a glass that has been dipped in sugar, flatten each cookie to form a round approximately 1¾ inches in diameter. Bake until the cookies are firm and crunchy through and through, 20 to 22 minutes. (To test for doneness, remove a cookie from the oven and cut it in half. There should be no doughy strip in the center.) Cool on the baking sheets.

10. Store the cookies in an airtight container at room temperature for a day or two if you think you will be snacking on them. After that, store the container in the freezer for up to 2 weeks. Bring the cookies to room temperature before eating.

Makes 40 cookies

Chocolate Orange Shortbread
❤ ❤ ❤ ❤ ❤ ❤   *refrigerator cookie*

I'm convinced that feasts of the gods on Olympus included chocolate and oranges since it's such a divine pairing. It's embodied here in a crunchy orange-flavored wafer, festooned with chunks of bittersweet chocolate.

INGREDIENTS

1 large egg
1 teaspoon pure vanilla extract
2¼ cups all-purpose flour
¼ teaspoon baking soda
½ teaspoon salt
6 tablespoons confectioners' sugar
2 tablespoons granulated sugar
1 tablespoon grated orange zest
1 cup (2 sticks) unsalted butter, cold,
    cut into 8 pieces
5 ounces bittersweet chocolate,
    chopped

1. Mix the egg and vanilla together in a cup and set aside.

2. Combine the flour, baking soda, salt, both sugars, and the orange zest in a food processor and process for 10 seconds.

3. Distribute the butter over the flour mixture, and process to form coarse crumbs, 5 seconds.

4. With the machine running, pour the egg mixture through the feed tube and process until the dough comes together, about 10 seconds. Stop the processor once during the blending to scrape the sides of the bowl with a rubber spatula.

5. Remove the dough from the processor and place it on a work surface. Knead the chocolate in by hand.

6. Place a 20-inch length of waxed paper or plastic wrap on a work surface. Shape the dough into a rough log 16 inches long and place it along one long side of the paper. Roll the dough up in the paper and twist the ends like a hard-candy wrapper. Refrigerate the dough for 2 hours.

7. Remove the log from the refrigerator. Using your hands, roll the wrapped dough gently back and forth on a work surface to smooth out the log. Refrigerate it again for 4 to 6 hours or as long as overnight.

8. Fifteen minutes before baking, preheat the oven to 325°F. Line several baking sheets with parchment paper, or leave them ungreased.

9. Remove the dough from the refrigerator, unwrap it, and cut the log into slices that are a slight ½ inch thick. Place the cookies 1 inch apart on the baking sheets.

10. Bake the cookies until they are firm and crisp, about 16 minutes. (To test for doneness, remove a cookie from the oven and cut it in half. There should be no doughy strip in the center.) Cool the cookies on the baking sheets.

11. Store the cookies in an airtight container at room temperature for a day or two if you think you will be snacking on them. After that, store the container in the freezer for up to 2 weeks. Bring the cookies to room temperature before eating.

Makes about 42 cookies

Chocolate-Glazed Chocolate Shortbread

❤ ❤ ❤ ❤ ❤ ❤ ❤ ❤ *formed cookie*

Good chocolate shortbread is hard to come by. This one is very chocolatey, delicious, and really easy to throw together. Cut it into rectangles, diamonds, strips, or squares to complement any cookie platter.

INGREDIENTS

THE COOKIE
1 cup all-purpose flour
⅔ cup sugar
⅓ cup unsweetened cocoa powder
8 tablespoons (1 stick) unsalted butter,
    cold, cut into 8 pieces

THE GLAZE
3 ounces bittersweet chocolate, chopped
1 teaspoon vegetable oil

1. Preheat the oven to 300°F. Lightly grease a 9 × 12-inch baking dish with vegetable oil, or line it with parchment paper.

2. Place the flour, sugar, and cocoa in a food processor and process for 10 seconds.

3. Scatter the butter over the flour mixture, and pulse 60 times to blend. (The mixture will still be crumbly.)

4. Press the mixture evenly into the baking dish. Place the dish on the center rack of the oven, and bake until the shortbread is firm to the touch, 40 to 45 minutes.

5. Remove the dish from the oven and place it on a cooling rack. Using a sharp knife, immediately cut the shortbread into 24 pieces (3 long slices by 8 crosswise). Then allow it to cool completely in the pan.

6. When the shortbread is cool, prepare the glaze: Melt the chocolate in the top of a double boiler placed over simmering water.

7. Whisk in the oil, stirring until the mixture is smooth, several seconds. Then pour the mixture into a small deep bowl.

8. Working quickly, dip the prongs of a fork into the glaze, and moving your wrist rapidly from side to side, drizzle lines of chocolate over the shortbread. Use the tip of a knife to go over the cut lines. Allow the shortbread to set for 4 to 6 hours, or place it in the refrigerator or freezer for 1 hour.

9. Any cookies not eaten on the first day should be layered in an airtight container, using plastic wrap, parchment, or waxed paper between the layers, and stored in the refrigerator for up to 2 days or in the freezer for up to 2 weeks.

Makes 24 cookies

Toasted Coconut Macadamia Shortbread

formed cookie

Delicate, crunchy, and chock-full of two of my favorite ingredients, these tropical cookies are good during any season.

INGREDIENTS

THE COATING
1 large egg white
2 cups flaked sweetened coconut

THE COOKIE
2 cups all-purpose flour
1/4 teaspoon baking powder
1/2 teaspoon salt
1 cup (2 sticks) unsalted butter at room temperature
7 tablespoons confectioners' sugar
4 tablespoons granulated sugar
2 teaspoons pure vanilla extract
1/2 cup flaked sweetened coconut
3/4 cup coarsely chopped macadamia nuts

1. Preheat the oven to 325°F. Line several baking sheets with parchment paper.

2. Place the egg white for the coating in a small bowl, and set it aside. Place the 2 cups coconut in another small bowl, and set aside.

3. Sift the flour, baking powder, and salt together into a small bowl, and set aside.

4. Using an electric mixer on medium-high speed, cream the butter, both sugars, and vanilla together in a medium-size mixing bowl until light and fluffy, 1½ minutes. Stop the mixer once during the process to scrape the bowl with a rubber spatula.

5. Add the flour mixture, and mix on low speed for 5 seconds. Scrape the bowl. Then increase the speed to medium-high and mix until fluffy, 1 minute. Scrape the bowl again.

6. Add the ½ cup coconut and mix for 10 seconds; scrape the bowl. Then add the nuts and mix until blended, 5 seconds.

7. Measure out generously rounded teaspoons of the dough, and roll them between your hands to form cylinders about 2 inches long by ½ inch thick. Press each cylinder between your palms to form an oval shape about 1½ by 2½ inches.

8. Dip each cookie into the egg white so that it is completely covered; then lift it up, allowing any excess white to slide off. Place the cookie in the bowl of coconut, and shake the bowl gently so that the cookie is completely coated with coconut.

9. Place the cookies 1 inch apart on the prepared baking sheets. Bake until the cookies are a deep golden color,

about 20 minutes. Then reduce the heat to 300°F, and continue to bake for 10 to 15 minutes (to ensure crispness). Allow the cookies to cool on the baking sheets.

10. Store the cookies in an airtight container at room temperature for a day or two if you think you will be snacking on them. After that, store the container in the freezer for up to 2 weeks. Bring the cookies to room temperature before eating.

Makes 58 cookies

Chunky Pecan Shortbread

♥ ♥ ♥ ♥ ♥ ♥ ♥ ♥   *formed cookie*

There are moments in baking when I feel like a matchmaker for the most obvious of unions. Here it's the natural trio of brown sugar, butter, and pecans. Together they create a solid, chunky cookie with incredible depth of flavor and a texture that's enhanced by the oats I threw in to keep them company.

INGREDIENTS

THE COOKIE
1¼ cups (2½ sticks) unsalted butter
    at room temperature
1 cup plus 2 tablespoons (lightly packed)
    light brown sugar
2 teaspoons pure vanilla extract
2½ cups all-purpose flour
¾ teaspoon salt
7 tablespoons rolled oats
6 tablespoons chopped pecans

THE GLAZE
1 large egg white
24 pecan halves

1. Preheat the oven to 325°F. Line two baking sheets with parchment paper, or leave them ungreased.

2. Using an electric mixer on medium speed, cream the butter, brown sugar, and vanilla together in a medium-size mixing bowl until light and fluffy, about 1½ minutes. Stop the mixer once or twice during the process to scrape the bowl with a rubber spatula.

3. Add the flour and salt, and blend on medium speed for about 1 minute. Scrape the bowl.

4. Add the oats and blend until incorporated, 30 seconds. Then scrape the bowl and add the nuts. Mix until blended, 5 seconds.

5. Measure out rounded tablespoons of dough, and form them into balls with your hands. Place the balls at least

1½ inches apart on the baking sheets. Flatten them with the palm of your hand to form cookies 2¼ inches in diameter and ½ inch thick.

6. Using a pastry brush, glaze each cookie with egg white. Place a pecan half in the center of each cookie. Bake until the cookies are firm and deep golden with darker edges, 35 minutes. Allow them to cool on the baking sheets.

7. Store the cookies in an airtight container at room temperature for a day or two if you think you will be snacking on them. After that, store the container in the freezer for up to 2 weeks. Bring the cookies to room temperature before eating.

Makes 24 cookies

Peanut Butter Shortbread Cookies

❤ ❤ ❤ ❤ ❤ ❤ ❤ *refrigerator cookie*

A sophisticated version of the peanut butter cookie, these small, crunchy refrigerator cookies are a cinch to make and a favorite for people of all ages.

INGREDIENTS

1¾ cups plus 2 tablespoons all-purpose flour
⅛ teaspoon baking powder
½ teaspoon salt
12 tablespoons (1½ sticks) unsalted butter at room temperature
7½ tablespoons smooth peanut butter
5 tablespoons granulated sugar
6 tablespoons (lightly packed) light brown sugar
¾ teaspoon pure vanilla extract
1 large egg

1. Sift the flour, baking powder, and salt together into a small bowl and set aside.

2. Using an electric mixer on medium speed, cream the butter, peanut butter, both sugars, and the vanilla together in a medium-size mixing bowl until light and fluffy, 1 or 2 minutes. Stop the mixer once or twice during the process to scrape the bowl with a rubber spatula.

3. Add the egg and mix on medium speed until incorporated, 15 to 20 seconds. Scrape the bowl.

4. Add the flour mixture and mix on low speed until the mixture is smooth, about 45 seconds. Divide the dough in half.

5. Place two 16-inch lengths of waxed paper or plastic wrap on a work surface. Shape each half of the dough into a rough log 10 inches long and place it along one long side of the paper. Roll the logs up in the waxed paper, and twist the ends like a hard-candy wrapper. Refrigerate the dough for 1½ to 2 hours.

6. Remove the dough from the refrigerator. Using your hands, roll the wrapped dough gently back and forth on a work surface to smooth out the logs. Refrigerate again for 1 to 2 hours.

7. Fifteen minutes before baking, preheat the oven to 300°F. Line several baking sheets with parchment paper, or leave them ungreased.

8. Remove the dough from the refrigerator, unwrap it, and cut the logs into slices that are ⅓ inch thick. Place the cookies 1 inch apart on the prepared baking sheets.

9. Bake the cookies until they are lightly golden and crisp to the touch, about 20 minutes. (To test for doneness, remove a cookie from the oven and cut it in half. There should be no doughy strip in the center.) Cool the cookies on the sheets.

10. Store the cookies in an airtight container at room temperature for a day or two if you think you will be snacking on them. After that, store the container in the freezer for up to 2 weeks. Bring the cookies to room temperature before eating.

Makes about 60 cookies

Ginger Shortbread

♥ ♥ ♥ ♥ ♥ ♥ ♥   *refrigerator cookie*

Instead of a tea cake, I like to offer this as a tea cookie. I save it for the true ginger lover because it's loaded both with ground and candied ginger. Like tea, it's an acquired taste—unless, of course, you hang out with very sophisticated children. Whatever the age of the palate, it's a shortbread that packs a punch.

INGREDIENTS

2 cups plus 2 tablespoons all-purpose flour
¼ teaspoon baking powder
¾ teaspoon salt
1 cup (2 sticks) unsalted butter at room temperature
⅔ cup plus 1 tablespoon (lightly packed) light brown sugar
¾ teaspoon pure vanilla extract
3 tablespoons ground ginger
1 cup coarsely chopped candied ginger (chopped by hand)

1. Sift the flour, baking powder, and salt together into a small bowl and set aside.

2. Using an electric mixer on medium speed, cream the butter, brown sugar, vanilla, and ground ginger together in a medium-size mixing bowl until light and fluffy, about 2 minutes. Stop the mixer once or twice during the process to scrape the bowl with a rubber spatula.

3. Add the flour mixture and mix on low speed until the mixture is fluffy again, about 45 seconds. Scrape the bowl.

4. Remove the dough from the bowl and place it on a work surface. Work the candied ginger into the dough with your hands.

5. Divide the dough in half. Place two 16-inch lengths of waxed paper or plastic wrap on a work surface. Shape each half of the dough into a rough log, about 10 inches long and 1½ inches in diameter, and place it along one long side of the paper. Roll the dough up in the paper, and twist the ends like a hard-candy wrapper. Refrigerate the dough for 1 to 2 hours.

6. Remove the dough from the refrigerator. Using your hands, roll the wrapped dough gently back and forth on the work surface to smooth out the logs. Refrigerate again for 4 to 6 hours.

7. Fifteen minutes before baking, preheat the oven to 350°F. Line several baking sheets with parchment paper, or leave them ungreased.

8. Remove the dough from the refrigerator, unwrap the logs, and cut them into slices that are a generous ⅓ inch thick.

9. Place the cookies 1 inch apart on the prepared baking sheets, and bake until they are golden and firm to the touch, 28 to 30 minutes. (To test for doneness, remove a cookie from the oven and cut it in half. There should be no doughy strip in the center.) Cool the cookies on the sheets.

10. Store the cookies in an airtight container at room temperature for a day or two if you think you will be snacking on them. After that, store the container in the freezer for up to 2 weeks. Bring the cookies to room temperature before eating.

Makes about 60 cookies

Cornmeal Shortbread Cookies

♥ ♥ ♥ ♥ ♥ ♥ *refrigerator cookie*

There's a lot to be said for cornmeal. The richness of its history, rooted in Native American culture, and the flavor reminiscent of one of our favorite holiday meals make this a very special ingredient. I put cornmeal in my kids' pancakes and cook them cornmeal mush for breakfast. With all that, why not cornmeal cookies, too? These have the crunchy butteryness of shortbread plus the texture of the cornmeal—light, delicious, and grainy.

INGREDIENTS

1 large egg

1 teaspoon pure vanilla extract

1¾ cups plus 2 tablespoons all-purpose
*   flour*

1 cup yellow cornmeal

⅛ teaspoon baking powder

½ teaspoon salt

¾ cup sugar

1 cup (2 sticks) unsalted butter, cold,
*   cut into 16 pieces*

1. Using a fork, stir the egg and vanilla together in a small cup and set aside.

2. Place the flour, cornmeal, baking powder, salt and sugar in a food processor and process to blend, 5 seconds.

3. Distribute the butter over the flour mixture and process until the mixture resembles coarse cornmeal, 20 to 30 seconds.

4. With the machine running, add the egg mixture through the feed tube; process for 30 seconds. Scrape the bowl, then process for 3 seconds more. Remove the dough and knead it for several seconds on a work surface.

5. Place a 16-inch length of plastic wrap on a work surface. Shape the dough into a rough log 11 inches long and 2 inches in diameter, and place it along one long side of the plastic wrap. Roll the dough up in the plastic wrap, and twist the ends like a hard-candy wrapper. Refrigerate the dough for 1 hour.

6. Remove the dough from the refrigerator. Using your hands, roll the wrapped dough gently back and forth on a work surface to smooth out the cylinder. Refrigerate it again for 4 to 6 hours or as long as overnight.

7. Fifteen minutes before baking, preheat the oven to 350°F. Line several baking sheets with parchment paper, or leave them ungreased.

8. Remove the dough from the refrigerator, unwrap it, and cut it into slices that are a generous ¼ inch thick. Place them 1 inch apart on the baking sheets.

9. Bake the shortbread cookies until they are firm and lightly golden around the edges, 20 minutes. Let them cool on the baking sheets.

10. Store the cookies in an airtight container at room temperature for a day or two if you think you will be snacking on them. After that, store the container in the freezer for up to 2 weeks. Bring the cookies to room temperature before eating.

Makes 44 cookies

CHAPTER 5

CAKEY

COOKIES

Sacher Tortes
Banana Cream Cheese Mounds
Lemon Orange Sour Cream Cookies
Carrot Cake Cookies
Lemon-Glazed Hermits
Maple Softies
Glazed Molasses Cake Cookies
Half Moons
Chippy Jaker Cakers

Glazed Molasses Cookies, Banana Cream Cheese Mounds, Half Moons. These luscious little heaps of cake, glazed or frosted and passed off as cookies, have a special place in my heart because they allow me to have my cake and eat my cookie too. It seems I'm not alone in this. When I told a friend I was writing a book of cookie recipes, the first thing he said was, "I certainly hope you plan to include Half Moons"—which reaffirmed for me why we're friends.

As my children have gone off to school, cakey cookies have risen even higher in my esteem, because they make wonderful child-size treats for school birthday parties. They're easier for the teacher to hand out and less messy than cake, but they taste just as good and are just as filling. They look great too, especially with a piece of candy or a birthday doodad perched atop the frosting. Best of all, they're separate but equal—and as anyone who has spent any time around kids knows, the child who has her own is a happy child.

Because these cookies are essentially miniature cakes, their batters require more delicate mixing than the other types of cookies. They're also

Cover-ups

Many of these cookies are topped with a glaze or frosting. I use a liquidy confectioners' sugar glaze, and if the glaze is loose enough, I dip the top of the cookie directly in it. If it's too dense for dipping, I spread the glaze with a small spatula or a butter knife. Frostings are always too thick for dipping, so you have to spread them, using the same utensils.

Frostings and glazes are most attractive when they're spread evenly over the cookie with a narrow border left around the edge. When toppings are left to dribble over the sides, they look more like a mistake than an adornment.

fussier about baking time and temperature, and they don't hang around well, so you need to eat them the day of or the day after baking, or you can freeze them for later on. Don't let their demands put you off, though. Once you've made any of these cookies, you'll know their quirks, and you'll agree that the effort is certainly worth it.

Sacher Tortes

❤ ❤ ❤ ❤ ❤ ❤ ❤ ❤ ❤ ❤   *drop cookie*

The Sacher torte is a Viennese specialty, a chocolate cake layered with apricot preserves and glazed with more chocolate. I've transformed it into a cookie, keeping all the original ingredients but making it more compact. If you're not a fan of apricots, you can still enjoy the essence of the torte; just leave the preserves out to create a great devil's food cookie with a fudge glaze.

INGREDIENTS

THE COOKIE
2 ounces unsweetened chocolate
1 cup all-purpose flour
1 cup cake flour
6 tablespoons unsweetened cocoa powder
½ teaspoon salt
1 teaspoon baking powder
¼ teaspoon baking soda
4 tablespoons (½ stick) unsalted butter at
    room temperature
¼ cup vegetable oil
1 cup (lightly packed) light brown sugar
3 tablespoons granulated sugar
1½ teaspoons pure vanilla extract
3 large eggs
1 cup sour cream

THE TOPPING
⅓ cup apricot preserves

THE GLAZE
8 ounces bittersweet chocolate
2 tablespoons light corn syrup
2 tablespoons unsalted butter
2 tablespoons hot water

1. Preheat the oven to 400°F. Line two baking sheets with parchment paper, or grease them lightly with vegetable oil.

2. Melt the chocolate in the top of a double boiler placed over simmering water. Remove it from the heat and set it aside.

3. Sift both flours, the cocoa powder, salt, baking powder, and baking soda together into a small bowl and set aside.

4. Using an electric mixer on medium-high speed, cream the butter, oil, both sugars, and the vanilla together in a medium-size bowl until light and fluffy, 1½ to 2 minutes. Stop the mixer once or twice during the process to scrape the bowl with a rubber spatula.

5. Add the eggs one at a time, blending on medium speed for 5 seconds after each addition and scraping the bowl with the rubber spatula each time.

6. Add the sour cream and beat on medium speed until blended, about 5 seconds, then on high speed for 3 seconds.

7. Using the spatula, fold in the melted chocolate, mixing until the batter is uniform in color.

8. Fold in the flour mixture with six or seven broad strokes of the spatula. Then mix with the electric mixer on low speed until the batter is velvety, about 10 seconds, stopping once to scrape the bowl with the rubber spatula.

9. Drop the batter by slightly rounded tablespoons about 2 inches apart on the prepared baking sheets.

10. Bake the cookies until they are puffed and just set, about 11 minutes.

11. As soon as the cookies come out of the oven, heat the apricot preserves in a saucepan over low heat just until liquid.

12. Drop a generous ½ teaspoon of the preserves on top of each cookie, and spread it over the surface with a pastry brush. Let the cookies sit for 5 minutes. Then slide the sheet of parchment onto the counter (or, using a spatula, carefully transfer each cookie to a sheet of aluminum foil or waxed paper on the counter) and let them cool further.

13. While the cookies are cooling, prepare the glaze: Melt the chocolate in the top of a double boiler placed over simmering water. Remove the pan from the heat.

14. Add the corn syrup, butter, and hot water to the chocolate, and whisk vigorously until smooth and shiny.

15. Loosen the cookies from the paper with a spatula, and dip their tops into the warm glaze; or use a spatula or a butter knife to spread the glaze over the top. Then return the cookies to the paper, and allow the glaze to set for 2 hours (or refrigerate for 1 hour to set quickly). If you plan to eat them the first day,

store them at room temperature on a plate. After that, place them in an airtight plastic container with plastic wrap, parchment, or waxed paper between the layers, and store them in the refrigerator for up to 3 days or in the freezer for up to 2 weeks. Bring the cookies to room temperature before eating.

Makes about 30 cookies

Banana Cream Cheese Mounds

❤ ❤ ❤ ❤ ❤ ❤ ❤ ❤ ❤ ❤   *drop cookie*

Soft and moist, these cookies are among my favorites in this book. It has to do with a cherished memory from my childhood: a banana layer cake my mother sometimes brought home as a treat. When I bite into these cookies, I'm transported back to our dining room table, with my feet not quite reaching the floor and my fork poised to let the glory begin.

INGREDIENTS

THE COOKIE

1½ cups plus 1 tablespoon sifted cake flour
1 teaspoon baking powder
⅛ teaspoon baking soda
¼ teaspoon salt
6 tablespoons (¾ stick) unsalted butter at
*   room temperature*
5 tablespoons granulated sugar
¼ cup (lightly packed) light brown sugar
1 teaspoon pure vanilla extract
1 large egg
½ cup plus 2 tablespoons mashed very ripe
*   bananas*

THE FROSTING

¾ cup cream cheese at room temperature
6 tablespoons confectioners' sugar
3 tablespoons unsalted butter at room
*   temperature*

1. Preheat the oven to 400°F. Line several baking sheets with parchment paper, or lightly grease them with vegetable oil.

2. Sift the flour, baking powder, baking soda, and salt together into a small bowl and set aside.

3. Using an electric mixer on medium speed, cream the butter, both sugars, and the vanilla in a medium-size bowl until light and fluffy, 1 to 1½ minutes. Scrape the bowl.

4. Add the egg and mix on medium speed until blended, about 15 seconds. Scrape the bowl.

5. Add the banana and mix on medium-low speed until blended, about 10 seconds. Scrape the bowl.

6. Fold in the flour mixture by hand. Then blend with the mixer on low speed for 5 seconds. Scrape the bowl with the rubber spatula, and mix on low speed until the batter is smooth and velvety, about 10 seconds. Give the batter a stir or two with the spatula.

7. Drop the batter by heaping table-spoons 2 inches apart onto the prepared baking sheets.

8. Bake the cookies until they are puffed and just firm to the touch (but not golden), about 10 minutes. Let the cookies sit for 2 to 3 minutes. Then slide the sheet of parchment onto the counter (or, using a spatula, carefully transfer each cookie to a sheet of aluminum foil or waxed paper on the counter), and let them cool further.

9. Meanwhile prepare the frosting: Place all the frosting ingredients in a food processor and process until smooth, 40 seconds.

10. Using a small spatula or a butter knife, spread a generous tablespoon of the frosting over the top of each cookie.

11. If you plan to eat the cookies that day, leave them sitting out. To store them, place them in an airtight plastic container with plastic wrap, parchment, or waxed paper between the layers. Store them in the refrigerator if you plan to eat them the next day. Otherwise, place the container in the freezer for up to 2 weeks. Bring the cookies to room temperature before eating.

Makes about 13 large cookies

Lemon Orange Sour Cream Cookies

♥ ♥ ♥ ♥ ♥ ♥ ♥ ♥ ♥ ♥ *drop cookie*

Does everyone have some food that makes them close their eyes and moan blissfully, or is it just me? That's certainly what happens when I bite into this cookie. It's so moist, tender, and flavorful—I feel as if I'm indulging in a sumptuous orange layer cake with lots of lemon frosting.

INGREDIENTS

THE COOKIE
1 cup plus 1 tablespoon cake flour
½ cup plus 2 tablespoons all-purpose flour
½ teaspoon baking powder
½ teaspoon baking soda
½ teaspoon salt
8 tablespoons (1 stick) unsalted butter at
*   room temperature*
1 cup minus 2 tablespoons sugar
1½ tablespoons grated orange zest
1½ teaspoons pure vanilla extract
1 large egg
½ cup plus 3 tablespoons sour cream

THE GLAZE
1 cup confectioners' sugar
2 tablespoons unsalted butter, melted
1 tablespoon plus 2 teaspoons fresh
*   lemon juice*

1. Preheat the oven to 400°F. Line several baking sheets with parchment paper, or lightly grease them with vegetable oil.

2. Sift both flours, the baking powder, baking soda, and salt together into a small bowl and set aside.

3. Using an electric mixer on medium speed, cream the butter, sugar, orange zest, and vanilla in a medium-size bowl until light and fluffy, about 1 minute. Scrape the bowl.

4. Add the egg and mix on medium speed until blended, about 10 seconds. Scrape the bowl.

5. Add the sour cream and mix on medium-low speed until blended, about 8 seconds.

6. Fold in the flour mixture by hand. Then blend with the mixer on low speed for 5 seconds. Scrape the bowl with the rubber spatula, and mix on low speed until the batter is smooth and velvety, 10 seconds. Give the batter a stir or two with the spatula.

7. Drop the batter by large rounded tablespoons about 2 inches apart onto the prepared baking sheets.

8. Bake until the cookies have puffed up, are firm to the touch, and are just beginning to turn golden around the edges, 10 minutes. Let the cookies sit for 2 to 3 minutes. Then slide the sheet of parchment onto the counter (or, using a spatula, carefully transfer each cookie to a sheet of aluminum foil or waxed paper on the counter), and let them cool further.

9. Meanwhile, prepare the glaze: Place the confectioners' sugar in a medium-size bowl. Add the butter and lemon juice, and beat vigorously with a whisk until the mixture is smooth and creamy.

10. Once the cookies have cooled, drop generously rounded ½ teaspoons of the glaze onto each cookie and spread with small butter knife. Allow them to sit until the glaze hardens, about 2 hours (or pop them into the refrigerator for 1 hour).

11. If you plan to eat the cookies that day, leave them sitting out. To store them, place them in an airtight plastic container with plastic wrap, parchment, or waxed paper between the layers. Store them in the refrigerator if you plan to eat them the next day. Otherwise, place the container in the freezer for up to 2 weeks. Bring the cookies to room temperature before eating.

Makes about 24 cookies

Carrot Cake Cookies

♥ ♥ ♥ ♥ ♥ ♥ ♥ ♥   *drop cookie*

Although carrot cake is not quite the hot ticket that it was in the 1970s, it still ranks as a favorite in the repertoire of American desserts. This moist, cakey cookie is topped appropriately with a cream cheese frosting—just like in the old days!

INGREDIENTS

THE COOKIE
2 cups all-purpose flour
1 teaspoon baking powder
¾ teaspoon baking soda
1 teaspoon salt
1 teaspoon ground cinnamon
½ teaspoon ground allspice
¾ teaspoon ground mace
½ teaspoon ground ginger
2 cups grated carrots (2 or 3 good-size
*   carrots)*
12 tablespoons (1½ sticks) unsalted butter
*   at room temperature*
7 tablespoons (lightly packed) light brown
*   sugar*
7 tablespoons granulated sugar
2 teaspoons pure vanilla extract
2 large eggs
1 cup drained crushed pineapple
*   (one 16-ounce can)*

THE FROSTING
1 cup cream cheese at room temperature
½ cup confectioners' sugar
4 tablespoons (½ stick) unsalted butter
*   at room temperature*

1. Preheat the oven to 425°F. Line several baking sheets with parchment paper or grease them lightly with vegetable oil.

2. Sift the flour, baking powder, baking soda, salt, and all the spices together into a medium-size bowl and set aside.

3. Place the grated carrots in a food processor and pulse 8 times to chop the shreds. Set aside.

4. Using an electric mixer on medium-high speed, cream the butter, both sugars, and vanilla in a medium-size bowl until light and fluffy, 1 minute. Stop the mixer once during the process to scrape the bowl with a rubber spatula.

5. Add the eggs one at a time, blending on medium speed for 10 seconds after each addition and scraping the bowl with the rubber spatula each time.

6. Add the carrots and the pineapple, and mix on medium speed until blended, 10 seconds, stopping the mixer once to scrape the bowl and then scraping it once again at the end.

7. Add the flour mixture with the mixer on low speed, and blend for 8 seconds. Scrape the bowl thoroughly, then turn the mixer to medium-high and blend for 5 more seconds. Scrape the bowl and finish mixing the batter by hand with a few additional turns of the spatula.

8. Drop the batter by heaping tablespoons onto the prepared baking sheets, and bake on the center rack of the oven until the centers are puffed, set, and lightly golden, about 13 minutes. Allow the cookies to cool 2 to 3 minutes on the baking sheets. Then slide the sheet of parchment onto the counter (or, using a spatula, carefully transfer each cookie onto a sheet of aluminum foil or waxed paper on the counter) and let them cool further.

9. Meanwhile, prepare the frosting: Place all the ingredients in a food processor and process until smooth, 40 seconds.

10. Using a small spatula or a butter knife, spread a generous tablespoon of the frosting over the top of each cookie.

11. If you plan to eat the cookies that day, leave them sitting out. To store them, place them in a single layer in large airtight plastic containers. Store them in the fridge if you plan to eat them the next day. Otherwise, store the container in the freezer for up to 2 weeks. Bring the cookies to room temperature before eating.

Makes about 20 cookies

Lemon-Glazed Hermits

♥ ♥ ♥ ♥ ♥ ♥ ♥ ♥ ♥ ♥ *drop cookie*

Hermits always seem misnamed to me because they're so popular, though it's true that they keep to themselves very well. This version is a moist cakey mound of molasses-and-spice-flavored cookie topped with a white glaze.

INGREDIENTS

THE COOKIE

2¼ cups all-purpose flour

1 teaspoon baking soda

½ teaspoon salt

14 tablespoons (1¾ sticks) unsalted butter
     at room temperature

1 cup plus 2 tablespoons (firmly packed)
     light brown sugar

1 tablespoon plus 1 teaspoon ground
     cinnamon

2 tablespoons ground ginger

2 teaspoons ground cloves

1 tablespoon plus 1 teaspoon instant
     coffee powder

1 whole large egg

2 large egg yolks

2 tablespoons dark molasses

THE GLAZE

1¼ cups confectioners' sugar

3 tablespoons fresh lemon juice

1. Preheat the oven to 400°F. Line several baking sheets with parchment paper, or lightly grease them with vegetable oil.

2. Sift the flour, baking soda, and salt together into a small bowl and set aside.

3. Using an electric mixer on medium-high speed, cream the butter, brown sugar, all the spices, and coffee powder together in a medium-size bowl until light and fluffy, about 2 minutes. Stop the mixer twice during the process to scrape the bowl with a rubber spatula. Scrape the bowl a third time before going on to the next step.

4. Add the whole egg and blend on medium speed for about 10 seconds. Scrape the bowl, and then add the yolks. Blend on medium speed for 20 seconds. Scrape the bowl again.

5. Add the molasses and mix on medium-low speed for about 5 seconds. Scrape the bowl.

6. Fold in the flour mixture by hand. Then turn the mixer on low speed and mix for about 5 seconds. Scrape the bowl with the rubber spatula, and mix on low speed until the batter is smooth and velvety, 10 seconds. Give the batter a stir or two with the spatula.

7. Drop the batter by generously rounded tablespoons about 2 inches apart onto the prepared baking sheets.

8. Bake the cookies until they are puffed but the tops are not set (they should leave an indentation when touched), about 12 minutes depending on how chewy you like your hermits. Using a metal spatula, carefully transfer the cookies to wire racks to cool completely.

9. Meanwhile, prepare the glaze: Place the confectioners' sugar and the lemon juice in a small bowl and beat vigorously with a whisk until the mixture is smooth and creamy.

10. Drizzle the glaze over the cooled cookies, or spread it over the surface with a butter knife. Allow the cookies to sit until the glaze hardens, 2 to 3 hours.

11. Then place the cookies, with plastic wrap, parchment, or waxed paper between the layers, in an airtight container and keep them at room temperature if you plan to eat them the first day. Otherwise, store them in the freezer for up to 2 weeks. Bring the cookies to room temperature before eating.

Makes about 22 hermits

Maple Softies

♥ ♥ ♥ ♥ ♥ ♥ ♥ ♥ ♥ *drop cookie*

One of my most vivid memories from my college years is my mornings at King Pin Donuts on Telegraph Avenue in Berkeley. I'd go there before classes and inhale a maple bar—a fresh-from-the-oven rectangular doughnut swathed in a maple glaze. This is a tribute to that memory: a tender, cakey drop cookie, finished off with a confectioners' sugar–maple glaze.

INGREDIENTS

THE COOKIE
2 cups plus 6 tablespoons cake flour
½ teaspoon plus ⅛ teaspoon baking powder
½ teaspoon plus ⅛ teaspoon baking soda
½ teaspoon salt
9 tablespoons (1 stick plus 1 tablespoon) unsalted butter at room temperature
¾ cup granulated sugar
6 tablespoons (lightly packed) light brown sugar
½ teaspoon pure vanilla extract
¾ teaspoon pure maple extract
2 large eggs
¾ cup sour cream

THE GLAZE
3 cups confectioners' sugar
¼ cup water
3 tablespoons pure maple syrup
1½ tablespoons light corn syrup
1½ tablespoons (lightly packed) light brown sugar
2 teaspoons pure maple extract

THE TOPPING
About 24 pecan halves

1. Preheat the oven to 400°F. Line several baking sheets with parchment paper, or lightly grease them with vegetable oil.

2. Sift the flour, baking powder, baking soda, and salt together into a small bowl and set aside.

355

3. Using an electric mixer on medium-high speed, cream the butter, both sugars, vanilla, and maple extract together until light and fluffy, 1 minute. Stop the mixer twice during the process to scrape the bowl with a rubber spatula. Scrape the bowl a third time before going on to the next step.

4. Add the eggs one at a time, blending for about 10 seconds on medium speed after each addition. Scrape the bowl.

5. Add one third of the flour mixture with the mixer on low speed, and blend for 5 seconds. Scrape the bowl.

6. Add half of the sour cream, and blend on low speed for 5 seconds. Scrape the bowl.

7. Repeat steps 5 and 6. Then add the remaining flour mixture and mix on low speed for 5 seconds.

8. Give the batter a few broad strokes with a rubber spatula.

9. Drop the batter by heaping tablespoons 2 inches apart on the prepared baking sheets.

10. Bake the cookies until they are just golden and firm to the touch but not crusty, 11 to 12 minutes.

11. Let the cookies sit for 2 to 3 minutes. Then slide the sheet of parchment onto the counter (or, using a spatula, carefully transfer each cookie to a sheet of aluminum foil or waxed paper on the counter), and let them cool further.

12. When the cookies have cooled, prepare the glaze: Place the confectioners' sugar in a medium-size bowl and set aside.

13. Place the water, maple syrup, corn syrup, and brown sugar in a small saucepan and bring to a boil over medium heat. Remove from the heat and add the maple extract.

14. Immediately add this hot mixture to the confectioners' sugar and beat it vigorously with a whisk until velvety smooth, 20 to 30 seconds.

15. Dip the rounded top of each cooled cookie into the glaze, and place a pecan half on top of the cookie. Return the cookies to the paper or foil, and allow them to sit until the glaze hardens, 2 to 3 hours (or pop them into the fridge for 1 hour to set quickly).

16. If you plan to eat the cookies that day, leave them sitting out. To store them, place them in an airtight plastic container with plastic wrap, parchment, or waxed paper between the layers. Store them in the refrigerator if you plan to eat them the next day. Otherwise, place the container in the freezer for up to 2 weeks. Bring the cookies to room temperature before eating.

Makes about 24 cookies

Glazed Molasses Cake Cookies

♥ ♥ ♥ ♥ ♥ ♥ ♥ ♥ ♥   *drop cookie*

This moist and flavorful molasses cookie is like a tasty piece of gingerbread in cookie form. Glaze a single cookie or sandwich two cookies together with Marshmallow Filling (see page 140). Either way, they're best on the day they are baked.

INGREDIENTS

THE COOKIE
1½ cups all-purpose flour
1 cup plus 2 tablespoons cake flour
1 teaspoon salt
¾ teaspoon baking soda
1 teaspoon ground ginger
1 teaspoon ground cinnamon
¼ teaspoon ground cloves
13 tablespoons (1½ sticks plus 1 table-
*   spoon) unsalted butter at room*
*   temperature*
2 teaspoons grated lemon zest
2 whole large eggs
2 large egg yolks
1 cup dark molasses

THE GLAZE
1½ cups confectioners' sugar
2 tablespoons plus 2 teaspoons heavy
*   (whipping) cream*
1 tablespoon plus 1 teaspoon fresh
*   lemon juice*

1. Preheat the oven to 400°F. Line several baking sheets with parchment paper, or grease them lightly with vegetable oil.

2. Sift both flours, the salt, baking soda, ginger, cinnamon, and cloves together into a small bowl and set aside.

3. With an electric mixer on medium-high speed, cream the butter and lemon zest together in a medium-size bowl until light and fluffy, 1 minute.

4. Add the whole eggs and the yolks, and mix on medium speed until blended, 20 seconds. Stop the mixer once to scrape the bowl.

5. Add the molasses and mix to blend, 10 seconds. Scrape the bowl.

6. Add half the flour mixture with the mixer on low speed, and blend for 10 seconds. Scrape the bowl with the rubber spatula, add the rest of the flour mixture, and blend on low speed for 10 seconds. Finish the mixing by hand until the batter is smooth.

7. Drop the batter by large rounded tablespoons about 2 inches apart on the prepared baking sheets.

8. Bake until the cookies have puffed up and are firm to the touch, about 13 minutes. Let the cookies sit for 2 to 3 minutes. Then slide the sheet of parchment onto the counter (or, using a spatula, carefully transfer each cookie to a sheet of aluminum foil or waxed paper on the counter), and let them cool further.

9. Meanwhile, prepare the glaze: Place the confectioners' sugar, cream, and the lemon juice in a small bowl and whisk vigorously until smooth.

10. Using a small spatula or a butter knife, frost the top of each cookie with a generously rounded teaspoon of glaze. Let the cookies set for 2 to 3 hours (or pop them into the fridge for 1 hour to set quickly).

11. If you plan to eat the cookies that day, leave them sitting out. To store them, place them in a large airtight plastic container in no more than two layers, with plastic wrap, parchment, or waxed paper between the layers. Store them in the refrigerator if you plan to eat them the next day. Otherwise, place the container in the freezer for up to 2 weeks. Bring the cookies to room temperature before eating.

Makes 20 to 24 cookies

Half Moons

♥ ♥ ♥ ♥ ♥ ♥ ♥ ♥ ♥ ♥ *drop cookie*

However many days there were in the academic years of 1961 to 1964 probably exactly equals the number of Half Moons I consumed. It was only a short jaunt from school

to the little neighborhood bakery that supplied me with these oversized yellow cake cookies, one half frosted in chocolate and one half in vanilla. Half Moons are close to perfection.

INGREDIENTS

THE COOKIE
1¼ cups cake flour
½ cup plus 1 tablespoon all-purpose flour
1¼ teaspoons baking powder
½ teaspoon salt
10 tablespoons (1¼ sticks) unsalted butter
    at room temperature
¾ cup plus 2 tablespoons sugar
1½ teaspoons pure vanilla extract
1 teaspoon grated lemon zest
2 large egg yolks
2 whole large eggs
1 tablespoon milk

THE VANILLA GLAZE
¾ cup confectioners' sugar
2 tablespoons plus 1 teaspoon heavy
    (whipping) cream
1½ teaspoons unsalted butter, melted

THE CHOCOLATE GLAZE
¼ cup heavy (whipping) cream, heated
    just to boiling
1 ounce unsweetened chocolate, melted
2 teaspoons unsalted butter
¼ cup confectioners' sugar

1. Preheat the oven to 400°F. Line several baking sheets with parchment paper, or lightly grease them with vegetable oil.

2. Sift both flours, the baking powder, and the salt together into a small bowl and set aside.

3. Using an electric mixer on medium-high speed, cream the butter, sugar, vanilla, and lemon zest together in a medium-size bowl until light and fluffy, about 2 minutes. Stop the mixer once during the process to scrape the bowl with a rubber spatula. Scrape the bowl a third time before going on to the next step.

4. Add the egg yolks and blend on medium speed until incorporated, 15 seconds, stopping the mixer once to scrape the bowl with a rubber spatula.

5. Add the whole eggs one at a time, blending on medium speed for 10 seconds after each addition. Stop the mixer once to scrape the bowl. Then blend on high speed for 5 seconds.

6. Fold in half of the flour mixture by hand. Then turn the mixer on low speed and mix for about 10 seconds. Add the milk. Scrape the bowl with the spatula. Then turn the mixer to medium speed and blend for 5 seconds. Scrape the bowl. With the mixer on low speed, add the remaining flour mixture and blend for 5 seconds. Scrape the bowl. Then turn the mixer to high speed and blend until velvety, 5 seconds.

7. Drop the batter by quarter-cupfuls about 3 inches apart on the prepared baking sheets.

8. Bake the cookies until they are just set and firm to the touch but not crusty, about 12 minutes. Let the cookies sit for 2 to 3 minutes. Then slide the sheet of parchment onto the counter (or, using a spatula, carefully transfer each cookie to a sheet of aluminum foil or waxed paper on the counter), and let them cool further.

9. While the cookies are cooling, prepare the glazes: Place all the ingredients for the vanilla glaze in a small bowl and stir vigorously with a whisk until smooth and velvety.

10. To make the chocolate glaze, place the hot cream in a small bowl and stir in the melted chocolate and the butter until blended. Add the confectioners' sugar and stir with a whisk until smooth and shiny. Allow both glazes to set for 10 minutes.

11. When the cookies are completely cool, turn them upside down, brush off any excess crumbs, and using a small spatula or a butter knife, spread half of the flat side with the vanilla glaze, half with the chocolate. Allow to set for 2 to 3 hours (or pop them into the fridge for 1 hour to set quickly).

12. If you plan to eat the cookies that day, leave them sitting out. To store them, place them in an airtight plastic container with plastic wrap, parchment, or waxed paper between the layers. Store them in the refrigerator if you plan to eat them the next day. Otherwise, place the container in the freezer for up to 2 weeks. Bring to room temperature before eating.

Makes about 10 very large cookies

Chippy Jaker Cakers

❤ ❤ ❤ ❤ ❤ ❤ ❤ ❤   *drop cookies*

Favorites of my son Jake, these cookies are a nice change from the classic chocolate chip. Their texture is like a soft, light cake, so they're best eaten the day they're baked— which hardly presents a problem in my household.

INGREDIENTS

1½ cups plus 2 tablespoons
    all-purpose flour
½ teaspoon baking soda
½ teaspoon salt
8 tablespoons (1 stick) unsalted butter
    at room temperature
1 cup (lightly packed) light brown sugar
2 teaspoons pure vanilla extract
1 large egg
¼ cup buttermilk
6 ounces (1 cup) semisweet chocolate
    chips

1. Preheat the oven to 400°F. Line several baking sheets with parchment paper, or grease them lightly with vegetable oil.

2. Sift the flour, baking soda, and salt together into a small bowl and set aside.

3. Using an electric mixer on medium speed, cream the butter, brown sugar, and vanilla together in a medium-size bowl until light and fluffy, 1½ to 2 minutes. Stop the mixer during the process twice to scrape the bowl with a rubber spatula.

4. Add the egg and beat on medium speed until blended, about 30 seconds. Scrape the bowl.

5. Add one third of the flour mixture, and mix on low speed for 5 seconds. Scrape the bowl.

6. Add the buttermilk and mix for 5 seconds. Then add the rest of the flour mixture and mix until blended, 5 seconds. Scrape the bowl.

7. Add the chocolate chips and blend until they are mixed in, 5 to 8 seconds.

8. Drop the dough by generously rounded tablespoons 2 inches apart on the prepared baking sheets.

9. Bake the cookies until the edges are light golden and the centers are slightly puffed, 11 to 12 minutes.

10. Allow any cookies that don't get eaten right away to cool completely on the sheets; then store them in an airtight plastic container. Leave them at room temperature for the first day if you plan to eat them. Otherwise, place the container in the freezer for up to 2 weeks. Bring the cookies to room temperature before eating.

Makes about 30 cookies

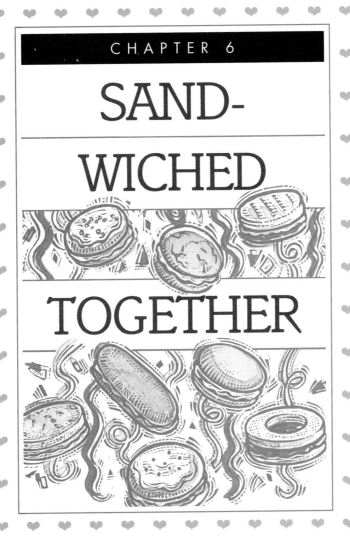

CHAPTER 6

SAND-WICHED TOGETHER

Boston Cream Pies

Birthday Cakes On The Go

Chocolate Minteos

Chocolate Raspberry Sandwiches

Double Crispy Sandwiches

Glazed Almond Raspberry Sandwiches

Katz Tongues

Shortbread Sandwiches

Little Princesses

Linzer Sandwiches

Almond Apricot Sandwiches

Chocolate Jam Sandwiches

Crispy Fingers

Summer's Day Sandwiches

Orange Almond Spritzes

Triple-Ginger Lemon Sandwiches

Pumpkin Whoopee Pies

Peanut Butter Sandwiches

Were there Nobel Prizes in his day, the Earl of Sandwich would surely have been nominated for his culinary contribution to lunch boxes everywhere. The same goes for the unknown genius who translated the Earl's invention into a cookie. I imagine her slaving over a hot Bunsen burner all those long nights in the laboratory, until one red-eyed dawn, just when it seems all has been in vain, she looks up from her calculations, whips off her glasses, and shouts, "Victory is mine! I've got it!"

There before her lies the perfect solution to the age-old problem of how to keep the filling inside the cookie—and on top of that, she's come up with the added prize of two cookies in one. Nothing stands between her and a bright future full of Nutter Butters, Oreos, and vanilla creams. Though history cruelly has denied our inventor immortality, it has given us the sandwich cookie to smoosh apart, lick the frosting off, and eat in pieces, or, being a democratic people, to eat in one piece if we're so inclined. And for that I am grateful.

Sandwich cookies can be made from many types of cookies: cakey, shortbread, and drops, both chewy and crispy. What are they, anyway, but tiny layer cakes in cookie form? Construction of the sandwich isn't hard, but

following certain steps helps. Before proceeding, be sure to read the tips in the box on this page.

Frosting the Sandwich

For all kinds of sandwiches, let the cookies cool before you fill them. Pair the cookies up, and turn half of them upside down to receive the filling; the other half will be tops.

For cookies that use buttercream, such as Peanut Butter Sandwiches, dab the right amount of filling in the center of an upside-down cookie and gently press the bottom of its partner down onto it. Let the filling ruffle slightly out the sides to give it a sumptuous look.

Cookies with jam, like Almond Apricot Sandwiches, look better and are easier to eat when they're neater. Spread the jam sparingly here, so that it doesn't ooze out.

For cookies with melted chocolate fillings, such as Shortbread Sandwiches, let the chocolate firm up just a bit after it has melted. Spoon the appropriate amount onto the center of the bottom cookie, and using a butter knife, spread the filling very gently toward the outer edge, stopping just short of it. Then carefully place the top cookie over the chocolate and press ever so lightly until the chocolate comes just to the edge. Allow cookies to set for several hours before eating, though refrigeration will speed up the process.

Boston Cream Pies

❤ ❤ ❤ ❤ ❤ ❤   *cakey drop cookie*

Boston cream pie isn't actually a pie—it's a cake. Variations have been floating around for at least a couple of centuries, and Fanny Farmer codified it as a "Favorite Cake" in her 1896 cookbook. For all that history, I remain loyal to my version: two buttery vanilla cake cookies sandwiched together with vanilla custard and topped with a glossy chocolate glaze.

INGREDIENTS

THE CUSTARD

1 cup milk
6 tablespoons heavy (whipping) cream
6 tablespoons sugar
3 tablespoons cornstarch
¼ teaspoon salt
1 large egg yolk
2 teaspoons pure vanilla extract

THE COOKIE

1 cup all-purpose flour
1 cup plus 2 tablespoons cake flour
¾ teaspoon baking soda
½ teaspoon salt
9 tablespoons (1 stick plus 1 tablespoon)
   unsalted butter at room temperature
1 cup plus 1 tablespoon sugar
2 teaspoons pure vanilla extract
½ teaspoon grated lemon zest
2 large egg yolks at room temperature
1 whole large egg at room temperature
½ cup plus 2 tablespoons buttermilk at
   room temperature

THE GLAZE

½ cup heavy (whipping) cream
2 ounces unsweetened chocolate, chopped
   fine or melted
1 tablespoon plus 1 teaspoon unsalted
   butter at room temperature
6 tablespoons confectioners' sugar

1. Prepare the custard: Place ½ cup plus 2 tablespoons of the milk, all the cream, and the sugar in a medium-size saucepan over medium-low heat and bring just to a boil. Remove from the heat.

2. Dissolve the cornstarch and salt in the remaining milk.

3. Add the egg yolk to the cornstarch mixture, and stir it rapidly with a fork or whisk. Add this to the scalded cream mixture and whisk over medium-low heat constantly until it thickens, 2 to 3 minutes. Then cook, stirring, for 30 seconds more.

4. Remove the custard from the heat, stir in the vanilla, and pour it into a ceramic or plastic bowl. Allow it to cool for 10 minutes, stirring it gently several times.

5. Puncture a piece of plastic wrap in several places, and place it directly over the surface of the custard. Refrigerate until completely chilled, 2 to 3 hours.

6. Meanwhile, make the cookies: Preheat the oven to 400°F. Line several baking sheets with parchment paper, or lightly grease them with vegetable oil.

7. Sift both flours, the baking soda, and the salt together in a small bowl and set aside.

8. With an electric mixer on medium-high speed, cream the butter, sugar, vanilla, and lemon zest together in a medium-size bowl until light and fluffy, about 2 minutes. Stop the mixer twice during the process to scrape the bowl with a rubber spatula. Scrape the bowl a third time before going on to the next step.

9. Add the egg yolks and blend on medium speed for about 10 seconds. Scrape the bowl. Then add the whole egg and mix until blended, about 10 seconds. Scrape the bowl again.

10. Add the buttermilk and mix on medium-low speed for about 10 seconds. The mixture will appear curdled. Scrape the bowl.

11. Fold in the flour mixture by hand. Then turn the mixer to low speed and mix for about 5 seconds. Scrape the bowl with the spatula, and mix on low speed until the batter is smooth and velvety, 10 seconds. Give the batter a stir or two with the spatula.

12. Drop the batter by generous tablespoons about 2 inches apart onto the prepared baking sheets.

13. Bake the cookies until they are just firm, yet spongy to the touch (not crusty), 10 to 11 minutes. Using a metal spatula, carefully transfer the cookies to wire racks to cool.

14. When the custard and the cookies have cooled, turn half the cookies upside down and spread each bottom half with a generously rounded tablespoon of custard. Top them with the remaining cookies.

15. Then prepare the glaze: Heat the cream in a small saucepan over medium-low heat just to the boiling point. Place the hot cream in a small bowl and add the chocolate and butter. Cover the bowl with a pot lid or a small plate and leave it for several minutes. Then uncover and stir with a small whisk until smooth. Add the confectioners' sugar and stir vigorously until smooth and velvety.

16. Frost each cookie by spreading a scant tablespoon of the chocolate glaze evenly across the top. If you plan to eat the cookies that day, leave them sitting out. To store them, first allow the glaze to set for several hours, then place the cookies in a large airtight plastic container, with parchment, plastic wrap, or waxed paper between the layers (no more than two layers). Store them in the refrigerator if you plan to eat them the next day. Otherwise, place the container in the freezer for up to 2 weeks. Bring the cookies to room temperature before eating.

Makes about 13 cookie sandwiches

Birthday Cakes On The Go

❤ ❤ ❤ ❤ ❤ ❤ *cakey drop cookie*

If your idea of the perfect birthday cake is the same as mine—a yellow cake with raspberry preserves and white frosting—then you'll love these sumptuous cookies. I find them ideal for school birthday treats. For an additional thrill, you can sprinkle colored jimmies or sugar confetti over the glaze immediately after spreading it.

INGREDIENTS

THE COOKIE
1 recipe Boston Cream Pies cookie batter (page 118)

THE GLAZE
1½ cups confectioners' sugar
6 tablespoons (¾ stick) unsalted butter at room temperature
3 tablespoons fresh lemon juice

THE FILLING
Approximately ¾ cup raspberry preserves

1. Preheat the oven to 400°F. Line several baking sheets with parchment paper, or lightly grease them with vegetable oil.

2. Prepare the cookie batter (steps 6 through 11), and drop it by generous tablespoons onto the prepared baking sheets. Bake until just firm, 10 or 11

minutes. Using a metal spatula, carefully lift the cookies from the sheet and place them on wire racks to cool.

3. Prepare the glaze: Place all the glaze ingredients in a food processor and process until smooth, about 10 seconds.

4. When the cookies are completely cool, turn half of them upside down, and spread each bottom half with a slightly rounded teaspoon of preserves. Top them with the remaining cookies.

5. Using a small spatula or a butter knife, frost the top of each cookie with a generously rounded teaspoon of the glaze. Allow the cookies to sit until the glaze has set, 2 hours.

6. You can store the cookies in an airtight container and eat them the next day. They will continue to soften overnight. Otherwise, store the cookies in an airtight plastic container in the freezer for up to 2 weeks. Bring them to room temperature before eating.

Makes about 13 cookie sandwiches

Chocolate Minteos

❤ ❤ ❤ ❤ ❤ ❤ *crispy drop cookie*

It is my firm belief that no matter how sophisticated our palates become and no matter how we hone our culinary skills, we will never lose the taste memory of Oreos. So here's a tribute to that cookie of our youth. It's thick and crunchy and filled with mint-flavored buttercream, and as my oldest son, Jake, does, you may eat the inside first. They are especially good when chilled in the fridge—I eat them cold all the time!

INGREDIENTS

THE COOKIE
2½ cups all-purpose flour
1 teaspoon baking soda
12 tablespoons (1½ sticks) unsalted butter
    at room temperature
1 cup plus 2 tablespoons sugar
2 teaspoons peppermint extract
2 large eggs
2 tablespoons water
12 ounces (2 cups) semisweet chocolate
    chips, melted

THE FILLING
8 tablespoons (1 stick) unsalted butter
    at room temperature
2 cups confectioners' sugar
2 tablespoons plus 2 teaspoons
    half-and-half or light cream
½ teaspoon peppermint extract

1. Preheat the oven to 375°F. Line several baking sheets with parchment paper, or grease them lightly with vegetable oil.

2. Sift the flour and baking soda together into a small bowl and set aside.

3. Using an electric mixer on medium speed, cream the butter, sugar, and peppermint extract together in a medium bowl until light and fluffy, 1 minute. Scrape the bowl with a rubber spatula.

4. Add the eggs and water and beat on medium speed until they are blended, about 20 seconds. Scrape the bowl.

5. Add the melted chocolate chips and mix until blended, 5 seconds. Scrape the bowl.

6. Add the flour mixture and mix on low speed for 15 seconds. Scrape the bowl.

7. Scoop rounded teaspoons of the batter 2 inches apart onto the prepared baking sheets. Using the bottom of a glass that has been dipped in water, press each cookie down so that it forms a round 1½ inches in diameter.

8. Bake the cookies until they are firm to the touch, 17 minutes. Cool them completely on wire racks.

9. Meanwhile, prepare the filling: Place all the filling ingredients in a small bowl and whisk until smooth.

10. When the cookies are completely cool, turn half of them upside down, and spread a rounded teaspoon of filling on each bottom half. Top them with the remaining cookies. Allow them to set for 2 to 3 hours or pop them into the refrigerator for 1 hour to set quickly. If you plan to eat the cookies that day, leave them sitting out. If not, store them in an airtight plastic con-

tainer in the freezer for up to 2 weeks, and bring to room temperature before eating. Or try eating them cold for a refreshing treat.

Makes about 40 cookie sandwiches

Chocolate Raspberry Sandwiches

❤ ❤ ❤ ❤ ❤ *rolled shortbread cookie*

Two delicate, crisp deeply chocolate wafers sandwiched with raspberry preserves: an elegant addition to a dessert of ice cream or fresh fruit. These cookies are also lovely as the chocolate component on a dessert platter, accompanying Lemon Curd Tartlets and Coconut Dainties.

INGREDIENTS

THE COOKIE
2 cups plus 2 tablespoons all-purpose flour
½ cup unsweetened cocoa powder
⅛ teaspoon baking soda
1 cup (2 sticks) unsalted butter at room temperature
¾ cup confectioners' sugar
½ cup granulated sugar
1 teaspoon pure vanilla extract

THE FILLING
1 cup raspberry preserves

THE GLAZE
12 ounces bittersweet chocolate

1. Sift the flour, cocoa powder, and baking soda together into a small bowl and set aside.

2. Using an electric mixer on medium speed, cream the butter, both sugars, and the vanilla together in a medium-size bowl until light and fluffy, 2½ to 3 minutes. Stop the mixer once or twice during the process to scrape the bowl with a rubber spatula.

3. Add the flour mixture and blend on low speed until the mixture is fluffy again, about 45 seconds. Scrape the bowl.

4. Divide the dough in half and shape it into two thick disks. Wrap each disk in plastic wrap and refrigerate for at least 2 hours or as long as overnight.

5. When you're ready to bake the cookies, preheat the oven to 325°F. Lightly grease several baking sheets with vegetable oil. Remove the dough from the refrigerator, unwrap it, and allow it to soften slightly, about 10 minutes.

6. Place each piece of dough between two new pieces of plastic wrap or waxed paper, and roll it out ⅛ inch thick.

7. Remove the top piece of plastic wrap, and using a 2-inch round cookie cutter, cut out approximately 20 rounds from each half. Place the rounds about ¾ inch apart on the prepared baking sheets. Gather up the scraps and reroll the dough to make as many cookies as possible.

8. Bake the cookies just until they are firm to the touch, 10 to 12 minutes. Cool the cookies on the sheets.

9. When the cookies are completely cool, turn half of them upside down, and spread each bottom half with a scant teaspoon of preserves. Top them with the remaining cookies.

10. Meanwhile, melt the chocolate in the top of a double boiler placed over simmering water.

11. Pour the melted chocolate into a small deep bowl, and dip half of each sandwich into the chocolate, using the rim of the bowl to scrape any excess chocolate off the bottom of the cookie. Or rotate just the outer edge of the cookie in the chocolate for an alternative design.

12. As they are dipped, place the cookies on a large sheet of waxed or parchment paper and allow them to sit until the chocolate hardens, 2 to 3 hours (or pop them into the fridge for 1 hour to set quickly, especially if it is a humid day).

13. If you plan to eat the cookies the first day, leave them sitting out. If not, store them in an airtight plastic container in the freezer for up to 2 weeks, and bring to room temperature before eating.

Makes 25 to 30 cookie sandwiches

Double Crispy Sandwiches

♥ ♥ ♥ ♥ ♥ ♥ ♥ *crispy drop cookie*

When my friend Allen Helschein told me that he had a great cookie recipe using cornflakes, I had my doubts. Well, Allen was right. Nothing besides cornflakes provides the satisfying crunch that contrasts so perfectly with the chocolate filling.

INGREDIENTS

THE COOKIE
1½ cups all-purpose flour
1 teaspoon baking soda
1 teaspoon salt
1½ cups quick-cooking oats
*1¼ cups (2½ sticks) unsalted butter
    at room temperature*
½ cup plus 2 tablespoons granulated sugar
*1 cup minus 2 tablespoons (lightly packed)
    light brown sugar*
2 teaspoons pure vanilla extract
2 large eggs
2 cups cornflakes

THE FILLING
*9 ounces (1½ cups) semisweet chocolate
    chips*

1. Preheat the oven to 375°F. Line several baking sheets with parchment paper, or lightly grease them with vegetable oil.

2. Sift the flour, baking soda, and salt together into a medium-size bowl. Stir in the oats and set aside.

369

3. Using an electric mixer on medium speed, cream the butter, both sugars, and the vanilla together in a medium-size bowl until light and fluffy, about 1½ minutes. Stop the mixer during the process to scrape the bowl with a rubber spatula.

4. Add the eggs one at a time, mixing on medium-low speed for 10 seconds each time, scraping the bowl after each addition and at the end.

5. Add the flour mixture and mix on medium-low speed for 10 seconds. Scrape the bowl, then mix until blended, about 5 seconds more. Scrape the bowl.

6. Add the cornflakes and mix until they're crushed and blended in, 10 seconds. Stop the mixer once during this process to scrape the bowl with a rubber spatula.

7. Drop the dough by rounded teaspoons about 2 inches apart onto the prepared baking sheets.

8. Bake until the cookies are crisp and lightly golden with darker golden edges, 12 to 14 minutes. Allow the cookies to cool completely on the sheets.

9. Prepare the filling: Melt the chocolate chips in the top of a double boiler placed over simmering water. Remove from the heat and allow to cool for 10 minutes.

10. Turn half the cookies upside down, and spread 1 rounded teaspoon of the chocolate on each bottom half. Place the other cookies over the filling, but don't press down. Allow the cookies to sit for 2 to 3 hours until the chocolate hardens (or refrigerate them for 1 hour to speed up the process).

11. If you plan to eat the cookies the first day, leave them sitting out. If not, store them in an airtight plastic container in the freezer for up to 2 weeks, and bring them to room temperature before eating.

Makes about 46 cookie sandwiches

Glazed Almond Raspberry Sandwiches

❤ ❤ ❤ ❤ ❤ ❤ ❤ ❤ ❤ *rolled cookie*

To me, almonds and raspberries are an inspired combination whose taste, texture, and color speak of luxury and abundance. They unite here in delicate almond butter cookies, held together with raspberry preserves and accented with a light lemon glaze.

INGREDIENTS

THE COOKIE
2 large egg yolks
1 teaspoon pure vanilla extract
½ cup sugar
1 package (7 ounces) almond paste (not marzipan)
1 cup (2 sticks) unsalted butter, cold, cut into 16 pieces
1 cup plus 3 tablespoons all-purpose flour
1 teaspoon salt
1 teaspoon grated lemon zest

THE FILLING
½ cup raspberry preserves

THE GLAZE
1 cup confectioners' sugar
1½ teaspoons almond extract
2 tablespoons hot water

1. Using a fork, stir the egg yolks and vanilla together in a cup. Set aside.

2. Process the sugar and almond paste in a food processor until the mixture looks like coarse sand, 25 seconds. Scatter the butter over the mixture and process for 15 seconds.

3. Add the flour, salt, and lemon zest, and pulse for 40 to 50 seconds to blend.

4. With the machine running, add the yolk mixture through the feed tube, and process for 5 seconds. Scrape the bowl. Then process just until the liquid is evenly absorbed, 5 to 8 seconds.

5. Remove the dough, place it on a work surface, and form it into two rectangular slabs. Wrap each in plastic wrap and refrigerate for an hour or two.

6. Place each slab of dough between two new pieces of plastic wrap, and roll it out ⅛ inch thick. Place the dough, still covered with the plastic wrap, in the freezer or refrigerator and allow it to chill again for 1 to 2 hours.

7. When you are ready to bake the cookies, preheat the oven to 375°F. Line several baking sheets with parchment paper, or grease them lightly with vegetable oil.

8. Remove the top piece of plastic wrap, and using a 2-inch round cookie cutter, cut out approximately 35 rounds from each half. Place the rounds about ¾ inch apart on the prepared baking sheets. Gather up the dough scraps and reroll the dough to make as many more cookies as possible.

9. Bake the cookies until the edges are just beginning to turn golden, about 8 or 9 minutes. Remove them from the oven and cool on the sheets.

10. When the cookies are completely cool, turn half of them upside down, and spread each bottom cookie with a scant ½ teaspoon of preserves. Top them with the remaining cookies.

11. Prepare the glaze: Place ingredients in a small bowl, and whisk until smooth.

12. Using a spoon, drizzle the glaze over the tops of the cookies. Allow to set for 2 to 3 hours (or place in the refrigerator for 1 hour to speed up the process).

13. If you plan to eat the cookies the first day, leave them sitting out. If not, store them in an airtight plastic container in the freezer for up to 2 weeks, and bring to room temperature before eating.

Makes about 40 cookie sandwiches

Katz Tongues
❤ ❤ ❤ ❤ ❤ ❤   *crispy piped cookie*

Within walking distance of my house is a great place called the Bentonwood Bakery and Cafe. Katz Tongues are owner and pastry chef, Rick Katz's rendition of the classic French *langues du chat,* so named because they resembled a cat's tongue. This version, made of two thin, crispy butter wafers sandwiched together with chocolate, is one of my favorites—particularly because their daintiness belies the ease with which they're made.

INGREDIENTS

THE COOKIE
¾ cup all-purpose flour
¾ teaspoon salt
8 tablespoons (1 stick) unsalted butter
    at room temperature
1 cup sugar
½ teaspoon pure vanilla extract
½ cup egg whites (from 3 or 4 large eggs),
    lightly beaten

THE FILLING
4 ounces bittersweet chocolate

1. Preheat the oven to 375°F. Line several baking sheets with parchment paper (do not grease them). If possible, have ready a pastry bag with a No. 9 tip; flatten the tip to form a thin oval so the batter comes out thin.

2. Sift the flour and salt together into a small bowl, and set aside.

3. Using an electric mixer on medium speed, beat the butter just until fluffy, 15 seconds. Scrape the bowl with a rubber spatula.

4. Turn the mixer to medium-low speed and gradually add the sugar, then the vanilla. Scrape the bowl.

5. Turn the mixer to low speed and gradually add the egg whites. Mix until blended, 30 seconds, stopping the mixer once to scrape the bowl.

6. Add the flour mixture, stirring it in by hand. Then blend thoroughly with the mixer on low speed for 10 seconds. Stop the mixer once during the process to scrape the bowl.

7. Place some of the batter in the pastry bag, and pipe out strips approximately 2½ inches long onto the parchment leaving 2 inches between cookies. Alternatively, use a spoon to drop the batter onto the baking sheet, and then flatten it to ⅛ inch thickness with a butter knife or spatula.

8. Bake the cookies until they are crisp to the touch in the center and rich golden around the edges, 14 to 16 minutes. Watch them carefully as they can overbake within seconds. Cool completely on the baking sheets. Then carefully loosen them with a thin spatula.

9. Prepare the filling: Melt the chocolate in the top of a double boiler placed over simmering water. Remove from the heat and let cool to spreading consistency.

10. Turn half the cookies upside down. Spread each bottom half with a teaspoon of chocolate, and top with the remaining cookies. Allow to set completely before eating, about 2 hours (or refrigerate to speed up the process).

11. If you plan to eat the cookies the first day, leave them sitting out. If not, store them in an airtight plastic container in the freezer for up to 2 weeks, and bring to room temperature before eating.

Makes about 24 cookie sandwiches

Shortbread Sandwiches

♥ ♥ ♥ *shortbread refrigerator cookie*

This perfect union of shortbread and chocolate offers two thick, not-too-sweet, crunchy cookies with bittersweet chocolate sandwiched between. Eat them as is or do as my son Jake does—pull them apart and devour the filling first.

INGREDIENTS

THE COOKIE
1 cup (2 sticks) unsalted butter, cold, cut into 16 pieces
1 cup confectioners' sugar
2 teaspoons pure vanilla extract
2½ cups cake flour
½ teaspoon baking powder
½ teaspoon salt

THE FILLING
8 ounces bittersweet chocolate
2 tablespoons plus 2 teaspoons vegetable oil

1. Place the flour, confectioners' sugar, baking powder, and salt in a food processor and process for 10 seconds.

2. Scatter the butter over the flour mixture, add the vanilla, and process until the dough just comes together, 30 to 40 seconds.

3. Place a 2-foot length of waxed paper on a work surface. Shape the dough into a rough log 13 or 14 inches long (or into two logs each 6 to 7 inches long) along the length of one side of the paper. Roll the dough up in the waxed paper, and twist the ends like a hard-candy wrapper. Refrigerate the dough for 2 hours.

4. Remove the log from the refrigerator. Using your hands, roll the wrapped dough gently back and forth on the work surface to smooth out and round the cylinder. Refrigerate for another 3 hours or overnight.

5. Fifteen minutes before baking, preheat the oven to 350°F. Line several baking sheets with parchment paper or leave them ungreased.

6. Remove the log from the refrigerator, unwrap it, and cut it into slices that are a scant ¼ inch thick.

7. Place the cookies 1 inch apart on the prepared baking sheets, and bake until the edges are golden and the centers are firm, 15 to 17 minutes. (To test for doneness, remove a cookie from the sheet and cut it in half. There should be no doughy strip down the center.) Cool on the baking sheets.

8. While the cookies are cooling, prepare the filling: Melt the chocolate in the top of a double boiler placed over simmering water. Remove from the heat and whisk in the oil until smooth. Let sit 15 to 20 minutes to reach spreading consistency.

9. When the cookies are completely cool, turn half of them upside down, making them the bottom half. Spread each bottom half with 1 teaspoon of the chocolate and top them with the remaining cookies. Do not press down. Allow to set for 2 to 3 hours. (They can be chilled in the refrigerator for 1 hour to speed up the process.)

10. If you plan to eat the cookies the first day, leave them sitting out. If not, store them in an airtight plastic con-

tainer in the freezer for up to 2 weeks, and bring to room temperature before eating.

Makes about 28 cookie sandwiches

Little Princesses

❤ ❤ ❤ ❤ *formed shortbread cookie*

These rich, buttery vanilla cookies, paired with raspberry preserves and then dusted with powdered sugar, truly live up to their name. Crisp the first day, they tend to soften a bit by the second day no matter how you store them—but either way, they are royally divine.

INGREDIENTS

THE COOKIE
6 large egg yolks
¾ teaspoon pure vanilla extract
2 cups all-purpose flour
⅔ cup sugar
½ teaspoon salt
1 tablespoon plus 1 teaspoon grated lemon zest
1 cup (2 sticks) unsalted butter, cold, cut into 16 pieces

THE FILLING
5 to 6 tablespoons raspberry preserves

THE COATING
¼ cup confectioners' sugar

1. Preheat the oven to 375°F. Line several baking sheets with parchment paper, or grease them lightly with vegetable oil.

2. Using a fork, stir the egg yolks and vanilla together in a small cup.

3. Place the flour, sugar, salt, and lemon zest in a food processor, and process for 5 seconds.

4. Scatter the butter over the flour and process until the mixture resembles coarse meal, 20 to 30 seconds.

5. With the machine running, add the yolk mixture through the feed tube and process for 5 seconds. Scrape the bowl. Then process until the dough comes together, 10 to 15 seconds.

6. Scoop out rounded teaspoons of the dough and roll them into balls with your hands. Place them 2 inches apart on the prepared baking sheets.

7. Using the bottom of a glass that has been lightly dipped in flour, flatten each ball to a generous ⅛-inch thickness, about 2¼ inches in diameter.

8. Bake the cookies until the edges are deep golden, 14 to 16 minutes. Allow them to cool on the baking sheets.

9. When the cookies are completely cool, turn half of them upside down. Spread each bottom half with a generous ½ teaspoon of the preserves, and top with the remaining cookies. Sift confectioners' sugar over the tops.

10. If you plan to eat the cookies the first day, leave them sitting out. If not, store them in an airtight plastic container in the freezer for up to 2 weeks, and bring to room temperature before eating.

Makes about 16 cookie sandwiches

Linzer Sandwiches

❤ ❤ ❤ ❤ ❤ ❤ ❤ ❤ *rolled cookie*

One of my most vivid food memories comes from the William Greenberg bakery in New York City, where I recall savoring the nutty crunch of a giant linzer cookie, then enjoying a second taste as I licked at the confectioners' sugar mustache it left on my upper lip. I tried to get the recipe from Greenberg's, but without success, so I worked and worked to come as close as I could on my own. I've made my version smaller than the original (a function of age), but other than that, it matches my memory cookie right down to the mustache.

INGREDIENTS

THE COOKIE

1 whole large egg
1 large egg yolk
1 teaspoon pure vanilla extract
1¾ cups all-purpose flour
1¼ cups confectioners' sugar
1¼ cups ground almonds
1 teaspoon ground cinnamon
¼ teaspoon ground cloves
½ teaspoon baking powder
1 tablespoon unsweetened cocoa powder
¾ teaspoon salt
2½ tablespoons grated lemon zest
*13 tablespoons unsalted butter, cold, cut
    into 13 pieces*

THE FILLING

½ cup raspberry preserves

THE COATING

2 to 3 tablespoons confectioners' sugar

1. Preheat the oven to 350°F. Line several baking sheets with parchment paper or grease them lightly with vegetable oil.

2. Using a fork, stir the egg, egg yolk, and vanilla together in a small cup. Set aside.

3. Place the flour, sugar, almonds, cinnamon, cloves, baking powder, cocoa powder, salt, and lemon zest in a food processor and process to blend, 5 seconds.

4. Distribute the butter over the surface of the flour mixture, and process until the mixture resembles coarse meal, 20 to 30 seconds.

5. With the machine running, add the egg mixture through the feed tube and process for 3 seconds. Scrape the bowl, then process for 3 more seconds.

6. Remove the dough from the machine and shape it into two disks. Place each piece of dough between two pieces of plastic wrap or waxed paper, and roll it out to a generous ⅛-inch thickness.

7. Remove the top piece of plastic wrap, and, using a 2-inch round cookie cutter, cut out approximately 20 rounds from each half. Using a smooth bottle cap, a sharp knife, or a tiny cookie cutter, make small holes in the center of half the rounds. Place all the rounds about ¾ inch apart on the prepared baking sheets. Gather up the dough scraps and reroll the dough to make as many more cookies as possible, again making small holes in the center of half of them.

8. Bake the cookies until they are firm, 14 minutes. Remove them from the oven and let them cool on the sheets.

9. When the cookies are completely cool, turn the cookies with no holes upside down. Spread each one with a level ½ teaspoon of raspberry preserves, then place another ½ teaspoon of the preserves in a mound in the center of each cookie. Sprinkle confectioners' sugar over the cookies with holes, and place them on top of the cookie bottoms so that the jam forms a perfect little mound in the middle.

10. If you plan to eat the cookies the first day, leave them out. If not, store them in an airtight plastic container in the freezer for up to 2 weeks, and bring to room temperature before eating.

Makes 20 to 25 cookie sandwiches

Almond Apricot Sandwiches

❤ ❤ ❤ *shortbread refrigerator cookie*

Apricot jam holds these rich, nutty cookies together, while a bittersweet chocolate drizzle over the top does double duty as decoration and decadent finishing touch.

I N G R E D I E N T S

THE COOKIE
1 large egg
1 teaspoon pure almond extract
2 cups all-purpose flour
¾ cup confectioners' sugar
6 tablespoons granulated sugar
1½ cups finely ground almonds
¾ teaspoon salt
1 cup (2 sticks) unsalted butter, cold, cut into 16 pieces

THE FILLING
¾ cup apricot preserves

THE GLAZE
3 ounces bittersweet chocolate
1 tablespoon vegetable oil

1. Using a fork, stir the egg and almond extract together in a cup and set aside.

2. Place the flour, all but 2 tablespoons of the confectioners' sugar, the granulated sugar, almonds, and salt in a food processor, and process for 5 seconds.

3. Scatter the butter over the flour mixture, and process until the mixture resembles coarse crumbs, 30 seconds.

4. With the machine running, add the egg mixture through the feed tube and process just until the dough comes together, 45 seconds.

5. Spread a 2-foot length of waxed paper on a work surface. With floured fingers, shape the dough into a rough log about 20 inches long along the length of one side of the paper. Roll the log in the waxed paper and twist the ends like a hard-candy wrapper. Refrigerate the dough for 2 hours. (You can cut the log in half in order to fit it in the refrigerator.)

6. Remove the log from the refrigerator, and with the dough still in the waxed paper, gently roll it back and forth on the work surface to smooth out and round the cylinder.

7. Place the log back in the refrigerator and chill it at least 3 hours more.

8. Fifteen minutes before baking, preheat the oven to 350°F. Line two baking sheets with parchment paper or leave them ungreased.

377

9. Place the log on the counter, unwrap it, and cut it into scant ¼-inch-thick slices.

10. Place the cookies 1 inch apart on the baking sheets and bake until they are firm and lightly golden around the edges, 20 minutes. Cool them completely on the sheets.

11. Turn half the cookies upside down, and spread 1 scant tablespoon of the preserves over each bottom half. Top them with the remaining cookies. Sift the remaining 2 tablespoons confectioners' sugar over the cookies.

12. Prepare the glaze: Melt the chocolate in the top of a double boiler placed over simmering water. Remove from the heat and whisk in the oil until smooth.

13. Using a spoon or fork, drizzle the chocolate over the tops of the cookies in a zigzag or crisscross fashion. Allow the glaze to set for 2 to 3 hours (or refrigerate for 1 hour to speed up the process).

14. If you plan to eat the cookies the first day, leave them sitting out. If not, store them in an airtight plastic container in the freezer for up to 2 weeks, and bring to room temperature before eating.

Makes about 42 cookie sandwiches

Chocolate Jam Sandwiches

❤ ❤ ❤ ❤ ❤   *rolled shortbread cookie*

Two crunchy, buttery shortbread cookies sandwiched together with a double dose of delectableness: chocolate and raspberry or orange. As an alternative, sandwich the cookies with the preserves or marmalade and use the chocolate as a glaze. You can either dip half the cookie in the glaze or drizzle the glaze over the top.

INGREDIENTS

THE COOKIE
1 large egg yolk
½ teaspoon pure vanilla extract
1¼ cups all-purpose flour
5 tablespoons confectioners' sugar
3 tablespoons granulated sugar
2 tablespoons grated orange zest
½ teaspoon salt
8 tablespoons (1 stick) unsalted butter,
    cold, cut into 8 pieces

THE FILLING
3 tablespoons heavy (whipping) cream
4 ounces bittersweet chocolate
Approximately 6 tablespoons raspberry
    preserves or orange marmalade

1. Using a fork, stir the egg yolk and vanilla together in a small cup. Set aside.

2. Place the flour, both sugars, the

orange zest, and salt in a food processor, and process for about 10 seconds.

3. Add the butter and process until the mixture resembles coarse meal, 20 to 30 seconds.

4. With the machine running, add the yolk mixture though the feed tube and process for 5 seconds. Scrape the bowl, then process until the liquid is evenly absorbed, about 10 seconds.

5. Place the dough on a work surface, and work it with your hands just until you can form it into a mass. Divide the dough in half and shape it into two thick disks. Wrap each disk in plastic wrap. Refrigerate the dough for at least 1½ hours or overnight.

6. When you're ready to bake the cookies, preheat the oven to 350°F. Line several baking sheets with parchment paper, or lightly grease them with vegetable oil. Remove the dough from the refrigerator and allow it to soften slightly, about 10 minutes.

7. Place each piece of dough between two new pieces of plastic wrap or waxed paper, and roll it out ⅛ inch thick. Slide the dough, still sandwiched in the plastic wrap, onto a plate or tray and refrigerate it for 15 minutes for easier handling.

8. Remove the top piece of plastic wrap, and using a 2-inch round cookie cutter, cut out approximately 16 rounds from each half. Place the cookies about ¾ inch apart on the prepared baking sheets. Gather up the scraps and reroll the dough to make as many more cookies as possible.

9. Bake the cookies just until the edges begin to turn golden, 14 to 15 minutes. Remove them from the oven and let them cool on the sheets.

10. Meanwhile, prepare the filling: Heat the cream in a small saucepan over medium heat just to the boiling point, about 40 seconds.

11. Remove the pan from the heat and stir in the chocolate. Cover and set aside until the chocolate is melted, about 3 minutes. Then stir until smooth, 10 seconds.

12. Turn half the cookies over, and spread ¾ teaspoon of the chocolate filling over each bottom half. Turn the remaining cookies over, and spread ½ teaspoon of the preserves over each one.

13. Sandwich the two filled halves together, and allow to set for 3 to 4 hours (or refrigerate for 1 hour to speed up the process).

14. If you plan to eat the cookies the first day, leave them sitting out. If not, store them in an airtight plastic container in the freezer for up to 2 weeks, and bring to room temperature before eating.

Makes about 26 cookie sandwiches

Crispy Fingers

❤ ❤ ❤ ❤ ❤ ❤ ❤ ❤ *piped cookie*

For fans of Pepperidge Farm's Brussels cookie, here's a home-made version. These thin, crispy almond oatmeal wafers sandwiched with bittersweet chocolate make a wonderful teatime cookie or a delicate, elegant garnish for a dish of ice cream at the end of a meal.

INGREDIENTS

THE COOKIE
¾ cup all-purpose flour
¼ teaspoon baking soda
¼ teaspoon cream of tartar
8 tablespoons (1 stick) unsalted butter
    at room temperature
¾ cup sugar
½ teaspoon orange extract
½ teaspoon pure vanilla extract
¼ teaspoon grated orange zest
2 large egg whites, lightly beaten
½ cup finely chopped almonds
¼ cup quick-cooking oats

THE FILLING
1 ounce unsweetened chocolate
4 ounces semisweet chocolate

1. Preheat the oven to 350°F. Line several baking sheets with parchment paper, or lightly grease them with vegetable oil. Have ready a pastry bag fitted with a ½-inch tip.

2. Sift the flour, baking soda, and cream of tartar together into a small bowl and set aside.

3. Using an electric mixer on medium speed, cream the butter, sugar, both extracts, and the orange zest together in a medium-size bowl until light and fluffy, 2 minutes. Stop the mixer twice during the process to scrape the bowl with a rubber spatula.

4. Add the egg whites and beat on medium-high speed until blended, about 1 minute.

5. Add the flour mixture to the batter, and mix by hand with a rubber spatula until blended.

6. Add the almonds and oats, and mix by hand until blended.

7. Fill the pastry bag with batter, and pipe 2-inch-long fingers 3 inches apart on the prepared baking sheets. Bake until lightly golden with darker golden edges, about 12 minutes. Using a spatula, immediately transfer the cookies to wire racks to cool.

8. When the cookies have cooled, prepare the filling: Melt the chocolates together in a double boiler placed over simmering water.

9. Turn half the cookies upside down, and using a small frosting spatula or a butter knife, spread a thin layer of chocolate over each bottom half. Immediately place the remaining cookies on top, pressing down gently.

10. Allow the cookies to set for 2 hours, or place them in the refrigerator for 1 hour to speed up the process.

11. If you plan to eat the cookies the first day, leave them sitting out. If not, store them in an airtight plastic container in the freezer for up to 2 weeks, and bring to room temperature before eating.

Makes about 24 cookie sandwiches

Summer's Day Sandwiches

♥ ♥ ♥ ♥ ♥ *piped shortbread cookie*

Little lemon wafers sandwiched together with white chocolate—perfect with a glass of iced mint tea on a summer's day.

I N G R E D I E N T S

THE COOKIE
1 cup all-purpose flour
Generous ¼ teaspoon salt
Pinch of baking powder
7 tablespoons confectioners' sugar
1½ tablespoons granulated sugar
1 tablespoon grated lemon zest
8 tablespoons (1 stick) plus 1 teaspoon
    unsalted butter at room temperature
¼ cup milk

THE FILLING
3½ ounces good-quality white chocolate,
    grated or chopped fine (do not use
    white chocolate chips)
1½ tablespoons vegetable oil

1. Preheat the oven to 375°F. Line several baking sheets with parchment paper, or grease them lightly with vegetable oil. Prepare a pastry bag fitted with a ½-inch round tip.

2. Place the flour, salt, baking powder, both sugars, and the lemon zest in a food processor and process for 10 seconds.

3. Add the butter and process until partially incorporated, 30 seconds. Scrape the bowl with a rubber spatula.

4. Add the milk and process until the batter comes together, 20 seconds. It will be quite wet.

5. Fill the pastry bag with batter, and pipe 1-inch-diameter cookies, approximately ⅜ inch thick, 2 inches apart on the prepared baking sheets.

6. Using the bottom of a glass that has been dipped in flour, press each cookie into a diameter of 1½ inches.

7. Bake the cookies until the edges are golden and the centers are firm, 14 minutes.

8. Cool the cookies on wire racks.

9. Meanwhile, prepare the filling: Bring a pot of water to a boil, and remove it from the heat. Set a small metal bowl inside a larger bowl, and pour the hot water around it. The water should come about halfway up the sides of the smaller bowl. Make sure the inside of the smaller bowl stays dry. Place the white chocolate in the small bowl, cover the small bowl, and allow the chocolate to sit until it is melted. (You may need to change the water a couple of times to keep it hot.)

10. Stir the oil into the melted chocolate, whisking until the mixture is smooth. Let this set for 30 minutes. It will be fairly loose in texture.

11. Turn half the cookies upside down and place a generous ½ teaspoon of the chocolate mixture on each bottom half. Place the remaining cookies on top, pressing just enough for the filling to come to the edge of the sandwich.

12. Refrigerate the cookies for 1 hour to harden the filling, or let them set at room temperature for 2 to 3 hours.

13. If you plan to eat the cookies the first day, leave them sitting out. If not, store them in an airtight plastic container in the freezer for up to 2 weeks, and bring to room temperature before eating.

Makes about 22 cookie sandwiches

Orange Almond Spritzes

❤ ❤ ❤ ❤   *piped shortbread cookie*

Spritzes are squeezed from a cookie press, so you find them in all different shapes and sizes. As I worked on this recipe, I discovered that spritzes made with vegetable shortening hold their shape and thickness best, but that spritzes made with butter taste better, even if they spread and flatten out a little more. For the best results, be sure to cream the butter and sugar well, so the batter is soft enough to squeeze through the cookie press. If you don't have a press, scoop the batter out by the teaspoonful and flatten the cookies slightly before baking them. Either way, these cookies are delicious.

I N G R E D I E N T S

THE COOKIE

2¼ cups all-purpose flour

¾ teaspoon baking powder

¼ teaspoon salt

4 ounces (7 tablespoons) almond paste (not marzipan), cut into 8 pieces

½ cup confectioners' sugar

5 tablespoons granulated sugar

1 cup (2 sticks) unsalted butter at room temperature, cut into 16 pieces

2 tablespoons grated orange zest

½ teaspoon orange extract

2 large egg yolks

THE FILLING
About ½ cup orange marmalade

THE GLAZE
Approximately 6 ounces bittersweet chocolate

1. Preheat the oven to 325°F. Line several baking sheets with parchment paper, or grease them lightly with vegetable oil. Have ready a cookie press. Choose your favorite tips.

2. Sift the flour, baking powder, and salt together into a medium-size bowl and set aside.

3. Place the almond paste, both sugars, butter, orange zest, and orange extract in a food processor and process until smooth, 25 to 30 seconds.

4. Transfer this mixture to a medium-size mixing bowl.

5. Add the flour mixture, and mix on medium speed until thoroughly blended, 1½ minutes. Stop the mixer once to scrape the bowl.

6. Add the egg yolks with the mixer on medium-low speed, and mix until blended, 30 seconds. Stop the mixer once to scrape the bowl.

7. Feed the dough into the cookie press, and pipe the cookies onto the prepared baking sheets, leaving 1 inch between cookies.

8. Bake the cookies until they are firm and lightly golden around the edge. The baking time will vary depending on shape, but the range will probably be 16 to 20 minutes. Cool the cookies on the sheets.

9. When the cookies have cooled completely, prepare the glaze: Melt the chocolate in the top of a double boiler placed over simmering water.

10. Turn half the cookies upside down on a piece of parchment paper. Spread each bottom half with a teaspoon (this may vary depending on the size and shape of cookie you have chosen) of marmalade, and top them with the remaining cookies.

11. Place the melted chocolate in a small deep bowl, and dip a portion of each sandwich into the glaze (or paint the chocolate on with a pastry brush).

12. Return the cookies to the parchment and allow them to set for 2 to 3 hours, or place them in the refrigerator for 1 hour to set quickly.

13. If you plan to eat the cookies the first day, leave them sitting out. If not, store them in an airtight plastic container in the freezer for up to 2 weeks, and bring to room temperature before eating.

Makes about 25 cookie sandwiches

Triple-Ginger Lemon Sandwiches

❤ ❤ ❤ ❤ ❤ ❤ ❤ *refrigerator cookie*

Here's a triple threat of ground, candied, and fresh ginger, combined to pack a genuine wallop. The lemon buttercream filling adds a wonderful accent. These small, stylish, and sophisticated refrigerator cookies may single-handedly change the perceived wisdom about the appropriateness of cookies as dinner party fare.

INGREDIENTS

THE COOKIE

⅓ cup grated fresh ginger
½ cup granulated sugar
1½ cups all-purpose flour
1½ teaspoons baking soda
½ teaspoon salt
1¼ teaspoons ground ginger
¼ teaspoon ground cloves
1 teaspoon ground cinnamon
13 tablespoons (1½ sticks plus 1 table-
     spoon) unsalted butter at room
     temperature
½ cup (lightly packed) light brown sugar
¼ cup molasses
1 large egg
1½ cups quick-cooking oats
⅓ cup minced candied ginger or stem ginger

THE FILLING

2 cups confectioners' sugar
3 tablespoons light corn syrup
3 tablespoons unsalted butter, melted
1½ teaspoons grated lemon zest
2 tablespoons fresh lemon juice

1. Place the fresh ginger and 2 tablespoons of the granulated sugar in a food processor and process for several seconds to break up the ginger strands.

2. Sift the flour, baking soda, salt, ground ginger, cloves, and cinnamon into a small bowl and set aside.

3. Using an electric mixer on medium speed, cream the butter, brown sugar, the remaining 6 tablespoons granulated sugar, and the fresh ginger mixture in a medium-size mixing bowl until light and fluffy, 1 minute. Stop the mixer once during the process to scrape the bowl with a rubber spatula.

4. Add the molasses and beat for 10 to 15 seconds on medium speed. Scrape the bowl. Then add the egg and beat to incorporate it, 10 seconds.

5. Add the flour mixture and beat on medium-low speed for 10 seconds. Scrape the bowl, then mix until blended, about 5 seconds more. Then scrape the bowl again.

6. Add the oats and candied ginger. Blend for several seconds on low speed.

7. Spread a 13-inch length of waxed paper or plastic wrap on a work surface.

Shape one fourth of the dough into a rough log 9 inches long and 1 inch in diameter along the length of one side of the paper. Roll the log up in the waxed paper and twist the ends like a hard-candy wrapper. Make three more logs with the remaining batter, wrap them, and refrigerate for at least 2 hours.

8. Remove the logs from the refrigerator, and with the dough still in the paper, gently roll them back and forth on the work surface to round them.

9. Chill the logs in the refrigerator for 2 to 3 more hours.

10. Fifteen minutes before baking, preheat the oven to 350°F. Line two baking sheets with parchment paper, or grease them lightly with vegetable oil.

11. Unwrap the logs and cut them into scant ¼-inch-thick slices.

12. Place the cookies 1 inch apart on the prepared baking sheets, and bake until they are a deep golden color and set but still soft to the touch, 8 to 10 minutes.

13. Allow the cookies to cool on the sheets for 3 or 4 minutes. Then remove the cookies carefully with a spatula, and place them on wire racks to cool completely.

14. Meanwhile, prepare the filling: Place the confectioners' sugar, corn syrup, melted butter, and lemon zest in a small saucepan over low heat, and stir constantly with a whisk until the mix-

ture is of pouring consistency, 4 minutes. Add the lemon juice and stir to mix. Cool for 5 minutes.

15. Turn half the cookies upside down. Drop a scant teaspoon of the filling onto the center of each bottom half. Then top them with the remaining cookies, pressing down just enough to bring the filling to the edge of the cookie. Allow to set for about 3 hours. If it's a very hot day, refrigerate them.

16. If you plan to eat the cookies the first day, leave them sitting out. If not, store them in an airtight plastic container in the freezer for up to 2 weeks, and bring to room temperature before eating.

Makes about 70 cookie sandwiches

Pumpkin Whoopee Pies

❤ ❤ ❤ ❤ ❤ ❤   *cakey drop cookie*

Yes, the day came when I got down from my high horse and used Marshmallow Fluff in a recipe. And you know what? The world didn't end. In fact, it's now all the richer for this yummy filling, which I use here to hold two pumpkin-flavored cakey cookies together. The result is a classic whoopie pie and then some.

INGREDIENTS

THE COOKIE

½ cup plus 1 tablespoon all-purpose
    flour
¾ cup plus 1 tablespoon cake flour
½ teaspoon baking soda
1 teaspoon baking powder
½ teaspoon salt
9 tablespoons (1 stick plus 1 tablespoon)
    unsalted butter at room temperature
½ cup plus 2 tablespoons (lightly packed)
    light brown sugar
7 tablespoons granulated sugar
2½ teaspoons ground cinnamon
2 teaspoons ground nutmeg
¾ teaspoon ground allspice
½ teaspoon ground cloves
½ teaspoon ground ginger
1 teaspoon pure vanilla
    extract
2 large eggs
1½ tablespoons molasses
½ cup plus 2 tablespoons
    canned puréed pumpkin
¼ cup buttermilk

MARSHMALLOW FILLING

8 tablespoons (1 stick) unsalted butter at
    room temperature
5 heaping tablespoons Marshmallow Fluff
1 cup confectioners' sugar, sifted
½ teaspoon pure vanilla extract

1. Preheat the oven to 400°F. Line several baking sheets with parchment paper, or lightly grease them with vegetable oil.

2. Sift both flours, the baking soda, the baking powder, and the salt together into a small bowl and set aside.

3. Using an electric mixer on medium-high speed, cream the butter, both sugars, the spices, and the vanilla together in a medium-size bowl until light and fluffy, about 1½ minutes. Stop the mixer twice during the process to scrape the bowl with a rubber spatula. Scrape the bowl a third time before going on to the next step.

4. Add the eggs, one at a time, blending on medium speed for about 10 seconds after each addition.

5. Add the molasses and pumpkin, and mix on medium-low speed until well blended, about 10 seconds. Scrape the bowl. Add the buttermilk and blend for 5 seconds.

6. Fold in the flour mixture by hand. Then turn the mixer to low speed and mix for about 5 seconds. Scrape the bowl with the spatula, and mix on low speed until the batter is smooth and velvety, 10 seconds. Give the batter a stir or two with the spatula.

7. Drop the batter by generously rounded tablespoons about 2 inches apart onto the prepared baking sheets.

8. Bake the cookies until they are risen and firm to the touch, but not crusty, about 12 minutes. Using a metal spatula, carefully transfer the cookies to wire racks to cool.

9. While the cookies are cooling, prepare the filling: Place all four filling ingredients in a small bowl and beat with an electric mixer on low speed until the sugar is absorbed, 15 to 20 seconds. Scrape the bowl with a rubber spatula, turn the mixer to medium-high, and beat until the mixture is light and fluffy, 3 minutes. Stop the mixer twice during the process to scrape the bowl with a rubber spatula.

10. When the cookies are completely cool, turn half of them upside down, and spread each bottom half with a heaping teaspoon of filling. Top them with the remaining cookies.

11. If you plan to eat the cookies the first day, leave them sitting out. If not, store them in an airtight plastic container in the freezer for up to 2 weeks, and bring to room temperature before eating.

Makes about 14 cookie sandwiches

Peanut Butter Sandwiches

♥ ♥ ♥ ♥ ♥ ♥ *crunchy drop cookie*

Time may do its work on me, but I'll never outgrow the thrill of a peanut butter cookie—especially this sandwich version, with its thick crunchy cookies and its layer of peanut butter filling to stick them to-gether (and to the roof of your mouth). A Girl Scout memory? A triumph for the makers of Skippy? Whatever, these cookies make me sorry I no longer carry a box lunch.

INGREDIENTS

THE COOKIE
¾ cup plus 1 tablespoon all-purpose flour
½ teaspoon baking soda
¼ teaspoon baking powder
½ teaspoon salt
8 tablespoons (1 stick) unsalted butter
    at room temperature
½ cup smooth or chunky peanut butter
½ cup granulated sugar
½ cup (lightly packed) light brown sugar
½ teaspoon pure vanilla extract
1 large egg
1 cup minus 2 tablespoons quick-cooking
    oats

THE BUTTERCREAM
1 cup confectioners' sugar
3 tablespoons unsalted butter at room
    temperature
½ cup smooth peanut butter
2 tablespoons plus 1 teaspoon heavy
    (whipping) cream

THE GLAZE
2 ounces bittersweet chocolate
2 teaspoons vegetable oil

1. Preheat the oven to 350°F. Line several baking sheets with parchment paper, or lightly grease them with veg-etable oil.

2. Sift the flour, baking soda, baking powder, and salt together into a small bowl and set aside.

3. Using an electric mixer on medium speed, cream the butter, peanut butter, both sugars, and the vanilla together in a medium-size bowl until light and fluffy, about 1½ minutes. Stop the mixer twice during the process to scrape the sides of the bowl with a rubber spatula.

4. Add the egg and mix on medium-low speed to incorporate it, about 20 seconds.

5. Add the flour mixture and mix on medium-low speed for 10 seconds. Scrape the bowl, then mix until blended, about 5 seconds more. Scrape the bowl again.

6. Add the oats and mix for several seconds on low speed to blend them in.

7. Drop the dough by generously rounded teaspoons about 2 inches apart onto the prepared baking sheets. Using the prongs of a fork (to create a crosshatch pattern), press them down to form ¼-inch-thick cookies about 2 inches in diameter.

8. Bake until the cookies are lightly golden with darker golden edges, about 10 to 12 minutes. Allow them to cool on the baking sheets.

9. Meanwhile, prepare the buttercream filling: Using an electric mixer on low speed, cream the confectioners' sugar, butter, and peanut butter together in a medium-size mixing bowl for 1 minute, stopping the mixer once to scrape the bowl with a rubber spatula.

10. Add the cream and mix until fluffy, 40 seconds, stopping the mixer once to scrape the bowl.

11. When the cookies are completely cool, turn half of them upside down. Spread each bottom half with a rounded teaspoon of filling and top with the remaining cookies.

12. Prepare the glaze: Melt the chocolate in the top of a double boiler placed over simmering water. Remove from the heat. Add the oil and stir until smooth.

13. Drizzle the glaze in a pattern over the top of the sandwiches, and allow to set for 2 to 3 hours (or pop them into the fridge for 1 hour to set quickly).

14. If you plan to eat the cookies the first day, leave them sitting out. If not, store them in an airtight plastic container in the freezer for up to 2 weeks, and bring to room temperature before eating.

Makes about 25 cookie sandwiches

CHAPTER 7

THE BAR CROWD

My New Brownie
Peanut Butter Topped Brownies
Chocolate Raspberry Brownies
New York Cheesecake Brownies
Sour Cherry Cheesecake Brownies
Chocolate Soufflé Brownies
Toasted Pecan Orange Brownies
Chocolate Hazelnut Brownies
Bourbon Brownies
Chocolate Almond Amaretto Brownies
Butterscotch Chocolate Chip Brownies
White Chocolate Macadamia Brownies
Pucker-Your-Lips Apricot Linzer Bars
Blond Linzer Bars
Chocolate Linzer Bars
Hazelnut Cranberry Linzers
Cinnamon Pecan Shortbread Bars
Semolina Shortbread Bars
Noah's Scotch Shortbread Bars
Tosca Bars
Almond Bars
Gooey Butter Bars
Cherry Crumb Bars
Cranberry Crumb Bars
Creamy Cranberry Orange Bars
Cranberry Walnut Squares
Dating Bars
Yummy Cheesecake Bars
Raspberry Cream Cheese Bars
Tropical Macadamia Bars
Caramel Pecan Bars
Pecan Delight Bars
Carrot Cake Cream Cheese Bars
Poppyseed Coffee Cake Bars

There have been moments in the history of Rosie's when I thought we ought to change our name to "Brownies R Us." Our various brownies are major sellers and recipients of numerous awards, and our Chocolate Orgasms featured in *Rosie's Bakery . . . Baking Book*—the fudgy, frosted favorite of family planners and abstention advocates alike—have brought us our share of notoriety. That's not why I created them, though. To me, brownies constitute one of the basic food groups, and these were simply the most luscious to be had.

As American as brownies may now be, they are said to have come to us originally from Holland. Farm wives of yore baked them for their hungry menfolk, who knew a good thing when they saw it. That perhaps was the last time anyone agreed on what a brownie should be. Line up any ten people and ask them about their ideal brownie and I'm willing to bet that you'll get ten, maybe twelve, different opinions: Cakey, fudgy, dense, packed with nuts, cinnamony, unadulterated . . . So many people consider themselves connoisseurs that I've considered setting up brownie tastings. I see them as similar to wine tastings, complete with their own esoteric vocabulary and ratings by year—though I'd vote against limiting samples to a single bite.

In this chapter I tried to create a brownie for every palate, but it seemed a shame to stop there. There are so many other kinds of bars, covering such a spectrum of tastes, textures, and combinations, that nothing would do but to include fruit bars, nut bars, non-chocolate brownies, cheesecake bars, crumbly bars, and bars that refuse categorization, if you please.

What all these bars have in common is the ease with which they're made and the speed with which they're eaten. Just in case I'm proven wrong on the latter, most bars will keep for a week or so in an airtight container and freeze well for a while longer.

As for how and when bars are served, you're limited only by your imagination and your cutting skill. The standard form is a square of generous proportions, but triangles or wedges are also easy to cut and provide a nice change, and long, narrow rectangles, like ingots of gold, make perfect samples for platters of cookies or to accompany ice cream or puddings.

My New Brownie

♥ ♥ ♥ ♥ ♥ ♥ ♥ ♥ ♥ ♥ *brownie bar*

Y ou wouldn't think there would be anything more for me to discover in my love affair with the basic brownie. I had tested and retested the recipe over the years, and we had settled into a comfortable middle age where companionship and dependability were more important than surprises. Sure, we still had our special moments, but not every day like at the beginning. So imagine my delight when I decided to rekindle that old feeling by trying something new and came up with what I think is absolutely the best brownie ever. Fudgy, bittersweet, simple to make . . . it'll bring a glow to your cheeks and a smile to your lips. Just like the first time.

INGREDIENTS

6 ounces unsweetened chocolate
1 cup (2 sticks) unsalted butter
2 cups sugar
1 teaspoon pure vanilla extract
4 large eggs
1 cup all-purpose flour
½ cup chopped walnuts (optional)

1. Preheat the oven to 350°F. Lightly grease a 9-inch square baking pan with butter or vegetable oil, or line the bottom with parchment paper.

2. Melt the chocolate and butter together in the top of a double boiler placed over simmering water. Let the mixture cool for 5 minutes.

3. Place the sugar in a medium-size mixing bowl, and pour in the chocolate mixture. Using an electric mixer on medium speed, mix until blended, about 25 seconds. Scrape the bowl with a rubber spatula.

4. Add the vanilla. With the mixer on medium-low speed, add the eggs one at a time, blending after each addition until the yolk is broken and dispersed, about 10 seconds. Then scrape the bowl and blend until the mixture is velvety, about 15 seconds more. Scrape the bowl.

5. Add the flour on low speed, and mix for 20 seconds, stopping the mixer once to scrape the bowl. Finish the mixing by hand, being certain to incorporate any flour at the bottom of the bowl. Stir in the nuts, if using.

6. Spread the batter evenly in the prepared pan.

7. Bake the brownies on the middle rack of the oven just until the center has risen to the level of the sides and a tester inserted in the center comes out with moist crumbs, about 35 minutes.

8. Remove the pan from the oven and place it on a rack to cool for 1 hour before cutting the brownies into 2¼-inch squares with a sharp knife.

9. Leave the brownies in the pan, at room temperature, covered, for up to 2 days. After that, layer them in an airtight plastic container with plastic wrap, parchment, or waxed paper between the layers, and store for another 2 days in the refrigerator or in the freezer for up to 2 weeks. They are delicious cold or at room temperature.

Makes 16 brownies

Pan Size Alert

Many of the recipes in this chapter call for a 9-inch square baking pan. If you have trouble finding one (Williams-Sonoma has one), bake the brownies in an 8-inch pan, reducing the heat in most cases by 25°F and adding 10 to 15 minutes to the cooking time.

Peanut Butter Topped Brownies

♥ ♥ ♥ ♥ ♥ ♥ ♥ ♥ ♥   *brownie bar*

In homage to the Reese's Peanut Butter Cup, I've combined a layer of peanut butter buttercream with a layer of brownie and then topped all of that with a bittersweet chocolate glaze. Rich enough, do you think? I recommend very small bites.

INGREDIENTS

1 recipe My New Brownie (facing page)

THE BUTTERCREAM
½ cup plus 2 tablespoons peanut butter (smooth or crunchy)
1 cup confectioners' sugar
2½ tablespoons unsalted butter at room temperature
½ teaspoon pure vanilla extract

THE GLAZE
5 ounces bittersweet chocolate
2 teaspoons light corn syrup
½ cup chopped unsalted peanuts (optional)

1. Prepare the brownies and let them cool completely (you can place the pan in the refrigerator or freezer to speed up the process).

2. Prepare the buttercream: Place all the ingredients in a food processor and process until smooth, 60 seconds, stopping the processor once to scrape the bowl with a rubber spatula. (Or use an electric hand mixer and beat on medium-high speed in a small mixing bowl until smooth.)

3. Using a spatula, spread the buttercream evenly over the brownie, and freeze for 1 hour.

4. When the hour is almost up, prepare the glaze: Melt the chocolate in the top of a double boiler placed over simmering water. Remove the pan from the heat and stir in the corn syrup.

5. Allow the glaze to cool to the point where it is no longer hot but is still loose and spreadable, 8 to 10 minutes. Using a frosting spatula, spread the glaze over the buttercream. Sprinkle the peanuts, if using, over the glaze. Refrigerate the pan and allow the chocolate to harden, 30 minutes.

6. Cut the brownies into 2¼-inch squares with a sharp thin knife, dipping it in hot water and drying it before each cut.

7. When cool, refrigerate the bars in the pan, covered with plastic wrap, for up to 2 days. After that, layer them in an airtight plastic container with plastic wrap, parchment, or waxed paper between the layers, and store for another 2 days in the refrigerator or in the freezer for up to 2 weeks. They are delicious either cold or at room temperature.

Makes 16 brownies

Chocolate Raspberry Brownies

♥ ♥ ♥ ♥ ♥ ♥ ♥ ♥ ♥ ♥ *brownie bar*

The divine combination of chocolate and raspberries is layered in this unforgettable taste experience. For a sophisticated dessert, serve small pieces garnished with whipped cream and fresh raspberries.

INGREDIENTS

1 cup fresh raspberries or thawed, drained frozen unsweetened raspberries
¼ cup raspberry preserves
1 recipe My New Brownie (page 146), sugar reduced by 1 tablespoon

1. Preheat the oven to 350°F. Lightly grease a 9-inch square baking pan with butter or vegetable oil, or line the bottom with parchment paper.

2. Using a spoon or fork, mix the raspberries and the preserves together in a small bowl until the mixture has a pourable consistency. Set it aside.

3. Prepare the batter for the brownies. Scoop half of it into the prepared pan. Shake the pan gently to distribute the batter evenly.

4. Pour or spoon the raspberry mixture over the batter, and spread it out very gently, leaving ¾ inch uncovered around the edges.

5. Spoon or pour the remaining batter in long ribbon-like strips over the filling and spread it gently with a spatula. (Your goal is for the three layers to remain separate.) Shake the pan gently back and forth to level the batter.

6. Bake on the center rack of the oven until a tester inserted in the center comes out clean or with some moist crumbs, approximately 45 minutes.

7. Allow the brownies to cool in the pan for 1 hour before cutting into 2¼-inch squares with a sharp thin knife.

8. Leave the brownies in the pan, at room temperature, covered with plastic wrap, for up to 2 days. After that, layer them in an airtight plastic container with plastic wrap, parchment, or waxed paper between the layers, and store for another 2 days in the refrigerator or in the freezer for up to 2 weeks. They are delicious either cold or at room temperature.

Makes 16 brownies

New York Cheesecake Brownies

♥ ♥ ♥ ♥ ♥ ♥ ♥ ♥ ♥ ♥ *brownie bar*

What better combo for a gal from New York City who grew up on cheesecake and brownies? A layer of cheesecake and a layer of bittersweet brownie, one creamy, one fudgy, and both utterly divine. Eat at room temperature like a brownie, or chilled just like cheesecake.

INGREDIENTS

THE BROWNIE
3½ ounces unsweetened chocolate
10 tablespoons (1¼ sticks) unsalted butter
1 cup sugar
3 whole large eggs
½ cup all-purpose flour

THE CHEESECAKE
1 pound cream cheese, cold
½ cup sugar
1 whole large egg
1 large egg yolk
1½ teaspoons fresh lemon juice

1. Preheat the oven to 300°F. Lightly grease a 9-inch square baking pan with butter or vegetable oil, or line the bottom with parchment paper.

2. Prepare the brownie: Melt the chocolate and butter together in the top of a double boiler placed over simmering water. Let the mixture cool for 5 minutes.

3. Place the sugar and the eggs in a medium-size mixing bowl, and using an electric mixer, beat on medium-high speed until pale yellow, 2 minutes. Scrape the bowl with a rubber spatula.

4. Add the flour on low speed and mix for 5 seconds. Scrape the bowl.

5. Add the cooled chocolate mixture on low speed and blend until mixed, 15 seconds, stopping the mixer once to scrape the bowl.

6. Spread the batter evenly in the prepared pan, and place the pan in the freezer for 10 minutes.

7. Meanwhile prepare the cheesecake topping: Place all the cheesecake ingredients in a food processor and process until smooth, 1 minute. Stop the machine once during the process to scrape the bowl.

8. Remove the pan from the freezer. Carefully spoon the cheesecake mixture over the brownie layer, and using a spatula, spread it over the brownie so as not to mix the two together.

9. Bake on the center rack of the oven until the top is set and the center is just about level with the edges, 1 hour and 5 to 10 minutes.

10. Cool the brownies in the pan for 30 minutes. Using a sharp thin knife, cut into 2¼-inch squares, dipping the knife in hot water and wiping it off after each cut.

11. When cut, refrigerate the bars in the pan, covered with plastic wrap, for up to 2 days. After that, layer them in an airtight plastic container with plastic wrap, parchment, or waxed paper between the layers, and store for another 2 days in the refrigerator or in the freezer for up to 2 weeks. They are delicious either cold or at room temperature.

Makes 16 brownies

Sour Cherry Cheesecake Brownies

❤ ❤ ❤ ❤ ❤ ❤ ❤ ❤ ❤ *brownie bar*

The tartness of the sour cherries cuts the sweetness of the chocolate and the cheesecake, sending a rush of contrasting flavors to your tongue. It's unusual to combine all three elements in one brownie, but I figured, why not? I tried it out and found the results to be sensational.

INGREDIENTS

THE FILLING
8 ounces cream cheese at room temperature
¼ cup sugar
1 tablespoon sour cream
2 large egg yolks

THE BROWNIE
3½ ounces unsweetened chocolate
12 tablespoons (1½ sticks) unsalted butter
1½ cups sugar
2 whole large eggs
¾ cup all-purpose flour
¾ cup canned sour cherries, drained

1. Preheat the oven to 325°F. Lightly grease a 9-inch square baking pan with butter or vegetable oil, or line the bottom with parchment paper.

2. Make the filling: Place the cream cheese, sugar, and sour cream in a medium-size bowl and beat on medium-high speed until blended, 30 seconds. Scrape the bowl with a rubber spatula.

3. Add the egg yolks and mix until blended, 20 seconds. Set aside.

4. Prepare the brownie batter: Melt the chocolate and butter together in the top of a double boiler placed over simmering water. Remove the chocolate mixture from the heat and let it cool for 5 minutes.

5. Place the sugar in a medium-size bowl, and pour in the chocolate mixture. Using an electric mixer on medium speed, mix until blended, about 25 seconds. Scrape the bowl.

6. With the mixer on medium-low speed, add the eggs one at a time, blending after each addition until the yolk is broken and dispersed, about 10 seconds. Then scrape the bowl and blend until velvety, about 15 seconds.

7. Add the flour on low speed and mix for 20 seconds. Finish the mixing with a rubber spatula, being certain to incorporate any flour at the bottom of the bowl.

8. Pour half of the batter into the prepared pan, and spread it evenly. Using a rubber spatula, scoop the cream cheese mixture onto the brownie batter and gently spread it evenly over the surface.

9. Distribute the cherries over the filling, and use your fingers to press them down gently into the cream cheese.

10. Drop the rest of the batter over the filling by large spoonfuls. Then, using a spatula, spread it as gently as possible over the surface (do not worry if the cream cheese shows in places).

11. Bake the brownies on the center rack of the oven until a tester inserted in the center comes out clean or with moist crumbs, about 50 minutes. Allow the brownies to cool for 30 minutes in the pan. Then cut them into 2¼-inch squares with a sharp thin knife.

12. Refrigerate the bars in the pan, covered with plastic wrap, for up to 2 days. After that, layer them in an airtight plastic container, with plastic wrap, parchment, or waxed paper between the layers, and store for another 2 days in the refrigerator or in the freezer for up to 2 weeks. They are delicious either cold or at room temperature.

Makes 16 brownies

Chocolate Soufflé Brownies

❤ ❤ ❤ ❤ ❤ ❤ ❤ ❤ *brownie bar*

This fudgy brownie with a thick layer of baked mousse is one of the richest, most luxurious chocolate desserts known to humankind, if I do say so myself. Cut them small or you'll be flying for hours after you eat one. They're delicious cold, at room temperature, or warmed up, topped with vanilla ice cream or whipped cream.

INGREDIENTS

THE BROWNIE

3½ ounces unsweetened chocolate
10 tablespoons (1¼ sticks) unsalted butter
1 cup sugar
½ teaspoon pure vanilla extract
3 large eggs
½ cup all-purpose flour

THE TOPPING

¾ cup heavy (whipping) cream
2 ounces unsweetened chocolate
4 ounces (¾ cup) semisweet chocolate
  chips
3 large eggs
5 tablespoons sugar

1. Preheat the oven to 325°F. Lightly grease a 9-inch square baking pan with butter or vegetable oil, or line the bottom with parchment paper.

2. Make the brownie batter: Melt the chocolate and butter together in the top of a double boiler placed over simmering water. Let the mixture cool for 5 minutes.

3. Place the sugar in a medium-size mixing bowl and pour in the chocolate mixture. Using an electric mixer on medium speed, mix until blended, about 25 seconds. Scrape the bowl with a rubber spatula.

4. Add the vanilla. With the mixer on medium-low speed, add the eggs one at a time, blending after each addition until the yolk is broken and dispersed, about 10 seconds. Then scrape the bowl and blend until the mixture is velvety, about 15 seconds.

5. Add the flour on low speed and mix for 20 seconds. Finish the mixing by hand, being certain to incorporate any flour at the bottom of the bowl.

6. Spread the batter evenly in the prepared pan, and set it aside.

7. Make the topping: Heat the cream in a medium-size saucepan over low heat until hot. Add the chocolate and the chocolate chips, stir, and remove the pan from the heat. Cover the pan to melt the chocolate. Meanwhile, with the electric mixer on medium-high speed, beat the eggs and sugar together in a medium-size bowl until pale and foamy, about 3 minutes.

8. Stir the chocolate mixture with a whisk until smooth. Then add the chocolate mixture to the egg mixture and mix at medium-low speed until well blended.

9. Pour the topping over the batter, and tip the pan gently from side to side so that it spreads evenly.

10. Bake the brownies on the center rack of the oven until the top is set, 40 to 45 minutes. (The center of the brownies should never quite rise to the height of the edges.)

11. Remove the pan from the oven and place it on a rack to cool for 1 hour before cutting the brownies into 1½-inch squares with a sharp thin knife.

12. Leave the brownies in the pan, at room temperature, covered with plastic wrap, for up to 1 day. After that, layer them in an airtight plastic container with plastic wrap, parchment, or waxed paper between the layers, and store for another 2 days in the refrigerator or in the freezer for up to 2 weeks. They are delicious either cold or at room temperature.

Makes 36 brownies

Toasted Pecan Orange Brownies

❤ ❤ ❤ ❤ ❤ ❤ ❤ ❤ ❤ ❤   *brownie bar*

I believe it was Maida Heatter's Mandarin Chocolate Cake that first put me in touch with the wonderful combination of chocolate and orange. This brownie takes that perfect union a couple of steps further by adding candied orange slices and pecans.

INGREDIENTS

THE CANDIED ORANGE
1 large orange, thinly sliced
½ cup water
⅔ cup sugar

THE BROWNIE
3 ounces unsweetened chocolate
12 tablespoons (1½ sticks) unsalted butter at room temperature
¾ cup plus 1 tablespoon all-purpose flour
3 tablespoons unsweetened cocoa powder
1½ cups sugar
3 large eggs
¾ teaspoon pure vanilla extract
2 cups chopped pecans, toasted (page 89)

THE GLAZE
3 ounces semisweet chocolate
1 ounce unsweetened chocolate
2 tablespoons unsalted butter

1. Make the candied orange: Place the orange slices and water in a small heavy saucepan over medium heat. Bring to a boil and simmer gently for 3 minutes.

2. Add the sugar and continue stirring until the mixture is slightly thickened and shiny, 5 to 10 minutes. Remove the saucepan from the heat and allow to cool for 15 to 20 minutes.

3. When the mixture has cooled, drain it, reserving the syrup (there should be approximately ⅓ cup). Chop the drained orange slices coarsely in a food processor (there will be about ⅔ cup), and set aside.

4. Preheat the oven to 325°F. Lightly grease an 8-inch square baking pan with butter or vegetable oil, or line the bottom with parchment paper.

5. Prepare the brownie batter: Melt the chocolate and butter together in the top of a double boiler placed over simmering water. Remove the pan from the heat and allow to cool slightly.

6. Sift the flour and cocoa powder into a small bowl and set aside.

7. Place the sugar and eggs in a medium-size mixing bowl, and using an electric mixer on medium speed, beat until the mixture is thick and pale, 2 to 3 minutes. Stop the mixer once during the process to scrape the bowl.

8. Add the vanilla and mix for several seconds on medium speed.

9. Add the flour mixture and mix until blended, 15 seconds, stopping the mixer once to scrape the bowl.

10. Turn the mixer to low speed and gradually add the chocolate mixture. Mix until blended, 15 seconds, stopping the mixer once to scrape the bowl.

11. Fold in the nuts and the chopped candied orange. Spread the batter evenly in the pan, and bake on the center rack of the oven until a tester inserted in the center comes out with moist crumbs, 35 to 40 minutes.

12. Transfer the pan to a cooling rack and prepare the glaze: Melt both chocolates and butter together in the top of a double boiler placed over simmering water. Using a whisk, vigorously stir in 2 tablespoons of the reserved orange syrup until the glaze is smooth and shiny. If it is too stiff, add more syrup until it reaches glaze consistency. Spread over the warm brownies.

13. Allow the brownies to set for 4 to 6 hours in the pan before cutting them; or to speed the process, chill them for 1 to 2 hours in the refrigerator and then cut them into 2¼-inch squares, with a sharp thin knife.

14. Refrigerate the bars in the pan, covered with plastic wrap, for up to 2 days. After that, layer them in an airtight plastic container with plastic wrap, parchment, or waxed paper between the layers, and store for another 2 days in the refrigerator or in the freezer for up to 2 weeks. They are delicious either cold or at room temperature.

Makes 16 brownies

Chocolate Hazelnut Brownies

brownie bar

Here's a news flash: America's favorite flavor is hazelnut. (As of today, that is. Who knows about tomorrow?) Far be it from me to let the moment pass without contributing this light, delicate brownie made with ground hazelnuts and accented with Frangelico liqueur. The liqueur is optional, but with or without it, these brownies are lovely served in small pieces with a cappuccino.

INGREDIENTS

2 ounces unsweetened chocolate
5 ounces semisweet chocolate
2 tablespoons all-purpose flour
2 tablespoons cornstarch
10 tablespoons (1¼ sticks) unsalted butter
 at room temperature
14 tablespoons sugar
½ teaspoon pure vanilla extract
5 large eggs, separated
1½ teaspoons instant coffee or espresso
 powder
2 tablespoons Frangelico liqueur plus 2
 tablespoons water, or ¼ cup water
½ cup hazelnuts, toasted (page 89), and
 finely ground
¼ teaspoon salt

1. Preheat the oven to 325°F. Lightly grease a 9-inch square baking pan with butter or vegetable oil, or line the bottom with parchment paper.

2. Melt both chocolates in the top of a double boiler placed over simmering water. Remove from the heat and allow to cool.

3. Sift the flour and cornstarch together into a small bowl and set aside.

4. Using an electric mixer on medium speed, cream the butter, 11 tablespoons of the sugar, and the vanilla in a medium-size mixing bowl until light and fluffy, 45 seconds. Scrape the bowl.

5. Add the egg yolks and beat on medium speed until blended, 20 seconds. Stop the mixer once to scrape the bowl. Add the chocolate and beat on low speed until blended, 5 seconds. Scrape the bowl again.

6. Dissolve the coffee powder in the Frangelico mixture, and add this to the butter mixture.

7. Add the flour mixture and the ground nuts, and beat on low speed for 10 seconds, stopping the mixer once to scrape the bowl.

8. Using an electric mixer on medium-low speed, beat the egg whites with the salt in a medium-size bowl until frothy, about 30 seconds. Increase the speed to medium-high and gradually add the remaining 3 tablespoons sugar. Beat until soft peaks form, about 30 seconds.

9. Using a wooden spoon, stir one third of the whites into the batter to loosen the mixture. Fold in the remaining whites with a rubber spatula.

10. Spread the batter evenly in the baking pan, and bake the brownies on the center rack of the oven until they are just set and a tester comes out with moist crumbs, 30 to 35 minutes. Let the brownies cool in the pan for 1 to 2 hours before cutting them into 2¼- or 1½-inch squares with a sharp thin knife.

11. Leave the brownies in the pan, at room temperature, covered with plastic

wrap, for up to 2 days. After that, layer them in an airtight plastic container with plastic wrap, parchment, or waxed paper between the layers, and store for another 2 days in the refrigerator or in the freezer for up to 2 weeks. They are delicious either cold or at room temperature.

Makes 16 large or 36 small brownies

Bourbon Brownies

♥ ♥ ♥ ♥ ♥ ♥ ♥ ♥ ♥ ♥ *brownie bar*

As a rule I like my chocolate unadulterated, but bourbon provides a wonderful accent that complements, rather than disguises, the chocolate taste of these brownies. They're rich and fudgy, so you'll probably want to cut them into small pieces. You may also want to brush the bourbon onto the baked brownie more sparingly than I do; try the recipe once to see.

INGREDIENTS

THE BROWNIE
5 ounces unsweetened chocolate
12 tablespoons (1½ sticks) unsalted butter
2 cups sugar
1 teaspoon pure vanilla extract
9 tablespoons bourbon
4 large eggs
1 cup all-purpose flour

THE GLAZE
3 tablespoons heavy (whipping) cream
3 ounces bittersweet chocolate, chopped fine or shaved

1. Preheat the oven to 325°F. Lightly grease an 8-inch square baking pan with butter or vegetable oil or line the bottom with parchment paper.

2. Melt the chocolate and butter together in the top of a double boiler placed over simmering water. Remove the mixture from the heat and let it cool for 5 minutes.

3. Place the sugar in a medium-size mixing bowl, and pour in the chocolate mixture. Using an electric mixer on medium speed, mix until blended, about 15 seconds. Scrape the bowl with a rubber spatula.

4. Add the vanilla and 6 tablespoons of the bourbon. With the mixer on medium-low speed, add the eggs one at a time, blending after each addition until the yolk is broken and dispersed, about 10 seconds. Then scrape the bowl and blend until the mixture is velvety, about 15 seconds.

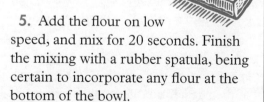

5. Add the flour on low speed, and mix for 20 seconds. Finish the mixing with a rubber spatula, being certain to incorporate any flour at the bottom of the bowl.

6. Spread the batter evenly in the prepared pan. Bake the brownies on the center rack of the oven until a thin crust forms on top and a tester inserted in the center comes out with moist crumbs, 45 to 50 minutes.

7. Transfer the pan to a wire rack, and using a small brush, glaze the surface of the brownies with the remaining 3 tablespoons bourbon. Allow them to cool for at least 1 hour.

8. When the brownies are cool, prepare the glaze: Heat the cream in a small saucepan over low heat just to the boiling point.

9. Remove the pan from the burner, add the chocolate, and cover the pan for 1 to 2 minutes. Then stir the mixture with a small whisk until smooth and shiny.

10. Using a frosting spatula, spread the glaze evenly over the surface of the brownies.

11. Place the pan in the refrigerator for 1 to 2 hours so the glaze will set. Then cut the brownies into 1½-inch squares with a sharp thin knife.

12. Refrigerate the bars in the pan, covered with plastic wrap, for up to 2 days. After that, layer them in an airtight plastic container with plastic wrap, parchment, or waxed paper between the layers, and store for another 2 days in the refrigerator or in the freezer for up to 2 weeks. They are delicious either cold or at room temperature.

Makes 36 brownies

Chocolate Almond Amaretto Brownies

❤ ❤ ❤ ❤ ❤ ❤ ❤ ❤ ❤   *brownie bar*

Almost flourless, these brownies are so elegant that they require only a single string of pearls to go anywhere. I recommend serving them in small pieces because they're also rich. You can opt not to add the Amaretto and still come out with a superb brownie. They're best made a day ahead so the flavor can settle.

INGREDIENTS

¾ cup plus 2 tablespoons all-purpose flour
½ teaspoon salt
3 ounces (½ cup) semisweet chocolate chips
3½ ounces unsweetened chocolate
1 cup (2 sticks) unsalted butter at room
    temperature
1½ cups sugar
1 teaspoon pure vanilla extract
1¼ teaspoons almond extract
4 large eggs
2 tablespoons Amaretto liqueur (optional)
1 cup coarsely chopped almonds, lightly
    toasted (page 89)

1. Preheat the oven to 325°F. Lightly grease a 9-inch square baking pan with butter or vegetable oil or line the bottom with parchment paper.

2. Sift the flour and salt together into a small bowl and set aside.

3. Melt both chocolates and butter together in the top of a double boiler placed over simmering water. Remove the mixture from the heat and let it cool for 5 minutes.

4. Place the sugar, vanilla, and almond extract in a medium-size bowl. Add the chocolate mixture, and using an electric mixer, mix on medium speed until blended, 30 seconds. Scrape the bowl with a rubber spatula.

5. With the mixer on medium-low speed, add the eggs one at a time, blending after each addition until the yolk is broken and dispersed, about 10 seconds. Then scrape the bowl and blend until velvety, about 15 seconds.

6. Add the flour mixture on low speed and mix for 10 seconds. Scrape the bowl with a rubber spatula, and complete the blending by hand with several strokes.

7. Spread the batter evenly in the pan, and sprinkle the Amaretto, if using, over the surface. Tip the pan from side to side to ensure even coverage.

8. Sprinkle the nuts over the surface, and bake the brownies on the center rack of the oven until a thin crust forms on top and a tester inserted in the center comes out with moist crumbs, 45 to 50 minutes.

9. Transfer the pan to a rack to cool for 1 hour. Then cut them into 1½- or 2¼-inch squares with a sharp thin knife. If possible, serve the brownies the next day.

10. Leave the brownies in the pan, at room temperature, covered with plastic wrap, for up to 2 days. After that, layer them in an airtight plastic container with plastic wrap, parchment, or waxed paper between the layers, and store for another 2 days in the refrigerator or in the freezer for up to 2 weeks. They are delicious eaten either cold or at room temperature.

Makes 16 large or 36 small brownies

Butterscotch Chocolate Chip Brownies

♥ ♥ ♥ ♥ ♥ ♥ ♥ ♥ ♥ *brownie bar*

These chewy bars offer the consistency of a fudgy brownie and the distinctive taste of butterscotch enhanced with chocolate chips. Though the recipe calls for a 9-inch pan, an 8-inch one works also. With the smaller pan, you'll get thicker bars, so you'll need to bake them a bit longer.

INGREDIENTS

1½ cups minus 1 tablespoon all-purpose
    flour
Generous ½ teaspoon baking powder
½ teaspoon salt
12 tablespoons (1½ sticks) unsalted butter
    at room temperature
1¾ cups plus 1 tablespoon (lightly packed)
    light brown sugar
2 teaspoons pure vanilla extract
3 large eggs
6 ounces (1 cup) semisweet chocolate chips

1. Preheat the oven to 350°F. Lightly grease a 9-inch square baking pan with butter or vegetable oil, or line the bottom with parchment paper.

2. Sift the flour, baking powder, and salt together into a small bowl and set aside.

3. Using an electric mixer on medium speed, cream the butter, brown sugar, and vanilla in a medium-size bowl until light and fluffy, about 1½ minutes. Scrape the bowl with a rubber spatula.

4. Add the eggs one at a time, beating on medium speed after each addition until partially blended, 5 seconds. Scrape the bowl. Then beat until the batter is blended, 20 seconds.

5. With the mixer on low speed, add the flour mixture and beat until almost blended, 15 seconds. Scrape the bowl.

6. Add the chocolate chips and mix on low speed until they are blended in,

about 5 seconds. Stir the batter several times with a rubber spatula, and spread it evenly in the prepared pan.

7. Bake on the center rack of the oven until the top has puffed and is just set, and is a golden color, 30 to 35 minutes. (The top won't spring back when touched; a depression remains.) Transfer the pan to a rack and allow to cool for 1 hour before cutting into 2¼-inch squares with a sharp thin knife.

8. Leave the brownies in the pan, at room temperature, covered with plastic wrap, for up to 2 days. After that, layer them in an airtight plastic container with plastic, parchment, or waxed paper between the layers, and store for another 2 days in the refrigerator or in the freezer for up to 2 weeks. They are delicious either cold or at room temperature.

Makes 16 brownies

White Chocolate Macadamia Brownies

♥ ♥ ♥ ♥ ♥ ♥ ♥ ♥ ♥   *brownie bar*

Customers at Rosie's clamor for this masterpiece of a bar: a chewy white chocolate base dotted with chunks of white and bittersweet chocolate and toasted macadamia nuts. What a way to gild the lily!

INGREDIENTS

12 ounces white chocolate
4 ounces bittersweet chocolate
1½ cups all-purpose flour
½ teaspoon baking powder
⅛ teaspoon salt
10 tablespoons (1¼ sticks) unsalted butter
¾ cup sugar
3 large eggs
2½ teaspoons pure vanilla extract
¾ cup coarsely chopped macadamia nuts, toasted (page 89)

1. Preheat the oven to 325°F. Lightly grease a 9-inch square baking pan with butter or vegetable oil, or line the bottom with parchment paper.

2. Chop 6 ounces of the white chocolate very fine and set it aside. Chop the remaining 6 ounces white chocolate and the bittersweet chocolate very coarse and set them aside.

3. Sift the flour, baking powder, and salt together into a small bowl and set aside.

4. Melt the butter in a small saucepan over low heat. Do not allow it to bubble. Remove the pan from the heat and add the finely chopped white chocolate, but *do not stir.* Set aside.

5. Using an electric mixer on medium-high speed, beat the sugar, eggs, and vanilla in a medium-size bowl until thick and pale, 5 minutes.

6. With the mixer on low speed, add the butter mixture and mix to blend, 15 to 20 seconds. Scrape the bowl.

7. Add the flour mixture and blend on low speed just to incorporate, 15 seconds. Stop the mixer once during the process to scrape the bowl.

8. Using a rubber spatula, fold in the coarsely chopped white and bittersweet chocolates and the nuts. Spread the batter evenly in the prepared pan.

9. Bake the brownies on the center rack of the oven until they are just set and a tester comes out with moist crumbs, 30 to 35 minutes. Allow them to cool in the pan for 1 hour, and then cut them into 2¼-squares with a sharp thin knife.

10. Leave the brownies in the pan, at room temperature, covered with plastic wrap, for up to 2 days. After that, layer them in an airtight plastic container with plastic wrap, parchment, or waxed paper between the layers, and store for another 2 days in the refrigerator or in the freezer for up to 2 weeks. They are delicious either cold or at room temperature.

Makes 16 brownies

Pucker-Your-Lips Apricot Linzer Bars

♥ ♥ ♥ ♥ ♥ ♥ ♥ ♥ *fine pastry bar*

For me, few fruits can rival the beauty and succulent tartness of apricots, so I created these bars to highlight those attributes. I placed a mixture of dried apricots and apricot preserves over a rich pastry crust, topped it with latticework, and came up with the perfect complement for afternoon tea.

INGREDIENTS

THE DOUGH
2 cups plus 3 tablespoons all-purpose flour
½ cup sugar
¼ teaspoon salt
2½ teaspoons grated lemon zest
15 tablespoons (2 sticks minus 1 table-
*   spoon) unsalted butter, cold,*
*   cut into 15 pieces*
2 large egg yolks
1 large egg white

THE FILLING
1 box (8 ounces) dried apricots, chopped
*   fine*
¾ cup apricot preserves
2 tablespoons fresh lemon juice

1. Preheat the oven to 375°F. Lightly grease a 9-inch square baking pan with butter or vegetable oil, or line the bottom with parchment paper.

2. Place the flour, sugar, salt, and lemon zest in a food processor, and process for 20 seconds. (Or whisk them together by hand in a large bowl.)

3. Distribute the butter evenly over the flour, and process until the mixture resembles coarse meal, 15 to 20 seconds. (Or rub the butter into the flour with your fingertips, or cut it in with a pastry blender.)

4. Whisk the egg yolks together. With the processor running, pour the yolks in a steady stream through the feed tube and process just until the dough comes together, 20 to 30 seconds. (Or sprinkle the yolks over the flour mixture while tossing with a fork.)

5. Divide the dough into two-thirds and one-third portions. Gently press the larger portion evenly in the bottom of the prepared pan and a scant ½ inch up the sides. Using a pastry brush, glaze the dough all over with some of the egg white. (Or pour the egg white over the dough, and tip the pan from side to side so the white spreads completely over the surface. Pour off and save the excess.)

6. Bake on the center rack of the oven until golden, 30 minutes.

7. While the base is baking, prepare the lattice dough: Roll out the remaining dough between two pieces of plastic wrap to form a 9½-inch square. Place this, still sandwiched in the wrap, in the freezer while you prepare the filling.

407

8. Place the apricots in a small sauce-pan and add water to cover. Bring to a boil over medium heat. Boil until soft, 2 to 3 minutes. Drain the apricots and pat them dry with paper towels. Place them in a small bowl along with the apricot preserves and lemon juice, and mix together.

9. Remove the pan from the oven, and raise the oven temperature to 400°F.

10. Spread the apricot filling over the baked base.

11. Remove the remaining dough from the freezer and peel off the top piece of plastic wrap. Cut the dough into 12 strips approximately ¾ inch wide.

12. Carefully place 6 of the strips across the filling, about 1 inch apart, with the first and last strip touching the sides of the pan. Repeat the procedure with the remaining 6 strips, placing them perpendicular to the first 6, in a lattice pattern. Press the ends of the strips into the dough border on the edge of the pan. Brush the remaining egg white over the lattice strips with a pastry brush.

13. Bake on the center rack of the oven until the lattice is golden, 40 minutes.

14. Remove the pan from the oven and place it on a rack to cool for at least 2 hours. Then cut into 2¼-inch squares, "sawing" the lattice carefully with the tip of a sharp thin knife.

15. Leave the bars in the pan, at room temperature, covered with plastic wrap, for up to 2 days, or layer the bars in an airtight plastic container with plastic wrap, parchment, or waxed paper between the layers, and store in the refrig-erator for 2 or 4 days or in the freezer for up to 2 weeks. Bring the bars to room temperature before eating.

Makes 16 bars

Blond Linzer Bars

♥ ♥ ♥ ♥ ♥ ♥   *linzer pastry bar*

For those of us who are linzer fans, here is another variation on the theme. This light-colored version of that classic dessert—made with a spicy dough and filled with apricot preserves—absolutely maintains its true linzer integrity.

INGREDIENTS

THE DOUGH
1½ cups all-purpose flour
¾ teaspoon baking powder
½ teaspoon salt
*10 tablespoons (1¼ sticks) unsalted butter
    at room temperature*
¼ cup (lightly packed) light brown sugar
½ cup granulated sugar
¾ teaspoon ground cinnamon
¼ teaspoon ground cloves
1 tablespoon grated lemon zest
1 large egg
½ teaspoon pure vanilla extract
1 cup finely chopped almonds

THE FILLING

¼ cup chopped dried apricots
½ cup plus 1 tablespoon apricot
    preserves
5 teaspoons fresh lemon juice

THE GLAZE

1 large egg white
2 tablespoons finely chopped almonds

1. Lightly grease an 8-inch square baking pan with butter, or line the bottom with parchment paper.

2. Sift the flour, baking powder, and salt together into a small bowl and set aside.

3. Using an electric mixer on low speed, cream the butter, both sugars, cinnamon, cloves, and lemon zest together in a medium-size bowl until just mixed. Scrape the bowl with a rubber spatula. Then mix on medium speed until smooth, 2 to 3 minutes, stopping the mixer twice to scrape the bowl.

4. Stir the egg and vanilla together in a small cup, and add to the butter mixture. Mix on medium speed until incorporated, about 10 seconds. Scrape the bowl.

5. With the mixer on low speed, blend in the flour mixture and the almonds until they are incorporated, 5 to 8 seconds.

6. Divide the dough into two-thirds and one-third portions. Gently press the larger portion into the prepared pan, cover with plastic wrap, and refrigerate it for 2 hours or freeze it for 1 hour.

7. Place the smaller portion of dough between two pieces of plastic wrap, and roll it out to form an 8-inch square. Slip the dough, still sandwiched between the wrap, onto a platter or baking sheet and refrigerate it for 2 hours or freeze it for 1 hour.

8. Preheat the oven to 350°F.

9. Prepare the filling: Place the apricots in a small saucepan, add water to cover, and bring to a boil over medium heat. Boil for 2 to 3 minutes, remove from the heat, and set aside for 10 minutes. Then drain the apricots, combine them with the preserves and lemon juice, and mix well.

10. Remove the pan from the refrigerator. Spread the apricot mixture evenly over the dough in the baking pan, leaving a ¼-inch border on all sides.

11. Remove the remaining dough from the refrigerator. Peel off the top piece of plastic wrap, and cut the dough into 12 strips about ½ inch wide (there will be leftover dough).

12. Carefully place 6 of the strips across the filling, about 1 inch apart, with the first and last strip touching the sides of the pan. Repeat the procedure with the remaining 6 strips, placing them perpendicular to the first 6, in a lattice pattern. Press the ends of the strips into the dough border on the edge of the pan.

13. Using a pastry brush, brush the egg white over the lattice strips. Then sprinkle the 2 tablespoons chopped almonds over the surface.

14. Bake on the center rack of the oven until the top is lightly golden and shiny and the filling is bubbling, about 35 minutes.

15. Remove the pan from the oven and place it on a rack to cool completely. Then cut into 2-inch squares, "sawing" carefully through the lattice with the tip of a sharp thin knife.

16. If you plan to snack on them that day, leave the bars in the pan at room temperature, covered with plastic wrap. At the end of the day, layer them in an airtight plastic container with plastic wrap, parchment, or waxed paper between the layers. They will stay fresh in the refrigerator for up to 3 days or in the freezer for up to 2 weeks. Bring the bars to room temperature before eating.

Makes 16 bars

Chocolate Linzer Bars

❤ ❤ ❤ ❤ ❤ ❤ ❤ *linzer pastry bar*

I'm a big fan of linzer bars and tortes, so I had fun trying out all kinds of variations. I knew that nuts

and chocolate go great together, and that raspberry goes well with chocolate, so when it came to variations on a linzer bar, I figured why not make a terrific trio? I put them all together, and this is the result.

INGREDIENTS

THE DOUGH
1 whole large egg
2 large egg yolks
1½ teaspoons pure vanilla extract
1¼ cups plus 2 tablespoons all-purpose flour
7 tablespoons unsweetened cocoa powder
¼ teaspoon baking powder
⅛ teaspoon salt
¾ cup plus 2 tablespoons sugar
1 cup coarsely ground almonds
14 tablespoons (1¾ sticks) unsalted butter, cold, cut into 14 pieces

THE FILLING
¾ cup raspberry preserves
1 tablespoon fresh lemon juice

THE GLAZE
1 large egg white

1. Preheat the oven to 350°F. Lightly grease a 9-inch square baking pan, or line the bottom with parchment paper.

2. Using a fork, stir the whole egg, egg yolks, and vanilla together in a small cup. Set aside.

3. Place the flour, cocoa powder, baking powder, salt, and sugar in a food processor and process to blend, 5 seconds.

4. Add the almonds and process several seconds to blend.

5. Distribute half the butter over the flour mixture and process until the mixture resembles coarse meal, 15 seconds. Then repeat with the remaining butter and process for 10 seconds.

6. With the machine running, add the egg mixture through the feed tube and process for 3 seconds. Scrape the bowl with a rubber spatula, and then process for another 3 seconds.

7. Divide the dough into two portions, one slightly larger than the other. Gently press the larger portion into the prepared pan. Bake on the center rack of the oven until the dough is firm to the touch, about 20 minutes. Then remove the pan from the oven, but leave the oven on.

8. While the base is baking, roll out the remaining dough between two pieces of plastic wrap to form a square approximately 9½ inches. Slip this dough, still sandwiched between the plastic wrap, onto a platter or baking sheet and refrigerate it for 45 minutes.

9. Stir the raspberry preserves and lemon juice together in a small bowl, and spread the mixture evenly over the baked crust.

10. Remove the chilled dough from the refrigerator, and peel off the top piece of plastic wrap. Cut the dough into 12 strips about ¾ inch wide.

11. Carefully place 6 of the strips across the filling, about 1 inch apart, with the first and last strip touching the sides of the pan. Repeat the procedure with the remaining 6 strips, placing them perpendicular to the first 6, in a lattice pattern. Press the ends of the strips into the dough border on the edge of the pan.

12. Brush the egg white over the lattice strips with a pastry brush.

13. Bake on the center rack of the oven until the lattice strips are firm and the filling is bubbling, 35 to 40 minutes. Let the pan cool completely on a wire rack; then cut carefully into 2¼-inch squares by "sawing" with a sharp thin knife.

14. If you plan to snack on them that day, leave the bars in the pan at room temperature, covered with plastic wrap. At the end of the day, layer them in an airtight plastic container with plastic wrap, parchment, or waxed paper between the layers. They will stay fresh in the refrigerator for up to 3 days or in the freezer for up to 2 weeks. Bring the bars to room temperature before eating.

Makes 16 bars

Hazelnut Cranberry Linzers

❤ ❤ ❤ ❤ ❤ ❤ ❤ *linzer pastry bar*

When you want something a little different, here's a linzer bar with a twist. To the spicy dough that's the calling card of a good Viennese linzertorte, I've added ground hazelnuts and the all-American cranberry.

INGREDIENTS

THE DOUGH
1½ cups all-purpose flour
¼ teaspoon baking powder
¼ teaspoon salt
1 tablespoon unsweetened cocoa powder
1⅛ teaspoons ground cinnamon
¼ teaspoon ground cloves
1 cup (2 sticks) unsalted butter at room
    temperature
½ cup granulated sugar
¼ cup (lightly packed) light brown sugar
1 tablespoon grated lemon zest
1 whole large egg
1 large egg yolk
⅔ cup finely chopped almonds
⅓ cup finely chopped hazelnuts

THE FILLING
¾ cup raspberry preserves
¾ cup fresh cranberries
1 tablespoon grated orange zest

THE TOPPING
1 large egg white
3 tablespoons chopped or slivered almonds

1. Lightly grease an 8-inch square baking pan with butter, or line the bottom with parchment paper.

2. Sift the flour, baking powder, salt, cocoa powder, cinnamon, and cloves together into a bowl and set aside.

3. Using an electric mixer on low speed, cream the butter, both sugars, and lemon zest together in a medium-size mixing bowl until just mixed. Scrape the bowl with a rubber spatula. Then mix on medium speed until smooth, 2 to 3 minutes, stopping the mixer once or twice to scrape the bowl with a rubber spatula.

4. Add the whole egg and the egg yolk, and mix on medium speed until incorporated, about 10 seconds. Scrape the bowl.

5. With the mixer on low speed, blend in the flour mixture, almonds, and hazelnuts until they are incorporated, 5 to 8 seconds.

6. Divide the dough into slightly uneven halves. Gently press the larger half into the prepared pan, cover with plastic wrap, and refrigerate it for 2 hours or freeze it for 1 hour.

7. Place the remaining dough between 2 pieces of plastic wrap and roll it out to form an 8-inch square. Slip the dough, still sandwiched between the plastic wrap, onto a platter or baking sheet and refrigerate it for 2 hours or freeze it for 1 hour.

8. Preheat the oven to 375°F.

9. Remove the pan from the refrigerator. Stir the filling ingredients together, and spread the mixture evenly over the dough in the baking pan, leaving a ¼-inch border on all sides.

10. Remove the remaining dough from the refrigerator, and peel off the top piece of plastic wrap. Cut the dough into 12 strips about ½ inch wide (there will be leftover dough).

11. Carefully place 6 of the strips across the filling, about 1 inch apart, with the first and last strip touching the sides of the pan. Repeat the procedure with the remaining 6 strips, placing them perpendicular to the first 6, in a lattice pattern. Press the ends of the strips into the dough border on the edge of the pan.

12. Brush the egg white over the lattice strips with a pastry brush. Sprinkle the chopped almonds over the entire surface.

13. Bake on the center rack of the oven until the top is shiny and golden and the filling is bubbling, 35 to 40 minutes.

14. Remove the pan from the oven and cool completely on a wire rack. Then cut the bars very carefully into 2-inch squares by "sawing" with the tip of a sharp thin knife.

15. If you plan to snack on them that day, leave the bars in the pan at room temperature, covered with plastic wrap. At the end of the day, layer them in an airtight plastic container with plastic wrap, parchment, or waxed paper between the layers. They will stay fresh in the refrigerator for up to 3 days or in the freezer for up to 2 weeks. Bring the bars to room temperature before eating.

Makes 16 bars

Cinnamon Pecan Shortbread Bars

♥ ♥ ♥ ♥ ♥ ♥ ♥ ♥ *shortbread bar*

A simple shortbread, flavored with cinnamon—the prince of spices—and covered with pecans.

INGREDIENTS

THE BASE
1 cup plus 1 tablespoon all-purpose flour
½ teaspoon plus ⅛ teaspoon ground
  cinnamon
⅛ teaspoon baking powder
¼ teaspoon salt
8 tablespoons (1 stick) unsalted butter at
  room temperature
3 tablespoons (lightly packed) light brown
  sugar
2 tablespoons granulated sugar

THE TOPPING
1 tablespoon granulated sugar
½ teaspoon ground cinnamon
¼ cup plus 1 tablespoon hand-chopped
  pecans

413

1. Preheat the oven to 300°F. Have ready an 8-inch square baking pan.

2. Sift the flour, cinnamon, baking powder, and salt together into a small bowl and set aside.

3. Using an electric mixer on medium speed, cream the butter and both sugars together in a medium-size bowl until light and fluffy, 1 to 1½ minutes. Stop the mixer once or twice during the process to scrape the bowl with a rubber spatula.

4. Add the flour mixture on medium-low speed, and mix for 20 seconds. Scrape the bowl. Then mix on medium-high speed until the batter is light and fluffy again, 2 to 2½ minutes, stopping the mixer three times to scrape the bowl.

5. Press the dough evenly over the bottom of the pan, and prick it all over with the tines of a fork.

6. Make the topping: Mix the sugar with the cinnamon. Sprinkle this mixture over the dough, and then scatter the nuts over the surface.

7. Bake on the center rack of the oven until the shortbread is firm to the touch, 55 to 60 minutes.

8. While the shortbread is still hot, cut it into 4 ×1-inch bars with the point of a sharp thin knife. Allow the bars to cool completely before eating.

9. If you plan to snack on them, store the bars in an airtight plastic container at room temperature for up to 4 days. After that, store the container in the freezer for up to 2 weeks. Bring the bars to room temperature before eating.

Makes 16 bars

Semolina Shortbread Bars

♥ ♥ ♥ ♥ ♥ ♥ ♥ ♥ *shortbread bar*

Semolina is the flour used in pasta; here it gives shortbread a grainy texture to add to its already divinely buttery flavor. This shortbread is thick, so be sure that it's baked through and through.

INGREDIENTS

1½ cups plus 2 tablespoons all-purpose flour
½ cup plus 3 tablespoons semolina flour
½ cup plus 2 tablespoons sugar
½ teaspoon salt
1 cup (2 sticks) unsalted butter, cold, cut into 10 pieces

1. Preheat the oven to 325°F. Have ready an 8-inch square baking pan.

2. Place both flours, the sugar, and salt in a food processor and pulse to blend, 5 seconds.

3. Distribute the butter over the flour mixture and process just until the dough comes together, 40 to 45 seconds. Stop the processor once during the mixing to scrape the bowl with a rubber spatula.

4. Place the dough on a work surface, and work it gently with your hands to bring it together. Pat the shortbread evenly into the pan. Using the tines of a fork, poke deep holes over the entire surface.

5. Bake the shortbread on the center rack of the oven for 45 minutes. Then lower the heat to 300°F and continue baking until it is crisp, firm, and richly golden, 30 minutes.

6. While the shortbread is still hot, cut it into 4 × 1-inch bars with the point of a sharp thin knife. Then let it cool in the pan.

7. Store the bars in an airtight container at room temperature for 3 to 4 days if you think you will be snacking on them. After that, store the container in the freezer for up to 2 weeks. Bring the shortbread to room temperature before eating.

Makes 16 bars

Noah's Scotch Shortbread Bars

♥ ♥ ♥ ♥ ♥ ♥ ♥ ♥ *shortbread bar*

When my son Noah's second-grade teacher asked the class to bring in easy-to-make ethnic recipes to conclude her section on other cultures, we chose this utterly delicious cookie that will be enjoyed by people of all ages. It's amazing how such a delicious treat can be so easy to prepare!

INGREDIENTS

1½ cups plus 1 tablespoon all-purpose flour
½ teaspoon salt
⅛ teaspoon baking powder
*12 tablespoons (1½ sticks) unsalted butter
    at room temperature*
7 tablespoons sugar

1. Preheat the oven to 325°F. Have ready an 8-inch square baking pan.

2. Sift the flour, salt, and baking powder together into a small bowl and set aside.

3. Using an electric mixer on medium-high speed, cream the butter and sugar together in a medium-size bowl until light and fluffy, 1 to 1½ minutes. Stop the mixer twice during the process to scrape the bowl with a rubber spatula.

4. Add the flour mixture with the mixer on low speed, and blend for 10 seconds. Scrape the bowl, and then beat at medium-high speed until fluffy, 2 to 2½ minutes, stopping the mixer twice during the process to scrape the bowl.

5. Pat the dough evenly into the pan, and pierce the surface all over with the tines of a fork. Bake until it is crisp and golden, about 45 minutes.

6. While the shortbread is still hot, cut it into 4 × 1-inch bars with the point of a sharp thin knife. Then allow it to cool completely in the pan.

7. Transfer the bars to an airtight container and store at room temperature for 3 to 4 days. After that, store the container in the freezer for up to 2 weeks.

Makes 16 bars

Tosca Bars

♥ ♥ ♥ ♥ ♥ ♥ ♥ ♥ *shortbread bar*

This crunchy shortbread bar is topped with a thin layer of raspberry preserves and a soft almond paste mixture.

INGREDIENTS

THE BASE
1⅓ cups all-purpose flour
⅓ cup sugar
8 tablespoons (1 stick) unsalted butter, cold, cut into 8 pieces
1 large egg, separated

THE FILLING
1 package (7 ounces) almond paste (not marzipan)
3 tablespoons sugar
9 tablespoons (1 stick plus 1 tablespoon) unsalted butter at room temperature, cut into 9 pieces
2 large eggs
¾ teaspoon pure vanilla extract
3 tablespoons all-purpose flour
¾ teaspoon baking powder
6 tablespoons raspberry preserves

THE TOPPING
3 tablespoons unsalted butter
6 tablespoons sugar
1½ tablespoons milk
1½ tablespoons all-purpose flour
¾ cup sliced almonds

1. Preheat the oven to 350°F. Lightly grease a 7 × 11-inch baking pan with butter, or line the bottom with parchment paper.

2. Place the flour and sugar in a food processor, and process the mixture for 5 seconds.

3. Distribute the butter evenly over the flour mixture, and process until the mixture resembles coarse meal, 15 to 20 seconds.

4. With the processor running, drop the egg yolk through the feed tube and process just until the dough comes together, 20 to 30 seconds.

5. Press the dough evenly over the bottom of the prepared pan and ½ inch up the sides. Using a pastry brush, glaze the dough all over with the egg white. (Or you can pour the egg white over the dough, tilt the pan so the white covers the dough completely, and pour off the excess.)

6. Place the pan on the center rack of the oven and bake until golden, 20 to 25 minutes. Set the pan aside, but leave the oven on.

7. Prepare the filling: Place the almond paste and sugar in a food processor and process until the mixture resembles coarse sand, 20 seconds.

8. Add the butter and process until evenly incorporated, 5 seconds.

9. Add the eggs and vanilla, and process until evenly incorporated, 5 seconds.

10. Add the flour and baking powder, and process 5 seconds more.

11. Spread the raspberry preserves over the baked base. Then gently pour

and spread the almond mixture over that. Return the pan to the center rack of the oven, and bake until the filling is set in the center, about 25 minutes. Remove the pan from the oven and preheat the broiler.

12. Meanwhile, prepare the topping: Melt the butter in a small saucepan over low heat. Add the sugar, milk, and flour, and bring to a simmer. Stir constantly over medium-low heat for about 1½ minutes. Do not boil. Remove the pan from the heat and stir in the almonds.

13. Pour the topping evenly over the filling, and spread it gently with a small spatula or a butter knife.

14. Broil the bars until golden, about 2 minutes. *Watch carefully!* Cool completely in the pan before cutting into 2¾ × 1¾-inch bars with a sharp thin knife.

15. If you plan to snack on them the first day. place the bars on a plate or simply leave them in the pan. After that refrigerate, covered, overnight, or layer the bars in an airtight plastic container with plastic wrap, parchment, or waxed paper between the layers. Store the container in the freezer for up to 2 weeks. Bring the bars to room temperature before eating.

Makes 16 bars

Almond Bars

♥ ♥ ♥ ♥ ♥ ♥ ♥   *shortbread bars*

Here is a first-class recipe from Kathleen Stewart (for her other recipe, Apple Galettes, see Index) of the Downtown Bakery and Creamery in Healdsburg, California. It's a bar made of a rich shortbread base covered with a creamy, buttery almond topping.

INGREDIENTS

THE BASE
1 cup all-purpose flour
1½ tablespoons sugar
¼ teaspoon salt
8 tablespoons (1 stick) unsalted butter,
    cold, cut into 8 pieces
1½ tablespoons cold water

THE TOPPING
1 cup heavy (whipping) cream
1 cup sugar
2 teaspoons Grand Marnier or Amaretto
¾ cup slivered almonds

1. Preheat the oven to 375°F. Lightly grease a 9-inch square baking pan with butter, or line the bottom with parchment paper.

2. Place the flour, sugar, and salt in a food processor, and process for 5 seconds. Scatter the butter over the flour and process until the mixture looks like coarse meal, about 20 seconds.

3. With the machine running, add the cold water through the feed tube and process just until the dough comes together, 10 to 15 seconds.

4. Press the dough evenly over the bottom of the prepared pan (it will be thin). Place the pan on the center rack of the oven and bake until lightly golden, about 20 minutes. Then remove the pan from the oven and raise the heat to 400°F.

5. Let the base cool while you prepare the topping: Place the cream, sugar, and Grand Marnier in a medium-size saucepan and cook over medium-low heat, whisking occasionally, until it comes to a rolling boil, 2 to 3 minutes.

6. Remove the pan from the heat, stir in the almonds, and allow the mixture to sit for 15 minutes.

7. Pour the warm topping mixture over the baked base, making sure that the almonds are evenly distributed.

8. Bake on the center rack of the oven until light golden, 25 to 30 minutes.

9. While the bars are still hot, use the point of a sharp thin knife to free the edges from the sides of the pan. Then allow the bars to sit for 15 to 20 minutes before cutting into 2¼-inch squares. After cutting, allow the bars to cool in the pan.

10. Leave the bars in the pan at room temperature, covered with plastic wrap, for up to 2 days, or layer the bars in an airtight container with plastic wrap, parchment, or waxed paper between the layers, and store in the refrigerator for up to 1 week or in the freezer for up to 2 weeks. Bring to room temperature before eating.

Makes 16 bars

Gooey Butter Bars

♥ ♥ ♥ ♥ ♥ ♥ ♥ ♥ ♥ *shortbread bar*

Herein lies a tale—or two tales, to be precise. The first involves my mother-in-law, Barbara, who served us a yellow cake bar soaked through with custard so scrumptious that I couldn't help but talk with my mouth full. I asked for the recipe, only to find that she had used a cake mix, and since I had decided that cake mix would never touch my cookbook, I fought temptation and put the recipe aside. Enter tale two. On my travels, I came across the same treat in St. Louis, Missouri, where, as the story goes, a baker working during World War II mistakenly doubled the sugar in a butter cake. Because sugar was rationed, he was loath to toss the cake out. So he sold it—and to his surprise, got rave reviews. The cake has assuaged the St. Louis sweet tooth ever since. I decided to come up with my own, made-from-scratch version,

which has a cakey bottom with a very sweet vanilla custard topping that sinks partway into the base.

INGREDIENTS

THE BASE
1 cup all-purpose flour
½ teaspoon salt
¼ teaspoon baking soda
8 tablespoons (1 stick) unsalted butter
    at room temperature
½ cup sugar
1 teaspoon pure vanilla extract
1 large egg

THE FILLING
12 tablespoons (1½ sticks) unsalted butter
    at room temperature
Pinch of salt
½ teaspoon pure vanilla extract
6 tablespoons sweetened condensed milk
⅓ cup light corn syrup
1 large egg
⅓ cup all-purpose flour

1. Preheat the oven to 350°F. Lightly grease a 9-inch square baking pan with butter, or line the bottom with parchment paper.

2. Sift the flour, salt, and baking soda together into a small bowl, and set aside.

3. Using an electric mixer on medium speed, cream the butter, sugar, and vanilla together in a medium-size bowl until light and fluffy, about 1 minute. Scrape the bowl with a rubber spatula.

4. Add the egg and beat until smooth, 10 seconds. Scrape the bowl.

5. Add the flour mixture and beat on low speed until blended, 10 seconds, stopping the mixer once to scrape the bowl.

6. Using floured fingertips or a spatula, spread the dough evenly over the bottom of the prepared pan. Set it aside.

7. Prepare the filling: With the mixer on medium speed, cream the butter, salt, and vanilla together until light and fluffy, about 1 minute. Scrape the bowl with a rubber spatula.

8. Add the condensed milk and beat on low speed until blended, 15 seconds. Scrape the bowl, then add the corn syrup and mix until blended, 10 seconds.

9. Add the egg and beat for 1½ minutes on medium-high speed until the mixture is light and fluffy again. Scrape the bowl.

10. With the mixer on medium-low speed, add the flour and beat until mixed, 30 seconds.

11. Pour the filling evenly over the base, and bake on the center rack of the oven until the edges appear set but the center is still jiggly, 25 to 27 minutes. Cool to room temperature; then refrigerate until set, about 4 hours. Cut into 2¼ × 1½-inch bars with a sharp thin knife, dipping it in hot water and wiping it clean before each new cut.

12. If you plan to snack on them the first day, place the bars on a plate or simply leave them in the pan. After that, refrigerate, covered with plastic wrap, overnight, or layer the bars in an airtight plastic container with plastic wrap, parchment, or waxed paper between the layers. Store the container in the freezer for up to 2 weeks. Bring the bars to room temperature before eating.

Makes 24 small bars

Cherry Crumb Bars
♥ ♥ ♥ ♥ ♥ ♥ ♥ ♥   *shortbread bar*

Just what the world has been clamoring for: a portable cherry crumb pie. Okay, maybe not clamoring, but this sure beats those commercial snack pies. It's built on a shortbread base, which is layered with a tart cherry filling, then finished off with a crunchy crumb topping.

INGREDIENTS

THE BASE
1 cup plus 2 tablespoons all-purpose flour
¼ cup granulated sugar
¼ teaspoon salt
8 tablespoons (1 stick) unsalted butter, cold, cut into 8 pieces
1 large egg white

420

THE FILLING

2¼ cups canned sour cherries, drained,
   but 1 cup juice reserved
3 tablespoons cornstarch
¾ cup granulated sugar
¼ teaspoon salt

THE TOPPING

5 tablespoons all-purpose flour
1 tablespoon granulated sugar
2 tablespoons (lightly packed) light brown
   sugar
6 tablespoons quick-cooking oats
Pinch of salt
3 tablespoons unsalted butter, cold, cut
   into 4 pieces

1. Preheat the oven to 350°F. Lightly grease an 8-inch square baking pan with butter, or line the bottom with parchment paper.

2. Place the flour, sugar, and salt in a food processor, and process for 5 seconds. Scatter the butter over the flour mixture, and process just until the dough comes together, 20 to 30 seconds.

3. Press the dough gently over the bottom of the prepared pan. Using a pastry brush, glaze the dough all over with the egg white. (Or you can pour the egg white over the dough, tilt the pan so the white covers the dough completely, and pour off the excess.)

4. Bake the base on the center rack of the oven until golden brown, 25 to 30 minutes.

5. While the base is baking prepare the filling: Place the drained cherries in a small bowl and set aside. Combine ¼ cup of the reserved juice with the cornstarch in a small bowl, and set aside.

6. Combine the remaining ¾ cup juice, the sugar, and salt in a small saucepan and bring to a boil over medium-low heat.

7. Pour the cornstarch mixture slowly into the boiling juice, whisking vigorously. Reduce the heat to low and continue whisking vigorously until the mixture turns clear, about 4 minutes.

8. Add the mixture to the cherries and set aside.

9. Prepare the topping: Place the flour, both sugars, the oats, and salt in a food processor and pulse briefly 4 times.

10. Add the butter and pulse 8 to 10 times, until it is incorporated evenly. Scrape the bowl.

11. Remove the base from the oven, and raise the oven temperature to 425°F. Spread the cherry filling evenly over the base, and sprinkle the topping evenly over the cherries.

12. Bake until the topping is lightly golden and crispy, about 25 minutes. Then preheat the broiler. Broil until the topping is a slightly deeper gold, 1 to 2 minutes. Watch the bars the entire time they are under the broiler.

13. Cool completely in the pan on a wire rack. Then cut into 2-inch squares.

14. Leave the bars in the pan, at room temperature, covered with plastic wrap, for up to 2 days, or layer the bars in an airtight plastic container with plastic wrap, parchment, or waxed paper between the layers, and store in the refrigerator for 3 to 4 days or in the freezer for up to 2 weeks. If frozen, the fruit may get a little wet in the thawing process, but the bars will still taste delicious.

Makes 16 bars

Cranberry Crumb Bars

❤ ❤ ❤ ❤ ❤ ❤   *crumb pastry bar*

If you love cranberries, then you'll enjoy making these bars during the fall and winter, when cranberries are at their peak. Two layers of a crunchy oatmeal crumb cookie are held together by a tart cranberry/raspberry mixture.

INGREDIENTS

THE DOUGH
½ cup whole wheat flour
1 cup all-purpose flour
½ teaspoon salt
½ cup plus 2 tablespoons (lightly packed) light brown sugar
1½ cups quick-cooking oats
½ cup walnuts, chopped small
12 tablespoons (1½ sticks) unsalted butter, melted
1 tablespoon hot water

THE FILLING
¾ cup raspberry preserves
2¼ cups fresh cranberries

1. Preheat the oven to 375°F. Lightly grease a 9-inch square baking pan with butter, or line the bottom with parchment paper.

2. Make the dough: Place all the dry ingredients in a medium-size bowl, and stir with a spoon to mix (or toss with your hands).

3. Add the melted butter and toss with the dry ingredients to distribute the butter evenly.

4. Take a little more than half of the dough and press it evenly into the prepared pan. Bake on the middle rack of the oven until lightly golden, about 14 minutes. Then remove the pan from the oven but leave the oven on.

5. Meanwhile, add the hot water to the remaining dough, and toss with a fork to distribute. Set aside.

6. Prepare the filling: Mix the preserves and cranberries in a medium-size bowl until the berries are evenly distributed.

7. Distribute the berry mixture over the baked base, and using a frosting spatula or the back of a spoon, spread it so that it covers the whole base evenly. Crumble the remaining dough over the filling.

8. Return the pan to the oven and bake until the top is golden and the filling is bubbling, about 45 minutes. Cool completely in the pan on a wire rack before cutting into 2¼-inch squares.

9. Leave the bars in the pan, at room temperature, covered with plastic wrap, for up to 2 days, or layer the bars in an airtight plastic container with plastic wrap, parchment, or waxed paper between the layers, and store in the refrigerator for 3 to 4 days or in the freezer for up to 2 weeks. Bring the bars to room temperature before eating. If frozen, the fruit may get a little wet in the thawing process, but the bars will still taste delicious.

Makes 16 bars

Creamy Cranberry Orange Bars

♥ ♥ ♥ ♥ ♥ ♥ ♥ *shortbread bar*

Start with a layer of crunchy short-bread, smooth it over with a creamy cheesecake mixture flavored with orange, and stud it with fresh cranberries for a deliciously sweet-tart treat.

INGREDIENTS

THE BASE

1 cup all-purpose flour
¼ cup confectioners' sugar
8 tablespoons (1 stick) unsalted butter, cold, cut into 8 pieces
1 large egg white

THE TOPPING

10 ounces cream cheese at room temperature
2 tablespoons granulated sugar
2 tablespoons sour cream
2 large eggs
1 teaspoon pure vanilla extract
5 tablespoons orange marmalade
½ cup plus 2 tablespoons fresh cranberries
2 tablespoons finely chopped orange zest

1. Preheat the oven to 350°F. Lightly grease an 8-inch square baking pan with butter, or line the bottom with parchment paper.

2. Place the flour and confectioners' sugar in a food processor, and process for 5 seconds. Scatter the butter over the flour mixture, and process until the dough comes together, 20 to 30 seconds.

3. Press the dough gently over the bottom of the prepared pan and about 1 inch up the side. Using a pastry brush, glaze the dough all over with the egg white. (Or you can pour the egg white over the dough, and tip the pan from side to side so the white spreads completely over the surface. Pour off the excess.)

4. Bake the base on the center rack of the oven until golden, about 25 minutes. Transfer the pan to the refrigerator to cool completely, 15 minutes. Keep the oven on.

5. Meanwhile, prepare the topping: Using an electric mixer on medium-high speed, cream the cream cheese and granulated sugar together in a medium-size bowl until light and fluffy, 2 to 3 minutes. Stop the mixer once or twice during the process to scrape the bowl with a rubber spatula.

6. Add the sour cream and beat the mixture on medium-high speed until smooth, about 1 minute. Scrape the bowl.

7. Add the eggs and vanilla and beat on medium-high speed until smooth and creamy, about 10 seconds.

8. Add the marmalade and beat on low speed until blended, 5 seconds. Then fold in the cranberries and orange zest by hand with a rubber spatula.

9. Pour the cream cheese mixture over the cooled base, and jiggle the pan to distribute it evenly.

10. Bake on the center rack of the oven until the top is slightly golden around the edges and a tester inserted in the center comes out dry, 35 to 40 minutes. If the topping bubbles up during baking, prick the bubbles with a toothpick or a thin knife.

11. Allow to cool completely in the pan on a rack. Then cut into 2-inch squares with the point of a thin sharp knife, dipping it in hot water and wiping it dry before each cut.

12. When cool, refrigerate the bars in the pan, uncovered, for the first day. At the end of the day, cover them. They will remain fresh in the refrigerator for 3 to 4 days. To freeze, chill the bars in the refrigerator first, then layer them in an airtight plastic container with plastic wrap, parchment, or waxed paper between the layers. Store in the freezer for up to 2 weeks. Bring the bars to room temperature before eating.

Makes 16 bars

Cranberry Walnut Squares

♥ ♥ ♥ ♥ ♥ ♥ ♥   *shortbread bar*

Patti Chase, an experienced Boston chef, passed the recipe for these squares on to me: a crunchy shortbread base that supports a sweet and gooey mix chock-full of walnuts and tart cranberries. They are a tribute to her talent.

INGREDIENTS

THE BASE
1 cup plus 2 tablespoons all-purpose flour
¼ teaspoon salt
5 tablespoons confectioners' sugar
8 tablespoons (1 stick) unsalted butter, cold, cut into 8 pieces
1 large egg white

THE TOPPING
2 cups fresh cranberries
½ cup light corn syrup
½ cup sugar
2 whole large eggs
2 tablespoons unsalted butter, melted
¾ teaspoon pure vanilla extract
1 tablespoon all-purpose flour
½ cup chopped walnuts

1. Preheat the oven to 350°F. Lightly grease an 8-inch square baking pan with butter, or line the bottom with parchment paper.

2. Place the flour, salt, and confectioners' sugar in a food processor, and process for 5 seconds. Scatter the butter over the flour mixture and process until the dough comes together, 20 to 30 seconds.

3. Press the dough gently over the bottom of the prepared pan. Using a pastry brush, glaze the dough all over with the egg white. (Or you can pour the egg white over the dough, and tip the pan from side to side so the white spreads completely over the surface. Pour off the excess.)

4. Bake on the center rack of the oven until golden, about 25 minutes.

5. Meanwhile, prepare the topping: Place the cranberries in a food processor and process for 3 seconds. Set aside.

6. Place the remaining topping ingredients, except the nuts, in a medium-size bowl and stir vigorously with a whisk to blend. Add the cranberries and the nuts, and stir well.

7. Pour the topping over the hot base, and return the pan to the oven. Bake until the topping is set, 40 to 45 minutes.

8. Cool in the pan on a wire rack. Then cut carefully into 2-inch squares, "sawing" with the tip of a long thin knife.

9. If you plan to snack on them, place the bars on a plate or simply leave them in the baking pan, covered, for up to 2 days, or layer the cut bars in an airtight container, with plastic wrap, parchment, or waxed paper between the layers, and place in the refrigerator for up to 4 days or the freezer for up to 2 weeks. If frozen, the fruit may get a little wet in the thawing process, but the bars will still taste delicious.

Makes 16 bars

Dating Bars

❤ ❤ ❤ ❤ ❤ ❤   *crumb pastry bar*

In my younger, sillier years, when Rosie's had just begun, I named this bar. My co-workers and I had a good chuckle, and the name has stuck around all these years. You'll find some version of these bars in nearly every American cookbook—which goes to show, I suppose, that dating never goes out of fashion. Two hearty, crunchy oatmeal layers with a gooey date filling in between.

INGREDIENTS

THE FILLING

1½ cups finely chopped dates

6 tablespoons (lightly packed) light brown
   sugar

¾ cup water

1½ teaspoons pure vanilla extract

½ teaspoon grated lemon zest

THE DOUGH

1½ cups plus 2 tablespoons all-purpose
   flour

5 tablespoons whole wheat flour

1¼ cups quick-cooking oats

½ cup plus 2 tablespoons rolled oats

½ teaspoon baking soda

¼ teaspoon salt

½ cup minus ½ tablespoon (lightly packed)
   light brown sugar

2½ tablespoons granulated sugar

12½ tablespoons (1½ sticks plus ½ tablespoon) unsalted butter, melted

1. Preheat the oven to 350°F. Lightly grease an 8-inch square baking pan with butter, or line the bottom with parchment paper.

2. Make the filling: Combine the dates, brown sugar, and water in a small saucepan and bring to a boil over medium heat. Reduce the heat to low and simmer until the mixture has thickened, 5 minutes.

3. Remove the pan from the heat, and stir in the vanilla and lemon zest. Set aside.

4. Make the dough: Combine all the ingredients in a medium-size bowl, and toss to mix.

5. Press half of the dough evenly over the bottom of the prepared baking pan. Spread the date mixture over this, and then sprinkle the remaining dough evenly on top, pressing it down lightly into the dates.

6. Bake on the center rack of the oven until the top is crunchy and golden, about 40 minutes.

7. Cool in the pan on a rack for 30 minutes, and then cut into 2-inch squares with a sharp thin knife.

8. Leave the bars in the pan, at room temperature, covered with plastic wrap, for up to 2 days, or layer the bars in an airtight plastic container with plastic wrap, parchment, or waxed paper between the layers, and store in the refrigerator for 3 to 4 days or in the freezer for up to 2 weeks. Bring the bars to room temperature before eating.

Makes 16 bars

Yummy Cheesecake Bars

♥ ♥ ♥ ♥ ♥ ♥ *crumb pastry bar*

A nd yummy they are. I've sand-wiched two soft crumb layers with a cream cheese and golden raisin mixture. These taste equally good served cold or at room temperature. They will turn a bit soggy after a couple of days in the fridge, but they are absolutely delicious that way too.

INGREDIENTS

THE DOUGH

1½ cups all-purpose flour
6 tablespoons confectioners' sugar
12 tablespoons (1½ sticks) unsalted
butter at room temperature,
cut into several pieces
2 tablespoons (lightly packed) light
brown sugar

THE FILLING

8 ounces cream cheese at room
temperature
3 tablespoons sour cream
2 tablespoons fresh lemon juice
¼ cup granulated sugar
1 large egg
1 teaspoon pure vanilla extract
1½ teaspoons grated lemon zest
¼ cup golden raisins

1. Preheat the oven to 350°F. Lightly grease an 8-inch square baking pan with butter, or line the bottom with parchment paper.

2. Place the flour and confectioners' sugar in a food processor, and process for 5 seconds.

3. Add the butter and pulse 8 times, until the mixture forms coarse crumbs.

4. Remove 1 cup of the mixture, add the brown sugar to it, and toss it with a fork to incorporate. Set it aside.

5. With floured fingertips, press the remaining dough firmly over the bottom of the pan and 1 inch up the sides of the pan.

6. Bake on the center rack of the oven until lightly golden, 20 minutes. Then remove the pan from the oven, leaving the oven on, and allow the base to cool to room temperature. Wash and dry the food processor bowl and blade for the next step.

7. While the base cools, make the filling: Place all the ingredients except the raisins in the food processor and process until smooth, 15 to 20 seconds. Stir in the raisins by hand.

8. Pour the filling over the cooled base, and top it with the reserved crumb mixture. Return it to the oven and bake until the crumbs are just beginning to turn golden and the bars are set, 45 minutes.

9. Allow to cool in the pan on a wire rack for 1 hour. Then cut into 2-inch squares with a sharp thin knife.

10. When cool, refrigerate the bars in the pan, uncovered, for the first day. At the end of the day, cover them. They will remain fresh in the refrigerator for 2 days. To freeze, layer the bars in an airtight plastic container with plastic wrap, parchment, or waxed paper between the layers. Store in the freezer for up to 2 weeks. Serve cold or at room temperature.

Makes 16 bars

Raspberry Cream Cheese Bars

❤ ❤ ❤ ❤ ❤ ❤ ❤ ❤ *shortbread bar*

Here raspberry preserves separate a shortbread base from a layer of cheesecake, which is topped with glazed fresh raspberries. When you cut these bars, try to slice between the berries so they don't get bruised.

INGREDIENTS

THE BASE
1 cup all-purpose flour
¼ teaspoon salt
½ cup minus 1 tablespoon sugar
6 tablespoons (¾ stick) unsalted butter, cold, cut into 6 pieces
1 large egg yolk
¼ teaspoon pure vanilla extract
1 tablespoon milk, half-and-half, or heavy (whipping) cream
1 large egg white

THE TOPPING
11 ounces cream cheese at room temperature
5 tablespoons sugar
1 teaspoon cornstarch
1 whole large egg
1 large egg yolk
¼ teaspoon grated lemon zest
¾ cup sour cream

TO FINISH
¾ cup raspberry preserves
1 pint fresh raspberries
⅓ cup red currant jelly

1. Preheat the oven to 350°F. Lightly grease an 8-inch square baking pan with butter, or line the bottom with parchment paper.

2. Place the flour, salt, and sugar in a food processor and process for 5 seconds. Scatter the butter over the flour and process until the mixture resembles coarse meal, 20 seconds.

3. Stir the egg yolk, vanilla, and milk together in a small cup. With the machine running, pour this mixture through the feed tube and process just until it is mixed in and the dough is starting to come together, 1 minute.

4. Press the dough gently over the bottom of the prepared pan. Using a pastry brush, glaze the dough all over with the egg white. (Or you can pour the egg white over the dough, tilt the pan so the white covers the dough completely, and pour off the excess.) Bake on the center rack of the oven until golden, about 30 minutes. Set the pan on a wire rack to cool slightly. Leave the oven on.

5. Meanwhile, prepare the topping: Place the cream cheese, sugar, cornstarch, egg and yolk, lemon zest, and sour cream in a food processor and process just until blended, 15 seconds. Stop the processor once during the process to scrape the bowl.

6. Using a frosting spatula, spread the raspberry preserves over the base. Then pour the cream cheese topping over the preserves and spread it gently.

7. Bake on the center rack of the oven until set, about 1 hour. Transfer the pan to the refrigerator and chill for 1 hour.

8. Top the cooled bars with the fresh raspberries, arranging them in rows (see step 11).

9. Heat the jelly in the top of a double boiler placed over simmering water until liquefied. Glaze the berries by brushing the jelly over them with a pastry brush. Chill for at least 1 hour in the refrigerator so the glaze can set.

10. Cut the bars into 2-inch squares with the tip of a sharp thin knife, dipping it in hot water and wiping it dry before each cut.

11. Once you put the raspberries on top of these luscious bars, they can only be stored in the pan or on a plate. No stacking, please. If you want to make the bars a couple of days before serving, don't dress them with the berries. Complete the bars through step 7. When cooled, cover with plastic wrap and store in the refrigerator until the day they are to be served, then add the berries.

Makes 16 bars

Tropical Macadamia Bars

shortbread bar

Hawaii's answer to the dream bar—that traditional shortbread-based bar topped with a gooey coconut mixture that's found in every classic American dessert book. This one is chock-full of toasted macadamias as well as coconut, and it's accented with rum.

INGREDIENTS

THE BASE
1 cup all-purpose flour
½ cup plus 1 tablespoon (lightly packed) light brown sugar
8 tablespoons (1 stick) unsalted butter at room temperature

THE TOPPING
¾ cup plus 2 tablespoons (lightly packed) light brown sugar
¼ cup light corn syrup
1½ teaspoons pure vanilla extract
2 tablespoons rum
3 tablespoons unsalted butter, melted
2 large eggs
3 tablespoons all-purpose flour
½ teaspoon baking powder
¼ teaspoon salt
1 cup macadamia nuts, toasted (page 89) and coarsely chopped
½ cup plus 2 tablespoons shredded coconut

1. Preheat the oven to 350°F. Lightly grease an 8-inch square baking pan with butter, or line the bottom with parchment paper.

2. Place the flour and brown sugar in a food processor and process for 5 seconds. Add the butter and process until the dough comes together, 20 to 30 seconds.

3. Press the dough gently over the bottom of the prepared pan.

4. Bake on the center rack of the oven, until golden around the edges, 20 to 25 minutes.

5. Meanwhile, prepare the topping: Using a whisk, beat the brown sugar, corn syrup, vanilla, rum, melted butter, eggs, flour, baking powder, and salt in a medium-size bowl until blended. Stir in the nuts and coconut with a rubber spatula.

6. Spread the topping evenly over the baked base.

7. Bake on the center rack of the oven until the top is golden and set, about 20 minutes. Allow to cool completely in the pan on a wire rack before cutting into 2-inch squares with a sharp thin knife.

8. Leave the bars in the pan at room temperature, covered with plastic wrap, for up to 2 days, or layer the bars in an airtight plastic container, with plastic wrap, parchment, or waxed paper between the layers, and store in the refrig-

erator for up to 1 week or in the freezer for up to 2 weeks. Bring to room temperature before eating.

Makes 16 bars

Caramel Pecan Bars

♥ ♥ ♥ ♥ ♥ ♥ ♥ ♥   *shortbread bar*

I was always crazy about those little Turtle candies that came in pink-and-white-striped bags, so I decided to capture their spirit in a cookie. A layer of shortbread is topped with a chewy caramel that's packed with pecans, and bittersweet chocolate is drizzled over the whole thing. You'll need a good candy thermometer to determine when the caramel is done, but otherwise the method is straight-forward. They're best if you keep them refrigerated until an hour before eating.

INGREDIENTS

THE BASE
1 cup all-purpose flour
½ cup granulated sugar
8 tablespoons (1 stick) unsalted butter, cold, cut into 8 pieces
1¼ cups pecans, very coarsely chopped

THE CARAMEL

¾ cup plus 2 tablespoons heavy
    (whipping) cream
⅔ cup light corn syrup
⅔ cup (lightly packed) light brown sugar
6 tablespoons granulated sugar
5½ tablespoons (⅓ cup) unsalted butter
¼ teaspoon salt
1¼ teaspoons pure vanilla

THE GLAZE

1 ounce bittersweet chocolate
1 teaspoon vegetable oil

1. Preheat the oven to 350°F. Lightly grease an 8-inch square baking pan with butter, or line the bottom with parchment paper.

2. Place the flour and sugar in a food processor, and process for 5 seconds. Scatter the butter over the flour mixture and process until the dough comes together, 20 to 30 seconds.

3. Press the dough gently over the bottom of the prepared pan and bake on the center rack of the oven until golden, 25 to 30 minutes. Place the pan in the refrigerator for 15 minutes to cool completely.

4. Sprinkle the nuts evenly over the base, and set it aside at room temperature while you prepare the caramel.

5. Place the cream, corn syrup, both sugars, butter, and salt in that order in a heavy 2½- to 3-quart saucepan fitted with a tight lid. Cook over medium heat without stirring for exactly 5 minutes.

6. Uncover the saucepan, reduce the heat to medium-low, clip a candy thermometer to the side of the pan (but not touching the bottom), and continue to cook, stirring very frequently, until the thermometer reads 238° to 240°F, about 30 minutes.

7. Remove the pan from the heat and allow the mixture to set for 2 minutes. Then stir in the vanilla.

8. Pour the caramel over the base, and allow it to set for about 3 hours at room temperature.

9. After the caramel has set, prepare the glaze: Melt the chocolate in the top of a double boiler placed over simmering water. Remove it from the heat and vigorously stir in the vegetable oil with a small whisk. Drizzle this mixture over the caramel in whatever pattern strikes your fancy, chill in the refrigerator for no more than 15 minutes, and then set out at room temperature for 1 hour. Cut into 2-inch squares with a sharp thin knife.

10. Store the bars in the pan in the refrigerator, covered with plastic wrap, for up to 1 week. To freeze, cut and remove the bars from the pan, and layer them in an airtight plastic container with plastic wrap, parchment, or waxed paper between the layers, and store for up to 2 weeks. Bring the bars to room temperature before eating.

Makes 16 bars

Pecan Delight Bars

♥ ♥ ♥ ♥ ♥ ♥ ♥ ♥   *shortbread bar*

A perfect ending to a meal when you crave a bite of something sweet. Not overly rich, this short-bread topped with an ever-so-thin coating of brown sugar suffused with pecans hits the spot.

INGREDIENTS

THE SHORTBREAD

1½ cups all-purpose flour
6 tablespoons sugar
12 tablespoons (1½ sticks) unsalted butter,
*   cold, cut into 12 pieces*
1 large egg white

THE TOPPING

1¼ cups plus 2 tablespoons (lightly packed)
*   light brown sugar*
3 tablespoons all-purpose flour
½ teaspoon salt
2 tablespoons pure maple syrup
3 tablespoons unsalted butter, melted
3 large eggs
1½ cups finely chopped pecans
Confectioners' sugar for sprinkling
*   (optional)*

1. Preheat the oven to 350°F. Lightly grease a 9-inch square baking pan with butter, or line the bottom with parchment paper.

2. Place the flour and sugar in a food processor, and process for 5 seconds. Scatter the butter over the flour mix-

ture and process until the dough comes together, 20 to 30 seconds.

3. Press the dough gently over the bottom of the prepared pan. Using a pastry brush, glaze the dough all over with the egg white. (Or you can pour the egg white over the dough, tilt the pan so the white covers the dough completely, and pour off the excess.)

4. Bake on the center rack of the oven until lightly golden, 35 minutes. Remove from the oven, but leave the oven on.

5. Meanwhile, prepare the topping: Using a hand-held whisk, beat the brown sugar, flour, salt, maple syrup, melted butter, and eggs together in a medium-size bowl until blended. Stir in the chopped pecans. Spread the topping evenly over the baked base.

6. Bake the bars on the center rack of the oven until golden and set, 40 minutes. Allow them to cool in the pan just to room temperature; then cut them into 2¼-inch squares with a sharp thin knife. Using a small strainer, sprinkle confectioners' sugar over the surface if desired.

7. Leave the bars in the pan at room temperature, covered with plastic wrap, for up to 2 days, or layer the bars in an airtight plastic container with plastic wrap, parchment, or waxed paper between the layers, and store in the refrigerator for up to 1 week or in the freezer for up to 2 weeks. Bring to room temperature before eating.

Makes 16 bars

Carrot Cake Cream Cheese Bars

♥ ♥ ♥ ♥ ♥ ♥ ♥ ♥ ♥ ♥ ♥ *cake bar*

Okay, it's true: carrot cake is passé. So what's a little passé among friends? Besides, this bar is so light and moist, and the layers of cream cheese so luscious, that I wouldn't be surprised if it ushered in a carrot cake renaissance all by itself.

INGREDIENTS

THE TOPPING
½ cup chopped walnuts
1 teaspoon ground cinnamon
2 tablespoons granulated sugar

THE FILLING
8 ounces cream cheese at room temperature
1 large egg
¼ cup granulated sugar
2 tablespoons unsalted butter at room temperature
1 tablespoon cornstarch
½ teaspoon pure vanilla extract
1 can (8 ounces) crushed pineapple, drained

THE CAKE
⅔ cup puréed cooked carrots (3 or 4 carrots; see Note)
⅓ cup grated raw carrot
1⅓ cups all-purpose flour
¾ teaspoon baking powder
¼ teaspoon baking soda
¾ teaspoon salt
1¾ teaspoons ground cinnamon
¾ teaspoon ground allspice
5½ tablespoons (⅓ cup) unsalted butter at room temperature
⅓ cup vegetable oil
1 cup (lightly packed) light brown sugar
1½ teaspoons pure vanilla extract
2 teaspoons fresh lemon juice
1 tablespoon plus 1 teaspoon fresh orange juice
2 large eggs
½ cup raisins

1. Preheat the oven to 350°F. Lightly grease a 13 × 9-inch square baking pan with butter, or line the bottom with parchment paper.

2. Toss all the topping ingredients together in a small bowl, and set aside.

3. Make the filling: Place all the filling ingredients except the crushed pineapple in a food processor and process until smooth, 10 seconds. Stir in the pineapple by hand and set aside.

4. Make the cake: Place the puréed and grated carrots in a small bowl, stir, and set aside. Sift the flour, baking powder, baking soda, salt, cinnamon, and allspice together into a small bowl, and set aside.

5. Using an electric mixer on

medium speed, cream the butter, oil, brown sugar, and vanilla together in a medium-size bowl until well blended, 1 minute. Stop the mixer once during the process to scrape the bowl with a rubber spatula. Add the lemon juice and orange juice, and blend for a couple of seconds.

6. Add the eggs one at a time, mixing on medium speed after each addition until blended, 10 seconds. Scrape the bowl each time.

7. Add the flour mixture and beat on low speed for 5 seconds. Scrape the bowl. Then mix the batter by hand until the dry ingredients are incorporated.

8. Blend in the carrot mixture with several turns of the mixer at low speed. Then add the raisins and blend for several seconds.

9. Spread approximately two thirds of the carrot cake batter in the prepared pan. Then pour the cream cheese mixture gently over the batter, and using a frosting spatula, spread it evenly over the batter.

10. Drop the rest of the cake batter by spoonfuls all over the filling and use a frosting spatula to gently spread the batter. The batter will not thoroughly cover the filling—(it's fine for the cream cheese to show here and there).

11. Sprinkle the topping mixture over the surface, and bake on the center rack of the oven until golden and set, about 35 minutes.

12. Cool in the pan on a rack, and then cut into 3¼ × 2¼-inch bars with a sharp thin knife.

13. If you plan to snack on them the first day, place the bars on a plate or simply leave them in the pan. After that, refrigerate, covered with plastic wrap, overnight, or layer the cut bars in an airtight plastic container with plastic wrap, parchment, or waxed paper between the layers. Store the container in the freezer for up to 2 weeks. Bring the bars to room temperature before eating.

Makes 16 bars

Note: To purée carrots, cut them into 1-inch chunks and steam them until tender, about 10 minutes. Then purée them in a food processor, 10 to 15 seconds.

Poppyseed Coffee Cake Bars

cake bar

With these bars, you get two layers of yeasted butter dough surrounding a thick layer of poppyseed filling studded with golden raisins. I originally intended them

to be breakfast food, but my friend Wendy Berenson, who tested the recipe, quickly told me that I was selling them short. "Morning, nothing," she announced. "It was 11 P.M. and there I was sitting in bed, the covers up to my chin, while I finished the whole pan!" I'll take her word for it and recommend them as a dessert and mid-afternoon snack too.

INGREDIENTS

THE FILLING
1½ cups canned poppyseed filling
¼ cup golden raisins

THE TOPPING
1 tablespoon (lightly packed) light brown sugar
1 tablespoon granulated sugar
2 tablespoon all-purpose flour
½ teaspoon ground cinnamon
1 tablespoon unsalted butter, cold

THE DOUGH
2 teaspoons dry yeast
¼ cup warm water
2 cups plus 2 tablespoons all-purpose flour
2 teaspoons granulated sugar
½ teaspoon salt
1 teaspoon grated orange or lemon zest
1 cup (2 sticks) unsalted butter at room temperature, cut into 16 pieces
2 large eggs
3½ tablespoons sour cream

THE GLAZE
1½ teaspoons unsalted butter, melted
1½ teaspoons milk
¼ teaspoon pure vanilla extract
6 tablespoons confectioners' sugar

1. Make the filling: Fold the raisins into the poppyseed mixture in a small bowl, and set aside.

2. Make the topping: Place both sugars, the flour, and cinnamon in a small bowl and stir with a whisk. Using your fingers, rub the butter into the dry ingredients until the mixture resembles coarse meal. Place the bowl in the refrigerator.

3. Preheat the oven to 250°F. Lightly grease a 9-inch square baking pan with butter, or line the bottom with parchment paper.

4. Make the dough: Sprinkle the yeast over the warm water in a small bowl. Stir with a spoon, and allow the mixture to sit for several minutes until it appears foamy.

5. Meanwhile, place the flour, sugar, salt, and zest in a food processor and process for 5 seconds.

6. Scatter the butter over the surface of the dry ingredients, and pulse until the mixture resembles coarse meal, 10 seconds.

7. Using a whisk, stir the eggs and sour cream together in a small bowl until blended.

8. Stir the yeast mixture into the egg mixture, and pour this over the flour mixture. Pulse 3 times, and scrape the bowl. Then pulse 4 more times, until the dough just comes together.

9. Spread half the dough evenly over the bottom of the prepared pan, using your fingers or a frosting spatula. Then distribute the poppyseed filling in spoonfuls over the surface of the dough, and spread it very gently with a frosting spatula.

10. Place the rest of the dough over the filling, and spread it very gently with a frosting spatula to distribute it evenly.

11. Sprinkle the topping over the dough. Then wet and wring out a clean kitchen towel, and stretch it over the top of the pan (don't allow it to touch the topping). Place the pan in the oven, turn the oven off, and leave the pan

there for 1 hour. Then remove the pan from the oven.

12. Preheat the oven to 350°F.

13. Bake the bars on the center rack until they are golden on top, about 45 minutes. Cool them in the pan on a wire rack for 45 minutes.

14. Stir together all the glaze ingredients, and drizzle the glaze over the cooled bars. Cut them into 2¼-inch squares using a sharp thin knife.

15. Leave the bars in the pan, at room temperature, covered with plastic wrap, for up to 2 days, or layer the cut bars in an airtight plastic container with plastic wrap, parchment, or waxed paper between the layers, and store in the refrigerator for 3 to 4 days or in the freezer for up to 2 weeks. Bring the bars to room temperature before eating.

Makes 16 bars

TIDBITS

Whenever I go out to dinner, I can never decide which dessert to order. I am forever tempted by chocolate, yet who can pass up a fruit tart or creamy cheesecake? The only solution for me is to make sure to dine with as many friends as possible. Then, when choosing, I try to convince everyone to order something different and to share bites. From my dessert indecision, was born the idea of tidbits.

Almost any cake, pie, tart, muffin, turnover, or strudel can be made in miniature form. Somehow, these mini pleasures seem less sinful and more inviting than their full-size counterparts, and a platter of them makes a dazzling end to a special occasion dinner. Serve Rosy Cranberry Tartlets and Apple Galettes for a sophisticated but homey winter's eve dinner party, and mini cakes, such as Maya's Little Butter Cupcakes and Coconut Fluff Babycakes for school birthday parties. Mini Eclairs and Lemon Curd Tartlets make an elegant presentation served with

Champagne at an anniversary party. Apple Turnovers and Rosie's Blueberry Muffins are luscious for afternoon tea or even a brunch or breakfast. For a dessert party extravaganza, you can serve them all!

Although it's always best to make tidbits on the day you plan to serve them, if you are making more than one or two kinds, you'll probably want to spread the baking out over a period of time. Most tidbits freeze well and can be made in advance. Tidbits that require frosting or glazing, such as Chocolate Babycakes or Almond Raspberry Gems, should be frozen unfrosted or unglazed; do that step on the day of serving. Flaky pastries containing fruit (for example, Apple Turnovers, Apple Galettes, and Rosy Cranberry Tartlets) can be reheated in the oven before serving in order to restore their crispness.

I find these mini dessert favorites so inviting, I keep a stock in the freezer. Then, when the mood to nibble strikes, I'm ready. Once you try them, I bet you'll want a freezer full, too.

Apple Turnovers

A miniature version of the old standard: rich, flaky pastry filled to bursting with a simple apple mixture. Make sure that you bake these until they're golden so the pastry reaches the right texture.

INGREDIENTS

THE DOUGH
2 cups minus 1 tablespoon all-purpose
    flour
1 tablespoon sugar
¼ teaspoon salt
12 tablespoons (1½ sticks) unsalted butter,
    cold, cut into 12 pieces
4 ounces cream cheese, cold, cut into 8
    pieces
1 large egg yolk, beaten
3 tablespoons fresh orange juice, cold

THE FILLING
4 cups finely diced peeled apples
    (from 2 or 3 large apples)
5 tablespoons sugar

THE GLAZE
1 tablespoon sugar

1. Place the flour, sugar, and salt in a food processor and process to blend, 5 seconds.

2. Scatter the butter and cream cheese over the flour mixture and pulse until the mixture is the size of small peas, 15 to 20 pulses.

3. Beat the egg yolk and orange juice together in a small cup. Pour this in a stream through the feed tube while pulsing quickly 20 to 25 times, until the dough forms large clumps.

4. Place the dough on a work surface and knead it for several seconds. Then divide the dough in half and form it into two disks. Wrap each in plastic wrap and refrigerate them for 20 minutes.

5. Toss the apples with the sugar. Set aside.

6. Remove one of the disks from the refrigerator and roll it out between two pieces of plastic wrap to form a round 12 inches in diameter. Slide the dough, still sandwiched in the plastic wrap, onto a plate and refrigerate it. Repeat this procedure with the second disk.

7. Preheat the oven to 400°F. Line several baking sheets with parchment paper, or grease them lightly with vegetable oil.

8. Remove one portion of dough from the refrigerator and slide it onto a work surface. Peel off the top piece of plastic wrap. Using a 3-inch round cookie cutter, cut out as many rounds as possible (10 to 12). Gather up the dough scraps and reroll them to make as many more rounds as possible.

9. Place a scant teaspoon of apple filling in the center of each round.

Then fold the dough in half to cover the filling, and using the tines of a fork that have been dipped in flour, press the edges to seal them. Poke the top of each turnover with the tines of the fork to create a vent.

10. Repeat steps 8 and 9 with the second portion of dough.

11. Place the turnovers 1 inch apart on the prepared baking sheets. Using a pastry brush, brush each one with water and sprinkle ⅛ teaspoon sugar over the top.

12. Bake the turnovers for 8 minutes. Then rotate the pan and bake until they are a rich golden color, an additional 8 to 10 minutes. Allow the turnovers to cool on the sheets.

13. These are best eaten on day one, when their texture is crispiest. If you have leftovers, place them in an airtight plastic container and refrigerate them for a day or two. To serve, recrisp them in a preheated 400°F oven for 8 to 10 minutes. For longer-term storage, freeze them; recrisp frozen turnovers at 400°F for 10 to 15 minutes.

Makes about 24 turnovers

Apple Galettes

Whenever I visit a new place, I seek out the best bakery in town. When my friend Allen Helschein introduced me to the Downtown Bakery and Creamery in the charming town of Healdsburg, in California's wine country, I went wild. After tasting widely, I decided that my favorite was the Apple Galette, a kind of fruit tartlet wrapped in a delicious crust. Kathleen Stewart, who owns and operates this bakery, shared the recipe. Make lots of these and freeze them as soon as they've cooled. Heat them up right from the freezer in a preheated 400°F oven and no one will guess they were anything but freshly baked.

INGREDIENTS

THE DOUGH
2 cups all-purpose flour
3 tablespoons sugar
¼ teaspoon salt
1 cup (2 sticks) unsalted butter, very cold, cut into 16 pieces
¼ cup ice water

THE FILLING
4 cups diced peeled apples (¼-inch dice, from 2 or 3 large apples)
¼ cup plus 2 teaspoons sugar
4 tablespoons (½ stick) unsalted butter, melted

1. Place the flour, sugar, and salt in a food processor and process for 10 seconds.

2. Distribute the butter evenly over the flour and pulse 40 times. Use a spatula to toss the dough so the butter is evenly distributed.

3. Pour the ice water in a steady stream through the feed tube while pulsing 20 more times. Use a spatula to toss the dough so the bottom doesn't stick. Then process for 15 seconds longer.

4. Place the dough on a work surface, and work it slightly to bring it together. Then divide it into four portions. Form each portion into a log approximately 1 to 2 inches in diameter. Wrap each log in plastic wrap, and refrigerate them for at least 2 to 3 hours or overnight.

5. When you are ready to make the galettes, preheat the oven to 400°F. Line several baking sheets with parchment paper, or grease them lightly with vegetable oil.

6. Toss the apples, 3 tablespoons plus 1 teaspoon of the sugar, and the melted butter together in a medium-size bowl. Set aside.

7. Remove one log from the refrigerator and cut it into 5 equal slices. Place each slice between two pieces of plastic wrap, and roll it out to form a round measuring 4¼ to 4½ inches in diameter.

8. Remove the dough rounds from the plastic wrap, and place them on a surface that has been lightly sprinkled with sugar.

9. Place a rounded tablespoon of the apple mixture in the center of each piece of dough, leaving a ¾- to 1-inch border around the edge. Fold the edge of the pastry over the outer edge of the apples, pleating it to make it fit. Then, using your thumb and index finger, pinch each pleat together to ensure that they will hold. The center of the apples should not be covered with dough.

10. Sprinkle a scant ¼ teaspoon of the remaining sugar over the edge of the pastry. Then place the galettes on the prepared baking sheets, leaving 1 inch between them. Repeat with the rest of the pastry and apples. When you have filled up a sheet, place the sheet in the freezer. Let the galettes freeze for 5 minutes before placing them in the oven.

11. Bake the galettes until they are crisp and golden, 30 to 35 minutes. Allow them to cool on the sheets.

12. These are best eaten the day they are made, when their texture is crispiest. If you have leftovers, place them in an airtight plastic container and refrigerate them for a day or two. To serve, recrisp them in a preheated 400°F oven for 8 to 10 minutes. For longer-term storage, freeze them; recrisp frozen galettes at 400°F for 10 to 15 minutes.

Makes 20 galettes

Almond Raspberry Gems

♥ ♥ ♥ ♥ ♥ ♥ ♥ ♥ ♥ ♥ ♥ ♥ ♥ ♥ ♥ ♥

The dazzle of these moist mini cupcakes earned them their name. They're made with lots of almond paste, filled with raspberry preserves, and crowned with an almond-flavored confectioners' sugar glaze. If you want to really gild the lily, garnish them with almond halves and raspberries.

INGREDIENTS

THE CAKE
¾ cup all-purpose flour
½ teaspoon baking powder
⅛ teaspoon salt
1 package (7 ounces) almond paste
    (not marzipan), cut into 8 pieces
1 cup minus 2 tablespoons sugar
1½ teaspoons grated lemon zest
12 tablespoons (1½ sticks) unsalted butter
    at room temperature, cut into
    12 pieces
½ teaspoon pure vanilla extract
½ teaspoon pure almond extract
4 large eggs at room temperature
Approximately 2 tablespoons raspberry
    preserves

THE GLAZE
10 tablespoons confectioners' sugar
1 teaspoon pure almond extract
1 tablespoon hot or boiling water

THE GARNISH (OPTIONAL)
18 almond halves
18 fresh raspberries

1. Preheat the oven to 350°F. Line 36 mini muffin cups with paper liners and set them aside.

2. Sift the flour, baking powder, and salt together into a small bowl and set aside.

3. Place the almond paste in a food processor, add ½ cup of the sugar, and process until the mixture looks like coarse sand, 25 seconds.

4. Add the lemon zest and pulse 5 times.

5. Scatter the butter pieces over the almond mixture and process until creamy, 40 seconds. Scrape the bowl with a rubber spatula. Then add the vanilla and almond extracts and process for 10 seconds.

6. Using an electric mixer on high speed, beat the eggs with the remaining 6 tablespoons sugar in a medium-size bowl until thick and pale, 5 to 6 minutes.

7. Sift the flour mixture over the almond paste mixture. Then pour in the egg mixture and pulse 25 quick pulses. Scrape the bowl, and then pulse 5 more times to blend. Do not overmix.

8. Place a slightly rounded teaspoon of batter in each cupcake liner. Center ⅛ teaspoon of raspberry preserves over this batter, and cover that with another slightly rounded teaspoon of batter. (The batter should reach to about ⅛ inch below the top of the cupcake liner.)

9. Bake until the cupcakes have risen and are set, 20 to 25 minutes. Let them cool in the pans.

10. Meanwhile, prepare the glaze: Place the confectioners' sugar, almond extract, and hot water in a small bowl and whisk vigorously until smooth.

11. Dip the tops of 18 cupcakes into the glaze and stand an almond half, if using, pointed end up, in the center of the top.

12. For the remaining cupcakes, use a fork or spoon to drizzle the glaze back and forth over the top. Top each of these with a fresh raspberry, if using. Allow the glaze to set for 2 to 3 hours.

13. Store the cupcakes at room temperature if you plan to eat them on the first or second day (cover them with plastic wrap if you're holding them over for day two). Otherwise refrigerate them (without the garnish) in an airtight plastic container with plastic wrap, parchment, or waxed paper between the layers, for up to 4 days. For longer storage, they can be frozen for up to 3 weeks.

Makes 36 cupcakes

Black-bottoms

❤ ❤ ❤ ❤ ❤ ❤ ❤ ❤ ❤ ❤ ❤ ❤ ❤ ❤

T he first time I heard about Black-bottoms, I was won over by the idea of a cupcake made of chocolate cake, cream cheese filling, and chocolate chips. Too bad that it tasted mediocre. Not so with this recipe, because its cake is moist and deeply chocolate. Blackbottoms are delicious when cooled just to room temperature and the chips are still soft enough to burst in your mouth.

INGREDIENTS

THE FILLING
8 ounces cream cheese at room temperature, cut into 8 pieces
¼ cup sugar
⅛ teaspoon salt
1 large egg
1 tablespoon all-purpose flour
6 ounces (1 cup) semisweet chocolate chips

THE CAKE
½ cup warm water
½ teaspoon white distilled vinegar
¾ cup all-purpose flour
3 tablespoons dark unsweetened cocoa powder
¼ teaspoon plus ⅛ teaspoon baking soda
⅛ teaspoon salt
4½ tablespoons unsalted butter at room temperature
½ cup plus 1 tablespoon sugar
½ teaspoon pure vanilla extract

1. Preheat the oven to 350°F. Line 24 mini muffin cups with paper liners.

2. Make the filling: Place all the filling ingredients except the chocolate chips in a food processor and process until completely smooth and blended, 30 seconds. Stop the processor once during the mixing to scrape the bowl with a rubber spatula.

3. Add the chips and blend by hand with a rubber spatula or wooden spoon. Set aside.

4. Make the cake: Stir the warm water and the vinegar together in a cup and set aside.

5. Sift the flour, cocoa powder, baking soda, and salt together into a small bowl and set aside.

6. Using an electric mixer on medium speed, cream the butter, sugar, and vanilla together in a medium-size bowl until light and fluffy, 1 minute. Scrape the bowl with a rubber spatula.

7. Add half the flour mixture and mix on medium speed until blended, 25 seconds, stopping the mixer once to scrape the bowl. Then scrape the bowl at the end.

8. With the mixer on low speed, add the water mixture in a stream and mix just until blended, 20 seconds, stopping the mixer once to scrape the bowl.

9. Add the remaining flour mixture and mix on low speed just until blended, 20 seconds. Stop the mixer once during the process to scrape the bowl.

10. Drop slightly rounded teaspoons of the batter into the paper cups. Then top them with rounded teaspoons of the cream cheese mixture (the cream cheese mixture should be mounded, not level).

11. Bake the blackbottoms until the tops are set and a tester inserted in the center comes out dry, 22 to 25 minutes. Cool in the pans before serving. Leave the blackbottoms at room temperature if you plan to eat them on the first day. After that, they can be stored in an airtight plastic container in the refrigerator for a day or two (with plastic wrap, parchment, or waxed paper between the layers), or you can freeze them for up to 2 weeks. Bring the blackbottoms to room temperature before serving.

Makes 24 cupcakes

Baby Cheesecakes

♥ ♥ ♥ ♥ ♥ ♥ ♥ ♥ ♥ ♥ ♥ ♥ ♥ ♥ ♥ ♥

These little cheesecakes with prebaked graham cracker crusts are made on top of the stove, then put in the refrigerator to set—which means they are a lot easier and quicker to make than the full-grown version. When you trim them with a mélange of berries, they look as stunning as they taste: the perfect ending to a dinner party.

INGREDIENTS

THE CRUST

1 cup minus 2 tablespoons graham cracker crumbs
2 tablespoons sugar
4 tablespoons (½ stick) unsalted butter, melted

THE FILLING

8 ounces cream cheese at room temperature
¼ cup sugar
2 tablespoons sour cream
½ teaspoon pure vanilla extract
2 teaspoons fresh lemon juice
6 tablespoons milk
1 teaspoon unflavored gelatin powder
1 large egg yolk

THE GARNISH

24 fresh berries (strawberries, raspberries, blueberries, blackberries, or a combination)

1. Preheat the oven to 375°F. Line 24 mini muffin cups with paper liners.

2. Place the graham cracker crumbs, sugar, and melted butter in a small bowl and toss together with a fork. The crumbs should be moistened with the butter.

3. Spoon 1 teaspoon of this mixture into each paper liner and press it down

with a finger (the mixture will naturally come a bit up the sides when you do this).

4. Place the muffin tins on the center rack of the oven and bake until the shells are crisp and golden, about 8 minutes. Remove from the oven and refrigerate.

5. Prepare the filling: Place the cream cheese, sugar, sour cream, vanilla, and lemon juice in a food processor and process until smooth, 10 seconds. Scrape the sides of the bowl with a rubber spatula.

6. Place the milk in a small saucepan, sprinkle the gelatin over it, and allow it to soften for 3 to 4 minutes, then stir with a whisk. Heat this mixture over medium heat, stirring constantly with a whisk, until it begins to boil, after about 2 minutes.

7. Add the egg yolk, break it with the whisk, and bring to a boil again, continuing to stir constantly.

8. Remove the mixture from the heat and pour it through a small strainer into the cream cheese mixture. Process for 5 seconds to blend.

9. Scoop a generous tablespoon of the cream cheese mixture into each crust-lined cup, and refrigerate until set, about 4 hours.

10. Remove the cheesecakes from the muffin tins, garnish each with a fresh berry, and serve (see step 11).

11. If not serving immediately, refrigerate the cheesecakes (without garnish) in an airtight plastic container with plastic wrap, parchment, or waxed paper between the layers for up to 2 days. For longer storage, they can be frozen for up to 2 weeks. Bring them to room temperature before garnishing and serving.

Makes 24 mini cheesecakes

Maya's Little Butter Cupcakes

♥ ♥ ♥ ♥ ♥ ♥ ♥ ♥ ♥ ♥ ♥ ♥

I named these for my daughter because they're as petite, adorable, and perfect as she is.

INGREDIENTS

THE CAKE
1 cup plus 3 tablespoons cake flour
¾ teaspoon baking powder
¼ teaspoon baking soda
¼ teaspoon salt
6 tablespoons buttermilk at room temperature
¼ cup milk at room temperature
7 tablespoons unsalted butter at room temperature
¾ cup plus 2 tablespoons sugar
1½ teaspoons pure vanilla extract
1 large egg at room temperature

THE FROSTING
½ cup heavy (whipping) cream
5 ounces bittersweet chocolate, broken into small chunks
6 tablespoons (¾ stick) unsalted butter at room temperature

1. Preheat the oven to 350°F. Line 24 mini muffin cups with paper liners.

2. Sift the flour, baking powder, baking soda, and salt together in a small bowl and set aside.

3. Stir the buttermilk and milk together in a cup and set aside.

4. With an electric mixer on medium speed, cream the butter, sugar, and vanilla together in a medium-size bowl until light and fluffy, 1 to 1½ minutes. Stop the mixer once during the process to scrape the bowl with a rubber spatula. Then scrape the bowl once again after mixing.

5. Add the egg and mix on medium speed until blended, 10 to 15 seconds. Scrape the bowl.

6. Add half the flour mixture and mix on low speed until partially blended, 10 seconds. Scrape the bowl. Then add half the milk mixture in a stream while the mixer is running on low speed, and mix just until the flour is absorbed, 5 to 10 seconds.

7. Add the remaining flour with the mixer on low speed, and blend just until the flour begins to get absorbed. Scrape the bowl. With the mixer on low speed again, add the rest of the milk mixture in a stream. Mix until smooth and velvety, about 10 seconds, stopping the mixer once to scrape the bowl.

8. Spoon rounded tablespoons of the batter into the prepared muffin cups and bake until the little cakes have risen and are set, 22 to 25 minutes.

9. Remove the cupcakes from the oven and allow them to cool in the pans.

10. If you are planning to serve the cupcakes today, prepare the frosting now (otherwise see step 14): Heat the cream in a small saucepan to the boiling point. Remove from the heat, stir in the chocolate, cover, and set aside for 5 minutes.

11. Transfer the chocolate mixture to a small bowl and refrigerate until set, 30 to 40 minutes.

12. Then add the butter to the chocolate mixture and beat until the mixture is light and fluffy, 2 to 3 minutes. Stop the mixer 3 times during the process to scrape the bowl with a rubber spatula.

13. When the cupcakes are cool, use a butter knife or a small spatula to frost the tops (use about 1½ teaspoons per cupcake); or pipe the frosting onto the cupcakes with a pastry bag fitted with a

½-inch tip. Leave the cupcakes at room temperature until serving.

14. If you do not plan to eat the cupcakes the day they are made, do not frost them. Place them on a baking sheet and cover them tightly with plastic wrap; then frost the next day. If you want to bake them further ahead of time, freeze the unfrosted cupcakes in an airtight container with plastic wrap, parchment, or waxed paper between the layers, for up to 2 weeks. Defrost them overnight before frosting and serving, so they'll be soft.

Makes 24 mini cupcakes

Coconut Fluff Babycakes

W hen I was applying to colleges, I attended a tea for prospective Wellesley students at a stunning townhouse in New York City. I remember the house, I remember being nervous, and I remember what we were served: white cake with white frosting and coconut. I didn't get into Wellesley, but no matter—that kind of cake is still my weakness. I've transformed it here into cupcakes, which I'm sure will raise all SAT scores by at least 100 points.

INGREDIENTS

THE BATTER

1 cup plus 2 tablespoons cake flour

1½ teaspoons baking powder

½ teaspoon salt

*2 tablespoons unsalted butter at room
    temperature*

2 tablespoons plus 1 teaspoon vegetable oil

¾ cup sugar

1½ teaspoons pure vanilla extract

½ cup milk

2 large egg whites

3 to 4 tablespoons fruit preserves

THE FROSTING

2 large egg whites at room temperature

6 tablespoons sugar

3 tablespoons light corn syrup

½ teaspoon pure vanilla extract

⅓ cup shredded coconut

1. Preheat the oven to 350°F. Line 24 mini muffin cups with paper liners.

2. Sift the flour with the baking powder and salt into a small bowl and set aside.

3. With an electric mixer on medium-high speed, cream the butter, oil, ½ cup of the sugar, and the vanilla in a medium-size bowl until light in color, 10 seconds. Stop the mixer once during the process to scrape the bowl with a rubber spatula.

4. Add one third of the flour mixture by stirring it in lightly with the rubber spatula. Then turn the mixer to low speed and blend partially, 5 seconds. Scrape the bowl.

5. Add half of the milk, and blend it in with several broad strokes of the spatula. Then fold in the remaining flour mixture by hand, followed by the remaining milk. Turn the mixer to low speed and blend until the batter is velvety, 5 to 10 seconds.

6. With the electric mixer on medium-high speed (and clean beaters), beat the egg whites in another bowl until frothy, 20 seconds. Gradually add the remaining ¼ cup sugar and continue beating until soft peaks form, 20 to 30 seconds.

7. Using a rubber spatula, gently fold the whites into the batter.

8. Fill each cupcake liner half full with batter. Then place ⅛ teaspoon of the preserves in the center of the batter, and fill the liner with more batter so that it reaches to ⅛ inch below the top of the liner.

9. Bake the cupcakes until they have risen and are set, 15 minutes. Set them aside to cool in the pan for 20 minutes. Then remove them from the pan and set them on wire racks to cool completely, about 40 minutes.

10. When the cupcakes have cooled, prepare the frosting (or see step 14): Place the egg whites, sugar, and corn syrup in the top of a double boiler placed over rapidly boiling water and beat with a hand-held mixer (electric or rotary) until soft peaks form, about 4 minutes.

11. Transfer the mixture to a medium-size bowl. Add the vanilla and beat with an electric mixer (whisk attachment if possible) on medium-high speed until soft peaks form again, about 30 seconds.

12. Scoop 1 tablespoon of the frosting onto each cupcake, and using a small spatula or a butter knife, spread it over the top of the cupcake.

13. Place the coconut in a small bowl, and dip the top of each cupcake lightly into the coconut. Leave the cupcakes at room temperature until serving.

14. If you do not plan to eat the cupcakes the day they are made, do not frost them. Place them on a baking sheet and cover them tightly with plastic wrap; then frost the next day. If you want to bake them further ahead of time, freeze the unfrosted cupcakes in an airtight container, with plastic wrap, parchment, or waxed paper between the layers, for up to 2 weeks. Defrost them overnight before frosting and serving, so they'll be soft.

Makes 24 cupcakes

Chocolate Babycakes

♥ ♥ ♥ ♥ ♥ ♥ ♥ ♥ ♥ ♥ ♥ ♥ ♥ ♥

Because they're practically flourless, these miniature chocolate sensations resemble a soufflé as much as a cookie. Their taste is bittersweet and their appearance lustrous, with a shiny chocolate glaze. I top each with a fresh raspberry in season and arrange them on an antique platter.

INGREDIENTS

THE CAKE
4 ounces unsweetened chocolate
6 tablespoons (¾ stick) unsalted butter at room temperature
9 tablespoons sugar
½ teaspoon pure vanilla extract
3 large eggs, separated
2 tablespoons all-purpose flour
6 tablespoons raspberry preserves

THE GLAZE
6 tablespoons heavy (whipping) cream
3 ounces bittersweet chocolate

THE TOPPING
24 fresh raspberries

1. Preheat the oven to 325°F. Grease 24 mini muffin cups with butter.

2. Melt the unsweetened chocolate in the top of a double boiler placed over simmering water. Remove it from the heat and let it cool to room temperature.

3. With an electric mixer on medium-high speed, cream the butter, 5 table-spoons of the sugar, and the vanilla in a medium-size bowl until light and fluffy, 30 seconds. Scrape the bowl with a rubber spatula.

4. Add the egg yolks and beat on medium speed until blended, 30 seconds, stopping the mixer once to scrape the bowl.

5. Add the flour on medium-low speed and blend for 15 seconds, stopping the mixer once to scrape the bowl. Then add the melted chocolate on medium speed and blend for 15 seconds, stopping the mixer once to scrape the bowl.

6. Beat the egg whites in a separate bowl on medium speed until foamy, 20 seconds. Increase the speed to medium-high and gradually add the remaining 4 tablespoons sugar, beating until the whites form firm but not dry peaks, about 45 seconds.

7. Using a rubber spatula, fold one third of the whites into the batter to loosen it. Then gently fold in the remaining whites.

8. Fill each muffin cup two-thirds full with batter. Then place a generous ¼ teaspoon of the preserves in the center of the batter, and spoon enough batter over the preserves to just fill the muffin cup.

9. Bake the babycakes until set, about 15 minutes. Cool them completely in the pan.

10. Meanwhile, prepare the glaze (or see step 12): Heat the cream in a small

saucepan to the boiling point. Remove the pan from the heat, add the chocolate, cover, and set aside for 5 minutes. When the chocolate is melted, stir with a whisk until shiny and smooth, about 5 seconds. Transfer the glaze to a small deep bowl.

11. Dip the top of each babycake into the glaze so it is well covered. Place the cakes on wire racks, and garnish the top of each one with a whole raspberry. Allow to set for 3 hours before serving, or place them in the refrigerator for 1½ hours to speed the process.

12. Serve the babycakes that day or store them overnight, uncovered, on a plate in the refrigerator. If you are making them more than 2 days ahead of time, do not frost them; freeze the un-frosted cakes in an airtight plastic container with plastic wrap, parchment, or waxed paper between the layers, for up to 2 weeks. Bring them to room temperature for glazing on serving day or the day before.

Makes about 24 babycakes

M-M-M-Madeleines

❤ ❤ ❤ ❤ ❤ ❤ ❤ ❤ ❤ ❤ ❤ ❤ ❤ ❤

S o called because they were the exact words uttered by my daughter, Maya, when she tasted these for the first time. I knew she would love them because, like me, she is a lover of basics—in this case a sweet, rich butter flavor accented with vanilla and lemon zest. It's all either of us needs to keep us happy.

INGREDIENTS

6 tablespoons (¾ stick) unsalted butter
½ cup sugar
Pinch of salt
2 large eggs at room temperature
¾ teaspoon pure vanilla extract
1 teaspoon grated lemon zest
½ cup plus 3 tablespoons cake flour, sifted

1. Preheat the oven to 375°F. Thoroughly grease 18 madeleine forms with butter, using a paper towel or a piece of plastic wrap to spread the butter into all the little grooves.

2. Melt the 6 tablespoons butter in a small saucepan over medium-low heat. Remove from the heat and allow it to cool to room temperature, 10 to 15 minutes.

3. Meanwhile, using the whisk attachment on an electric mixer, beat the sugar, salt, eggs, vanilla, and lemon zest together in a medium-size bowl until thick and pale, 4 to 5 minutes. Stop the mixer twice during the process to scrape the sides of the bowl with a rubber spatula.

4. Resift half of the flour over the egg mixture, and fold it in gently with the rubber spatula so that it is almost, but not completely, incorporated. Repeat with the remaining flour.

5. Pour the melted butter over the batter in a thin stream, folding it in with gentle strokes.

6. Scoop approximately 2 tablespoons of batter into each madeleine cup, so the batter reaches to about ⅛ inch from the top. Then jiggle the pan slightly to distribute the batter evenly.

7. Place the pans on the center rack of the oven and bake until the cakes are puffed and set, with deep golden edges, 12 to 14 minutes.

8. Cool the madeleines in the pans for 10 minutes. Then use a small spatula or butter knife to gently loosen them, and transfer them to wire racks to cool, flat side down.

9. When the madeleines are cool, place them in an airtight plastic container, layered with plastic wrap, parchment, or waxed paper, and keep them at room temperature for 2 to 3 days. (Their flavor enhances with time.) For longer storage, place the container in the freezer for up to 1 week; bring to room temperature before eating.

Makes 18 madeleines

Rosy Cranberry Tartlets

♥ ♥ ♥ ♥ ♥ ♥ ♥ ♥ ♥ ♥ ♥ ♥ ♥ ♥ ♥

Tart in shape, tart in taste, these tiny pies hold a cranberry-raisin filling inside a flaky sour cream pastry. Sprinkle them lightly with confectioners' sugar before serving.

INGREDIENTS

THE DOUGH
1⅓ cups all-purpose flour
1½ tablespoons sugar
Scant ½ teaspoon salt
10½ tablespoons (1 stick plus 2½ table-
spoons) unsalted butter, cold, cut
into 12 pieces
⅓ cup sour cream, cold

THE FILLING
1 tablespoon all-purpose flour
½ cup plus 2 tablespoons sugar
⅛ teaspoon salt
⅓ cup water
1 tablespoon plus 1 teaspoon cornstarch
1½ cups fresh cranberries
½ cup golden or dark raisins
1 teaspoon grated lemon zest
1 tablespoon unsalted butter
2 tablespoons fresh lemon juice

THE TOPPING
1 tablespoon confectioners' sugar

1. Place the flour, sugar, and salt in a food processor and process for 5 seconds.

2. Scatter the butter over the flour mixture, and pulse until the mixture resembles coarse meal, 20 to 30 pulses.

3. Distribute the sour cream evenly over the mixture, and process for 5 seconds. Scrape the bowl with a rubber spatula, then process until the liquid is evenly distributed, 10 seconds. Do not let the dough come together into a ball.

4. Place the dough on a work surface, and divide it in half. Form each half into logs about 1½ inches in diameter. Wrap each log in plastic wrap and refrigerate for 2 to 3 hours or overnight.

5. Make the filling: Combine the flour, sugar, and salt in a medium-size saucepan.

6. In a small cup, stir the water into the cornstarch. Then add this to the flour mixture, stirring it with a whisk.

7. Stir in the cranberries, raisins, and lemon zest. Cook, covered, stirring occasionally, over medium heat until the cranberries start to pop and the liquid is rosy colored and bubbling furiously, 5 minutes.

8. Remove the pan from the heat, and add the butter and lemon juice.

Stir until the butter has melted. Cool the filling in the refrigerator.

9. To make the tarts: Generously grease 24 mini muffin cups with butter. Remove one log of dough from the refrigerator and cut it into 12 equal slices. Place each slice between two pieces of plastic wrap, and roll them out to form rounds about 3¼ inches in diameter.

10. Remove the rounds from the plastic wrap and press them gently into the muffin cups, making sure not to make a hole or tear the dough. Repeat with the second log.

11. Place 1 slightly rounded teaspoon of the filling in each tart. Then fold the excess dough inward to form a ruffly crust around the edges of the cranberry mixture.

12. When all the tartlets have been made, place the pans in the freezer for 10 minutes. Preheat the oven to 425°F.

13. Remove the pans from the freezer and bake on the center rack of the oven until the pastry is a rich golden color, about 35 minutes.

14. Let the pans cool on a wire rack for 10 minutes. Then run a little butter knife around the top edge of each tart, and use the knife to gently lift the tart out of the pan. Cool the tarts completely on the rack. Before serving, sift the confectioners' sugar over the tartlets.

15. These are best eaten on the day they are baked. Otherwise, store them in an airtight plastic container in the refrigerator for a day or two or freeze them for up to 2 weeks. To serve, recrisp them in a preheated 400°F oven for 8 to 10 minutes, or if frozen, for 10 to 15 minutes.

Makes 24 tartlets

Joyce Miller's Pecan Tartlets

❤ ❤ ❤ ❤ ❤ ❤ ❤ ❤ ❤ ❤ ❤ ❤ ❤ ❤

My friend Michael Miller swears by his mother's pecan tartlets, and so does his wife, Alisa. So here they are, straight from Joyce's Long Island kitchen—sweet, crunchy, portable perfections designed for pecan pie lovers.

INGREDIENTS

THE DOUGH
1 cup all-purpose flour
2 tablespoons sugar
¼ teaspoon salt
8 tablespoons (1 stick) unsalted butter,
    cold, cut into 8 pieces
3 tablespoons cream cheese, cold

THE FILLING
½ cup (firmly packed) light brown sugar
3 tablespoons dark corn syrup
1 large egg
2 teaspoons pure vanilla extract
⅛ teaspoon salt
2 tablespoons unsalted butter, melted
Generous ¾ cup chopped pecans

1. Place the flour, sugar, and salt in a food processor and process to blend, 5 seconds.

2. Scatter the butter and cream cheese over the flour mixture, and process until the mixture is the size of small peas, 20 pulses. Then process just until the mixture comes together, 15 seconds.

3. Place the dough on a piece of plastic wrap and form it into a mass. Pinch off 24 pieces of dough and roll them into balls with the palms of your hands. Place them on a plate and refrigerate, uncovered, for 30 minutes.

4. Preheat the oven to 375°F. Lightly grease 24 mini muffin cups with butter.

5. Remove the balls from the refrigerator and flatten each one with your fingers. Press them gently into the muffin cups so that the edge of each comes ⅛ inch above the rim. Make sure not to make a hole or tear the dough. Place the pans in the refrigerator or freezer while you prepare the filling.

6. Place the brown sugar, corn syrup, egg, vanilla, salt, and melted butter in a small bowl, and whisk until smooth.

7. Remove the muffin tins from the refrigerator. Place a slightly rounded teaspoon of filling in the bottom of each cup, then spoon a generous teaspoon of nuts over the filling.

8. Bake on the center rack of the oven until the pastry is a rich golden color and the top of the filling has risen and cracked (this will happen before the pastry color is right), 25 to 30 minutes.

9. Cool the tartlets completely in the pan. Run a little butter knife around the top edge of each tart, and use the knife to gently lift the tart out of the pan.

10. These are best eaten on the day they are baked. Otherwise, store them in an airtight plastic container in the refrigerator for up to 1 week or the freezer for up to 2 weeks.

Makes 24 tartlets

Lemon Curd Tartlets

❤ ❤ ❤ ❤ ❤ ❤ ❤ ❤ ❤ ❤ ❤ ❤ ❤ ❤ ❤

Here's a mouthful of tart lemon curd held in a sweet pastry crust and finished off with a dollop of whipped cream.

INGREDIENTS

THE CRUST

1 cup all-purpose flour

3 tablespoons sugar

⅛ teaspoon salt

6 tablespoons (¾ stick) unsalted butter,
very cold, cut into 6 pieces

1 tablespoon cold water

1 large egg yolk

THE CURD

¼ teaspoon unflavored gelatin powder

⅓ cup plus 1 tablespoon fresh lemon juice

4 large egg yolks

½ cup plus 1 tablespoon sugar

1 tablespoon unsalted butter

THE TOPPING

¼ cup heavy (whipping) cream

1 tablespoon confectioners' sugar

1. Place the flour, sugar, and salt in a food processor and process for 20 seconds. (Or whisk them together by hand in a large mixing bowl.)

2. Distribute the butter evenly over the flour, and process until the mixture resembles coarse meal, 15 to 20 seconds. (Or rub the butter into the flour with your fingertips, or cut it in with a pastry blender.)

3. In a small cup, whisk together the cold water and egg yolk. With the processor running, pour the egg mixture in a steady stream through the feed tube and process just until the dough comes together, 20 to 30 seconds. (Or sprinkle the egg mixture over the flour mixture while tossing with a fork.)

4. Place the dough on a lightly floured work surface and knead it several times to bring it together.

5. Shape the dough into a thick disk, wrap it in plastic wrap, and refrigerate it for 2 hours.

6. When you are ready to roll out the dough, generously grease 18 mini muffin cups with vegetable oil.

7. Place the disk between two fresh pieces of plastic wrap and roll it out to form a 12-inch round, a generous ⅛ inch thick.

8. Using a 2½-inch cookie cutter or the rim of a glass that has been dipped in flour, cut out approximately 14 rounds. Gather up the dough scraps and reroll the dough to make an additional 4 rounds.

9. Press each round of dough into a muffin cup so that it rises about ⅛ inch above the rim. Prick the bottom once with the tines of a fork, and place the pans in the freezer for 30 minutes.

10. Meanwhile, preheat the oven to 375°F.

11. Bake the shells until they are a rich golden color with darker golden edges, 18 to 20 minutes. Set them aside while you prepare the curd.

12. Dissolve the gelatin in the lemon juice in a small bowl.

13. Using a whisk, stir the egg yolks

and sugar together in a small bowl until blended.

14. Combine the lemon juice mixture and the egg mixture in a small heavy saucepan and stir with a whisk to blend. Place the pan over medium-low heat, and stirring constantly with the whisk, bring the mixture just to the boiling point.

15. Press the mixture through a strainer into a small bowl, stir in the butter, and let it cool slightly, 15 to 20 minutes.

16. Pour the mixture into the cooled shells, and place the trays in the refrigerator so that the curd can set, about 2 hours.

17. Remove the tartlets from the refrigerator 1 hour before serving. Fifteen minutes before serving, make the topping: Place the cream and the confectioners' sugar in a small bowl, and beat with an electric mixer on medium-high speed until firm peaks form, 1 to 1½ minutes. Garnish each tartlet with a dollop of whipped cream (see step 18).

18. Do not put whipped cream on any tarts that you plan to store. Place these tarts on a plate, cover with plastic wrap, and refrigerate for up to 2 days. For longer storage, place them in an airtight plastic container with plastic wrap, parchment, or waxed paper between the layers and freeze for up to 2 weeks. Defrost the tarts and dollop with whipped cream before serving.

Makes about 18 tartlets

Rosie's Blueberry Muffins

♥ ♥ ♥ ♥ ♥ ♥ ♥ ♥

Our full-size blueberry muffins are a favorite at Rosie's. This mini version, chock full of fresh blueberries and accented with lemon zest, are a perfect little snack any time of day and a lovely teatime treat.

INGREDIENTS

THE TOPPING
1 tablespoon all-purpose flour
1 teaspoon quick-cooking oats
1½ teaspoons (lightly packed) light brown sugar
⅛ teaspoon ground cinnamon
2 teaspoons unsalted butter, cold

THE MUFFIN
½ cup plus 2 tablespoons all-purpose flour
½ cup plus 3½ tablespoons cake flour, or another ½ cup plus 2 tablespoons all-purpose flour
1½ teaspoons baking powder
¼ teaspoon salt
4 tablespoons (½ stick) unsalted butter at room temperature
5 tablespoons sugar
1¼ teaspoons pure vanilla extract
¼ teaspoon grated lemon zest
1 large or extra large egg at room temperature
5 tablespoons milk
¾ cup fresh blueberries

1. Make the topping: Place the flour, oats, brown sugar, and cinnamon in a small bowl and stir to mix with a whisk or fork.

2. Place the butter in the bowl, and using a small knife, cut it repeatedly into the dry ingredients until the mixture forms coarse crumbs. Place in the refrigerator while you prepare the muffin batter.

3. Preheat the oven to 375°F. Line 20 mini muffin cups with paper liners or grease them generously with butter or vegetable oil.

4. Sift both flours, the baking powder, and salt together into a medium-size bowl and set aside.

5. Using an electric mixer on medium speed in a medium-size bowl, cream the butter, sugar, vanilla, and lemon zest together until light and fluffy, 45 to 60 seconds.

6. Add the egg and beat for 10 seconds. Scrape the bowl with a rubber spatula. The mixture should be fairly smooth at this point.

7. Add half of the flour mixture and beat on medium-low speed for 10 seconds while adding half the milk in a stream. Scrape the bowl.

8. Repeat step 7 with the remaining flour and milk. Scrape the bowl, then turn the mixer to medium-high speed and beat until smooth, 10 seconds. Scrape the bowl again.

9. Gently fold in the blueberries with the rubber spatula. Then scoop the batter by generously rounded tablespoons into the muffin cups. Pour a little water into each of the unfilled cups in the pan to prevent burning during baking.

10. Sprinkle the topping over the muffins. Place the pans on the middle rack of the oven, and bake until the muffins are firm and lightly golden, about 17 minutes. Cool the muffins in the pan.

11. Leave the muffins at room temperature for the first day. To hold them for the following day, simply cover them with plastic wrap. To store them longer place them in an airtight container in the freezer for up to 2 weeks. Before eating, bring them to room temperature or wrap them in foil and heat them in a 275°F oven for 15 to 20 minutes.

Makes 20 muffins

Mini Eclairs
♥ ♥ ♥ ♥ ♥ ♥ ♥ ♥ ♥ ♥ ♥ ♥ ♥ ♥

Voilà! Here's the solution to the problem of how to eat éclairs so that the filling doesn't spurt out the other end: You make them bite-size and put the whole thing in your mouth at once. These miniatures have all the goodness of full-size éclairs: they're filled with custard and coated with either a bittersweet chocolate glaze or a coffee glaze.

INGREDIENTS

THE CUSTARD

1 whole large egg

1 large egg yolk

⅓ cup sugar

2 tablespoons all-purpose flour

2 tablespoons cornstarch

Pinch of salt

1¼ cups whole milk, scalded

1 tablespoon unsalted butter

½ teaspoon pure vanilla extract

THE ECLAIRS

½ cup plus 1 tablespoon all-purpose flour

½ teaspoon salt

1½ teaspoons sugar

Pinch of baking powder

½ cup water

4 tablespoons (½ stick) unsalted butter

2 large eggs at room temperature

THE CHOCOLATE GLAZE

¼ cup heavy (whipping) cream

1½ teaspoons sugar

1½ teaspoons unsalted butter

4 ounces bittersweet chocolate, finely chopped

THE COFFEE GLAZE

1¾ cups confectioners' sugar

1½ teaspoons instant coffee powder

2 tablespoons boiling water

1 tablespoon light corn syrup

¼ teaspoon pure vanilla extract

1. Make the custard: Place the whole egg, yolk, sugar, flour, cornstarch, and salt in a blender and blend for 30 seconds.

2. With the motor running, add the scalded milk through the lid hole, and blend for 5 seconds.

3. Pour this mixture into a 1-quart saucepan and bring to a boil over medium heat, stirring constantly. Let boil for 1 minute, continuing to stir.

4. Then, pour the custard mixture into a medium-size bowl, add the butter and vanilla, and stir until the butter has completely melted. Place a piece of plastic wrap directly over the surface of the custard, and refrigerate until it is cold, about 3 hours.

5. When the custard has chilled, make the éclairs: Preheat the oven to 375°F. Line two baking sheets with parchment paper, and fit a pastry bag with a ½-inch tip.

6. Sift the flour, salt, sugar, and baking powder together into a small bowl and set aside.

7. Bring the water to a boil in a medium-size saucepan over medium-high heat. Add the butter and bring to a second rolling boil. Boil for 2 to 3 minutes.

8. Remove the pan from the heat and add the flour mixture, stirring vigorously with a wooden spoon.

9. Return the pan to the stove and cook over medium heat, stirring constantly until the mixture leaves the sides of the pan and forms a ball, 1 to 2 minutes. Cook for 30 to 60 seconds more, until a slight film forms on the bottom of the pan.

10. Let the mixture cool for 1 minute. Then place it in a medium-size bowl, and using an electric mixer on medium speed, beat the dough until the steam stops rising, 1 to 1½ minutes.

11. Add the eggs one at a time, beating until glossy, about 1 minute, after each addition.

12. Transfer the dough to the pastry bag, and pipe 2-inch fingers onto the prepared baking sheets, leaving 1½ inches between éclairs.

13. Bake the éclairs until they are puffed and nicely browned, about 20 minutes. Then open the oven door, pull out the oven rack, and puncture each éclair once to allow the steam to escape (to prevent soggy éclairs). Return the éclairs to the oven for another 3 minutes. Allow them to cool completely on the baking sheets before filling, about 30 minutes.

14. Meanwhile, prepare your choice of glaze: For the chocolate glaze, place the cream, sugar, and butter in a small saucepan and bring to a boil over medium heat, stirring with a wooden spoon, 3 to 4 minutes. Remove from the heat. Add the chocolate, and stir until it has melted and the mixture is smooth and shiny.

15. To make the coffee glaze, sift the confectioners' sugar into a medium-size bowl. Dissolve the coffee powder in the boiling water in a small bowl. Then mix in the corn syrup and vanilla. Pour this mixture into the center of the confec-

tioners' sugar, and whisk vigorously until smooth. If the glaze seems too thick, add an additional teaspoon of hot water until the mixture is a good spreading consistency.

16. Finish the éclairs: Have ready a pastry bag fitted with a ½-inch tip. Spread sheets of parchment or waxed paper on a work surface. Using a sharp serrated knife, cut off the top third of each éclair. Dip these tops in the glaze, and set them aside on the parchment paper to dry.

17. Fill the pastry bag with custard, and pipe a line of custard down the middle of each éclair bottom.

18. Set the dry tops gently on top of the filling. Serve immediately or within several hours for the best results.

Makes 30 éclairs

Note: The glaze should be warm when you dip the éclair tops into it. If it has cooled, place the bowl of glaze in a larger bowl of hot water, and stir to loosen it.

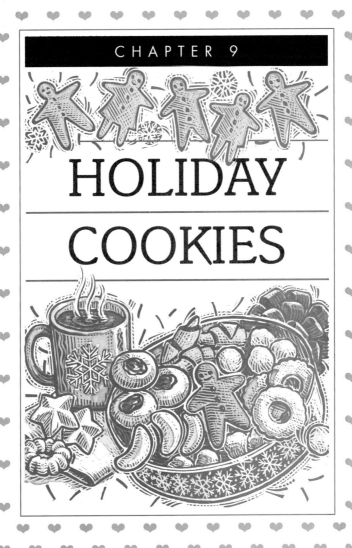

CHAPTER 9

HOLIDAY

COOKIES

Molasses Ginger Cookies

Jan Hagels

Gingerbread People

Orange Pecan Ginger Florentines

Almond Chocolate Praline Crisps

Pecan Crescents

Vanilla Kipfel

Butter Wreaths

Classic Spritzes

Dutch Almond Butter Rings

Mini Fruit Cakes

Chocolate Snowballs

Oatmeal Thumbprints

Classic Sugar Cookies

Poppyseed Hamantaschen

Cream Cheese Rugalach

Sour Cream Rugalach

Buttermilk Doughnut Holes

The Marks's Matzoh Crunch

O f course I'm partial to holiday baking. After all, were it not for those heart-shaped Valentine's Day sugar cookies so long ago, Rosie's might never have existed. Any holiday is an excuse for me to bake—although *my* personal baking doesn't usually begin until the night before the big day, after I'm freed from a week of hustle and bustle at the bakery.

For many people, holidays are the most fun time of the year for pulling out the baking sheets. It's an important part of the family ritual and joins us all together—moms, dads, sisters, brothers, cousins, aunts, uncles, grandparents—in joyous anticipation of the upcoming day.

There is no cookie that cannot be baked for any holiday (other than Passover, when flour is not permitted), but certain cookies have come to symbolize particular holidays. What is Christmas without gingerbread people,

Valentine's Day without sugar cookies, Purim without hamantaschen? We favor the shapes and flavors that we remember from our childhood, so it is always important to include those in our holiday fare.

Cookies can be wonderful gifts, expressions of our love. What a heartwarming feeling it is when a friend bestows on you a Christmas tin filled with cookies they have made or when a Purim basket filled with fruits and nuts and hamantaschen is left on your doorstep. Have you not cherished a sugar cookie heart given to you by your sweetheart?

So open up your cupboard around holiday time, don your favorite apron, get out your mixing bowls, and pass the spirit of holiday joy on to friends and family.

Molasses Ginger Cookies

❤ ❤ ❤ ❤ ❤ ❤ ❤ ❤ ❤ ❤ *drop cookie*

Divinely chewy in the center, crunchy around the edges, dark and gingery with a strong molasses flavor, these are a perfect cookie for the night before Christmas. Just be sure to leave some out for Santa.

INGREDIENTS

2 cups all-purpose flour
1 teaspoon baking soda
1 tablespoon ground ginger
2½ teaspoons ground cinnamon
¾ teaspoon ground nutmeg
¾ teaspoon ground cloves
½ teaspoon ground allspice
¾ teaspoon salt
*12 tablespoons (1½ sticks) unsalted butter
    at room temperature*
1 cup granulated sugar
¼ cup (lightly packed) dark brown sugar
¼ cup dark molasses
1 large egg

1. Preheat the oven to 375°F. Line several baking sheets with parchment paper, or grease them lightly with vegetable oil.

2. Sift the flour, baking soda, all of the spices, and salt together into a small bowl and set aside.

3. Using an electric mixer on medium speed, cream the butter and both sugars together until light and fluffy, 1 minute. Scrape the bowl with a rubber spatula.

4. Add the molasses and mix until blended, 10 seconds. Scrape the bowl. Then add the egg and mix until it is incorporated, 10 seconds.

5. Add the flour mixture and blend on low speed for 15 seconds. Stop the mixer to scrape the bowl, and then blend until the dough is smooth, about 5 seconds more.

6. Drop the dough by heaping tablespoons 2 inches apart onto the prepared baking sheets. Bake the cookies until they are still slightly soft, 15 to 16 minutes. Let them cool completely on the baking sheets.

7. If you plan to snack on them the first day, leave the cookies out on the baking sheet or on a plate. After that, place them in an airtight plastic container with plastic wrap, parchment, or waxed paper between the layers, and store them in the freezer for up to 2 weeks. Bring the cookies to room temperature before eating.

Makes about 16 cookies

Jan Hagels

♥ ♥ ♥ ♥ ♥ ♥ ♥ ♥ ♥ *rolled cookie*

Taste is one of the most evocative senses, and these cookies are among the most evocative I know. They conjure up visions of a wintry Christmas Eve—thin, buttery, and loaded with spices—perfect for snuggling in front of a fire with a mug of hot cider and a plate of these delicacies (and maybe a person to snuggle with, so long as he doesn't eat too many of your cookies).

INGREDIENTS

THE COOKIE
2¼ cups plus 3 tablespoons all-purpose
    flour
¾ teaspoon salt
2¼ teaspoons ground cinnamon
¾ teaspoon ground cloves
1 cup (2 sticks) plus 2 tablespoons unsalted
    butter at room temperature
½ cup plus 1 tablespoon (lightly packed)
    light brown sugar
½ cup plus 1 tablespoon granulated sugar

THE GLAZE
1 large egg white
½ cup slivered almonds, coarsely chopped

1. Sift the flour, salt, and both of the spices together into a bowl and set aside.

2. Using an electric mixer on medium speed, cream the butter and both sugars together in a medium-size bowl until light and fluffy, about 1 minute. Scrape the bowl.

3. Add the flour mixture and mix on low speed for 20 seconds. Scrape the bowl. Then turn the mixer to medium speed and beat just until the dough is blended, about 15 seconds.

4. Turn the dough out onto a work surface and knead it with your hands for several seconds so that it comes together just a bit more.

5. Divide the dough in half, form each half into a slab, and wrap them in plastic wrap. Refrigerate for 2 to 3 hours.

6. Fifteen minutes before baking, preheat the oven to 350°F. Line two baking sheets with parchment paper, or grease them lightly with vegetable oil.

7. Remove the dough from the refrigerator and roll each slab out between two fresh pieces of plastic wrap to form a rough rectangle ⅛ inch thick and approximately 15×10 inches.

8. Remove the plastic wrap and transfer each rectangle to a baking sheet. Using a pastry brush, glaze the rectangles with the egg white, and sprinkle the almonds over the glaze.

9. Bake until golden with darkening edges, about 20 minutes. Remove the baking sheets from the oven, and reduce the oven temperature to 325°F. Cut each rectangle, still on the sheets, into 24 pieces (4 lengthwise slices, then 6 crosswise slices), and return them to the oven. Bake until a deeper golden

color, about 15 minutes. Let the cookies cool completely on the baking sheets.

10. Store the cookies in an airtight plastic container for a day or two at room temperature if you think you will be snacking on them. After that, store the container in the freezer for up to 2 weeks. Bring the cookies to room temperature before eating.

Makes 48 cookies

Gingerbread People

❤ ❤ ❤ ❤ ❤ ❤ ❤ ❤ *rolled cookie*

It's hard to improve on this classic recipe, or on the classic shape of pudgy little people in their three-button uniforms. My kids love them; they are a part of our holiday ritual each winter. Sometimes we poke little holes in them before we bake them, so they can be displayed as ornaments on a Christmas tree. Despite their name, this dough can be used to cut out all kinds of shapes, depending on the time of year or simply the mood you're in!

INGREDIENTS

THE COOKIE
2 tablespoons dark molasses
1 tablespoon water
1 large whole egg
3¼ cups all-purpose flour
1 teaspoon baking soda
½ teaspoon salt
1½ cups (lightly packed) light brown sugar
1½ tablespoons grated orange zest
2 teaspoons ground cinnamon
1 tablespoon ground ginger
½ teaspoon ground cloves
¼ teaspoon ground nutmeg
1 cup (2 sticks) unsalted butter, cold, cut into 16 pieces

THE DECORATIONS
Currants
Red-hot cinnamon candies

THE ICING
2¾ cups sifted confectioners' sugar, plus 2 tablespoons if needed
2 large egg whites at room temperature

1. Using a whisk, vigorously stir the molasses, water, and egg together in a small bowl or cup, and set aside.

2. Place the flour, baking soda, salt, brown sugar, orange zest, and all of the spices in a food processor and process for 10 seconds.

3. Distribute the butter over the flour mixture, and process until the dough resembles coarse meal, about 30 seconds.

4. Pour the molasses mixture over the flour mixture, and process just until the dough comes together, about 35 seconds.

5. Remove the dough from the processor, place it on a work surface, and knead it for several seconds.

6. Divide the dough into two slabs, wrap each in plastic wrap, and refrigerate for 1 to 2 hours.

7. When you're ready to bake the cookies, preheat the oven to 350°F. Line several baking sheets with parchment paper.

8. Remove one slab of dough from the refrigerator and place it between two new pieces of plastic wrap. Roll it out ⅛ inch thick.

9. Remove the top piece of plastic wrap, and using a 5-inch cookie cutter, cut out as many "people" as you can. Using a spatula, place the cookies on a prepared baking sheet, leaving about 1 inch between them. Place currants for the eyes and little cinnamon candies for buttons and the mouth, pressing them down slightly into the dough.

10. Repeat with the second slab. Then reroll the scraps and repeat with that dough.

11. Place the cookies in the oven and bake until firm, 12 to 14 minutes. Cool completely on the baking sheet or on wire racks.

12. While the cookies are cooling, prepare the icing: Place a writing tip on a pastry bag. Set the bag in a tall glass, tip side down, and set it aside. Place the confectioners' sugar and the egg whites in a medium-size bowl, and beat with the paddle attachment on low speed for 30 seconds. Then change to medium-high speed and beat until smooth, 3 minutes. The icing should be stiff enough to pipe. If it's not, add up to 2 tablespoons additional confectioners' sugar.

13. Fill the bag with the icing and pipe decorations, as desired, onto the completely cooled cookies. Allow the icing to set for several hours.

14. Although it's hard to imagine that there would be any gingerbread people left over with kids around, leave the cookies out for a day so the glaze is totally hard, then store them at room temperature for 1 week in an airtight plastic container with plastic wrap, parchment, or waxed paper between the layers. If they are not frosted, the gingerbread people can be stored at room temperature for up to 1 week or frozen for up to 2 weeks.

Makes about fifteen 5-inch-tall gingerbread people

Orange Pecan Ginger Florentines

♥ ♥ ♥ ♥ ♥ ♥ ♥ ♥ ♥ ♥ *drop cookie*

Most kids loathe florentines. For starters, they're full of nuts, and then, even if you can pick those out, they still have red and yellow things and bumpy little bits. One of the benefits of adulthood is that you can change your mind, which in this case is a distinct advantage because these lacelike caramel crunch cookies, full of almonds, candied ginger, and orange peel, are as divine as the city they're named after and a perfect festive treat at Christmas. Glaze them with chocolate as the recipe suggests, or eat them unadorned. Either way, you'll be a convert.

INGREDIENTS

THE COOKIE

⅓ cup chopped candied orange peel
    (¼-inch pieces)
1 cup plus 1 tablespoon very finely chopped
    almonds
¼ cup whole almonds, sliced in thirds
⅓ cup chopped crystallized ginger
¼ cup all-purpose flour
3 tablespoons unsalted butter
6 tablespoons plus 2 teaspoons sugar
6 tablespoons plus 2 teaspoons heavy
    (whipping) cream
3 scant tablespoons good-quality honey
¼ cup light corn syrup

THE GLAZE

6 or 12 ounces bittersweet or semisweet
    chocolate (see Note)

1. Preheat the oven to 350°F. Line 3 baking sheets with parchment paper (do not grease).

2. Place the candied orange peel, chopped and sliced almonds, and crystallized ginger in a medium-size bowl.

3. Sift the flour over the fruit-nut mixture, and toss to coat. Set aside.

4. Combine the butter, sugar, cream, honey, and corn syrup in a medium-size heavy saucepan and place over low heat. Stirring constantly, bring the mixture to a boil and boil for 1 minute. Remove from the heat.

5. Add the fruit-nut mixture to the butter mixture, and stir with a wooden spoon just to evenly coat.

6. Drop the batter by rounded teaspoons onto the prepared baking sheets, placing only 5 cookies on each sheet.

7. Dip a fork in water, and use it (redipping as needed) to flatten each cookie so it is 2 inches in diameter.

8. Bake the cookies until they are bubbling all over and golden in color, 11 to 13 minutes.

9. Let the cookies cool slightly on the baking sheets, and then remove the paper and transfer to a wire rack. Allow the cookies to cool completely. Then carefully remove the cookies from the paper by hand. Repeat with the remaining batter.

10. Meanwhile, prepare the glaze: Melt the chocolate in the top of a double boiler placed over simmering water. Remove from the heat and allow to cool to spreading consistency.

11. Using a frosting spatula, spread the bottom of each cookie with ¾ teaspoon of the melted chocolate; then make a fancy design by running the tines of a fork over the chocolate in a zigzag pattern.

12. Set the cookies aside, chocolate side up, on wire racks for the glaze to set, about 3 hours; or place them in the refrigerator or freezer for 1 hour to set quickly.

13. It's really best to eat these the day they're made in order to enjoy them at their peak of crispness. If this isn't possible, layer them in an airtight plastic container with plastic wrap, parchment, or waxed paper between the layers. They will keep this way for 2 days at room temperature and for up to 1 week if frozen.

Makes about 25 cookies

Note: If you prefer less chocolate on your cookie, use only 6 ounces and using a spoon, drizzle the chocolate in a crisscross pattern on the bottom of the cookies.

Almond Chocolate Praline Crisps

❤ ❤ ❤ ❤ ❤ ❤ ❤ ❤ ❤ *drop cookie*

This is a cookie that should be served to you in a fancy restaurant as an accent to a gourmet dinner—on New Year's Eve, perhaps—and yet these lacelike toffee wafers, studded with almonds and sandwiched with chocolate, are surprisingly easy to make. Just watch them carefully while they're baking, because they burn easily.

INGREDIENTS

THE COOKIE
8 tablespoons (1 stick) unsalted butter
1¼ cups chopped almonds
½ cup sugar
2 tablespoons all-purpose flour
3 tablespoons milk
¼ teaspoon pure vanilla extract

THE FILLING
4 ounces bittersweet chocolate, melted

1. Preheat the oven to 400°F. Line several baking sheets with parchment paper (do not grease).

2. Melt the butter in a small saucepan over low heat. Then add the almonds, sugar, flour, milk, and vanilla. Bring the mixture to a simmer and remove from the heat. Allow it to sit for 5 to 10 minutes.

3. Drop the batter by teaspoons onto the prepared baking sheets, spacing them about 4 inches apart. Bake until the cookies are deep golden, 7 to 8 minutes (watch carefully—they burn easily).

4. Remove the cookies from the oven and allow them to cool on the sheets for 1 minute. Then transfer the cookies to wire racks to cool.

5. When they are completely cooled, turn half the cookies upside down and spread the bottoms with ½ teaspoon of chocolate each. Top them with the re-maining cookies. Refrigerate until the chocolate is set, about 2 hours.

6. It's really best to eat these the day they're made in order to enjoy them at their peak of crispness. If this isn't pos-sible, layer them in an airtight plastic container with plastic wrap, parch-ment, or waxed paper between the lay-ers. They will keep this way for 2 days at room temperature and for up to 1 week if frozen.

Makes about 18 cookie sandwiches

Pecan Crescents

❤ ❤ ❤ ❤ ❤ ❤ ❤ ❤ *formed cookie*

C rispy. Crunchy. Buttery. These cookies, made with lots of ground pecans, have all the bases covered. They are wonderful choices to pack in holiday tins. And, oh, did I mention that they melt in your mouth?

INGREDIENTS

THE COOKIE
2 cups all-purpose flour
½ teaspoon salt
½ teaspoon ground cinnamon
*1 cup (2 sticks) unsalted butter at room
    temperature*
⅓ cup plus 1 tablespoon sugar
1½ teaspoons pure vanilla extract
1½ cups finely ground pecans

THE COATING
½ cup sugar
1 teaspoon ground cinnamon

1. Preheat the oven to 325°F. Line several baking sheets with parchment paper, or grease them lightly with vegetable oil.

2. Sift the flour, salt, and cinnamon together into a small bowl and set aside.

3. Using an electric mixer on medium speed, cream the butter, sugar, and vanilla in a medium-size bowl until the ingredients are light and fluffy, about 4 minutes. Scrape the bowl with a rubber spatula.

4. Add the flour mixture and the pecans, and beat on medium-low speed for 20 seconds. Scrape the bowl. Then beat until the flour and nuts are completely incorporated, about 15 seconds.

5. Break off generously rounded teaspoons of the dough, and roll them between your palms to form crescents.

6. In a small bowl, stir together the sugar and cinnamon for the coating. Dip the cookies in the coating and place them 2 inches apart on the prepared baking sheets.

7. Bake the cookies until they are lightly golden and firm to the touch, 30 minutes. Cool completely on the sheets.

8. Store these cookies in an airtight plastic container at room temperature for up to 3 days. They become even more delicious as the flavors have a chance to meld. Or freeze for up to 2 weeks.

Makes about 48 cookies

Vanilla Kipfel

♥ ♥ ♥ ♥ ♥ ♥ ♥ ♥ ♥ *formed cookie*

When I was a little girl, my mother knew a German dressmaker named Martha, who

made the most unbelievable vanilla kipfel—nutty, buttery crescents rolled in vanilla sugar—and presented them to us every Christmas in a decorative tin. I hoped to get the recipe from her, but learned to my regret that she had passed away. So here is my homage to Martha; my attempt to re-create those childhood treats in honor of a fine dressmaker and a fine baker. These make a wonderful gift for the holidays and store beautifully in an airtight tin, the vanilla sugar flavor permeating the cookies more and more each day.

INGREDIENTS

6 tablespoons granulated sugar
2 vanilla beans, each approximately
9 inches long
1½ cups whole unblanched almonds
1¼ cups all-purpose flour
1 teaspoon salt
12 tablespoons (1½ sticks) unsalted butter, cold, cut into 12 pieces
2 large egg yolks, lightly beaten
1½ cups confectioners' sugar or vanilla sugar, sifted (see Note)

1. Preheat the oven to 325°F. Line several baking sheets with parchment paper, or grease them lightly with vegetable oil.

2. Place the granulated sugar in a small bowl. Split the vanilla beans open lengthwise. Using the point of a knife, gently scrape the seeds into the bowl of sugar.

3. Place the almonds in a food processor and process till fine, 45 seconds; do not overprocess. Add the sugar mixture, flour, and salt, and process to mix, 5 seconds.

4. Scatter the butter pieces over the flour mixture and process until the dough resembles coarse meal, 15 seconds.

5. With the processor running, pour the yolks through the feed tube. Stop the processor, then pulse 5 times. Scrape the bowl with a rubber spatula, and then process until the dough comes together, 5 to 10 seconds.

6. Pinch off tablespoons of the dough and form each of them into crescents. Place the crescents 1½ inches apart on the prepared baking sheets, and bake until firm and just beginning to turn golden, 30 minutes. (To test for doneness, remove a cookie from the sheet and cut it in half. The center should not be doughy.)

7. Allow the cookies to cool for 5 to 10 minutes on the baking sheets. Then roll them in the confectioners' sugar, and set them on wire racks to cool completely before eating.

8. Store the cookies in an airtight plastic container at room temperature for a day or two if you think you will be snacking on them. After that, store the container in the freezer for up to 2 weeks. Bring the cookies to room temperature before eating.

Makes about 36 cookies

Note: To make vanilla sugar, place a whole vanilla bean in 3 to 4 cups granulated sugar and let it sit for a minimum of 1 week.

Butter Wreaths

♥ ♥ ♥ ♥ ♥ ♥ ♥ ♥   *rolled cookie*

These little wreaths made of crispy puff pastry literally melt in your mouth. Their flaky texture is best the first day, so if you're planning to serve them for Christmas dinner, prepare the dough up to two days ahead and then bake them on the day you'll be eating them.

INGREDIENTS

THE COOKIE
2 cups all-purpose flour
⅛ teaspoon salt
3 tablespoons sugar
8 tablespoons (1 stick) unsalted butter, cold, cut into 8 pieces
⅓ cup ice water

THE GLAZE
1 large egg, beaten with a fork
½ cup sugar in a small bowl

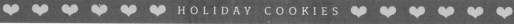

1. Place the flour, salt, and 3 tablespoons sugar in a food processor and process for 5 seconds.

2. Distribute the butter over the flour mixture, and pulse 25 to 30 times, until the mixture resembles coarse crumbs. Scrape the bowl with a rubber spatula.

3. With the machine running, pour the water in a stream through the feed tube. Then pulse quickly several times just to distribute.

4. Place the dough (it will be crumbly) on a work surface, and press it just enough to form a rough 6-inch square. Wrap it in plastic wrap, and refrigerate for 1 hour.

5. Remove the dough from the refrigerator and leave it at room temperature for 20 to 30 minutes, until it becomes workable. Place it between two fresh pieces of plastic wrap, and roll it out to a 12-inch square. Remove the top piece of plastic wrap.

6. Take the right-hand third of the dough and fold it over the middle third: then take that double thickness and fold it over again onto the remaining third so that you have a 4 × 12-inch rectangle that is three folds deep. Rewrap in plastic and refrigerate for about 3 hours.

7. When you are ready to bake the cookies, remove the dough from the refrigerator and leave it at room temperature for 20 to 30 minutes. Preheat the oven to 450°F. Line several baking sheets with parchment paper, or grease them lightly with vegetable oil.

8. Roll the dough out ⅛ inch thick. Using a 2½- or 2¾-inch cookie cutter with a hole in the center, or a doughnut cutter, cut out the cookies. (If you do not have either of these, use a round cookie cutter to make the cookies, and then use a metal bottle cap to cut out the center hole.) Discard the scraps.

9. Place the cookies 1½ inches apart on the prepared baking sheets, and place the hole cutouts on the sheets too. Cover the baking sheets with plastic wrap, and refrigerate for 15 minutes.

10. Remove one baking sheet from the refrigerator, and using a pastry brush, glaze each cookie wreath and hole with some of the beaten egg. Turn the cookies upside down into the bowl of sugar, and place them back on the sheet, sugar side up. Place the sheet on the center rack of the oven and bake until the cookies are a rich golden color, about 12 minutes. Repeat with the remaining cookies.

11. Cool the cookies completely on the baking sheets.

12. Try to eat these the first day; the delicate flaky texture can't sustain itself much longer than that. If need be, place them in an airtight plastic container and leave them at room temperature for a day or two.

Makes about 30 cookies (wreaths and holes)

473

Classic Spritzes

❤ ❤ ❤ ❤ ❤ ❤ ❤ ❤ *piped cookie*

Spritzes are great holiday cookies because they can be squeezed into an endless number of festive shapes. You can also sandwich them with chocolate, or sandwich them with jam and then dip half the cookie in melted chocolate. As I worked on this recipe, I discovered that spritzes made with vegetable shortening hold their shape and thickness best, but that spritzes made with butter taste better, even if they spread and flatten out a little more. For the best results, be sure to cream the butter and sugar so the dough is soft enough to squeeze through the press (use whatever decorative tip you like). If you don't have a press, scoop the batter out by the teaspoonful and flatten them slightly before baking.

INGREDIENTS

1 whole large egg
1 large egg yolk
2¼ cups plus 2 tablespoons all-purpose
    flour
1¼ teaspoons baking powder
¼ teaspoon salt
1 cup (2 sticks) unsalted butter at room
    temperature
1 cup confectioners' sugar
¼ cup granulated sugar
2 teaspoons pure vanilla extract
1 teaspoon grated lemon zest

1. Preheat the oven to 350°F. Line several baking sheets with parchment paper, or grease them lightly with vegetable oil.

2. Stir the egg and the yolk together in a cup and set aside.

3. Sift the flour, baking powder, and salt together in a small bowl and set aside.

4. Using an electric mixer on medium speed, cream the butter, both sugars, vanilla, and lemon zest together in a medium-size mixing bowl until fluffy, 1 to 1½ minutes. Scrape the bowl with a rubber spatula.

5. Add the flour mixture and continue to mix on medium speed until thoroughly blended, 3 minutes, stopping the mixer once to scrape the bowl.

6. With the mixer on medium-low speed, add the egg mixture and mix until blended, 30 seconds. Stop the mixer once to scrape the bowl.

7. Feed the dough into the cookie press and press the cookies out onto the prepared baking sheets, leaving 1 inch between them.

8. Bake the cookies for 10 minutes. Then lower the oven temperature to 325°F and bake until they are firm and lightly golden around the bottom edge. The baking time will vary depending on their shape, but the range will probably be 16 to 22 minutes. Cool the cookies on the baking sheets.

9. If you plan to snack on them the first day, leave the cookies out on the baking sheet or on a plate. After that, place them in an airtight plastic container and store them in the freezer for up to 2 weeks. Bring the cookies to room temperature before eating.

Makes 60 to 70 cookies

Dutch Almond Butter Rings

♥ ♥ ♥ ♥ ♥ ♥ ♥ ♥ ♥ *piped cookie*

It seems only appropriate that our word "cookie" comes from the Dutch word *koekje,* since the Dutch have given the world some of its most glorious butter delicacies. The recipe for this crisp piped cookie with its brittle caramel center is an adaptation of a recipe from Corrie Wittenberg, owner of the noteworthy Bakery Butter in Zaandam, who generously shared her knowledge with my recipe tester, Beverly Jones, when she last visited the Netherlands.

INGREDIENTS

THE FILLING
3½ tablespoons unsalted butter at room
 temperature
6 tablespoons confectioners' sugar
3 tablespoons light corn syrup
½ cup slivered or sliced almonds

THE COOKIE
1 cup plus 1 tablespoon sifted all-purpose
 flour
1 teaspoon salt
7 tablespoons unsalted butter at room
 temperature
¾ cup plus 2 tablespoons confectioners'
 sugar, sifted
¼ cup egg whites (about 2 large eggs)
1 teaspoon pure vanilla extract

THE TOPPING
Generous ½ cup crushed sliced almonds

1. Make the filling: Using an electric mixer on medium speed, cream the butter, confectioners' sugar, and corn syrup together in a small bowl until blended. Add the slivered almonds and blend until they are broken up.

2. Preheat the oven to 350°F. Line several baking sheets with parchment paper, and fit a pastry bag with a ¼-inch tip.

3. Make the cookie dough: Sift the flour and salt together into a small bowl and set aside.

4. Using the mixer on medium-high speed, cream the butter, confectioners' sugar, egg whites, and vanilla in a medium-size bowl until smooth, 30 seconds. Stop the mixer twice during the process to scrape the bowl with a rubber spatula.

5. Sift the flour mixture over the butter mixture and mix on low speed just until blended, 5 seconds. Scrape the bowl, then blend for several seconds. Fill the pastry bag with the dough.

6. Pipe the dough onto the prepared baking sheets, forming 1½-inch-diameter circles 1½ inches apart. Drop ½ teaspoon of the almond filling in the center of each circle, and sprinkle each cookie with ½ teaspoon of the crushed almonds.

7. Bake the cookies on the center rack of the oven until the filling is brown and bubbling and the edges of the cookies are golden brown, 12 to 14 minutes.

8. Allow the cookies to cool on the baking sheets. Then carefully remove them with a spatula.

9. Store the cookies in an airtight plastic container at room temperature for a day or two if you think you will be snacking on them. After that, store the container in the freezer for up to 2 weeks. Bring the cookies to room temperature before eating.

Makes about 50 cookies

Mini Fruit Cakes

❤ ❤ ❤ ❤ ❤ ❤ ❤ ❤ ❤ *tidbit cookie*

These miniature cakes are jammed with rum-soaked fruit, then glazed twice with more rum. Add them to Christmas cookie tins or holiday dessert platters and I guarantee that they'll be appreciated more than their full-size counterparts. If you can, soak the fruit for 3 to 5 days, tossing it occasionally, before preparing the fruitcakes.

INGREDIENTS

THE CAKE
*10 ounces assorted dried fruit (raisins,
     cranberries, apricots, dates, etc.), cut
     into ¼-inch pieces (about 2 cups)*
1 cup rum or brandy
½ cup boiling water
1 cup plus 3 tablespoons all-purpose flour
⅜ teaspoon baking soda
⅜ teaspoon ground cinnamon
⅜ teaspoon ground cloves
⅜ teaspoon ground mace
⅜ teaspoon ground allspice
¼ teaspoon salt
*10 tablespoons (1¼ sticks) unsalted butter
     at room temperature*
½ cup granulated sugar
½ cup (lightly packed) light brown sugar
½ teaspoon pure vanilla extract
1½ teaspoons grated lemon or orange zest
2 tablespoons molasses
2 large eggs
½ cup chopped pecans (¼-inch pieces)
½ cup chopped almonds (¼-inch pieces)

THE GLAZE

1 tablespoon plus 1 teaspoon granulated
  sugar
½ cup rum or brandy

THE FROSTING

¾ cup confectioners' sugar
2 tablespoons plus ¾ teaspoon rum or
  brandy

1. Combine the dried fruits and the rum in a small bowl, cover, and allow to sit for 8 hours, tossing occasionally. Then add the boiling water, toss, and allow to sit for at least 1½ to 2 days, or up to 5 days.

2. Preheat the oven to 350°F. Generously grease 36 mini muffin cups with butter.

3. Sift the flour, baking soda, all of the spices, and salt together into a small bowl and set aside.

4. With an electric mixer on medium speed, beat the butter, both sugars, vanilla, and zest in a medium-size bowl until light and fluffy, about 1 minute. Scrape the bowl with a rubber spatula.

5. Add the molasses and beat on medium speed until incorporated, 10 seconds.

6. Add the eggs one at a time, mixing on low speed after each addition for 10 seconds. Scrape the bowl each time.

7. Drain the fruits and pat them dry.

8. Add the flour mixture to the butter mixture and mix until blended, 10 seconds. Scrape the bowl, then mix 5 seconds more.

9. Add the dried fruits and both nuts, and blend by hand with a rubber spatula.

10. Spoon the batter into the muffin cups so that it is slightly mounded (see Note). Bake the mini-fruitcakes until puffed and set, 25 to 30 minutes.

11. Allow the fruitcakes to cool in the pan for 20 minutes. Then run a small butter knife around the edge of each muffin to loosen it slightly, and gently remove them from the pan. Place the muffins on a rack or plate.

12. Meanwhile, make the glaze: Place the sugar and the rum in a small bowl, and stir to dissolve the sugar.

13. Using a small pastry brush, paint all sides of the mini cakes with the glaze.

14. Make the frosting: Place the confectioners' sugar and rum in a small bowl, and whisk vigorously until creamy.

15. Turn each fruitcake upside down and dip its top in the frosting. Then turn it right side up and allow to set for 1 hour.

16. Leave the fruitcakes on a plate, uncovered, if you plan on snacking on them the first day. To store longer, layer them in an airtight plastic container with plastic wrap, parchment, or waxed paper between the layers and place in the refrigerator for up to 1 week or the freezer for up to 2 weeks.

Makes about 36 fruitcakes

Note: If you do not have enough batter to fill all the cups, pour a little water into each unused cup to prevent burning during baking.

Chocolate Snowballs

♥ ♥ ♥ ♥ ♥ ♥ ♥ ♥   *formed cookie*

A chocolate version of Mexican wedding cakes—those rich little balls of butter, sugar, flour, and pecans rolled in powdered sugar. I've substituted chocolate for the nuts and rolled them in cocoa.

INGREDIENTS

2 cups sifted all-purpose flour
½ cup plus 1 tablespoon granulated sugar
½ cup plus 2 tablespoons unsweetened
    cocoa powder
1 teaspoon instant coffee powder
14 tablespoons (1¾ sticks) unsalted butter
    at room temperature, cut into 10
    pieces
1 large egg yolk
3 ounces (½ cup) semisweet chocolate
    chips
5 tablespoons confectioners' sugar

1. Preheat the oven to 350°F. Line several baking sheets with parchment paper, or grease them lightly with vegetable oil.

2. Place the flour, granulated sugar, ¼ cup of the cocoa, and the coffee powder in a food processor and process for 10 seconds.

3. Scatter the butter over the flour mixture and process until the mixture resembles coarse crumbs, 15 seconds.

4. While the machine is running, add the egg yolk through the feed tube. Then pulse 15 times until it is incorporated. Scrape the bowl with a rubber spatula.

5. Add the chips and process 5 seconds more.

6. Measure out rounded teaspoons of the dough, and roll them into balls with your hands. Place them 2 inches apart on the prepared baking sheets.

7. Bake the cookies until they are firm to the touch, about 24 minutes. Allow them to cool on the baking sheets.

8. Meanwhile, sift the remaining ¼ cup plus 2 tablespoons cocoa and the confectioners' sugar together into a small bowl. Then transfer to a plastic bag.

9. Place 2 or 3 cookies at a time in the bag and shake the bag gently to coat them with the mixture.

10. If you plan to snack on them the first day, leave the cookies out on the baking sheet or on a plate. After that, place them in an airtight plastic container with plastic wrap, parchment, or waxed paper between the layers, and store them in the freezer for up to 2 weeks. Bring the cookies to room temperature before eating.

Makes about 60 cookies

Oatmeal Thumbprints

❤ ❤ ❤ ❤ ❤ ❤ ❤ ❤ ❤ *formed cookie*

Prominent among cookie classics are these small butter cookies with their red jam centers—a festive holiday treat for Valentine's Day or Christmas. For this version I've kept that bright dollop of color and taste but added oats to the batter, which makes the cookies just a little bit heartier. Have no fear, though: they have the same melt-in-your-mouth quality as the originals.

INGREDIENTS

1 cup (2 sticks) unsalted butter at room temperature
½ cup plus 2 tablespoons sugar
2 teaspoons pure vanilla extract
1 cup plus 2 tablespoons all-purpose flour
¼ teaspoon salt
1¼ cups quick-cooking oats
½ cup raspberry or apricot jam

1. Preheat the oven to 350°F, and line several baking sheets with parchment paper.

2. Using an electric mixer on medium-high speed, cream the butter, sugar, and vanilla together in a medium-size bowl until light and fluffy, about 2 minutes. Stop the mixer twice during the process to scrape the bowl with a rubber spatula.

3. Add the flour and salt, and mix on low speed for several seconds. Scrape the bowl. Then turn the mixer to high speed and beat until the batter is light and fluffy, about 1 minute. Add the oats and beat on low speed for 20 seconds, stopping the mixer once to scrape the bowl.

4. Measure out rounded teaspoons of dough, and roll them into balls with your hands.

5. Place the balls about 1½ inches apart on the prepared baking sheets. Then make a firm indentation in the center of each cookie with your thumb or index finger.

6. Bake the cookies until lightly golden, 20 minutes. Remove the baking sheets from the oven, place ½ teaspoon of the jam in the center of each cookie, and return the sheets to the oven.

7. Bake the cookies just until the jam melts and spreads slightly, about 10 minutes. Allow the cookies to cool on the sheets.

8. If you will be snacking on them, store the cookies in an airtight plastic container at room temperature for a day or two. After that, store the container in the freezer for up to 2 weeks. Bring the cookies to room temperature before eating.

Makes about 50 cookies

Classic Sugar Cookies

❤ ❤ ❤ ❤ ❤ ❤ ❤ ❤ ❤   *rolled cookie*

L et's hear it for the plain old sugar cookie. It has a special place in my heart and on my palate, partly because it tastes great, partly because it played a big part in Rosie's history, and partly because it's so versatile. Sugar cookies are what got me into the baking biz to begin with, and sugar cookies are what keep me creative. You can adorn them with colored sugars and frosting, send them as Valentines with endearing messages written on top, throw a decorating party for the kids on your block, deliver them as gifts in satin-lined boxes, or use them as Christmas tree ornaments by forming small holes in them before baking. The sky's the limit!

INGREDIENTS

THE COOKIE
2¼ cups all-purpose flour
½ cup granulated sugar
½ cup confectioners' sugar
⅛ teaspoon baking soda
⅛ teaspoon cream of tartar
½ teaspoon salt
12½ tablespoons (1½ sticks plus ½ tablespoon) unsalted butter, cold, cut into 12 pieces
1 large egg
1 tablespoon pure vanilla extract

THE GLAZE
1 cup minus 2 tablespoons confectioners' sugar
¼ cup heavy (whipping) cream
Food coloring (optional)

THE DECORATIONS
Colored sugars
Sugar confetti
Tiny candies

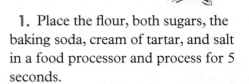

1. Place the flour, both sugars, the baking soda, cream of tartar, and salt in a food processor and process for 5 seconds.

2. Distribute the butter over the flour mixture, and process until the dough resembles coarse meal, about 30 seconds. Scrape the bowl with a rubber spatula once during the process to make certain the butter is evenly distributed.

3. Stir the egg and vanilla together in a cup. With the processor running, pour this mixture through the feed tube and process until the dough comes together, about 35 seconds.

4. Remove the dough from the processor, place it on a work surface, and knead it for several seconds.

5. Divide the dough into two slabs, wrap each in plastic wrap, and refrigerate for 1 to 2 hours.

6. When you're ready to bake the cookies, preheat the oven to 375°F. Line several baking sheets with parchment paper.

7. Remove one slab of dough from the refrigerator and place it between two fresh pieces of plastic wrap. Roll it out ⅛ inch thick.

8. Remove the top piece of plastic wrap, and using the cookie cutter of your choice, cut out as many cookies as you can. Using a spatula, place the cookies on a prepared baking sheet, leaving about 1 inch between cookies. Gather up the scraps and refrigerate them for rerolling. Repeat with the second slab: then reroll and cut out the scraps.

9. Bake the cookies until firm with lightly golden edges, 15 to 20 minutes depending on their size. Cool them on the sheets.

10. Meanwhile make the glaze: Place the confectioners' sugar and the cream in a medium-size bowl and whisk vigorously until smooth and creamy. If you are using food coloring, divide the glaze among as many bowls as you have colors, and whisk in a drop at a time to get the desired color.

11. With the cookies still on the baking sheets, use a spoon to drizzle the glaze, or a small butter knife or paintbrush to spread it on the cookies. Then sprinkle colored sugar, sugar confetti, or candies on the glaze (see step 12).

12. Place the baking sheets in the refrigerator to speed up the setting of the glaze, or allow the cookies to set for 4 to 6 hours at room temperature.

13. Unfrosted sugar cookies should be stored in an airtight plastic container at room temperature for up to 3 days or in the freezer for up to 3 weeks. When glazed or frosted, it's best to store them in the container, with plastic wrap, parchment, or waxed paper between the layers.

Makes 15 large or 25 small cookies

Poppyseed Hamantaschen

❤ ❤ ❤ ❤ ❤ ❤ ❤   *formed cookie*

I went through a lot of hamantaschen—a fall favorite, served often in celebration of the Jewish holiday of Purim—before I came up with this one. The rejects were dry or tasteless, their dough was impossible to work with, or they called for incongruous ingredients like ginger ale or orange juice. This one is simple to make, rich in taste, and filled with a poppyseed mixture, which you should be able to find in the baking section of major supermarkets (it's made by Solo). If poppyseeds aren't to your taste, use any thick preserves for the filling.

INGREDIENTS

THE DOUGH

2 cups plus 3 tablespoons all-purpose flour
½ cup sugar
⅛ teaspoon baking powder
1 teaspoon grated lemon or orange zest
¾ teaspoon salt
¾ cup (1½ sticks) unsalted butter at room
    temperature, cut into 12 pieces
2 tablespoons cold water
2 large egg yolks

THE FILLING

1¼ cups poppyseed filling (see headnote)

1. Place the flour, sugar, baking powder, zest, and salt in a food processor and process for 20 seconds. (Or whisk them together by hand in a large mixing bowl.)

2. Distribute the butter evenly over the flour and process until the mixture resembles coarse meal, 15 to 20 seconds. (Or rub the butter into the flour with your fingertips, or cut it in with a pastry blender.)

3. In a small cup, whisk together the cold water and egg yolks. With the processor running, pour the egg mixture in a steady stream through the feed tube and process just until the dough comes together, 20 to 30 seconds. (Or sprinkle the egg mixture over the flour mixture while tossing with a fork.)

4. Place the dough on a lightly floured work surface, and knead it several times to bring it together.

5. Shape the dough into two thick disks, wrap each one in plastic wrap, and refrigerate them for 1 hour.

6. Line several baking sheets with parchment paper, or grease them lightly with vegetable oil.

7. Remove one disk from the refrigerator and roll it out to form a round approximately 12 inches in diameter and a generous ⅛ inch thick.

8. Using a 2½-inch cookie cutter, cut out as many rounds as possible. Place them ¼ inch apart on the prepared baking sheets. Repeat with the second disk.

9. Place 1 rounded teaspoon of filling in the center of each round. Then fold the edges of the dough toward the center to form a triangle, leaving a bit of the filling showing in the center. Pinch the edges in three places to seal them. Place the baking sheets in the refrigerator for 30 minutes, or in the freezer for 15 minutes, to chill the triangles.

10. Fifteen minutes before baking, preheat the oven to 375°F.

11. Bake the hamantaschen until they are crisp, firm to the touch, and golden around the edges, 20 minutes. Let them cool completely on the baking sheets.

12. If you plan on snacking on them on the first day, leave the hamantaschen on a plate, uncovered, at room temperature. After that, layer them in an airtight plastic container with plastic wrap, parchment, or waxed paper between the layers and place in the refrigerator for up to 3 days or the freezer for up to 2 weeks.

Makes about 40 hamantaschen

Cream Cheese Rugalach

♥ ♥ ♥ ♥ ♥ ♥ ♥ ♥ ♥ ♥   *rolled cookie*

R ugalach and I first met in my childhood, when my mother used to bring it home with her after visiting my grandmother in Queens. Determined to make it more readily available, I've sold it at Rosie's for twenty years, and it has never lost its appeal. That may be because it is perfect served at the end of almost any meal—holiday or not. Making rugalach isn't a simple undertaking, but the dough in this recipe is easier to work with than many I've come across, and the result is certainly

worth the effort. Just remember that you can keep refrigerating the dough intermittently while you're working with it, which makes the whole enterprise less daunting. Also, the filling can be made with fruit-juice-sweetened jam if you're avoiding sugar.

INGREDIENTS

THE DOUGH
1¼ cups all-purpose flour
⅛ teaspoon salt
8 tablespoons (1 stick) unsalted butter at room temperature
4 ounces cream cheese at room temperature

THE FILLING
¾ cup apricot or raspberry preserves
½ cup chopped pecans or walnuts
½ cup golden or dark raisins

THE GLAZE
1 large egg
1 tablespoon sugar
¼ teaspoon ground cinnamon

1. Sift the flour and salt together in a small bowl and set aside.

2. Using an electric mixer on medium speed, cream the butter and cream cheese together in a medium-size bowl until light and fluffy, 1½ to 2 minutes. Stop the mixer once or twice during the process to scrape the bowl with a rubber spatula.

3. Add the flour mixture and mix until blended, about 20 seconds, stopping the mixer once to scrape the bowl. Place the dough on a work surface and work it with your hands until it comes together.

4. Shape the dough into two thick rectangles, wrap each one in plastic wrap, and refrigerate them for 3 hours.

5. Remove one dough rectangle from the refrigerator, and roll it out between two fresh pieces of plastic wrap to form a rectangle about 14 × 8 inches.

6. Peel off the top piece of plastic wrap and turn the dough so one long side is facing you. Spread 6 table-spoons of the preserves evenly over the dough, leaving uncovered a ½-inch strip along the long edge farthest away from you.

7. Sprinkle ¼ cup of the nuts and ¼ cup of the raisins over the preserves.

8. Loosen the filled long edge of the dough from the plastic wrap with a knife or spatula, and roll it toward the uncovered edge like a jelly roll, peeling off the plastic wrap as you roll. The seam should be on the underside. Wrap the roll in fresh plastic and refrigerate it. Repeat the process with the other dough rectangle. Keep the filled rolls refrigerated for 2 hours.

9. Fifteen minutes before baking, preheat the oven to 375°F. Line two baking sheets with parchment paper, or lightly grease them with vegetable oil.

10. For the glaze, lightly beat the egg with a fork. Stir the sugar and cinna-mon together in a small cup. Using a pastry brush, brush the egg over the outside of both rolls. Then sprinkle the cinnamon-sugar mixture over the rolls.

11. Using a thin sharp knife, carefully cut the rolls into pieces about 1 inch thick. Place the rugalach, seam side down, about 1 inch apart on the pre-pared baking sheets.

12. Bake until the rugalach are golden, 18 to 20 minutes. (Some of the jam will ooze out and start to darken.) Use a spatula to immediately transfer the rugalach to wire racks to cool.

13. Layer the rugalach in an airtight plastic container with plastic wrap, parchment, or waxed paper between the layers and store at room tempera-ture for 1 day before serving. Their fla-vor and consistency will be enhanced by the day of rest. The rugalach can re-main at room temperature for up to 3 days. After that place the container in the freezer for up to 2 weeks.

Makes about 26 rugalach

Sour Cream Rugalach

❤ ❤ ❤ ❤ ❤ ❤ ❤ ❤ *rolled cookie*

This recipe is slightly different from the Cream Cheese Rugalach: You form the dough into little crescents rather than long rolls, and you use sour cream to create a light and flaky dough. As my daughter, Maya, would say, "Awesome!"

INGREDIENTS

THE DOUGH

1 large egg yolk
¾ cup sour cream
2 cups all-purpose flour
½ teaspoon salt
1 cup (2 sticks) unsalted
*   butter, cold, cut into 12 pieces*

THE FILLING

4½ tablespoons sugar
1½ teaspoons ground cinnamon
1 cup raspberry or apricot preserves
Scant 1 cup chopped walnuts
*   or pecans*
Scant 1 cup golden or dark raisins

1. Stir the egg yolk and sour cream together in a small bowl.

2. Place the flour and salt in a food processor and process for 5 seconds.

3. Distribute the butter over the flour mixture, and process until the mixture resembles coarse cornmeal, 15 seconds.

4. With the machine running, pour the sour cream mixture through the feed tube. Stop the processor, then pulse 12 times. Scrape the bowl, then pulse another 20 times.

5. Place the dough on a work surface and knead it several times.

6. Divide the dough into four disks, wrap each one in plastic wrap, and refrigerate them for 6 to 8 hours or overnight.

7. Remove one disk from the refrigerator and roll it between two fresh pieces of plastic wrap to form a round 9 inches in diameter and approximately ⅛ inch thick. Trim the edges to make a perfect circle. Place the dough, still sandwiched in the plastic wrap, on a plate and refrigerate it for 1 hour. Repeat with the remaining disks.

8. In a small bowl, stir together the sugar and the cinnamon. Set aside.

9. Line several baking sheets with parchment paper, or grease them lightly with vegetable oil.

10. After the dough has chilled, remove one round from the refrigerator. Peel off the top piece of plastic wrap. Spread ¼ cup of the preserves over the dough. Then sprinkle it with approximately 4 teaspoons of the cinnamon-sugar mixture, 3 tablespoons of the raisins, and 3 tablespoons of the nuts.

11. Using the point of a sharp thin knife, cut the disk into 12 wedges. Carefully lift the wide end of each wedge, roll up the triangle toward the tip, and with the point on the bottom, curve in the sides to form a crescent shape. Place the rugalach 1½ inches apart on the baking sheet. Refrigerate for 30 minutes before baking. Repeat with the remaining dough and filling.

12. Fifteen minutes before baking, preheat the oven to 375°F.

13. Bake the rugalach until they are crisp and golden, 18 to 20 minutes.

14. Cool the rugalach for several minutes on the sheets. Then using a spatula, carefully transfer each rugalach to a wire rack (do this before any jam that has seeped out starts to harden). Cool the rugalach completely before eating.

15. Layer the rugalach in an airtight plastic container with plastic wrap, parchment, or waxed paper between the layers and store at room temperature for 1 day before serving. Their flavor and consistency will be enhanced by the day of rest. The rugalach can remain at room temperature for up to 3 days. After that, place the container in the freezer for up to 2 weeks.

Makes 48 rugalach

Buttermilk Doughnut Holes

❤ ❤ ❤ ❤ ❤ ❤ ❤ ❤ ❤ ❤ ❤ ❤ ❤ ❤ ❤

I bow to no one in my love of doughnuts. Not the fancy-schmancy ones, mind you, but your basic, old-fashioned doughnutty doughnut that's crunchy on the outside and soft on the inside—like these doughnut holes. My family devours them in bulk at Chanukah, when tradition calls for doughnuts (for any fried food, actually) to commemorate the oil that miraculously kept the Temple's sacred light burning for eight days and nights. Even divine intervention wouldn't keep these doughnut holes around my house that long, so it's a good thing that they're quick to prepare.

INGREDIENTS

1½ quarts pure vegetable oil

THE COATINGS
1 cup sifted confectioners' sugar
1 cup granulated sugar
2 tablespoons ground cinnamon

THE BATTER
1 cup all-purpose flour
⅔ cup cake flour
½ teaspoon baking soda
1 teaspoon baking powder
½ teaspoon salt
½ teaspoon ground nutmeg
1 large egg
½ cup sugar
1 tablespoon unsalted butter, melted
½ teaspoon pure vanilla extract
½ cup buttermilk at room temperature

1. Attach a candy thermometer to the side of a 4- or 5-quart saucepan placed over medium heat. Pour in the oil (it should be 3 to 4 inches deep) and heat until the oil reaches 375° to 380°F.

2. Prepare one or both coatings: Place the confectioners' sugar in a plastic bag. Place the granulated sugar and the cinnamon in another plastic bag, and shake (with the bag tightly closed) to mix thoroughly. Set the bags aside.

3. Sift both flours, baking soda, baking powder, salt, and nutmeg together into a small bowl and set aside.

4. Using a whisk, blend the egg and sugar together in a medium-size bowl. Stir in the melted butter, vanilla, and buttermilk.

5. Resift the flour mixture over the egg mixture, and using a rubber spatula, fold gently until mixed.

6. Using a 1½-inch diameter ice cream scoop, drop five level scoops of the batter, one at a time, into the oil and cook until they are crunchy and deep golden, 4 to 5 minutes.

7. Using a slotted spoon, remove a doughnut hole from the oil and cut it in half. If the center seems gooey, the doughnut holes need to cook for another minute or two. Remove the doughnuts with the slotted spoon and place them on paper towels to drain. Continue frying the remaining batter in this fashion.

8. To coat the doughnut holes in the cinnamon-sugar mixture: About 1 minute after removing them from the oil, place one doughnut at a time in the bag and toss to coat. Return it to the paper towel to cool.

9. To coat with the confectioners' sugar, allow the doughnut holes to cool completely. Then place them one by one in the bag and toss to coat.

10. These doughnuts should be eaten as soon as possible.

Makes about 20 doughnut holes

Variation: Cider Doughnuts
Substitute ½ cup cider for the buttermilk, and add 1 tablespoon ground cinnamon, ¾ teaspoon ground cardamom, and ¾ cup finely chopped peeled apples to the batter.

The Marks's Matzoh Crunch

❤ ❤ ❤ ❤ ❤ ❤ ❤ ❤ ❤ ❤ ❤ ❤ ❤ ❤

This recipe was plucked from the pages of the self-published *Father and Son Cookbook*, a delightful book by the talented father-and-son team of my good friends Roger and Gabriel Marks. The crunch created a sensation at Rosie's and became a staple at Passover, even for those who don't celebrate the holiday. I'm honored to add it to my repertoire and thank Roger and Gabriel again.

INGREDIENTS

6 boards plain matzoh
1¼ cups (2½ sticks) unsalted butter
1¼ cups (firmly packed) light brown sugar
6 ounces (1 cup) semisweet chocolate chips
or chopped semisweet chocolate

1. Preheat the oven to 350°F. Lightly grease a rimmed baking sheet with butter.

2. Line the baking sheet with the matzoh, breaking the pieces where necessary to fill in all the spaces.

3. Combine the butter and brown sugar in a medium-size saucepan over medium heat. Stir constantly with a wooden spoon until the mixture boils, 5 minutes. Then continue to cook 3 minutes more, stirring constantly.

4. Remove the butter mixture from the heat, and pour it evenly over the matzoh.

5. Bake until the matzoh is deep golden in color, 10 to 12 minutes. (After the first 8 minutes, check every 2 minutes to make sure it doesn't burn.)

6. Remove the pan from the oven and sprinkle the chocolate over the matzoh. Allow it to melt. Then use a frosting spatula to spread the chocolate over the matzoh. Place the pan in the refrigerator for the chocolate to set, 1 to 2 hours.

7. When the matzoh is completely chilled, break it into pieces.

Makes 6 boards of matzoh crunch

COOKIE
■CHEF■

488

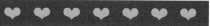

T